The Works of William James

Editors
Frederick H. Burkhardt, General Editor
Fredson Bowers, Textual Editor
Ignas K. Skrupskelis, Associate Editor

Advisory Board

Max H. Fisch	Eugene T. Long
John J. McDermott	Edward H. Madden
Maurice Mandelbaum	H. S. Thayer

*This edition of the Works of William James
is sponsored by the American Council of
Learned Societies*

William James

photograph by Pach; courtesy Houghton Library, Harvard University

Essays in Religion and Morality

William James

HARVARD UNIVERSITY PRESS
Cambridge, Massachusetts
and London, England
1982

Copyright © 1982 by the President and Fellows of Harvard College

Printed in the United States of America

CENTER FOR
SCHOLARLY EDITIONS
AN APPROVED EDITION
MODERN LANGUAGE
ASSOCIATION OF AMERICA

Library of Congress Cataloging in Publication Data

James, William, 1842–1910.
Essays in religion and morality.

(The works of William James)
Includes index.
1. Religion—Addresses, essays, lectures. 2. Ethics
—Addresses, essays, lectures. I. Burkhardt, Frederick
Henry, 1912–   . II. Bowers, Fredson Thayer.
III. Skrupskelis, Ignas K., 1938–   . IV. Title.
V. Series: James, William, 1842–1910. Works. 1975.
BL50.J35   1982   200   81–7040
ISBN 0–674–26735–4   AACR2

Foreword

Essays in Religion and Morality is the ninth title, and the eleventh
volume, to be published in THE WORKS OF WILLIAM JAMES. In it
are collected those of James's writings on religion and morality that
he did not himself assemble and publish in books like *The Will to
Believe* and *The Varieties of Religious Experience*. That he did not
do so has no relation to their intrinsic worth or to their importance
in James's philosophical work. Two of them, *Human Immortality*
and "The Moral Equivalent of War," are among the best known of
his writings, and the longest piece, James's Introduction to *The
Literary Remains of the Late Henry James*, is of particular interest
and importance because of its adumbration of themes that were
more fully developed in later philosophical works, and especially
in *The Varieties of Religious Experience*.

All of the essays, varied as they are in their subjects, are consistently and characteristically Jamesian in the freshness of their attack on
the perennial problems of humankind and in their steady faith in
human powers.

The text of *Essays in Religion and Morality* has been established
in accordance with the editorial policy of the edition as a whole,
which, briefly stated, seeks to provide the reader with an authoritative text that represents as closely as possible James's final intentions.
The principles and techniques of modern textual criticism involved
in the preparation of such a text are set forth in the Note on the Edi-

torial Method by Fredson Bowers, Linden Kent Professor of English, Emeritus, at the University of Virginia, the Textual Editor of the WORKS. Professor Bowers also provides a discussion of the text and the authority of its source documents, together with a textual apparatus that will enable scholars to reconstruct the documents used in the editing. The availability of manuscript material for some of the essays, and particularly the manuscript stages of "The Moral Equivalent of War," assisted in the formation of an authentic text and also illuminated the creative process by which James arrived at the final form.

The Associate Editor, Professor Ignas K. Skrupskelis of the University of South Carolina, prepared the reference Notes to the text and the General Index. In addition, he contributed to the documentation of the publishing history of the essays.

The Advisory Board of scholars listed in the front matter was appointed by the American Council of Learned Societies, which is the sponsor of this edition of the WORKS. Its members have supplied the editors with general policy guidance and many specific suggestions on substantive questions.

One of the members of the Advisory Board, Professor John J. McDermott, Distinguished Professor of Philosophy and Medical Humanities, Texas A&M University, has written the Introduction, which discusses the essays and their relation to James's philosophical development.

It remains for the editors to acknowledge their indebtedness to the institutions and individuals that have helped make this volume possible.

The National Endowment for the Humanities has generously continued its support of this edition of THE WORKS OF WILLIAM JAMES by providing funds for the editorial work and for the preparation of camera-ready copy for the apparatus and other end matter. Dr. George F. Farr, Jr., of the Division of Research Grants, has given steady friendly support to the entire project.

The editors are also grateful to the Barra Foundation and to its President, Robert L. McNeil, Jr., for a generous and timely matching grant in support of the edition.

Alexander James and Dr. William Bond of the Houghton Library have granted permission to use and reproduce both printed and manuscript texts and illustrations in the James Collection at Harvard University. Marte-Eliza Shaw and the members of the staff of the Houghton Library Reading Room were unfailingly helpful and patient in making the James Papers available to the editors.

The Reference Room staff of the Alderman Library at the University of Virginia have provided assistance with foreign-language quotations and with locating materials pertinent to the textual work.

The University of South Carolina has provided the Associate Editor with research assistance and working space.

Colby College provided three letters to Katharine James Prince bearing on *The Literary Remains of the Late Henry James*.

The Sterling Memorial Library and the Beinecke Library of Yale University made available letters and a card from James to Lutoslawski. Also, the Havelock Ellis Collection, Yale University, supplied correspondence from James to Ellis dealing with James's preface to Starbuck's *Psychology of Religion*.

The Stanford University Libraries provided a letter from James to F. C. S. Schiller concerning Lutoslawski.

Walter R. Benjamin Autographs, Inc., furnished a letter from James to Parke Godwin.

The editors also acknowledge their indebtedness to the following individuals:

Signora Anna Casini provided a letter from James to Giovanni Papini, who translated "The Energies of Men" for *Leonardo*.

Eugene Taylor supplied information about the manuscripts of Henry James, Senior.

G. Thomas Tanselle examined the volume for the seal of the Center for Scholarly Editions.

Audrone Skrupskelis assisted the Associate Editor in tracing quotations in the works of Henry James, Senior, and in the preparation of the Index.

Charlotte Bowman contributed her services as Administrative Assistant to the General Editor.

Finally, Anne McCoy, Chief Research Assistant to the Textual Editor, and her staff, Elizabeth Berkeley, Mary Mikalson, Wilma Bradbeer, Judith Nelson, Richard Rainville, and Ann Tuley, prepared the manuscript for publication with their usual skill and meticulous attention to detail.

F.H.B.

Contents

Foreword   v

Introduction by John J. McDermott   xi

Essays in Religion and Morality   1
  Introduction to *The Literary Remains of*
    the Late Henry James   3
  Robert Gould Shaw: Oration by Professor William James   64
  Human Immortality:
    Two Supposed Objections to the Doctrine   75
  Preface to Starbuck's *Psychology of Religion*   102
  Preface to Lutoslawski's *World of Souls*   105
  Emerson   109
  Introduction to Fechner's *Life After Death*   116
  Remarks at the Peace Banquet   120
  Reason and Faith   124
  The Energies of Men   129
  The Powers of Men   147
  The Moral Equivalent of War   162

Notes   175

Appendixes
  I. Notes for "The Energies of Men"   199
  II. Notes for an Unidentified Lecture   201

A Note on the Editorial Method   205

The Text of *Essays in Religion and Morality*   214

Apparatus
  Emendations   267
  Textual Notes   281
  Historical Collation   284
  Alterations in the Manuscripts   307
  Word-Division   333

General Index   335

Introduction

by

John J. McDermott

Julius Seelye Bixler was prescient when he wrote in 1926 that "the isolated reference from James is always unreliable."[1] So too must we be careful in our assessment of the essays, introductions, and prefaces contained in the present volume, *Essays in Religion and Morality*.[2] The chronological range of these materials extends from 1884 until 1910, the year of James's death, and although they are gathered under the generic heading of "religion and morality," they also touch on many other issues of interest to James. To be fully appreciated, *Essays in Religion and Morality* must be read in the context of James's major writings on these matters, especially *The Varieties of Religious Experience* and his essay "The Will to Believe."

As with *Essays in Philosophy*, an earlier volume in this edition of James's collected works, and *Essays in Psychology*, a volume that will be published in the near future, the present collection of essays was never published by James in this unified format. The Editors of THE WORKS OF WILLIAM JAMES have been confronted by a difficult

[1] Julius Seelye Bixler, *Religion in the Philosophy of William James* (Boston: Marshall Jones Company, 1926), p. xi.

[2] References to *Essays in Religion and Morality*, designated in these pages as *ERM*, are to the present volume. References to *A Pluralistic Universe* are to this edition of THE WORKS OF WILLIAM JAMES. All other references to James's work are to first printings.

organizational problem. Arrangement of all of James's essays and incidental pieces according to disciplines, such as philosophy, religion, and psychology, gives rise to the danger that the interdisciplinary character of James's thought may be somewhat obscured. James, more than most philosophers, did not honor hard and fast distinctions among the academic disciplines, but rather regarded them as names given to varieties of human behavior and patterns of inquiry. On the other hand, a merely chronological arrangement of these varied essays would have made it difficult for the reader to follow the ways in which James developed the basic themes in each of the fields that engaged his attention. As a compromise, it was decided to arrange the essays by fields, but to publish them in chronological order within each field. In this way the student of the Works might read all that James wrote, including previously unpublished material, year by year, as well as in the more conventional way, volume by volume.

By way of introducing this volume, it is convenient to divide the material into five separate areas of concern: first, William James's presentation of his father's *Literary Remains*; second, James's interest in human immortality, the relation between reason and faith, and his brief prefaces to the works of Starbuck, Lutoslawski, and Fechner; third, his two memorial pieces, one on Robert Gould Shaw and the other on Emerson; fourth, James's writing on the energies and powers of human life; last, his writings on the possibilities of peace, especially as found in his famous essay "The Moral Equivalent of War."

In 1884 William James wrote a very long Introduction to an edition of his father's *Literary Remains*. Much of this Introduction consists of quotations from the writings of Henry James, Senior, although the interpolations of William James are representative of some of his most deeply held beliefs. As it is William James who is the subject of the present volume, I shall concentrate on these interpolations, for they provide some insight into the development of his mature religious thought.

Henry James, Senior (1811–1882), was a garrulous and fascinating man. The son of William James of Albany (1771–1832), Henry lost a leg in an accident when he was twelve years old. This event, which left him unfit for manual work, intensified his deeply speculative nature. A seeker of the truth, his restless mind and spirit indulged many of the salvation nostrums of his time. In addition to being influenced by the American transcendentalists and the Brook Farm experiment, Henry James also had an abiding interest in the work of the Scottish religious thinker Robert Sandeman (1718–1778), in the ideas of the Utopian Socialist Charles Fourier (1772–1837), and especially in the mysticism of Emmanuel Swedenborg (1686–1772). Despite the significant dissimilarities in these rivulets of influence on him, Henry seized upon a common theme and made it his own: salvation was a temporal affair, and for him the divine experience was divine precisely because it was immanent and not distant from human activity.

If Henry's physical accident when a boy dramatically altered his vocational future, so also did a profound spiritual experience at the age of thirty-three alter his reflective future (*ERM*, pp. 30–33). Finding solace in the writings of Swedenborg, he developed a theology that joined two unlikely propositions. The Divine, the Godhead, was significant precisely and only because it penetrated human life, whereas human life was meaningful only to the extent that it abandoned the aggrandizing of the self and opened to the presence of the Divine. Furthermore, this transaction was to take place in the arena of time and not in a world beyond. This was not a denial of the transcendent; rather, somewhat paradoxically, the transcendent was to be found in the affairs of human time.

What is of interest here to students of William James is that he had an experience strikingly similar to that of his father and that he came to an opposite conclusion. Under the pseudonym of a French correspondent, James presents what we now know to be an autobiographical version of an event that took place, probably in 1870, when he was twenty-eight years of age.

Whilst in this state of philosophic pessimism and general depression of spirits about my prospects, I went one evening into a dressing-room in the twilight to procure some article that was there; when suddenly there fell upon me without any warning, just as if it came out of the darkness, a horrible fear of my own existence. Simultaneously there arose in my mind the image of an epileptic patient whom I had seen in the asylum, a black-haired youth with greenish skin, entirely idiotic, who used to sit all day on one of the benches, or rather shelves against the wall, with his knees drawn up against his chin, and the coarse gray undershirt, which was his only garment, drawn over them inclosing his entire figure. He sat there like a sort of sculptured Egyptian cat or Peruvian mummy, moving nothing but his black eyes and looking absolutely non-human. This image and my fear entered into a species of combination with each other. *That shape am I*, I felt, potentially. Nothing that I possess can defend me against that fate, if the hour for it should strike for me as it struck for him. There was such a horror of him, and such a perception of my own merely momentary discrepancy from him, that it was as if something hitherto solid within my breast gave way entirely, and I became a mass of quivering fear. After this the universe was changed for me altogether. I awoke morning after morning with a horrible dread at the pit of my stomach, and with a sense of the insecurity of life that I never knew before, and that I have never felt since. It was like a revelation; and although the immediate feelings passed away, the experience has made me sympathetic with the morbid feelings of others ever since. It gradually faded, but for months I was unable to go out into the dark alone.[3]

The trauma was remarkably similar to that experienced by James's father: a vastation characterized by an appearance of another self, terrifying, loathsome, and yet somehow familiar. For Henry James, Senior, it crystallized his determination to abandon the aggrandizing self in favor of an opening to divine influence. For William James, on the contrary, his experience pressed upon him the need to generate, *de novo*, a promethean self worthy of the hidden but repressed possibilities of consciousness that all of us harbor but fail to energize.[4]

On April 30, 1870, William James made an entry in his diary affirming his new-found, albeit halting, confidence in the powers of the human self to build a distinctively human world independent of the burdens of the familial inheritance and social mores.

Not in maxims, not in *Anschauungen*, but in accumulated *acts* of thought lies salvation. *Passer outre*. Hitherto, when I have felt like taking a free initiative, like daring to act originally, without carefully waiting for contemplation of the external world to determine all for me, suicide seemed the most manly form to put my daring into; now, I will go a step further with my will, not only act with it, but believe as well; believe in my individual reality and creative power. My belief, to be

[3] William James, *The Varieties of Religious Experience* (New York: Longmans, Green and Co., 1902), pp. 160–161.

[4] For support of the intriguing claim that James suffered from acedia, or moral torpor, during this period from 1868 to 1870, see William Clebsch, *American Religious Thought* (Chicago: University of Chicago Press, 1973), pp. 138–148. The most exhaustive and scholarly treatment of William James's religious thought is found in Henry Levinson, *The Religious Investigations of William James* (Chapel Hill: University of North Carolina Press, 1981).

sure, *can't* be optimistic—but I will posit life (the real, the good) in the self-governing *resistance* of the ego to the world. Life shall [be built in] doing and suffering and creating.[5]

This affirmation of human possibility will be discussed later when we consider James's essays on the powers and energies of men, but I return now to his analysis of his father's literary remains. In sifting through Henry James's writings, William repeatedly emphasizes certain themes. It is difficult to know whether these interests of William James are due to his father's influence or whether he arrived at his conclusions independently and thereby isolated them in his father's writings either as an anticipation of or as a foil for his own position. Two of these themes merit our attention. First, William is sympathetic to his father's view that redemption, if it is to occur at all, will occur in the fabric of society and not in a realm separate from the affairs of human life. He writes of his father that "to speak very oracularly, *Nature* is for Mr. James the movement of formation, the first quickening of the void unto itself; and *Society* is the movement of redemption, or the finished spiritual work of God" (*ERM*, p. 9). So strong is this commitment of Henry James, Senior, that he can write: "I literally mean what I say, that creation is absolutely contingent upon the Divine ability to humble Himself to the creature's level, to diminish Himself to the creature's *natural* dimensions" (*ERM*, p. 17). It is no wonder, then, that the James family was fond of repeating Henry's remark that if there were to be a heaven, it would be like a crowded horse-car.

A second theme that occupies William James in his commentary on his father's writings has to do with religious monism. Although William is impressed with his father's formulation, he subtly parts from it, for as early as 1884 he had begun to develop what was to become a life-long commitment to pluralism. He stresses the fact that his father's position is not a "*bald* monism, yet it makes of God the one and only *active* principle; and that is practically all that monism demands" (*ERM*, p. 61). He further praises his father for convincing the reader that "anthropomorphism and metaphysics seem for the first time in these pages to go harmoniously hand in hand. The same sun that lights up the frozen summits of abstraction, lights up life's teeming plain,—and no chasm, but an open highway lies between" (*ERM*, p. 61).

[5] See William James, "Diary," in *The Writings of William James*, ed. John J. McDermott (Chicago: University of Chicago Press, 1977), p. 8.

Nonetheless, he has reservations about this position. Hidden in this text is William's *bête noire*, monism, by which he meant the utilization of a single principle to account for the "varieties" of experience. By contrast, William James was a pluralist, for whom each of the "varieties" had its own, irreducible meaning. In a statement of gentle opposition, he presages a position that he was to defend with increasing intensity until the end of his life. Speaking of religious monists, of whatever stripe, he writes:

Their most serious enemy will be the *philosophic* pluralist. The naïf practical pluralism of popular religion ought, as I have said, to have no quarrel with the monism they teach. There is however a pluralism hardened by reflection, and deliberate; a pluralism which, in face of the old mystery of the One and the Many, has vainly sought peace in identification, and ended by taking sides against the One. It seems to me that the deepest of all philosophic differences is that between this pluralism and all forms of monism whatever. Apart from analytic and intellectual arguments, pluralism is a view to which we all practically incline when in the full and successful exercise of our moral energy. The life we then feel tingling through us vouches sufficiently for itself, and nothing tempts us to refer it to a higher source. Being, as we are, a match for whatever evils actually confront us, we rather prefer to think of them as endowed with reality, and as being absolutely alien, but, we hope, subjugable powers. Of the day of our possible impotency we take no thought; and we care not to make such synthesis of our weakness and our strength, and of the good and evil fortunes of the world, as will reduce them all to fractions, with a common denominator, of some less fluctuating Unity, enclosing some less partial and more certain form of Good. The feeling of *action*, in short, makes us turn a deaf ear to the thought of *being*; and this deafness and insensibility may be said to form an integral part of what in popular phrase is known as "healthy-mindedness." Any absolute moralism must needs be such a healthy-minded pluralism; and in a pluralistic philosophy the healthy-minded moralist will always feel himself at home (*ERM*, pp. 61–62).

In a judicious conclusion to his version of his father's thought, William James sides with the reflective pluralists against his father's monism, but hopes that they bring to their position "a spirit even remotely resembling the life-long devotion of his faithful heart" (*ERM*, p. 63). In James's judgment, such a hope seems to be a modest request, for he writes of his father as follows:

He was a religious prophet and genius, if ever prophet and genius there were. He published an intensely positive, radical, and fresh conception of God, and an intensely vital view of our connection with him. And nothing shows better the altogether lifeless and unintellectual character of the professional theism of our time, than the fact that this view, this conception, so vigorously thrown down, should not have stirred the faintest tremulation in its stagnant pool (*ERM*, p. 6).

Our next group of writings features one major piece, *Human Immortality*, as well as three brief prefaces to works by authors with whom James is sympathetic and a short but important piece, "Reason and Faith." William James's position on human immortality is more a hope than a belief. He writes: "I have to confess that my own personal feeling about immortality has never been of the keenest order, and that, among the problems that give my mind solicitude, this one does not take the very foremost place" (*ERM*, p. 78). Yet James was struck by two aspects of the possibility of human immortality: first, that it is such a deep and pervasive concern of human life and, second, the possibility that we can communicate with the dead. Although James did not share the first concern, it was characteristic of him to represent the position of ordinary people against the allegedly sophisticated objections of intellectuals. As for the second aspect of his interest in human immortality, this was to occupy much of his time in the later years of his life, when he was concerned with psychical research.[6]

Human Immortality: Two Supposed Objections to the Doctrine was published in 1898. The objections that James discusses are, first, "the absolute dependence of our spiritual life, as we know it here, upon the brain" (*ERM*, p. 79), and, second, "the incredible and intolerable number of beings which, with our modern imagination, we must believe to be immortal, if immortality be true" (*ERM*, p. 96). James devotes most of the essay to the first objection. It is not that he denies the contention that "thought is a function of the brain" (*ERM*, p. 81); rather, he contends that this physiological version of our human experience is conceived too narrowly. "The fatal conclusion of the physiologist flows from his assuming offhand another kind of functional dependence, and treating it as the only imaginable kind" (*ERM*, p. 82). To this limited view, James adds the "permissive or transmissive function" (*ERM*, p. 86). The gist of this position is that energies exist which the traditional brain-

---

[6] His essays on psychical research will be brought together in a forthcoming volume in the Works. Selections have been published in Gardner Murphy and Robert O. Ballou, eds., *William James on Psychical Research* (New York: Viking Press, 1960).

dependent production theory fails to acknowledge—that is, there are potentially available to us sensations that in normal experience are denied access to our consciousness. Of these sensations, James writes: "On the transmission-theory, they don't have to be 'produced,'—they exist ready-made in the transcendental world, and all that is needed is an abnormal lowering of the brain-threshold to let them through" (*ERM*, p. 93).

James believed in the transmission theory, and he pursued its implications in his work on psychical research. There was a tension, however, in James's approach to this issue of a wider range of consciousness. On the one hand, he was forthright on the existence of possibilities beyond our present sight. In *A Pluralistic Universe* he wrote: "In a word, the believer is continuous, to his own consciousness, at any rate, with a wider self from which saving experiences flow in."[7] Yet earlier, in *The Varieties of Religious Experience*, James had written that "so long as we deal with the cosmic and the general, we deal only with the symbols of reality, but *as soon as we deal with private and personal phenomena as such, we deal with realities in the completest sense of the term.*"[8] The result of this tension is that it can be resolved only by the pragmatic maxim, which would contend that the significance of the wider range of experience is precisely proportionate to the change it makes in our active life. For James, the possibility of such a change reverts to his doctrine of "The Will to Believe." If we regard the transmission theory as impossible, then, a priori, no change can take place. If, on the contrary, we admit to its possibility, then we entertain the "chance" of having access to a wider range of experience than that foreordained by our conceptual apparatus.

James's response to the second objection to human immortality is less technical. Indeed, it is frankly romantic. In effect, he denies that the immortality of human life should be blocked by a simply quantitative objection. His argument is somewhat old-fashioned, as he contends that an infinite God has infinite resources and thereby satiety is an impossibility. In an expansive mood, even for James, he concludes his essay with these overbeliefs: "I hope now that you agree with me that the tiresomeness of an over-peopled Heaven is a purely subjective and illusory notion, a sign of human incapacity, a remnant of the old narrow-hearted aristocratic creed. . . .

[7] *A Pluralistic Universe*, WORKS, p. 139.
[8] James, *Varieties*, p. 498.

For my own part, then, so far as logic goes, I am willing that every leaf that ever grew in this world's forests and rustled in the breeze should become immortal'' (*ERM*, pp. 100–101). James's appeal to "logic" is misplaced, for it is not logic that he invokes so much as it is his hope that the significance we feel in our own life will have perpetuity, as will the significance felt by others (*ERM*, p. 101).

The Prefaces to E. D. Starbuck's *Psychology of Religion* (1899) and to W. Lutoslawski's *World of Souls* (1899), as well as the Introduction to G. T. Fechner's *Little Book of Life After Death* (1904), take up fewer than twelve pages in this volume. In the Starbuck piece James affirms the importance of the psychology of religion and notes the prevalence of conversion (*ERM*, p. 103), a theme he was to emphasize in his *Varieties of Religious Experience*. James praises the vitality of Lutoslawski's presentation, and although he views it as utopian and romantic (*ERM*, p. 107) he welcomes the book as another pluralist venture. As for Fechner, James had a long-standing interest in his thought and was subsequently to devote a chapter to him in *A Pluralistic Universe*. In this brief Introduction to Fechner's book, James is especially attracted to the notion that "God has a genuine history" and that consciousness is much like a changing threshold, allowing us access to the inner life of earth and to "the total cosmic life of God" (*ERM*, p. 119). It is such offhand, enthusiastic remarks that feed those commentators who contend that James was a pan-psychist, despite his disclaimers to the contrary.

In the last essay of this second set of concerns, "Reason and Faith" (1905), James stresses the importance of religious experience in any judgment by reason that attempts to cast light on the nature of our actual situation. James admits that to reason, ordinarily considered, the bald facts are clear: "The *last* word everywhere, according to purely naturalistic science, is the word of Death, the death-sentence passed by Nature on plant and beast, and man and tribe, and earth and sun, and everything that she has made" (*ERM*, p. 127). But for James, this is only the obvious part of the story. As he contended in his chapter "Mysticism" in *The Varieties of Religious Experience*, there is "a supersensuous meaning to the ordinary outward data of consciousness."[9] The certitude of reason pales before these experiences and must find a way to take them into account if an authentic religious philosophy is to be developed. In his

[9] Ibid., p. 427.

time, as in ours, there are claims to be assessed and if found empirically true, they have to be integrated into any detailed version of human life. "The phenomenon is that of new ranges of life succeeding on our most despairing moments. There are resources in us that naturalism, with its literal virtues, never recks of, possibilities that take our breath away, and show a world wider than either physics or philistine ethics can imagine" (*ERM*, p. 128).

Our third set of essays contains two memorial addresses, the first in honor of Robert Gould Shaw (1897) and the second in honor of the centenary of Ralph Waldo Emerson (1903). The occasion of James's Oration was the unveiling of a monument to Robert Gould Shaw, the commander of the Fifty-Fourth Regiment of Massachusetts Volunteers, the first regiment of black soldiers to fight for the Union Army. James was both a likely and an unlikely candidate for the honor of giving this address. It was fitting for James to speak, for his younger brother Garth Wilkinson James had been an adjutant in the Fifty-Fourth Regiment and had been wounded in the assault on Fort Wagner. Yet William James, though of age and surrounded by peers who enlisted, chose not to serve in the Civil War and offered no excuses or explanations.[10]

James was nervous on this occasion—so much so, that for the first and only time in his career as a public lecturer, he memorized his address.[11] His trepidation seemed to proceed from the presence of the Governor and assorted military dignitaries rather than from that of the remnant of gallant blacks who had survived the war. In a letter to his brother Henry, William reveals some of his condescension to the blacks of his time, a position strikingly inappropriate for a third-generation descendant of an Irish immigrant.

The day was an extraordinary occasion for sentiment. The streets were thronged with people, and I was toted around for two hours in a barouche at the tail end of the procession. There were seven such carriages in all, and I had the great pleasure of being with St. Gaudens, who is a most charming and modest man. The weather was cool and the skies were weeping, but not enough to cause any serious discomfort. They simply formed a harmonious background to the pathetic sentiment that reigned over the day. It was very peculiar, and people have been

---

[10] See Gay Wilson Allen, *William James: A Biography* (New York: Viking Press, 1967), pp. 71–73.

[11] See Henry James, ed., *The Letters of William James* (Boston: Atlantic Monthly Press, 1920), vol. II, p. 59.

speaking about it ever since—the last wave of the war breaking over Boston, everything softened and made poetic and unreal by distance, poor little Robert Shaw erected into a great symbol of deeper things than he ever realized himself,—"the tender grace of a day that is dead,"—etc. We shall never have anything like it again. The monument is really superb, certainly one of the finest things of this century. Read the darkey [Booker T.] Washington's speech, a model of elevation and brevity. The thing that struck me most in the day was the faces of the old 54th soldiers, of whom there were perhaps about thirty or forty present, with such respectable old darkey faces, the heavy animal look entirely absent, and in its place the wrinkled, patient, good old darkey citizen.[12]

As for the Oration, it is, understandably, a paean of praise for Robert Gould Shaw and his willingness to lead this Regiment at a time when, even in the North, blacks were subject to derision. Missing, however, is any sense of the enormous importance of the abolition movement and of the end of slavery in the United States. Not having participated in that movement in either a military or political manner, he seems to view the Civil War at too great a distance, a distance that no doubt contributed to his estrangement from his two military brothers, Garth Wilkinson and Robertson.

Despite any misgivings one may have concerning the significance of this Oration in the canon of James's writings, it does offer in its penultimate paragraph an eloquent statement on the majesty of America: "The civic genius of our people is its only bulwark, and neither laws nor monuments, neither battleships nor public libraries, nor great newspapers nor booming stocks; neither mechanical invention nor political adroitness, nor churches nor universities nor civil-service examinations can save us from degeneration if the inner mystery be lost" (*ERM*, p. 74). That inner mystery is the ability to generate tolerance, coupled with the steadfast refusal to brook any opposition that threatens the public peace.

The second memorial piece in this volume concerns Ralph Waldo Emerson. In the life of William James, the influential role of Emerson, who had known the James family prior to William's infancy, was presaged early on. In 1873 James wrote in his diary: "I am sure that an age will come . . . when Emerson's philosophy will be in our bones, not our dramatic imagination."[13] Despite the more prolix and often fey style of Emerson, there is a continuity of theme

---

12 Ibid., pp. 60–61.
13 Allen, *William James*, pp. 186–187.

and concern with the thought of James. The source of this bond is their attitude toward the significance of the individual. James writes: "This faith that in a life at first hand there is something sacred is perhaps the most characteristic note in Emerson's writings" (*ERM*, p. 111). A corollary to their concern for the individual is their affection for the experience of the ordinary, the often despised everyday. "Thus does 'the deep today which all men scorn' receive from Emerson superb revindication. 'Other world! there is no other world.' All God's life opens into the individual particular, and here and now, or nowhere, is reality. The present hour is the decisive hour, and every day is doomsday" (*ERM*, p. 114). Although not as daring as James, Emerson could not only "perceive the full squalor of the individual fact, but he could also see the transfiguration" (*ERM*, p. 114). Emerson offered the promise, whereas James spent much of his life and thought diagnosing the "transfigurations."

Aside from this important focus on Emerson's concern for "individuals and particulars," James's essay is taken up with praise of Emerson's style as a literary artist. There is a certain irony here, for such praise of style is precisely what has occupied much of the commentaries on the thought of James, often to the detriment of an analysis of his serious philosophical intent. It is unfortunate that James never undertook a systematic study of Emerson, especially one directed to his notions of experience, relations, and symbol. James would have found Emerson far more congenial and helpful than many of the other thinkers he chose to examine. More than James cared to admit, Emerson was his master.[14]

In January of 1907 James published an essay in *The Philosophical Review* entitled "The Energies of Men," which was originally given in 1906 as the Presidential Address before the American Philosophical Association. Later that year, this essay with some omissions and some additions was published as "The Powers of Men." In this volume, both versions are reprinted. Since they have a common theme, I shall treat them as one piece.

Energies, powers, and possibilities are central to the philosophical anthropology of William James. Readers of James's famous essay

14 For the pervasive, if often unsung, influence of Emerson, see John J. McDermott, "Spires of Influence: The Importance of Emerson for Classical American Philosophy," in *History, Religion and Spiritual Democracy*, ed. Maurice Wohlgelernter (New York: Columbia University Press, 1980), pp. 181–202.

"The Will to Believe" know that one of his most controversial contentions is that there are cases in which belief helps create the fact. James did not intend to adhere to a simplistic optimism by this claim. He writes: "Of course there are limits: the trees don't grow into the sky. But the plain fact remains that men the world over possess amounts of resource, which only very exceptional individuals push to their extremes of use" (*ERM*, p. 133). Rather, he assumed a number of human characteristics as potentially operative but comparatively dormant. James believed that human beings are at their peak when they are active and that the human mind is as much a constructing agency as it is a denoting one. He also deeply believed in human powers and energies, which, when called upon by the will, make empirically possible what seems impossible when viewed in terms of some a priori conceptual framework. In "The Energies of Men," James acknowledges two obstacles to this position:

> The first of the two problems is *that of our powers*, the second *that of our means of unlocking them or getting at them*. We ought somehow to get a topographic survey made of the limits of human power in every conceivable direction, something like an ophthalmologist's chart of the limits of the human field of vision; and we ought then to construct a methodical inventory of the paths of access, or keys, differing with the diverse types of individual, to the different kinds of power. This would be an absolutely concrete study, to be carried on by using historical and biographical material mainly. The limits of power must be limits that have been realized in actual persons, and the various ways of unlocking the reserves of power must have been exemplified in individual lives (*ERM*, p. 145).

Throughout his essay, James cites instances of human beings reaching for previously untapped powers and accomplishing goals that ordinarily would seem out of reach. One such instance involved Colonel Baird Smith, wounded in battle and afflicted with scurvy, who carried on despite the severe weakness of his body. Of his experience, Colonel Smith wrote: "The excitement of the work was so great that no lesser one seemed to have any chance against it and I certainly never found my intellect clearer or my nerves stronger in my life" (*ERM*, p. 135). To this account, James responds, "How profound is the alteration in the manner in which, under excitement, our organism will sometimes perform its physiological work" (*ERM*, p. 135). He is especially attracted to the implications of physical regimen as found in the varieties of Yoga (*ERM*, pp. 137–141). And in "The Powers of Men" he isolates the reasons for the fact that some people can release energies that are denied to the remainder. "Either some unusual stimulus fills them with emotional excitement, or some unusual idea of necessity induces them to make an extra effort of will. *Excitements, ideas, and efforts*, in a word, are what carry us over the dam" (*ERM*, p. 151).

One of the most important of these efforts is our ability to say "no" to our encrusted habits (*ERM*, p. 136). In fact, it is by such negations that we cleanse our affirmations of their habitual character and throw them into positive relief. "Our philosophic and religious development proceeds thus by credulities, negations and the negating of negations" (*ERM*, p. 157). James's final message in these two essays is that we should not allow social conventions to prevent us from being true to ourselves. He notes that "conscience makes cowards of us all" (*ERM*, p. 160). The conscience of which he speaks, is, of course, a false conscience, one that responds more to the opinions of society than to the needs of the individual. James believes that in the long run we are capable of far more creative activity than we now reveal; this would be evident if we but had the will to energize ourselves independently of what others have come to expect of us, since then expectations are sure to fall short of our potentialities. Ralph Barton Perry, James's student and intellectual biographer, summarized James's attitude toward untapped possibilities:

There is thus a common thread running through James's observations on religion, neurasthenia, war, earthquakes, fasting, lynching, patriotism —an interest, namely, in human behavior under high pressure, and the conclusion that exceptional circumstances generate exceptional inner power. These phenomena have a bearing on metaphysics because such exceptional power suggests the sudden removal of a barrier and the tappings of a greater reservoir of consciousness; and they have a bearing on ethics, since this power differs in degree rather than in kind from that moral power—that fighting and adventurous spirit, that heroic quality— which gives to life the color and radiance of value.[15]

The last two essays in this volume, "Remarks at the Peace Banquet" (1904) and "The Moral Equivalent of War" (1910), are devoted to a crucial personal, social, and political event recurring

---

[15] Ralph Barton Perry, *The Thought and Character of William James* (Boston: Little, Brown, 1935), vol. II, p. 273.

in human history: war. They are also consistent with all that James believed, temperamentally and philosophically. He opens his address to the Thirteenth International Congress of Peace Societies by stating that "reason is one of the very feeblest of Nature's forces, if you take it at any one spot and moment. It is only in the very long run that its effects become perceptible" (*ERM*, p. 120). But James does admit that both reason and experience tell us that "our permanent enemy is the noted bellicosity of human nature" (*ERM*, p. 121). In the face of this appalling but inescapable situation, we must "foster rival excitements and invent new outlets for heroic energy" (*ERM*, p. 123). This commitment was not new to James. In an unlikely context, the chapter on "Saintliness" in *The Varieties of Religious Experience*, James had earlier raised the question of finding compensating outlets for war. At that time, in 1902, he wrote: "One hears of the mechanical equivalent of heat. What we now need to discover in the social realm is the moral equivalent of war: something heroic that will speak to men as universally as war does, and yet will be as compatible with their spiritual selves as war has proved itself to be incompatible."[16]

James's essay "The Moral Equivalent of War" is a provocative statement. Even its faults demand our response. James opens the essay with the forthright contention that "the war against war is going to be no holiday excursion or camping party. The military feelings are too deeply grounded to abdicate their place among our ideals until better substitutes are offered than the glory and shame that come to nations as well as to individuals from the ups and downs of politics and the vicissitudes of trade" (*ERM*, p. 162).

Although James claims to be a pacifist (*ERM*, p. 165), he is not naive about the persistent belligerence of modern nation-states. His commentary on the intentions of Japan are extraordinarily prescient: thirty-one years from the date of his essay, the Japanese set out to realize what he anticipated to be their intentions (*ERM*, pp. 166–167). It is this awareness that leads James to the conclusion that what is needed is an "equivalent" or a "substitution" for the martial urge, rather than an unrealistic banishment of such energies (*ERM*, pp. 171–172).

The martial type of character can be bred without war. Strenuous honour and disinterestedness abound elsewhere. Priests and medical men

16 James, *Varieties*, p. 367.

are in a fashion educated to it, and we should all feel some degree of it imperative if we were conscious of our work as an obligatory service to the state. We should be *owned*, as soldiers are by the army, and our pride would rise accordingly. We could be poor, then, without humiliation, as army officers now are. The only thing needed henceforward is to inflame the civic temper as past history has inflamed the military temper (*ERM*, p. 172).

These suggestions by James were taken up in the United States on two occasions. First, during the depression of the 1930s the Civilian Conservation Corps was modeled after James's plan. (In fact, under the leadership of a philosopher, Eugene Rosenstock-Huessy, one such camp in New Hampshire was called Camp William James.) A second affirmation of James's viewpoint occurred with the founding of the Peace Corps during the presidential administration of John F. Kennedy. The Peace Corps was structured as an alternative to conscription, and the influence of James's essay was cited on behalf of that bold political move.[17]

Not all commentators were enthusiastic about James's essay. For example, in private correspondence as yet unpublished,[18] John Dewey held that James was unfeeling with respect to the vast majority of citizens who deserved neither war nor social service as a conscriptive alternative to war service. In Dewey's judgment, most lives are lived at the edge of economic and social peril. Rather than siphoning off alleged martial energies, his position was that we should effect a transformation of the social and economic inequities of our society so that our citizens would have access to a creative life without the officiousness of conscription.

James understood Dewey's diagnosis but did not understand Dewey's projected solution. In his response to the socialist literature of the time, James wrote that "high wages and short hours are the only forces invoked for overcoming man's distaste for repulsive kinds of labor. Meanwhile men at large still live as they always have lived, under a pain-and-fear economy—for those of us who live in an ease-economy are but an island in the stormy ocean—and the whole atmosphere of present-day utopian literature tastes mawkish

---

17 See "Moral Equivalent," an editorial in the *New York Times*, March 5, 1961, p. 10, and a confirming letter of James's influence by Kay Holland, *New York Times*, March 12, 1961, p. 10.

18 Dewey's papers are to be found in The Center for Dewey Studies at Southern Illinois University.

and dishwatery to people who still keep a sense for life's more bitter flavors. It suggests, in truth, ubiquitous inferiority" (*ERM*, p. 169).

For Dewey and for others who propose an ameliorative social philosophy, such inferiority will be assuaged only with a proper transformation of society. James has none of this confidence in social and political transformation. He states unabashedly that "inferiority is always with us, and merciless scorn of it is the keynote of the military temper" (*ERM*, p. 169). And then in a passage that one can regard as either condescending or realistic, James sets out what he takes to be the range of possibilities for the average person. "The best thing about our 'inferiors' to day is that they are as tough as nails, and physically and morally almost as insensitive. Utopianism would see them soft and squeamish, while militarism would keep their callousness, but transfigure it into a meritorious characteristic, needed by 'the service,' and redeemed by that from the suspicion of inferiority. All the qualities of a man acquire dignity when he knows that the service of the collectivity that owns him needs them. If proud of the collectivity, his own pride rises in proportion" (*ERM*, p. 169).

There is a painful truth in this description by James, but I find missing both his distinctive emphasis on the individual's "will to believe" and his otherwise celebrated stress on the capacity of human beings to draw on energies and powers, hidden but accessible to the creative life. Is it necessary to be in the service of one collectivity or another for these capacities to be unleashed, unveiled, or even acknowledged? Are we caught between the bourgeois life, which James regards as humdrum, and the proletarian life, which he finds in need of stimulation by appeal to a collective demand, military or civilian? It would seem so, although in his writings as a whole, James fortunately transcends this dichotomy and joins those thinkers for whom every individual life is called upon to be and to do something distinctive, novel, and undying.

The essays in this volume were written over a period of twenty-four years. The dominant themes center on religious experience and on human moral obligations and moral possibilities. James had an indefatigable commitment to possibilities beyond our present sight and to the importance of events that remained unsung by the traditional canons of observation, acceptance, and evaluation. Immortality, cosmic consciousness, reserves of human strength, nostrums for renewed energy, and solutions to the habituation of violence and war all come within the ken of these essays. Never dull, usually imaginative, always brilliantly written, and frequently controversial, they represent William James as a thinker of importance, and they call upon us to study his major works with care and in detail.

Despite the fact that I opened this Introduction with Julius Bixler's wise admonition that the isolated reference from James is unreliable, I cannot resist suggesting that the most pregnant single line in this volume is to be found in his Introduction to his father's *Literary Remains*: "The sanest and best of us are of one clay with lunatics and prison-inmates" (*ERM*, p. 62). Excessive perhaps, but this trenchant admonition, at the least, should keep us from arrogance, philosophical and otherwise.

Essays in
Religion and Morality

Introduction to *The Literary Remains of the Late Henry James*

The longer of the works that follow was left by its author almost finished, and, as far as it goes, in completed form,—the proofs having been corrected and the electrotype plates made, under his own direction, during the last year of his life.

The autobiographic fragment dates from an earlier period. He had often been urged by members of his family to express his religious philosophy under the form of a personal evolution of opinion. But egotistic analysis was less to his taste than enunciation of objective results; so that, although he sat down to the autobiographic task a good many times, it was at long intervals; and the work, *Society the Redeemed Form of Man*, as well as the one now first published, were both written after the Autobiography was begun. The Stephen Dewhurst, whose confessions it is supposed to be, is an entirely fictitious personage. The few items of personal and geographic fact he gives have been rectified in footnotes, so as to be true of Mr. James rather than of his imaginary mouthpiece. The fragments were set up in type as fast as written, and the proofs preserved and much revised. A good deal of manuscript has been interpolated. The editor has used some discretion in the printing of this, some passages being diffuse. Probably no one will read what is here printed without a deep regret that the work should not have extended over later years of the author's life. To atone for the loss, I have tried to weave into the quotations later to be made in this Introduction all the autobiographic passages and references that are found scattered through his other works.

It is judged best to publish, for the present at any rate, none of the manuscript lectures or other fragments left by Mr. James. And of his contributions to periodical literature, only one, the article on Carlyle, sees the light again in this volume. Exception was made in favor of that article, because of its exceptional "popularity" at the time of its original publication.

It has seemed to me not only a filial but a philosophic duty, in giving these posthumous pages to the world, to prefix to them some such account of their author's ideas as might awaken, in readers hitherto strangers to his writings, the desire to become acquainted with them. I wish a less unworthy hand than mine were there to do the work. As it is, I must screen my own inadequacy under the language of the original, and let my father speak, as far as possible, for himself. It would indeed be foolish to seek to paraphrase anything once directly said by him. The matter would be sure to suffer; for, from the very outset of his literary career, we find him in the effortless possession of that style with which the reader will soon become acquainted, and which, to its great dignity of cadence and full and homely vocabulary, united a sort of inward palpitating human quality, gracious and tender, precise, fierce, scornful, humorous by turns, recalling the rich vascular temperament of the old English masters, rather than that of an American of to-day.

With all the richness of style, the ideas are singularly unvaried and few. Probably few authors have so devoted their entire lives to the monotonous elaboration of one single bundle of truths. Whenever the eye falls upon one of Mr. James's pages,—whether it be a letter to a newspaper or to a friend, whether it be his earliest or his latest book,—we seem to find him saying again and again the same thing; telling us what the true relation is between mankind and its Creator. What he had to say on this point was the burden of his whole life, and its only burden. When he had said it once, he was disgusted with the insufficiency of the formulation (he always hated the sight of his old books), and set himself to work to say it again. But he never analyzed his terms or his data beyond a certain point, and made very few fundamentally new discriminations; so the result of all these successive re-editings was repetition and amplification and enrichment, rather than reconstruction. The student

of any one of his works knows, consequently, all
in the rest. I must say, however, that the later fo
philosophically, if not always rhetorically, the best.
Redeemed Form of Man, which was composed whil
effects of an apoplectic stroke had not passed away, th
unsurpassed in any former writing. And in the work
lished, although most of it was written when my f
mental powers were visibly altered by a decay of stren
with his death, I doubt if his earlier readers wil
signs of intellectual decrepitude. His truths were his
the companions of his deathbed; and when all else ha
his grasp of them was still vigorous and sure.

As aforesaid, they were truths theological. This is
a theological age, as we all know; and so far as it perm
theological at all, it is growing more and more to distr
that aim at abstract metaphysics in dogma, or pretei
their terms. The conventional and traditional acquies
in the older dogmatic formularies is confined to thos
tellectually hardly vitalized enough either to apprehe
a novel and rival creed; whilst those of us who hav
vitality are either apt to be full of bias against theism
or if we are theistic at all, it is in such a tentative and
sort of way that the sight of a robust and dogmatizin
sends a shiver through our bones. A man like my fat
on such a time, is wholly out of his element and atm
is soon left stranded high and dry. His effectiveness as
is null; and it is wonderful if his voice, crying in the wil
getting no echo, do not soon die away for sheer disco
That my father should not have been discouraged, but
remained serene and active to the last, is a proof both
ness of his heart and of the consolations of his creed. Ho
known persons may have received help and suggestio
writings it is impossible to say. Of out-and-out disciples l
few who ever named themselves. Few as they were, his
dence with them was perhaps his principal solace and re

I have often tried to imagine what sort of a figure my fa
have made, had he been born in a genuinely theologica
the best minds about him fermenting with the mystery
vinity, and the air full of definitions and theories an
theories, and strenuous reasonings and contentions, abou

lations to mankind. Floated on such a congenial tide, furthered by sympathetic comrades, and opposed no longer by blank silence but by passionate and definite resistance, he would infallibly have developed his resources in many ways which, as it was, he never tried; and he would have played a prominent, perhaps a momentous and critical, part in the struggles of his time, for he was a religious prophet and genius, if ever prophet and genius there were. He published an intensely positive, radical, and fresh conception of God, and an intensely vital view of our connection with him. And nothing shows better the altogether lifeless and unintellectual character of the professional theism of our time, than the fact that this view, this conception, so vigorously thrown down, should not have stirred the faintest tremulation on its stagnant pool.

The centre of his whole view of things is this intense conception of God as a creator. Grant it, accept it without criticism, and the rest follows. He nowhere attempts by metaphysical or empirical arguments to make the existence of God plausible; he simply assumes it as something that must be confessed. As has been well said in a recent little work,[1] "Mr. James looks at creation instinctively from the creative side, and this has a tendency to put him at a remove from his readers. The usual problem is: Given the creation, to find the Creator; to Mr. James it is: Given the Creator, to find the creation. God is; of His being there is no doubt, but who and what are *we*?"

To sceptics of theism in any possible form, this fundamental postulate may naturally prove a barrier. But it is difficult to see why it should be an obstacle to professedly Christian students. They also confess God's existence; and the way in which Mr. James took it *au grand sérieux*, and the issues he read in it, ought, one would suppose, to speak to them with some accent of reality. Like any early Jewish prophet, like the Luther described in a recent work of genius,[2] he went back so far and so deep as to find the religious sentiment in its purest and most unsophisticated form. He lived and breathed as one who knew he had not made himself, but was the work of a power that let him live from one moment to the next, and could do with him what it pleased. His intellect reacted on his sense of the presence of this power, so as to form a *system* of the most

1 *Philosophy of Henry James: A Digest.* By J. A. Kellogg. New York, John W. Lovell Company, 1883 [pp. 4–5].

2 J. Milsand: *Luther et le serf-arbitre.* Paris, Fischbacher, 1884. *Passim.*

radical and self-consistent, as well as of the most simple, kind. I will essay to give the reader a preliminary notion of what its main elements and outlines were, and then try to build up a more adequate representation of it by means of quotations from the author's own pen.

It had many and diverse affinities. It was optimistic in one sense, pessimistic in another. Pantheistic, idealistic, hegelian, are epithets that very naturally arise on the reader's lips to describe it; and yet some part there is of the connotation of each of these epithets that made my father violently refuse to submit to their imposition. The ordinary empirical ethics of evolutionary naturalism can find a perfect *permis de séjour* under the system's wings; and yet close alongside is an insistence on the need of the death of the natural man and of a supernatural redemption, more thorough-going than what we find in the most evangelical protestantism. Dualism, yet monism; antinomianism, yet restraint; atheism (as we might almost name it,—that is, the swallowing up of God in Humanity) as the last result of God's achievement,—such are some of the first aspects of this at bottom very simple and harmonious view of the world.

It all flowed from two perceptions, insights, convictions, whatever one pleases to call them, in its author's mind. In the first place, he felt that the individual man, as such, is nothing, but owes all he is and has to the race nature he inherits, and to the society into which he is born. And, secondly, he scorned to admit, even as a possibility, that the great and loving Creator, who has all the being and the power, and has brought us as far as *this*, should not bring us *through*, and *out*, into the most triumphant harmony.

I beseech the reader from now onwards to listen to my stammering exposition in a very uncritical mood of mind. Do not *squeeze* the terms or the logic too hard! And if you are a positivist, do not be too prompt to throw the book down with an ejaculation of disgust at Alexandrian theosophizing, and of wonder that such brain-spinning should find a printer at the present day. My father's own disgust at any abstract statement of his system could hardly be excelled by that of the most positivistic reader. I will not say that the logical relations of its terms were with him a mere afterthought; they were more organic than that. But the core and centre of the thing in him was always instinct and attitude, something realized at a stroke, and felt like a fire in his breast; and all attempts at articulate verbal formulations of it were makeshifts of a more or less desperately impotent kind. This is why he despised every formulation he made as soon as it was uttered, and set himself to the Sisyphus-labor of producing a new one that should be less irrelevant. I remember hearing him groan, when struggling in this way, "Oh, that I might thunder it out in a single interjection that would tell the *whole* of it, and never speak a word again!" But he paid his tribute to necessity; and few writers in the end were more prolix than he.

To begin then,—trying to think the matter in as simple, childlike, and empirical a fashion as possible,—the negativity and dearth of the creature (which is surely a part of the truth we livingly feel every day of our lives)[3] is an elementary and primitive factor in the creative problem. It plays an active and dynamic part through Mr. James's pages, and is the feature which made me say, a moment back, that "hegelian" would be a very natural epithet to use in describing the doctrine they set forth. Hegel sometimes speaks of the Divinity making an illusion first, in order to remove it; setting up his own antithesis in order to the subsequent neutralization thereof. And this will also very well describe the creative drama as pictured by Mr. James, provided one bear in mind that the preliminary production of an illusory stage of being is *forced* upon the Creator by the character of that *positively yawning emptiness*

---

3 Empirically, we know that we are creatures with a lack, a destitution, a death, an ultimate helplessness. Which of us but sometimes "lifts a pallid face in prayer to God lest some hideous calamity engulf his fairest hopes? . . . We are all without real selfhood, without the selfhood which comes from God alone. We have only the shewy and fallacious one . . . which is wholly inadequate to guarantee us against calamity. We shiver in every breeze, and stand aghast at every cloud that passes over the sun. When our ships . . . go down at sea, what shrieks we hear from blanched and frenzied lips peopling the melancholy main, perturbing the sombre and sympathetic air, for months afterwards! When our children die, and take back to heaven the brimming innocence which our corrupt manhood feels no use for, and therefore knows not how to shelter; when our friends drop off; when our property exhales; when our reason totters on its throne, and menaces us with a downfall; who then is strong? Who, in fact, if he were left in these cases for a moment to himself, that is, if he were not steadied in his own despite by the mere life of routine and tradition, but would be ready to renounce God and perish? So too our *ennui* and prevalent disgust of life, which lead so many suffering souls every year to suicide, which drive so many tender and yearning and angel-freighted natures to drink, to gambling, to fierce and ruinous excess of all sorts: what are these things but the tacit avowal (audible enough however, to God!) that we are nothing at all and vanity, that we are absolutely without help in ourselves, and that we can never be blessed and tranquil until God take compassion on us, and conjoin us livingly and immortally with Himself?"— *Christianity the Logic of Creation*, pp. 132–134.

8

which is the opposite of himself, and with which he has to deal.

The ordinary orthodox view of creation is that Jehovah explodes the universe absolutely out of what was previously pure blank; his *fiat* whacks it down upon the *tabula rasa* of time and space, and there it remains. Such simple, direct, and "magical" creation is always derided by Mr. James as a childish idea. The *real* nothingness cannot become thus promptly the seat of real being; it must taint with its own "abysmal destitution" whatever first comes to fill it, and reduce it to the status of a sham, or unreal magic-lantern picture projected on the dark inane.

This first result of the intercourse of the creative energy with the void may *become* however, by decaying unto itself, a surface of rebound for *another* movement, of which the result is real. Creation is thus made up of two stages, the first of which is mere scaffolding to the second, which is the final work. Mr. James's terminology is a little vacillating with regard to these two stages. On the whole, "formation" is the word he oftenest applies to the first stage, and "redemption" to the second. His view of the matter is obviously entirely different from the simple, direct process taught by natural theology and by the Jewish Scripture; and it as obviously agrees in point of form with the composite movement of the Christian scheme.

All this is verbally simple enough; but what are the facts it covers? To speak very oracularly, *Nature* is for Mr. James the movement of formation, the first quickening of the void unto itself; and *Society* is the movement of redemption, or the finished spiritual work of God.

Now, both "Nature" and "Society" are words of peculiar and complex meaning in Mr. James's writings, so that much explanation is needed of the assertions just laid down.

"Nature" and "Society," if I understand our author correctly, do not differ from each other at all in substance or material. Their substance is the Creator himself, for he is the sole positive substance in the universe, all else being nothingness.[4] But they differ in form;

---

[4] This is why I said one might call the system pantheistic. Mr. James denounces pantheism, however; for he supposes it to exclude a dualism even of *logical* elements, and to represent the Divine as manifesting itself in phenomena by a simple outward movement without subsequent recoil. It is a matter of verbal definition after all. One might say that the gist of his differences, both with pantheism and with ordinary theism, is that while the latter represent creation to be essentially the formation of Two out of an original One, to Mr. James it is something more like the union into One of an original Two.

for while Nature is the Creator immersed and lost in a nothingness self-affirming and obstructive, Society is the same Creator, with the nothingness saved, determined to transparency and self-confession, and traversed from pole to pole by his life-giving rays.

The *matter* covered by both these words is Humanity and the totality of its conditions, nothing short of the entire world of phenomenal experience,—mineral, vegetable, animal, and human,— "Nature" culminating in, whilst "Society" starts from, the moral and religious consciousness of man. This is why I said the system could hospitably house anything that naturalistic evolutionism might ever have to say about man; for, according to both doctrines, man's morality and religion, his consciousness of self and his moral conscience, are natural products like everything else we see. Now, for Mr. James, the consciousness of self and the conscience are the hinges on which the process of creation turns, as it slowly revolves from its formative and natural to its redeemed and spiritual position of equilibrium. What I say will still be dark and unreal enough to those who know nothing of the original; but the exercise of a little patience will erelong make things clear.

What is self-consciousness or morality? and what is conscience or religion?—for our author uses synonymously the terms within each pair. The terminology is at first bewildering, and the metaphysical results confounding; for whilst the *stuff* of both morality and religion is, so to speak, the very energy, the very being, of God himself, yet in morality that being takes wholly, and in religion it takes partly, the form of a lie. Let us consider the matter *naïvely* and mythically, so as to understand. Remember, that for Mr. James a mere resistless "bang" is no creative process at all, and that a *real* creation means nothing short of a real *bringing to life* of the essential nothingness, which is the eternal antithesis to God,—a *work*, therefore, upon that nothingness actually performed. Well, then, God must work upon the void; but how can the trackless void be wrought upon? It must first be vivified and quickened into some kind of substantiality of its own, and made existential and phenomenal instead of merely logical and essential that it was, before any further fashioning of it can take place. God then must, *in the first instance*, make a being that has the void for its other parent, and *involves* nothingness in itself. To make a long story short, then, God's first product is a Nature *subject to self-consciousness or selfhood*,—that is, a Nature essentially good, as being divine, but the several members whereof *appropriate* the goodness, and egoistically and atheistically[5] seek to identify it with their private selves. This selfishness of the several members is the trail of the serpent over creation, the coming to life of the ancestral void. It negates, because it entirely inverts, God's own energy, which is undiluted altruistic love; it intercepts the truth of his impartial flowing tides; it is an utter lie, and yet a lie under the dense and unsuspecting mask of which alone "the great and sincere creator of men" is able gradually to conciliate our instincts, and win us over to the truth.

This happens whenever we are weaned from the lie; for the abandoning of the lie in this instance coalesces in the same conscious act with the confessing of the truth. "I am nothing as substantive,—I am everything as recipient"; this is a thought in which both I and the Creator figure, but in which we figure in perfectly harmonious and truthful guise. It is accordingly the threshold of spiritual life; and instead of obstructing and striving to intercept, it welcomes and furthers all that the divine Love may have in store for every member of the created family.

The agents of the *weaning* are conscience and religion. In the philosophy before us, these faculties are considered to have no other function than that of being ministers of death to the fallacious selfhood. They have no positive worth or character, and are mere clearers of the way. They bring no new content upon the scene; they simply permit the pre-existing content to settle into a new and truer form. The facts of our nature with every man in it blinded with pride and jealousy, and stiffened in exclusiveness and self-seeking, are one thing,—that thing whose destinies Church and State are invoked to control, and whose tragic and discordant history we partly know. Those very same facts, after conscience and religion have played their part, and undermined the illusion of the self, so

5 "That is to say: the only hindrance to men's believing in God as a creator, is their inability to believe in *themselves* as created. Self-consciousness, the sentiment of personality, the feeling I have of life in myself, absolute and underived from any other save in a natural way, is so subtly and powerfully atheistic, that no matter how loyally I may be taught to insist upon creation as a mere traditional or legendary fact, I never feel inclined personally to believe in it, save as the fruit of some profound intellectual humiliation, or hopeless inward vexation of spirit. My inward *afflatus* from this cause is so great, I am conscious of such superabounding personal life, that I am satisfied, for my own part at least, that my sense of selfhood must in some subtle exquisite way find itself wounded to death—find itself *become death* in fact, *the only death I am capable of believing in*—before any genuine spiritual resuscitation is at all practicable for me."—*Society the Redeemed Form of Man*, pp. 165–166.

that men acknowledge their life to come from God, and love each other as God loves, having no exclusive private cares, will form the kingdom of heaven on earth, the regenerate social order which none of us yet know. In a word, God will be fully incarnated at last in a form that no longer contradicts his character, in what Mr. James calls, with Swedenborg, the Divine-Natural Humanity. God's real creature is this aggregate Humanity. He cannot be partial to one fractional unit of us more than to another. And the only difference between the unredeemed and the regenerate social form lies in the simple fact, that in the former the units *will* not fall into relations accordant with this truth, while in the latter, such an attitude is the one they most spontaneously assume. One Substance, extricating itself by finding at last a true form,—such is the process, once begun! And no one *part* is either "lost" or "saved" in any other sense than that it either arrests or furthers the transmission through itself to others of God's life-giving tides.

This probably sounds to most ears thin and cold and mythical enough,—the "Divine-Natural Humanity" especially, with its abolition of selfishness, appearing quite as shallow and insipid a dream as any other paradise excogitated by imaginative man. This is the inevitable result of trying to express didactically and articulately, in the form of a story, what in its origin is more like an intuition, sentiment, or attitude of the soul. The matter shall be immediately thickened and filled out to the reader's understanding by quotations from Mr. James himself, touching successively the various elements of the scheme. But if I may be permitted an opinion here, I should say that in no such successive shape as this did the scheme have *authority* over Mr. James's own mind. I fancy that his belief in its truth was strongest when the dumb sense of human life, sickened and baffled as it is forever by the strange unnatural fever in its breast of unreality and dearth struggling with infinite fulness and possession, became a sort of voice within him, and cried out, "This *must* stop! The good, the good, is really *there*, and *must* see to its own! Who is its own? Is it this querulous usurping, jealous *me*, sickened of defeat and done to death, and glad never to raise its head again? Never more! It is some sweeter, larger, more innocent and generous receptacle of life than that cadaverous and lying thing can ever be.[6] Let *that* but be removed, and the other may come in.

---

[6] "Just in proportion accordingly as a man's spiritual knowledge improves, will his contempt for himself as an unmixed spiritual tramp, and irredeemable vagabond,

And there must be a way to remove it, for God himself is there, and cannot be frustrated forever of his aim,—least of all by such an obstacle as that! He must *somehow,* and by eternal necessity he *shall,* bring the kingdom of heaven about!"

I may as well say here, once for all, that the kingdom of heaven postulated in this deep and simple way, and then more articulately formulated as the "Divine-Natural Humanity," remained to the end a mere postulate or programme in my father's pages, and never received at his hands any concrete filling out. It was what *must* come to be, if God truly exist,—an assumption we *owe* to his power and his love, and that any man with a sense of God's reality will scorn to hesitate to make. That, moreover, the kingdom was to be made of no other stuff than the actual stuff of human nature, was but another tribute,—a tribute of manly loyalty to the real divinity of the Good existing in the human bosom now. In his earlier years, between 1842 and 1850, when Mr. James's ideas were being settled by the reading of Swedenborg, he also became interested in the socialistic fermentations then so rife, and in particular in the writings of Fourier. His first two works shadow forth the Divine-Natural Humanity as about to be born, through the yoking of the passions into harmonious social service, by the growth of socialistic organization, in place of the old régime of Church and State, among men. Since then, there have been many disappointments, in which he shared; and although Fourier's system was never displaced from his mind as at least a provisional representation of possible redeemed life, I think that at the last he cared little to dispute about matters of detail, being willing to cast the whole burden upon God, who would be sure to order it rightly when all the conditions were fulfilled.

I will now let the author speak as much as possible for himself. And perhaps the best way to begin is to cull a few of the numerous passages in which he succinctly states the necessities which, by its own intrinsic logic, the problem of creation involves.

---

increase and abound. We might very well bear with an uninstructed or inexperienced child, who, shut up to the companionship of its doll, constructed all of sawdust and prunella, looks upon it as spiritually alive . . . . But one has no patience with an experienced instructed man or churchman, who undergoes precisely the same hallucination with regard to his own worthless doll of a selfhood—which is destitute even of so much as a sawdust and prunella reality—and conceives that the Divine being has nothing better to do than literally to bestow Divine and immortal life upon that dead, corrupt, and stinking thing."—*New Church Independent,* September, 1879, p. 414.

"Nothing can be so intensely antagonistic to the conception of a creator as that of a creature. To create is one thing, to be created is the total and exact opposite of that thing. For what is one's *nature* as a creature? It is abject want or destitution. To be created is to be void of all things in one's self, and to possess them only in another; and if I am the creature accordingly of an infinite creator, my want of course must be infinite. The nature of a thing is what the thing is in itself, and apart from foreign interference. And evidently what the creature is in himself and apart from the creator is sheer nothingness, that is to say, sheer want or destitution, destitution of all things, whether of life, of existence, or even of being. So that to give the creature natural form or selfhood, is merely to vivify the infinite void he is in himself; is merely to organize in living form the universal destitution he is under with respect to the creative fulness."[7]

[7] *Secret of Swedenborg*, p. 47. Another statement may here be given:—

"Swedenborg's doctrine summarily stated is, that what we call nature, and suppose to be exactly what it seems, is in truth a thing of strictly human and strictly divine dimensions both as being at one and the same moment a just exponent of the creature's essential want or finiteness, and of the creator's essential fulness or infinitude. . . .

"In all true creation the creator is bound, by the fact of his giving absolute being to the creature, to communicate himself—make himself over—without stint to the creature; and the creature, in his turn, because he gives phenomenal form or manifestation to the creative power, is bound to absorb the creator in himself, to *appropriate* him as it were to himself, to reproduce his infinite or stainless love in all manner of finite egotistic form; so that the more truly the creator alone *is*, the more truly the creature alone *appears*. Now in this inevitable immersion which creation implies of creative being in created form, we have, according to Swedenborg, the origin of nature. It grows necessarily out of the obligation the creature is under by creation to *appropriate* the creator, or reproduce him in his own finite lineaments. It overtly consecrates the covert marriage of infinite and finite, creator and creature. By the hypothesis of creation the creator gives sole and absolute being to the creature; and unless therefore the creature reverberate the communication, or react towards the creator, the latter will inevitably swallow him up, or extinguish him. . . . Thus in the hierarchical marriage of creator and creature which we call creation, the creator yields the creature the primary place by spontaneously assuming himself a secondary or servile one; gives him absolute or objective being, in fact, only by stooping himself to the limitations of the created form. . . .

"It is a necessary implication, then, of the truth of the Divine-Natural Humanity, that while the creator gives invisible spiritual being to the creature, the creature in his turn gives natural form—gives visible existence—to the creator; or, more briefly, while the creator gives reality to the creature, the creature gives phenomenality to the creator. In other words still, we may say, that while the creator supplies the essential or properly creative element in creation, the creature supplies its existential or properly constitutive element—that element of hold-back or resistance without which it could

"If accordingly the creative love should scruple to permit *proprium* or selfhood to its creature—scruple to endow him with moral consciousness—it would withhold from him all conscious life or joy, and leave him a mere form of vegetative existence. Creation, to allow of any true fellowship or equality between creator and creature, demands that the creature be *himself*, that is, be *naturally* posited to his own consciousness, and he cannot be thus posited save in so far as the creative love vivifies his essential destitution, organizes it in living form, and by the experience thus engendered in the created bosom lays a basis for any amount of free or spiritual reaction in the creature towards the uncreated good.

"One sees at a glance, then, how very discreditable a thing creation would be to the creator, and how very injurious to the creature, if it stopped short in itself, i.e. contented itself with simply giving the creature natural selfhood, or antagonizing him with the creator. Nothing could be more hideous to conceive of than a creation which should end by exhibiting the subjective antagonism of its two factors, without providing for their subsequent objective

---

never put on manifestation. Nature is the attestation of this ceaseless give-and-take between creator and creature; the nuptial ring that confirms and consecrates the deathless espousals of infinite and finite. In spite, therefore, of its fertile and domineering actuality to sense, it is as void of all reality to reason as the shadow of one's person in a glass. It is, in fact, only the outward image or shadow of itself which is cast by the inward or spiritual world upon the mirror of our rudimentary intelligence. And inasmuch as the shadow or subjective image of itself which any object projects of necessity reproduces the object in inverse form, so nature, being the subjective image or shadow of God's objective and spiritual creation, turns out a sheer inversion of spiritual order; exhibits the creator's fulness veiled by the creature's want, the creator's perfection obscured, or negatively revealed, by the creature's imperfection. Spiritual or creative order affirms the essential unity of every creature with every other, and of all with the creator. Natural or created order must consequently exhibit the contingent or phenomenal oppugnancy of every creature with every other, and of all with the creator; or else furnish no adequate foothold or flooring to the spiritual world. . . .

"The logic of the case is inexorable. If creation at its culmination be an exact practical equation of creator and creature, the *minus* of the latter being rigidly equivalent to the *plus* of the former, then it incorporates as its needful basis a sphere of experience on the creature's part, in which he may feel himself utterly remote from the creator, and abandoned to his own resources; an empirical sphere of existence, in fine, which may unmistakably identify him with all lower things, and so alienate him from (i.e. make him consciously *another than*) his creator. Thus creation with Swedenborg, being at its apogee a rigid equation of the creator's perfection and the creature's imperfection, necessitates *a natural history*, or provisional plane of projection upon which the equation may be wrought out to its most definite issues."—*Secret of Swedenborg*, pp. 22–30.

reconciliation; which should show every cupidity incident to the abstract *nature* of the creature inflamed to infinitude, while the helpless creature *himself* at the same time was left to be the unlimited prey of his nature."[8]

"I attempt no apology, accordingly, for Swedenborg's doctrine on this subject, but applaud it with all my heart. I perfectly agree with him that *redemption* and not creation avouches the proper glory of the divine name. Creation is not, and cannot be, the final word of the divine dealings with us. It has at most a rigidly subjective efficacy as affording us self-consciousness, and not the least objective value as affording us any spiritual fellowship of the divine perfection. To be naturally created indeed—to be created an image of God—is to be anything except a spiritual likeness of him. The law of the image is subjectively to invert the lineaments of its original . . . . And to be spiritually *like* God is inwardly to undo this subjective inversion of the divine perfection to which we find ourselves naturally born or created, and put on that direct or objective presentation of it to which we are historically re-born or re-created."[9]

"You see, in short, how infinitely remote from spiritual sonship to God our natural creation leaves us, and how obligatory it is upon him therefore, if he would ever spiritually affiliate us to himself, to give us redemption from our own nature. And this great redemption, how shall it ever be able to come about? By the very nature of the case, *the sphere of its evolution is restricted to the limits of the created consciousness*, so that the creator can command absolutely no enginery to effect it, which is not supplied exclusively by the resources of that consciousness."[10]

The tragic evolution of the selfhood itself, "a limitation upon human life, which *on its face* is one of inconceivable malignity," is the only enginery required. But of its tragedy anon. Meanwhile—

"In truth, this altogether unobtrusive fact of selfhood or natural life which we are all born to, and which we therefore think nothing of but accept as a mere matter of course, is itself the eternal marvel of creation. We ourselves can modify existence almost at pleasure; we can change the form of existing things; i.e. can convert natural

[8] *Secret of Swedenborg*, p. 132.
[9] *Secret of Swedenborg*, p. 48.
[10] *Ibid.*, p. 57.

forms into artificial ones. But we cannot confer life; cannot make these artificial forms self-conscious or living. We can turn a block of wood into a table, a block of stone into a statue; but our work in no wise reflects the vivacity of Nature, because we not being life in ourselves, cannot possibly communicate life to the work of our hands. We frame a beautiful effigy of life; but the effigy remains forever uninhabited, forever irresponsive to the love which fashions it; in short forever unconscious or dead.

"Now the splendor of the creative activity is, that it makes even this effigy of itself alive with the amplest life; its product being no cold inanimate statue, but a living breathing exulting person. In short the everlasting miracle is that God is able, in giving us Himself, to endow us with our own finite selfhood as well; leaving us thereby so unidentified with Himself, so utterly free and untrammelled to our own consciousness as to be able very often seriously to doubt, and not seldom permanently to deny His own existence. And this miracle I say is utterly inexplicable upon any *datum* but that I have alleged, namely: that God is so truly infinite in love as not to shrink from shrouding His uncreated splendor in His creature's lineaments, from eternally humiliating Himself to the lowest possibilities of creaturely imbecility and iniquity, in order that the creature may thus become freely or spiritually elevated to the otherwise impracticable heights of His majestic wisdom and goodness.

"I ask no indulgence of my reader for this language. I literally mean what I say, that creation is absolutely contingent upon the Divine ability to humble Himself to the creature's level, to diminish Himself to the creature's *natural* dimensions. Language is incapable of painting too vividly the strength of my convictions on this subject. If the creature by the bare fact of his creatureship be demonstrably void of life in himself, then the creator can only succeed in rescuing him from this intrinsic death, and elevating him to Himself, by first abasing Himself to the creature; i.e. allowing His proper infinitude or perfection to be so swallowed up in the other's proper finiteness or imperfection, as never by any possibility to come into the least overt collision with it. Thus whenever I draw a breath or perform any automatic function; when I see or hear or smell or taste or touch; when I hunger or thirst; when I think or take cognizance of any truth; when I glow with passion; when I do good or evil to my fellow-man; my ability in all these cases is due exclusively to the great truth ... that God's love to me is so truly *infinite, i.e.* untainted by the least admixture of love to Himself, as to permit Him within the entire periphery of my consciousness physical intellectual and moral, to veil Himself so effectually from sight, to obscure and as it were annihilate Himself so completely on my behalf, that I cannot help *feeling* myself to exist absolutely or irrespectively of Him, and enjoy a conscious ability not only to do what is congruous with His ultimate good pleasure in me, but to abound if I please at any moment in all manner of profane injurious and filthy behavior."[11]

"There is no alternative if creation is really to take place. The creative love must either disavow its infinitude, and so renounce creation, or else it must frankly submit to all the degradation the created nature imposes upon it, i.e. it must consent to be converted from infinite love in itself to an altogether finite love in the creature," namely, the love of self. "This is the only true or philosophic conception of creation, namely, the abandonment of yourself to what is not yourself in a manner so intimate and hearty, as that you thenceforth shall utterly disappear within the precincts of its existence—shall become phenomenally extinct within the entire realm of its personality—while it alone shall appear to be." The divine creation is no exception to this law, which "necessitates that the creature shall not even appear to be, save by the creator's actual or objective disappearance within all the field of his subjective consciousness; save by the creator's becoming objectively merged, obscured, drowned out, so to speak, in the created subjectivity."[12]

---

11 *Substance and Shadow*, pp. 82–84.

12 "Thus there is no way open to us philosophically of accounting for selfhood in the human bosom, save upon the postulate of its being the mask of an *infinite spiritual substance now imprisoned, but eventually to be set free, in our nature*: a substance whose proper energy consists in its incessantly going out of itself, or communicating itself to what is not itself, to what indeed is infinitely alien and repugnant to itself, and *dwelling there infinitely and eternally as in its very self.* That is to say, the Divine being or substance is Love, love without any the least set-off or limitation of self-love, infinite or creative love in short; and it communicates itself to the creature accordingly in no voluntary or finite but in purely spontaneous or infinite measure, in a way so to speak of overwhelming *passion*: so that we practically encounter no limit to our faculty of appropriating it, but on the contrary sensibly and exquisitely feel it to be our own indisputable being, feel it to be in fact our inmost, most vital and inseparable *self*, and unhesitatingly call it *me* and *mine*, *you* and *yours*, cleaving to it as inmost bone of our bone, and veritable flesh of our flesh, and incontinently renouncing all things for it."—*Society the Redeemed Form of Man*, pp. 162–163.

Elsewhere the same truth is expressed in a way which to ordinary ears might sound almost revoltingly paradoxical, but which can alone bring out the full depth of its meaning.

"Creator and creature then are strictly correlated existences, the latter remorselessly implicating or involving the former, the former in his turn assiduously explicating or evolving the latter. The creator is in truth the inferior term of the relation, and the creature its superior term; although in point of appearance the relationship is reversed, the creator being thought to be primary and controlling, while the creature is thought secondary and subservient. The truth incurs this humiliation, undergoes this falsification, on *our* behalf exclusively, who, because we have by nature no perception of God as a spirit, but only as a person like ourselves, are even brutally ignorant of the divine power and ways. But it *is* a sheer humiliation nevertheless. For in very truth it is the creator alone who gives subjective constitution to us, only that we, appearing to ourselves thereupon absolutely to be, may ever after give objective reality to him.[13] Thus creation is not a something outwardly achieved by God in space and time, but a something inwardly wrought by him within the compass exclusively of human nature or human consciousness; a something subjectively conceived by his love, patiently borne or elaborated by his wisdom, and painfully brought forth by his power; just as the child is subjectively conceived, patiently borne, and painfully brought forth by the mother. Creation is no brisk activity on God's part, but only a long-patience or suffering. It is no ostentatious self-assertion, no dazzling parade of magical, irrational, or irresponsible power; it is an endless humiliation or prorogation of himself to all the lowest exigencies of the created consciousness. In short, it is no finite divine action, as we stupidly dream, giving the creature objective or absolute projection from his creator; it is in truth and exclusively an infinite divine passion, which, all in giving its creature subjective or phenomenal existence, contrives to convert this provisional existence of his into objective or real being, by freely endowing the created nature with all its own pomp of love, of wisdom, and of power."

These two conceptions, of God's unendingly patient self-surrender to us, and of our intrinsic nothingness, formed the deepest

[13] As *effective* Creator, namely. A few redundant words have been omitted from the passage, which will be found in the *Secret of Swedenborg*, pp. 185–186.—Ed.

springs of Mr. James's view of life. He has no words of scorn too deep for the venerable notion of Christian theology that God creates for his own glory; and when he vindicates his own idea of the divine character, it is in language by whose passionate fervor all must be impressed.

Here are some passages in point:—

"It is an easy enough thing to find a holiday God who is all too selfish to be touched with the infirmities of his own creatures—a God, for example, who has naught to do but receive assiduous court for a work of creation done myriads of ages ago, and which is reputed to have cost him in the doing neither pains nor patience, neither affection nor thought, but simply the utterance of a dramatic word; and who is willing, accordingly, to accept our decorous sunday homage in ample quittance of obligations so unconsciously incurred on our part, so lightly rendered and so penuriously sanctioned on his. Every sect, every nation, every family almost, offers some pet idol of this description to your worship. But I am free to confess that I have long outgrown this loutish conception of deity. I can no longer bring myself to adore a characteristic activity in the God of my worship, which falls below the secular average of human character. In fact, what I crave with all my heart and understanding—what my very flesh and bones cry out for—is no longer a sunday but a weekday divinity, a working God, grimy with the dust and sweat of our most carnal appetites and passions, and bent, not for an instant upon inflating our worthless pietistic righteousness, but upon the patient, toilsome, thorough cleansing of our physical and moral existence from the odious defilement it has contracted, until we each and all present at last in body and mind the deathless effigy of his own uncreated loveliness." [14]

"Accordingly when orthodoxy commends God, the universal creator, to our rational reverence and affection, under the guise of a great melodramatic being so essentially heartless as to live for untold eternities without feeling any desire for companionship; so essentially irrational that it cost him no effort of thought to summon the universe into absolute being"; when "natural religion represents creation as an act of pure will on God's part, a movement of simple caprice, involving not one particle of the honest labor and sweat which go to the execution of any humane enterprise: say, the

[14] *Secret of Swedenborg*, pp. vi–vii.

growing or the making or the baking of a loaf of bread,"—"I will
not acknowledge a God so void of human worth; so every way level
to the character of a mere ostentatious showman or conjuror. It is
just such a childish caricature of Deity as Byron might paint to
match those childish caricatures of manhood with which his puru-
lent imagination runs riot. I am constrained by every inspiration of
true manhood to demand for my worship a perfectly human Deity;
that is to say, a Deity who is so intent upon rescuing every creature
He has made from the everlasting death and damnation he bears
about in himself *as finitely constituted*, as not to shrink if need be
from humbling Himself to every patient form of ignominy, and
feeding contentedly year in and year out, century after century,
and millennium after millennium, upon the literal breath of our
self-righteous contempt." [15]

"We laugh, as I said awhile ago, at an inventor who should ask
us to take his genius on trust, or without any evidence of its reality.
And there can be no more offensive tribute to the Divine name
than to show Him a deference we deny to the rankest charlatan.
How infinitely unworthy of God it would be to exact or expect of
the absolute and unintelligent creatures of His power a belief out
of all proportion to their sensible knowledge, or unbacked by anything but tradition! . . . I am free to confess for my own part that I
have no belief in God's absolute or irrelative and unconditional
perfection. I have not the least sentiment of worship for His name,
the least sentiment of awe or reverence towards Him, considered as
a perfect person sufficient unto Himself. That style of deity exerts
no attraction either upon my heart or understanding. Any mother
who suckles her babe upon her own breast, any bitch in fact who
litters her periodical brood of pups, presents to my imagination a
vastly nearer and sweeter Divine charm. What do I care for a goodness which boasts of a hopeless aloofness from my own nature—
except to hate it with a manly inward hatred? And what do I care
for a truth which professes to be eternally incommunicable to its
own starving progeny—but to avert myself from it with a manly
outward contempt? Let men go on to cherish under whatever name
of virtue, or wisdom, or power they will, the idol of Self-Sufficiency:
I for my part will cherish the name of Him alone whose insufficiency
to Himself is so abject that He is incapable *of realizing Himself
except in others*. In short I neither can nor will spiritually confess

15 *Substance and Shadow*, pp. 73, 72, 73.

any deity who is not essentially *human,* and existentially thence exclusively *natural,* that is to say, devoid of all distinctively personal or limitary pretensions."[16]

It is plain enough that a God like this can be neither a judge, nor a respecter, of persons; that every creature, as such, must be as dear to him as every other; and that private differences must be melted down in the warmth of his charity, as dust disappears in a furnace blast. *Our* desperate clinging to private differences is what makes us the great enemies we are to the Creator, and is the next point it will be well to take up.

Mr. James uses the words "proprium" and "selfhood" to designate what more properly should be called selfishness or self-love; for the faculty in question is evidently not the mere cognitive awareness of one's self as a special part of all existence,—which would be self-consciousness merely,—but an active emotional interest in the part so singled out, to the exclusion of the rest. Mr. James calls it sometimes the deliverance of our "consciousness," sometimes that of our "sense." Sometimes he calls it our "morality,"—a very unusual use of the word, but one which has deep reasons in his system. On the whole, however, he has no properly psychological doctrine on the subject, but merely takes his stand upon the empirical fact that this surly and jealous principle exists within us, and then proceeds to tell its function and its fate.

"Morality expresses the sentiment I have of my own absoluteness, the feeling I have of a selfhood strictly independent of that of any other man. . . . It gives us that ample individual development and nursing, that affluent preliminary experience of our finite selves, which is necessary to base or engender our subsequent unlimited social expansion. It lifts us out of the mud of animality, out of the mire of mere natural passion and appetite, and endows us with selfhood or soul, that is, with the sense of a life so much more intimate and near than that of the body, as to lead us to identify ourselves with it or to cleave to it alone, cheerfully forsaking all things for it . . . so allying us to our own inexperienced imaginations with God; giving us that sentiment of individual power and glory which is unknown to the animal nature, and which is the coarse rude germ

[16] *Society the Redeemed Form of Man,* pp. 333–334.

of all our subsequent conceptions of spiritual things; whispering in short in our fondest hearts, *Ye shall be as God knowing good and evil....*

"Self-assertion is thus so clearly the fundamental law, the vital breath, of our moral life, that it is no wonder we cling to that life as the true end of our being, and require an internal Divine quickening, or the denunciatory voice of conscience, before we consent to regard it simply as a means to an infinitely higher end, which is our unity with all mankind. The inspiration of the moral sentiment, the sentiment of selfhood, is so powerful within us; it is so sweet to feel this delicious bosom inmate disengage itself from its gross carnal envelope, and come forth a radiant white-armed Eve full formed in all Divine vigor and beauty, that we cannot help clasping it to our bosoms as thenceforth bone of our bone and flesh of our flesh, cheerfully forsaking for it father and mother; or all we have traditionally loved and traditionally believed; and cleaving undismayed to its fortunes though it lead us through the gloom of death and the fires of hell....

"Self-love is the vital atmosphere of morality and there can be no extrication from it but by honest conflict with it, conflict if need be even unto death. Some men have been more grievously lacerated in this conflict than others, going down to their graves scourged by the contempt of the proud and unthinking, with banners once so lofty now all trailing in the dust of men's reproach. But this is not because they were spiritually any worse than other men; probably the exact contrary: it is only because they had fifty times the ordinary amount of moral or self-righteous force to start with, and it could only become spiritually weakened and overcome by this terrific personal humiliation."[17]

If the creature's *nature* were anything other than the mere provisional scaffolding it is, there would be no need of extrication, of conflict, of the quickening within it of a self doomed to humiliation and defeat. In that case there might be no consciousness of self at all. All flesh might "*sensibly* perceive God to be the sole life of the universe. [But were this so,] we should sit like stocks and stones, leaving Him who *obviously* was life, to the exclusive appropriation and enjoyment of it." On the other hand, we might imagine our-

17 *Substance and Shadow*, pp. 137–140.

selves endowed with a prosperous and harmonious self from the start, and creation beginning and ending with the Garden of Eden,[18] —"a state of blissful infantile delight unperturbed as yet by those fierce storms of the intellect which are soon to envelope and sweep it away, but also unvisited by a single glimpse of that Divine and halcyon calm of the heart, in which these hideous storms will finally rock themselves to sleep. Nothing can indeed be more remote (except in pure imagery) from distinctively *human* attributes, or from the spontaneous life of man, than this sleek and comely Adamic condition, provided it should turn out an abiding one: because man in that case would prove a mere dimpled nursling of the skies, without ever rising into the slightest Divine communion or fellowship, without ever realizing a truly Divine manhood and dignity ... mere unfermented dough, insipid and impracticable .... He would have mineral body and consequent inertia, no doubt: he would have vegetable form and consequent growth; he would have animal life and consequent motion: but he would be without all power of human action, because he would lack that constant permeation and interpenetration of his spirit by the living spirit of God, which weaves his pallid natural annals into the purple tissue of history, and separates man from nature by all the plenitude and power of incarnate Deity."[19]

But the consciousness of self *cannot* be innocent and prosperous. Being, as it is, a mere magic-lantern-phantom cast by the divine love upon essential nothingness, it must reveal the void on which it is based, and have a *tragic* history, if it have a history at all. The experience of the working out of the tragedy of the self is called by our author sometimes "conscience," and sometimes "religion."

"By religion I mean—what is invariably meant by the term where the thing itself still exists—such a conscience on man's part of a forfeiture of the Divine favor, as perpetually urges him to make sacrifices of his ease, his convenience, his wealth, and if need be his life, in order to restore himself, if so it be possible, to that favor. This is religion in its literal form; natural religion; religion as it

---

18 Mr. James, following Swedenborg, often calls the creature abstracted from moral consciousness, the Adam; the moral consciousness being the Eve. *Homo* and *vir* are terms symbolizing the same distinction.

19 *Christianity the Logic of Creation*, pp. 120–121.

stands authenticated by the universal instincts of the race, before it has undergone a spiritual conversion into life, and while claiming still a purely ritual embodiment."[20]

"Every man who has reached even his intellectual teens begins to suspect this; begins to suspect that life is no farce; that it is not

[20] Mr. James scorned to apply the word religion to any experience whose starting point was not pessimistic. Our modern optimism made him complain that "religion in the old virile sense of the word has disappeared from sight, and become replaced by a feeble Unitarian sentimentality. The old religion involved a conscience of the profoundest antagonism between God and the worshipper, which utterly refused to be placated by anything short of an unconditional pledge of the utmost Divine mercy. The ancient believer felt himself sheerly unable to love God, or do anything else towards his salvation, were it only the lifting of a finger. To un-love was his only true loving, to un-learn his only true learning, to un-do his only true doing. The modern religionist is at once amused and amazed at these curious archæological beginnings of his own history. He feels towards them as a *virtuoso* does towards what is decidedly *rococo* in fashion, and not seldom bestows a word of munificent Pharisaic patronage upon them, such as the opulent Mr. Ruskin dispenses to uncouth specimens of early religious Art. He has not the slightest conception of himself as a spiritual form inwardly enlivened by all God's peace and innocence. On the contrary, he feels himself to be a strictly moral or self-possessed being, vivified exclusively by his own action, or the relations he voluntarily assumes with respect to human and Divine law. The modern believer aspires to be a saint; the ancient one abhorred to be anything but a sinner. The former looks back accordingly to some fancied era of what he calls conversion: i.e. when he passed from death to life. The latter was blissfully content to forget himself, and looked forward exclusively to his Lord's promised spiritual advent in all the forms of a redeemed nature. The one is an absolutely changed man, no longer to be confounded with the world, and meet for the Divine approbation. The other is a totally unchanged one, only more dependent than he ever was before upon the unmitigated Divine mercy. The one feels sure of going to heaven if the Lord observes the distinctions which his own grace ordains in human character. The other feels sure of going to hell unless the Lord is blessedly indifferent to those distinctions."—*Substance and Shadow*, pp. 14–15.

Again: "Religion has undergone so sheer a demoralization since her pure and holy prime—has sunk into such a brazen handmaid to worldliness, such a painted and bedizened courtesan and street-walker, proffering her unstinted favors to every sentimental fop, or clerical *beau diseur*, who has the smallest change of self-conceit in his pocket wherewith to pay for them—that one finds himself secretly invoking the advent of some grand social renovation in order to blot it *as a profession* out of remembrance, and leave it extant only as a spiritual life. Religion was once a spiritual life in the earth, though a very rude and terrible one; and her conquests were diligently authenticated by the divine spirit. Then she meant terror and amazement to all devout self-complacency in man; then she meant rebuke and denial to every form of distinctively *personal* hope and pretension towards God; then she meant discredit and death to every breath of a pharisaic or quaker temper in humanity, by which a man could be led to boast of a 'private spirit' in his bosom, giving him a differential character and aspect in God's sight to that of other men, especially the great and holy and unconscious mass of his kind."—*Secret of Swedenborg*, p. 221.

genteel comedy even; that it flowers and fructifies on the contrary out of the profoundest tragic depths . . . the depths of the essential dearth in which its subject's roots are plunged. . . . The natural inheritance of every one who is capable of spiritual life, is an unsubdued forest where the wolf howls and every obscene bird of night chatters.[21] . . . The only valid natural superiority I can claim to the animal lies in the fact that I have *conscience*, and he has not. And the only valid moral superiority I can claim to my fellow-man is, that I am more hearty in my allegiance to it, and he less hearty. Thus deeper than my intellect, deeper than my heart, deeper in fact than aught and all that I recognize as myself, or am wont to call emphatically *me*, is this dread omnipotent power of conscience which now soothes me with the voice, and nurses me with the milk of its tenderness, as the mother soothes and nurses her child, and anon scourges me with the lash of its indignation, as the father scourges his refractory heir.

"But this is only telling half the story. It is very true that conscience is the sole arbiter of good and evil to man; and that persons of a literal and superficial cast of mind—persons of a good hereditary temperament—may easily fancy themselves in spiritual harmony with it, or persuade themselves and others that they have fully satisfied every claim of its righteousness. But minds of a deeper quality soon begin to suspect that the demands of conscience are not so easily satisfied, soon discover in fact that it is a ministration of death exclusively, and not of life, to which they are abandoning themselves. For what conscience inevitably teaches all its earnest adepts erelong is, to give up the hopeless effort to reconcile good and evil in their own practice, and learn to identify themselves, on the contrary, with the evil principle alone, while they assign all good exclusively to God. Thus no man of a sincere and honest intellectual make has ever set himself seriously to cultivate conscience with a view to its spiritual emoluments—i.e. with a view to placate the divine righteousness—without speedily discovering that every such hope is illusory, that peace flees from him just in proportion to the eagerness with which he covets it. In other words, no man, not a fool, since the beginning of history, has ever deliberately set himself 'to eat of the tree of the knowledge of good and evil'—i.e. *to prosecute his moral instincts until he should become inwardly as-*

[21] *Substance and Shadow*, p. 75.

sured of God's personal complacency in him—without finding death and not life to his soul, without his inward and spiritual obliquity being sooner or later made to abound in the exact ratio of his moral or outward rectitude. I have no idea, of course, that a man may not be beguiled by the insinuating breath of sense into believing himself spiritually or in the depths just what he appears to be morally or in the shallows. Vast numbers of persons, indeed, are to be found in every community, who—having as yet attained to no spiritual insight or understanding—are entirely content with, nay, proud of, the moral 'purple and fine linen' with which they are daily decked out in the favorable esteem of their friends, and are meanwhile at hearty peace with themselves. All this in fact is strictly inevitable to our native and cultivated fatuity in spiritual things; but I am not here concerned with the fact in the way either of denial or of confirmation. What I here mean specifically to say is, that every one in whom, to use a common locution of Swedenborg, 'the spiritual degree of the mind has been opened,' finds conscience no friend, but an impassioned foe to his moral righteousness or complacency in himself, and hence to his personal repose in God. . . . A stream cannot mount above its source, and . . . when I earnestly aspire to fulfil the divine law—when I earnestly strive after moral or personal excellence—my aim unquestionably is to lift myself above the level of human nature, or attain to a place in the divine regard unshared by the average of my kind; unshared by the liar, the thief, the adulterer, the murderer. But the same law which discountenances false-witness, theft, adultery, and murder binds me also *not to covet*: i.e. *not to desire for myself what other men do not enjoy*: so that the law which I fondly imagined was designed to give me life turns out a subtle ministry of death, and in the very crisis of my moral exaltation fills me with the profoundest spiritual humiliation and despair. It is an instinct doubtless of the divine life in me to hate false-witness, theft, adultery, and murder, and actually to avert myself from these evils whenever I am naturally tempted to do them. But then I must hate them *for their own sake*, exclusively, or because of their contrariety to infinite goodness and truth, and not with a base view to tighten my hold upon God's personal approbation. I grossly pervert the spirit of the law, and betray its infinite majesty to shame, if I suppose it capable of ratifying in any degree my private and personal cupidity towards God, or lending even a moment's sanction to the altogether frivolous and odious separation which I devoutly hope to compass between myself and other men in his sight.

"The entire historic function of conscience has been to operate an effectual check upon our gigantic natural pride and cupidity in spiritual things, by avouching a total contrariety between God and ourselves, so long as we remain indifferent to the truth of our essential society, fellowship, or equality with our kind, and are moved only by selfish or personal considerations in the devout overtures we make to the divine regard. . . . The only respect it ever pays to the private votary is to convince him of sin, through a conviction of God's wholly *impersonal* justice . . . [and make him] frankly disavow every title to the divine esteem which is not quite equally shared by publican and harlot." [22]

Selfhood and conscience, then, or "Morality and Religion together constitute the subject-earth of self-love which revolves now in light now in shade; morality being the illuminated side of that love, religion its obscured side; the one constituting the splendor of its day, the other the darkness of its night. Morality is the summer lustihood and luxuriance of self-love, clothing its mineral ribs with vegetable grace, permeating its rigid trunk with sap, decorating its gnarled limbs with foliage, glorifying every reluctant virgin bud and every modest wifely blossom into rich ripe motherly fruit. Religion is the icy winter which blights this summer fertility, which arrests the ascent of its vivifying sap, and humbles its superb life to the ground, in the interests of a spring that shall be perennial, and of autumns bursting with imperishable fruit. In other words, religion has no substantive force. Her sole errand on earth has been to dog the footsteps of morality, to humble the pride of selfhood which man derives from nature, and so soften his interiors to the reception of Divine Truth, as that truth shall stand fulfilled in the organization of human equality or fellowship." [23]

"Self-conceit and self-reproach, pride and penitence, thus make up the fever and the chill into which that great intermittent, which we call our moral and religious experience, ordinarily resolves itself." My father seems in his early years to have had an unusually lively and protracted visitation of this malady, and his philosophy indeed is but the statement of his cure. In the autobiographic pages

[22] *Secret of Swedenborg*, pp. 161–165.
[23] *Substance and Shadow*, pp. 10–11.

28

to be found further on, there is a full account of his boyish evolution in this respect. And here and there in his other writings we get glimpses of later states of mind which it will be profitable now to transcribe. Here is one of them:

"I had never for a moment *intellectually* realized my moral consciousness to be that mere steward or servant of the Divine inheritance in our nature, which Swedenborg showed it to be. On the contrary with the intellect, and in spite of the heart's misgiving, I had always quietly allowed it to be the undeniable lord of the inheritance, and beheld it accordingly whipping the men-servants and the maid-servants at its pleasure, without a suspicion. Far from supposing my natural selfhood or *proprium* to constitute a strictly *negative* token, an essentially *inverse* attestation, of God's spiritual and infinite presence in our nature, I habitually viewed it as the church taught me to view it, that is, as the only direct and positive manifestation of His power; and my religious life accordingly became one of incessant conflict and perturbation.

"How could it have been otherwise? Having as I supposed a purely moral *status* by creation—never dreaming that my selfhood possessed only a formal or subjective validity—I attributed to myself an objective or substantial reality in God's sight, and of course sought to attract His approbation to me, by the unswerving pursuit of moral excellence, by studiously cultivating every method of personal purity. It was all in vain. The more I strove to indue myself in actual righteousness, the wider gaped the jaws of hell within me; the fouler grew its fetid breath. A conviction of inward defilement so sheer took possession of me, that death seemed better than life. I soon found my conscience, once launched in this insane career, acquiring so infernal an edge, that I could no longer indulge myself in the most momentary deviation from an absurd and pedantic literal rectitude—could not for example bestow a sulky glance upon my wife, a cross word upon my child, or a petulant objurgation on my cook—without tumbling into an instant inward frenzy of alarm, lest I should thereby have provoked God's personal malignity to me. There is indeed no way of avoiding spiritual results so belittling, but by ceasing to regard morality as a direct, and looking upon it as an inverse, image of God's true life in us. If my moral consciousness constitute the true and eternal bond of intercourse between me and God; that is to say, if He attribute to me all the good and evil which I in my insane pride attribute to myself: then it will be impossible for me to avoid all eternity, either a most conceited and disgusting conviction of His personal complacency in me; or else a shuddering apprehension of His personal ill-will. If I have a naturally complacent temper my religious life will reflect it, and array me spiritually in all manner of nauseous Pharisaism and flunkeyism. If I have what is called a 'morbid' natural temperament, on the other hand, leading me to self-distrust and self-depreciation, my religious life will deepen these things into despair, by making my self-condemnation confess itself a feeble reflection of God's profounder vindictiveness."[24]

In a couple of long passages of his latest published work, he tells as follows of the manner in which he became acquainted with the writings of Swedenborg, and began to get relief:—

"In the spring of 1844 I was living with my family in the neighborhood of Windsor, England, much absorbed in the study of the Scriptures. Two or three years before this period I had made an important discovery, as I fancied, namely: that the book of Genesis was not intended to throw a direct light upon our natural or race history, but was an altogether mystical or symbolic record of the laws of God's *spiritual* creation and providence. I wrote a course of lectures in exposition of this idea, and delivered them to good audiences in New York. The preparation of these lectures, while it did much to confirm me in the impression that I had made an interesting discovery, and one which would extensively modify theology, convinced me, however, that a much more close and studious application of my idea than I had yet given to the illustration of the details of the sacred letter was imperatively needed. During my residence abroad, accordingly, I never tired in my devotion to this aim, and my success seemed so flattering at length that I hoped to be finally qualified to contribute a not insignificant mite to the sum of man's highest knowledge. I remember I felt especially hopeful in the prosecution of my task all the time I was at Windsor; my health was good, my spirits cheerful, and the pleasant scenery of the Great Park and its neighborhood furnished us a constant temptation to long walks and drives.

"One day, however, towards the close of May, having eaten a com-

24 *Substance and Shadow*, pp. 125–127.

fortable dinner, I remained sitting at the table after the family had dispersed, idly gazing at the embers in the grate, thinking of nothing, and feeling only the exhiliration incident to a good digestion, when suddenly—in a lightning-flash as it were—'fear came upon me, and trembling, which made all my bones to shake.' To all appearance it was a perfectly insane and abject terror, without ostensible cause, and only to be accounted for, to my perplexed imagination, by some damnèd shape squatting invisible to me within the precincts of the room, and raying out from his fetid personality influences fatal to life. The thing had not lasted ten seconds before I felt myself a wreck, that is, reduced from a state of firm, vigorous, joyful manhood to one of almost helpless infancy. The only self-control I was capable of exerting was to keep my seat. I felt the greatest desire to run incontinently to the foot of the stairs and shout for help to my wife,—to run to the roadside even, and appeal to the public to protect me; but by an immense effort I controlled these frenzied impulses, and determined not to budge from my chair till I had recovered my lost self-possession. This purpose I held to for a good long hour, as I reckoned time, beat upon meanwhile by an ever-growing tempest of doubt, anxiety, and despair, with absolutely no relief from any truth I had ever encountered save a most pale and distant glimmer of the Divine existence,—when I resolved to abandon the vain struggle, and communicate without more ado what seemed my sudden burden of inmost, implacable unrest to my wife.

"Now, to make a long story short, this ghastly condition of mind continued with me, with gradually lengthening intervals of relief, for two years, and even longer. I consulted eminent physicians, who told me that I had doubtless overworked my brain, an evil for which no remedy existed in medicine, but only in time, and patience, and growth into improved physical conditions. They all recommended by way of hygiene a resort to the water-cure treatment, a life in the open air, cheerful company, and so forth, and thus quietly and skilfully dismissed me to my own spiritual medication. At first, when I began to feel a half-hour's respite from acute mental anguish, the bottomless mystery of my disease completely fascinated me. The more, however, I worried myself with speculations about the cause of it, the more the mystery deepened, and the deeper also grew my instinct of resentment at what seemed so needless an interference with my personal liberty. I went to a famous water-cure, which did nothing towards curing my malady but enrich my memory with a few morbid specimens of English insularity and prejudice, but it did much to alleviate it by familiarizing my senses with the exquisite and endless charm of English landscape, and giving me my first full rational relish of what may be called England's pastoral beauty. To be sure I had spent a few days in Devonshire when I was young, but my delight then was simple enthusiasm, was helpless æsthetic intoxication in fact. The 'cure' was situated in a much less lovely but still beautiful country, on the borders of a famous park, to both of which, moreover, it gave us unlimited right of possession and enjoyment. At least this was the way it always struck my imagination. The thoroughly disinterested way the English have of looking at their own hills and vales,—the indifferent, contemptuous, and as it were *disowning* mood they habitually put on towards the most ravishing pastoral loveliness man's sun anywhere shines upon,—gave me always the sense of being a discoverer of these things, and of a consequent right to enter upon their undisputed possession. At all events the rich light and shade of English landscape, the gorgeous cloud-pictures that forever dimple and diversify her fragrant and palpitating bosom, have awakened a tenderer chord in me than I have ever felt at home almost; and time and again while living at this dismal water-cure, and listening to its endless 'strife of tongues' about diet, and regimen, and disease, and politics, and parties, and persons, I have said to myself: *The curse of mankind, that which keeps our manhood so little and so depraved, is its sense of selfhood, and the absurd abominable opinionativeness it engenders. How sweet it would be to find oneself no longer man, but one of those innocent and ignorant sheep pasturing upon that placid hillside, and drinking in eternal dew and freshness from nature's lavish bosom!*

"But let me hasten to the proper upshot of this incident. My stay at the water-cure, unpromising as it was in point of physical results, made me conscious erelong of a most important change operating in the sphere of my will and understanding. It struck me as very odd, soon after my breakdown, that I should feel no longing to resume the work which had been interrupted by it; and from that day to this—nearly thirty-five years—I have never once cast a retrospective glance, even of curiosity, at the immense piles of manuscript which had erewhile so absorbed me. I suppose if any one had designated me previous to that event as an earnest seeker after truth, I should myself have seen nothing unbecoming in the appellation. But now—within two or three months of my catastrophe —I felt sure I had never caught a glimpse of truth. My present consciousness was exactly that of an utter and plenary destitution of truth. Indeed an ugly suspicion had more than once forced itself upon me, that I had never really wished the truth, but only to ventilate my own ability in discovering it. I was getting sick to death in fact with a sense of my downright intellectual poverty and dishonesty. My studious mental activity had served manifestly to base a mere 'castle in the air,' and the castle had vanished in a brief bitter moment of time, leaving not a wrack behind. I never felt again the most passing impulse, even, to look where it stood, having done with it forever. Truth indeed! How should a beggar like me be expected to discover it? How should any man of woman born pretend to such ability? Truth must *reveal itself* if it would be known, and even then how imperfectly known at best! For truth is God, the omniscient and omnipotent God, and who shall pretend to comprehend that great and adorable perfection? And yet who that aspires to the name of man, would not cheerfully barter all he knows of life for a bare glimpse of the hem of its garment?

"I was calling one day upon a friend (since deceased) who lived in the vicinity of the water-cure—a lady of rare qualities of heart and mind, and of singular personal loveliness as well—who desired to know what had brought me to the water-cure. After I had done telling her in substance what I have told you, she replied: 'It is, then, very much as I had ventured from two or three previous things you have said, to suspect: you are undergoing what Swedenborg calls a *vastation*; and though, naturally enough, you yourself are despondent or even despairing about the issue, I cannot help taking an altogether hopeful view of your prospects.' In expressing my thanks for her encouraging words, I remarked that I was not at all familiar with the Swedenborgian technics, and that I should be extremely happy if she would follow up her flattering judgment of my condition by turning into plain English the contents of the very handsome Latin word she had used. To this she again modestly replied that she only read Swedenborg as an *amateur*, and was ill-qualified to expound his philosophy, but there could be no doubt about its fundamental postulate, which was, that a new birth for man, both in the individual and the universal realm, is the secret of the Divine creation and providence: that the other world, ac-

33

cording to Swedenborg, furnishes the true sphere of man's spiritual or individual being, the real and immortal being he has in God; and he represents *this* world, consequently, as furnishing only a preliminary theatre of his natural formation or existence in subordination thereto; so making the question of human regeneration, both in grand and in little, the capital problem of philosophy: that, without pretending to dogmatize, she had been struck with the philosophic interest of my narrative in this point of view, and had used the word *vastation* to characterize one of the stages of the regenerative process, as she had found it described by Swedenborg. And then, finally, my excellent friend went on to outline for me, in a very interesting manner, her conception of Swedenborg's entire doctrine on the subject.

"Her account of it, as I found on a subsequent study of Swedenborg, was neither quite as exact nor quite as comprehensive as the facts required; but at all events I was glad to discover that any human being had so much even as proposed to shed the light of positive knowledge upon the soul's history, or bring into rational relief the alternate dark and bright—or infernal and celestial—phases of its finite constitution. For I had an immediate hope, amounting to an almost prophetic instinct, of finding in the attempt, however rash, some diversion to my cares, and I determined instantly to run up to London and procure a couple of Swedenborg's volumes, of which, if I should not be allowed on sanitary grounds absolutely to read them, I might at any rate turn over the leaves, and so catch a satisfying savor, or at least an appetizing flavor, of the possible relief they might in some better day afford to my poignant need. From the huge mass of tomes placed by the bookseller on the counter before me, I selected two of the least in bulk—the treatise on the *Divine Love and Wisdom,* and that on the *Divine Providence.* I gave them, after I brought them home, many a random but eager glance, but at last my interest in them grew so frantic under this tantalizing process of reading that I resolved, in spite of the doctors, that, instead of standing any longer shivering on the brink, I would boldly plunge into the stream, and ascertain, once for all, to what undiscovered sea its waters might bear me.

"I read from the first with palpitating interest. My heart divined, even before my intelligence was prepared to do justice to the books, the unequalled amount of truth to be found in them. Imagine a fever patient, sufficiently restored of his malady to be able to think

34

of something beside himself, suddenly transported where the free airs of heaven blow upon him, and the sound of running waters refreshes his jaded senses, and you have a feeble image of my delight in reading. Or, better still, imagine a subject of some petty despotism condemned to die, and with—what is more and worse— a sentiment of death pervading all his consciousness, lifted by a sudden miracle into felt harmony with universal man, and filled to the brim with the sentiment of indestructible life instead, and you will have a true picture of my emancipated condition. For while these remarkable books familiarized me with the angelic conception of the Divine being and providence, they gave me at the same time the amplest *rationale* I could have desired of my own particular suffering, as inherent in the profound unconscious death I bore about in my *proprium* or selfhood."[25]

"I had always, from childhood, conceived of the Creator as bearing an outside relation to the creature, and had attributed to the latter consequently the power of provoking His unmeasured hostility. Although these crude traditional views had been much modified by subsequent reflection, I had nevertheless on the whole been in the habit of ascribing to the Creator, so far as my own life and actions were concerned, an outside discernment of the most jealous scrutiny, and had accordingly put the greatest possible alertness into His service and worship, until my will, as you have seen— thoroughly fagged out as it were with the formal, heartless, endless task of conciliating a stony-hearted Deity—actually collapsed. This was a catastrophe far more tragic to my feeling, and far more revolutionary in its intellectual results, than the actual violation of any mere precept of the moral law could be. It was the practical abrogation of the law itself, through the unexpected moral inertness of the subject. It was to my feeling not only an absolute decease of my moral or voluntary power, but a shuddering recoil from my conscious activity in that line. It was an actual acute loathing of the moral pretension itself as so much downright charlatanry. No idiot was ever more incompetent, practically, to the conduct of life than I, at that trying period, felt myself to be. It cost me, in fact, as much effort to go out for a walk, or to sleep in a strange bed, as it would an ordinary man to plan a campaign or write an epic poem. I have told you how, in looking out of my window at the time at a flock of silly sheep which happened to be grazing in the

25 *Society the Redeemed Form of Man*, pp. 43–54.

Green Park opposite, I used to envy them their blissful stupid ignorance of any law higher than their nature, their deep unconsciousness of self, their innocence of all private personality and purpose, their intense moral incapacity, in short, and indifference. I would freely, nay, gladly have bartered the world at the moment for one breath of the spiritual innocence which the benign creatures outwardly pictured, or stood for to my imagination; and all the virtue, or moral righteousness, consequently, that ever illustrated our specific human personality, seemed simply foul and leprous in comparison with the deep Divine possibilities and promise of our common nature, as these stood symbolized to my spiritual sight in all the gentler human types of the merely animate world. There seemed, for instance—lustrously represented to my inward sense— a far more heavenly sweetness in the soul of a patient overdriven cab-horse, or misused cadger's donkey, than in all the voluminous calendar of Romish and Protestant hagiology, which, sooth to say, seemed to me, in contrast with it, nothing short of infernal.

"You may easily imagine, then, with what relish my heart opened to the doctrine I found in these most remarkable books, *of the sheer and abject phenomenality of selfhood in man*; and with what instant alacrity my intellect shook its canvas free to catch every breeze of that virgin unexplored sea of being, to which this doctrine, for the first time, furnished me the clew. Up to this very period I had lived in the cheerful faith, nor ever felt the slightest shadow of misgiving about it—any more, I venture to say, than you at this moment feel a shadow of similar misgiving in your own mind—that my being or substance lay absolutely in myself, was in fact identical with the various limitations implied in that most fallacious but still unsuspected quantity. To be sure, I had no doubt that this being or self of mine (whether actually burdened, or not burdened, with its limitations, I did not stop to inquire, but unquestionably with a capacity of any amount of burdensome limitation) came originally as a gift from the hand of God; but I had just as little doubt that the moment the gift had left God's hand, or fell into my conscious possession, it became as essentially independent of Him in all spiritual or subjective regards as the soul of a child is of its earthly father; however much in material or objective regards it might be expedient for me still to submit to His external police. My moral conscience, too, lent its influence to the same profound illusion; for all the precepts of the moral law being objectively so good and real, and intended in the view of an unenlightened conscience to make men righteous in the sight of God, I could never have supposed, even had I been tempted on independent grounds to doubt my own spiritual or subjective reality, that so palpably Divine a law contemplated, or even tolerated, a wholly infirm and fallacious subject; much less that it was, in fact, altogether devised for the reproof, condemnation, and humiliation of such a subject. I had no misgiving, therefore, as to the manifest purpose of the Law. The Divine intent of it at least was as clear to me as it ever had been to the Jew, namely, to serve as a ministry of plain moral life or actual righteousness among men, so constructing an everlasting heaven out of men's warring and divided personalities: and not at all, as the apostles taught, a ministry of death, *to convince those who stood approved by it of* SIN, thereby shutting up all men, good and evil alike, but especially the good, to unlimited dependence upon the sheer and mere mercy of God.

"It was impossible for me, after what I have told you, to hold this audacious faith in selfhood any longer. When I sat down to dinner on that memorable chilly afternoon in Windsor, I held it serene and unweakened by the faintest breath of doubt. Before I rose from table it had inwardly shrivelled to a cinder. One moment I devoutly thanked God for the inappreciable boon of selfhood; the next that inappreciable boon seemed to me the one thing damnable on earth, seemed a literal nest of hell within my own entrails."[26]

The reader who shall have persevered as far as this, is now well emerged from the *apriori* logical atmosphere in which our quotations concerning the creative process began. He sees that those cold accounts were but a garb, a vehicle of introduction to the intellect, of experiences of the heart of the most living kind. He sees, if he be of a generalizing turn of mind, that Mr. James was one member of that band of saints and mystics, whose rare privilege it has been, by the mere example and recital of their own bosom-experience, to prevent religion from becoming a fossil conventionalism, and to keep it forever alive. The experience in question has always been an acute despair, passing over into an equally acute optimism, through a passion of renunciation of the self and surrender to the higher power. Doubtless it would be easy enough to muster pages

[26] *Society the Redeemed Form of Man*, pp. 70–74. These pages are headed, "My Moral Death and Burial."

of quotations from spiritual literature,—pagan, catholic, and protestant,—which would tally in all essential respects with what my
father felt and said about the relation of the Self and the Divine.
But every man carries his signature stamped upon him, and my
father's was, I think, very peculiar indeed.

The common run of mystics seem less to let their Self expire than
to get it calmed and appeased and made innocent on their hands,
so that it still remains extant to taste the delights of God's renewed
conversation with it. This gives to much of their writing that
voluptuous tinge, that perfume of spiritual sensuality, which makes
it impossible to many readers, even religious ones, to get any edification from their pages. One feels rebuked and distanced, and kept
out of the pale. It is the *I*, and not the *we*, that speaks. Now, my
father, with all the mystical depth of experience, and all the mystical
unction, had not a trace of the mystical egotism or voluptuousness,
but was as drastic and unsentimental as old Epictetus or even Diogenes himself. A calm and clarified and triumphantly peaceful self
was still a self, as much as a bitter and grievous one. And not if he
could help it, would he dally and toy with the enemy in any shape.
Universal Man is God's one creature: only in Man and through
Man would he be saved. "When Swedenborg called the selfhood
the realm of our *uncreation*, he by that unexpected word sent a
breath of health to the deepest heart of hell." Uncreated then shall
my self become! Accordingly it was a strange thing to see him, when
in a depressed mood, murmur the psalms of David to himself by the
hour, apparently without a feeling of personal application. He fairly
revelled in the emotion of humanity, and lost himself in the sentiment of unity with his kind, like a river in the sea.

The following passage may be quoted here:

"All the science or knowledge of life to which I am begotten,
born, and bred by our existing civilization, tells me with an un-
deviating persistency, that there is nothing so Divinely true, because so Divinely sweet and sufficing, as selfhood: and the consequence is that I actually succeed in giving the real Divinity in my
great race or nature only a scant and drowsy recognition. Indeed
if I should freely yield to instinct within me, or abandon myself
to the current inspiration of culture about me, I doubt not I should
end by altogether sacrificing that patient Divinity to the unscrupu-
lous idol and counterfeit enshrined in myself. For then my senses

authenticated and unchecked, would be free to tell me that my life or being is strictly identical with my finite personality, and that the only death and hell I shall ever have to dread is one which menaces that personality with desolation: namely, the death and hell wrapped up in my intimate Divine-natural innocence, truth, and chastity. I confess though that when once one's eyes are opened to a glimmer of eternal truth on the subject, one has no hesitation in hoping that ere he is caught hearkening to this gospel of an atheistic and drunken self-conceit, he may actually perish out of life, and the great lord of life know him no more forever. I for one should distinctly prefer forfeiting my self-consciousness altogether, to being found capable, in ever so feeble a degree, of identifying my being with it. My being lies utterly outside of my*self*, lies in utterly forgetting my*self*, lies in utterly unlearning and disusing all its elaborately petty schemes and dodges now grown so transparent that a child is not deceived by them: lies in fact *in honestly identifying myself with others.* I know it will never be possible for me to do this perfectly, that is, attain to self-extinction, because being created, I can never hope actually to become Divine; but at all events I shall become through eternal years more and more intimately one in nature, and I hope in spirit, with a being who *is* thoroughly destitute of this finiting principle, that is, a being who is without selfhood save in His creatures. And certainly the next best thing to being God, is to know Him, for this knowledge makes one content with any burden of personal limitation."[27]

Nothing so endlessly besotted in Mr. James's eyes, as the pretension to possess personally any substantive merit or advantage whatever, any worth other than your unconscious uses to your kind! Nothing pleased him like exploding the bubbles of conventional dignity, unless it was fraternizing on the simplest and commonest plane with all lowly persons whom he met. To exalt humble and abase proud things was ever the darling sport of his conversation,— a conversation the somewhat reckless invective humor of which, when he was in the *abasing* mood, often startled the good people of Boston, who did not know him well enough to see the endlessly genial and humane intuition from which the whole mood flowed. A friend, in a private letter received during this writing, says of

[27] *Society the Redeemed Form of Man*, pp. 361–362.

him: "He was of such an immense temperament, that when you took him to task for violating the feelings of others in his talk, he would score you black and blue for your distinctions; and all the while he made you feel that the origin of the matter was his divine rage with *himself* at still being so dominated by his natural selfhood which would not be shaken off. I have felt in him at times, away down at bottom of the man, so sheer a humility and self-abasement as to give me an idea of infinity."

The theology that went with all this was the passionate conviction that the *real* creature of God—human *nature* at large, *minus* the preposterous claims of the several selves—must be wholly good. For is it not the work of the good God, or rather the very substance of the good God, there *being* nought beside?

"What sort of a creator would he be who could allow, for a single moment, such an imputation to rest upon his creative power, as that his creature was *really* bad? Evidently a most beggarly sort. For if God's creature were *really* bad—that is, if his badness be, as the philosophers say, not only *subjective*, spiritual, formal, but *objective*, natural, substantial—why then no man can even begin to form an estimate of how much worse than the creature the creator himself must be, in order simply to account for the devilish atrocity of such a creation. The creature, you know, by the hypothesis of his creation, is absolute nought *in himself*; and if therefore he be *really* evil, where does this evil reality of his come from, if not from Him in whom alone he lives and moves and has his being?"

In another autobiographic passage he defends the rights of our nature as being the very incarnation of God:—

"As well as I can remember, in fact, the spring of all my intellectual activity in the past was to know for certain whether our felt finiteness was a necessity of our spiritual creation, or simply an incident of our natural constitution: whether, for example, it was to be interpreted as having been arbitrarily imposed upon us by the Divine will, or as inherent merely in the sentiment we so inordinately cherish of personal independence. For in the former case my hope in God necessarily dies out by the practical decease of His infinitude, while in the latter case it is not only left unimpaired but is revived and invigorated. . . .

"Here, in fact, was the veritable secret source of all my intellectual unrest. During all my early intellectual existence I was haunted by so keen a sense of God's *natural* incongruity with me—of his *natural* and therefore invincible alienation, otherness, externality, distance, remoteness to me—as to breed in my bosom oftentimes a wholly unspeakable heartsickness or homesickness. The sentiment to be sure masked its ineffable malignity from my perception under the guise of an alleged *super*natural limitation on God's part; but it none the less filled my soul with the tremor and pallor of death. I have no doubt indeed that if it had not been for my excessive 'animal spirits' as we say, or the extreme good-will I felt towards sensuous pleasure of every sort, which alternated my morbid conscientiousness and foiled its corrosive force, I should have turned out a flagrant case of arrested intellectual development. I could have borne very well, mind you, a conviction of God's *personal* antipathy to me carried to any pitch you please; for my person does not go with my nature as man, and a personal condemnation therefore which should not cut me off from a natural resurrection, would not deprive me of hope toward God. But my conviction of God's personal alienation had been hopelessly saddled, through the incompetency of my theologic sponsors, with the senseless tradition of His inveterate estrangement also from *human nature*. Thus unhappily although my person did not go with human nature they made human nature to go with my person, or managed so perfectly to confound the two things to my unpractised sense, that whenever I felt a superficial or intrinsically evanescent pang of mere personal remorse, it was sure to pass by a quick diabolical chemistry into a sense of the deadliest *natural* hostility between me and the source of my life.

"It is in fact this venomous tradition of a natural as well as a personal disproportion between man and his maker—speciously cloaked as it is under the ascription of a *super*natural being and existence to God—that alone gives its intolerable odium and poignancy to men's otherwise healthful and restorative conscience of sin. That man's personality should utterly alienate him from God—that is to say, make him infinitely other and opposite to God—this I grant you with all my heart, since if God were the least like me personally all my hope in Him would perish. . . . But that God should be also an infinitely alien *substance* to me—an infinitely other or foreign *nature*—this wounds my spontaneous faith in Him to its core, or leaves it a mere mercenary and servile homage. I perfectly understand how He should disown all private or personal relation to me, because I am . . . to all the extent of my distinctively personal interests and ambitions, the impassioned foe and rival of universal man. This is one thing. But it is quite a different and most odious thing that He should feel an envenomed animosity also to my innocent nature, or what binds me in indissoluble unity with every man of woman born." [28]

Some sort of antinomianism, or indifference to outward human contrasts, is the logical outcome of every creed which makes the Deity's love so impartial, and lays such stress upon the prominence of the *whole* to his regard. I cannot say that my father succeeded in practice in keeping faithful to this consequence; but in theory he did; and great was his delight in those pages of Swedenborg in which he found the doctrine of indifference clearly set down. First, concerning the angels:—

"The angel would be incontinently overcome of hell, if he were not sedulously preserved by the Divine power, vanquishing his incessant natural gravitation towards it. Swedenborg affirms that he found no angel in any heaven, however elevated, who was not in himself, or intrinsically, of a very shabby pattern, and who did not, therefore, cordially refer all his goodness and wisdom to the Lord; and he sets it down as the fundamental principle of their intelligence, that they ascribe all their good to the Lord, and all their evil to the devil. No matter what heights of manly virtue the angel may have reached, no matter what depths of Divine peace and contentment he may have sounded, Swedenborg invariably reports that in himself, or intrinsically, he is replete with every selfish and worldly lust, being in fact utterly undistinguishable from the lowest devil. Was ever testimony so loyal as this? Was ever honest heart or seeing eye so unseduced before by the most specious shows of things? I confess the wonder to me is endless. What other man in that rotten and degraded generation was capable of such devotion to humanity? Of which one of his contemporaries could you allege,

[28] *Society the Redeemed Form of Man*, pp. 314–318.

that being admitted to the most lustrous company in the universe . . . he would never for an instant lose his balance, or duck his servile head in homage, but stedfastly maintain his invincible faith in the great truth of human equality? George Washington is doubtless an unblemished name to all the extent of his commerce with the world; but how puny that commerce was, compared with this grand interior commerce of the soul; and how juvenile and rustic his virtue seems beside the profound, serene, unconscious humanity of this despised old soldier of truth! To gaze undazzled upon the solar splendours of heaven, to gaze undismayed upon the sombre abysses of hell, to preserve one's self-respect, or one's fidelity to the Divine name, unbribed by the subtlest attractions of the one sphere, and unchilled by the nakedest horrors of the other, implies a heroism of soul which in no wise belongs to the old Church, even in its highest sanctities, and which leaves the old State, even as to its most renowned illustrations, absolutely out of sight."[29]

Here are a couple of soberer passages:—

"The true or spiritual creation ignores the sentiment of morality in its subjects, i.e. disallows the distinction of good and evil among men, as at all pertinent to the divine mind. No angel that Swedenborg encountered was ever so foolish as to attribute the good which was visible in him to himself; and no devil was ever wise enough not to do so. The fundamental difference, in short, between Swedenborg's angels and devils was the difference between humility and loftiness; the latter always cherishing an unsubdued selfhood, or pride of character, the former being always more or less cultivated out of it."[30]

"Swedenborg shows, accordingly, throughout all his books, from their beginning to their close, that God has no joy in the angel, nor any grief in the devil, save as they . . . tend to enforce or enfeeble . . . the universality and the particularity of his presence and providence throughout the earth. The lord's love, as Swedenborg invariably reports it, is a universal love, being the salvation of the whole human race; and no form of his church, therefore, can satisfy his regard, which is not practically identical with the interests of human society; that is, which does not in itself structurally

[29] *Christianity the Logic of Creation*, pp. 17–18.
[30] *Secret of Swedenborg*, pp. 106–107.

43

reproduce and avouch the intimate and indissoluble fellowship, equality, brotherhood of universal man."[31]

And here is an abstract statement about good and evil:—

"Good and evil, heaven and hell, are not facts of creative, but of purely constitutive order. They bear primarily upon man's natural destiny, and have no relation to his spiritual freedom save through that. They are the mere geology of our natural consciousness, and this is all they are. They have no distinctively supernatural quality nor efficacy whatever. They have a simply constitutional relevancy to the earth of man's associated consciousness, and disavow therefore any properly creative or controlling relation to his spiritual or individual freedom. We have been traditionally taught that good and evil, heaven and hell, were objective realities, having an absolute ground of being in the creative perfection. But this is the baldest, most bewildering nonsense. They have not a grain of objective reality in them, and are noway vitalized by the absolute Divine perfection. They are purely subjective appearances, vitalized exclusively by the created imperfection, or the uses they subserve to our provisional moral and rational consciousness. When accordingly this consciousness—having more than fulfilled its legitimate office, and become as it now is a mere stumbling-block or rock of offence to the regenerate mind of the race—finally expires in its own stench, or else frankly allows itself to be taken up and disappear in our advancing social and æsthetic consciousness, good and evil, heaven and hell, will cease to be appearances even. For angel and devil, saint and sinner, will then find themselves perfectly fused or made over in a new or comprehensive race-manhood which will laugh to scorn our best empirical or tentative manhood, that is, our existing civic and ecclesiastic manhood so-called."[32]

One more quotation may conclude our illustrations of this aspect of Mr. James's philosophy:

"There are no fundamental differences in men. All men have one and the same Creator, one and the same essential being, and what formally differences one man from another, what distinguishes

31 *Ibid.*, pp. 78–79.
32 *Society the Redeemed Form of Man*, pp. 251–252.

hell from heaven, is that they are differently related to the Divine *natural* humanity, or to the life of God in nature, which is a life of perfect freedom or spontaneity. In that life self-love freely subordinates itself to neighbourly love, or promotes its own ends by promoting the welfare of all mankind. But so long as this life is wholly unsuspected by men, so long as no man dreams of any other social destiny for the race than that which it has already realized, and which leaves one man out of all fellowship or equality with another, self-love is completely unprovided for, except in subtle and hypocritical forms, and is consequently driven to these disorderly assertions of itself by way of actually keeping itself alive. . . . The liar, the thief, the adulterer, the murderer, no doubt utterly perverts the Divine life which is latent in every human form: he degrades and defiles self-love, in lifting it out of that free subordination which it will evince to brotherly love in the Divine *natural* man: but he nevertheless does all this in the way of a mute unconscious protest against an overwhelming social tyranny, which would otherwise crush out the distinctive life of man under the machinery of government and caste. Accordingly, I am profoundly convinced that if it had not been for these men, if we had not had some persons of that audacious make which would qualify them to throw off their existing social subjection, and so ventilate, even by infernal airs, the underlying life and freedom of humanity, that life and freedom would have been utterly stifled, and we should now be a race of abject slaves, without hope towards God, without love to our fellow-man, contentedly kissing the feet of some infallible Pope of Rome, contentedly doing the bidding of some unquestionable Emperor of all the Russias. These men have been, unknown to themselves, the forlorn hope of humanity, plunging headlong into the unfathomable night, only that we by the bridge of their desecrated forms might eventually pass over its hideous abysses into the realms of endless day. Let us, then, at least manfully acknowledge our indebtedness to them: let us view them as the unconscious martyrs of humanity, dying for a cause so Divinely high as to accept no conscious or voluntary adhesion, and yet so Divinely sure and sweet and human as ultimately to vindicate even their dishonoured memory, and rehabilitate them in the love and tenderness of eternal ages. In short, let us agree with Swedenborg, that odious and fearful as these men have seemed in merely celestial light, they have yet borne the unrecognized livery of the Divine NATURAL humanity, and will not fail in the end to swell the triumphs of His majestic patience. And this simply because by an undying Divine instinct, under every depth of degradation celestially viewed, they have always been true to themselves, feeling themselves to be men and not devils, and over their scarred and riven legions have ever indestructibly waved the banner of a conscious freedom and rationality."[33]

Such being Mr. James's intellectual destiny, there was no fending off the catastrophe that had to occur in his relations with the church in which he was born. For the church, the particular person is the unit, wherewith, in the last resort, God deals. Whatever theological formulas the sects may use, whatever reasons for the damning, whatever means for the saving, they may assign, still it is always *one* of us who becomes God's vessel of honor, and another who is lost from out his sight. He thus stands over against us, an *imputer*, an outward and eventually a hostile power, consecrating, by the absolute distinctions he makes, that whole seething life of private jealousy and exclusion which is the bane of this world's estate.

Here is an autobiographic passage which may usher in some of the drastic remarks on the bad stewardship of the church which our author scatters about with so profuse a hand:—[34]

"I never questioned the absoluteness of all the *data*, good and evil, of my moral experience. I never doubted the infinite and eternal consequences which seemed to me to be wrapped up in my consciousness of personality, or the sentiment I habitually cherished of my individual relations and responsibility to God. I had never, to my own suspicion, been arrayed in any overt hostility to the divine name. On the contrary, I reckoned myself an unaffected friend of God, inasmuch as I was a most eager and conscientious aspirant after moral perfection. And yet the total unconscious current of my religious life was so egotistic, the habitual color of my piety was so bronzed by an inmost selfishness and indifference to all mankind,

33 *Christianity the Logic of Creation*, pp. 104–107.

34 His earlier writings were largely taken up with negative criticisms on Orthodoxy in its practice as well as its teaching. The essay entitled "The Old and the New Theology" (in the volume of *Lectures and Miscellanies*), and the work called the *Church of Christ Not an Ecclesiasticism*, are masterpieces in this vein. The last named work seems to have been written in a peculiarly happy hour, and is distinguished by a charming freshness and geniality of tone.

save in so far as my action towards them bore upon my own salvation, that I never reflected myself to myself, never was able to look back upon any chance furrow my personality had left upon the sea of time, without a shuddering conviction of the abysses of spiritual profligacy over which I perpetually hovered, and towards which I incessantly gravitated. . . . From the day of my birth I had not only never known what it was to have an honest want, a want of my nature, ungratified, but I had also been able to squander upon the will of my personal caprice, an amount of sustenance equal to the maintenance of a virtuous household. And yet thousands of persons directly about me, in all respects my equals, in many respects my superiors, had never in all their lives enjoyed an honest meal, an honest sleep, an honest suit of clothes, save at the expense of their own personal toil, or that of some parent or child, and had never once been able to give the reins to their personal caprice without an ignominious exposure to severe social penalties. It is, to be sure, perfectly just that I should be conveniently fed and lodged and clad, and that I should be educated out of my native ignorance . . . . But it is a monstrous affront to the divine justice or righteousness, that I should be guaranteed, by what calls itself society, a life-long career of luxury and self-indulgence, while so many other men and women, my superiors, go all their days miserably fed, miserably lodged, miserably clothed, and die at last in the same ignorance and imbecility, though not, alas! in the same innocence, that cradled their infancy. . . .

"Now I had long felt this deep spiritual damnation in myself growing out of an outraged and insulted divine justice, had long been pent up in spirit to these earthquake mutterings and menaces of a violated conscience, without seeing any clear door of escape open to me. That is to say, I perceived with endless perspicacity that if it were not for the hand of God's providence visiting with constant humiliation and blight every secret aspiration of my pride and vanity, I should be more than any other man reconciled to the existing most atrocious state of things. I knew no outward want, I had the amplest social recognition, I enjoyed the converse and friendship of distinguished men, I floated in fact on a sea of unrighteous plenty, and I was all the while so indifferent if not inimical in heart to the divine justice, that save for the spiritual terrors it ever and anon supplied to my lethargic sympathies, to my swinish ambition, I should have dragged out all my days in that complacent sty, nor have ever so much as dreamed that the outward want of my fellows—their want with respect to nature and society—was in truth but the visible sign and fruit of my own truer want, my own more inward destitution with respect to God. Thus my religious conscience was one of poignant misgiving towards God, if not of complete practical separation, and it filled my intellect with all manner of perplexed speculation and gloomy foreboding. Do what I might I never could attain to the least religious self-complacency, or push my devout instincts to the point of actual fanaticism. Do what I would I could never succeed in persuading myself that God almighty cared a jot for me in my personal capacity, i.e. as I stood morally individualized from, or consciously antagonized with, my kind; and yet this was the identical spiritual obligation imposed upon me by the church. Time and again I consulted my spiritual advisers to know how it might do for me to abandon myself to the simple joy of the truth as it was in Christ, without taking any thought for the church, or the interests of my religious character. And they always told me that it would not do at all; that my church sympathies, or the demands of my religious character, were everything comparatively, and my mere belief in Christ comparatively nothing, since devils believed just as much as I did. The retort was as apt as it was obvious, that the devils believed and trembled, while I believed and rejoiced; and that this joy on my part could not be helped, but only hindered, whenever it was allowed to be complicated with any question about myself. But no: the evidently foregone conclusion to be forced upon me in every case was, that a man's religious standing, or the love he bears the church, takes the place, under the gospel, of his moral standing, or the love he bore the state, under the law; hence that no amount of delight in the truth, for the truth's sake alone, could avail me spiritually, unless it were associated with a scrupulous regard for a sanctified public opinion.

"Imagine, then, my glad surprise, my cordial relief, when in this state of robust religious nakedness, with no wretchedest fig-leaf of ecclesiastical finery to cover me from the divine inclemency, I caught my first glimpse of the spiritual contents of revelation, or discerned the profoundly philosophic scope of the christian truth. This truth at once emboldened me to obey my own regenerate intellectual instincts without further parley, in throwing the church overboard, or demitting all care of my religious character to the devil, of whom alone such care is an inspiration. The christian truth indeed . . . teaches me to look upon the church's heartiest malison as God's heartiest benison, inasmuch as whatsoever is most highly esteemed among men—namely, that private or personal righteousness in man, of which the church is the special protagonist and voucher—is abomination to God. . . . In other words, spiritual christianity means the complete secularization of the divine name, or its identification henceforth only with man's common or natural want, that want in which all men are absolutely one, and its consequent utter estrangement from the sphere of his private or personal fulness, in which every man is consciously divided from his neighbor: so that I may never aspire to the divine favor, and scarcely to the divine tolerance, save in my social or redeemed natural aspect; i.e. as I stand morally identified with the vast community of men of whatever race or religion, cultivating no consciousness of antagonist interests to any other man, but on the contrary frankly disowning every personal hope towards God which does not flow exclusively from his redemption of human nature, or is not based purely and simply upon his indiscriminate love to the race."[35]

[35] *Secret of Swedenborg*, pp. 170–176 (abridged). I append a couple of other passages which carry out the same idea:—

"The church-spirit is *par excellence* the evil-spirit in humanity, source of all its profounder and irremediable woes. Don't, I beg of you, interpret me to your own thought as saying that the church stimulates any of man's actual or moral evils. I say no such stupid thing. For it is notorious that the church studiously fosters the sentiment of moral worth or dignity in its disciples, the sentiment of distinction or difference between them and other men. It is only by so doing indeed that she *fixes* or hardens them in that tendency to *proprium* or selfhood to which they are naturally inclined, and thus delivers them over bound hand and foot to spiritual pride . . . . However selfish or worldly a man may be, these are good honest natural evils, and you have only to apply a motive sufficiently stimulating in either case and you will induce the subject to forbear them. But spiritual pride is inward evil exclusively, pertaining to the selfhood of the man, or livingly appropriated by him as his own, and cannot therefore become known to him save in the form of an outward natural representation; for it is not like moral evil mere oppugnancy to good, but it is the actual and deadly profanation of good, or the lavish acknowledgment of it with a view of subordinating it to personal, or selfish and worldly, ends. It is the only truly formidable evil known to God's providence, being that of *self*-righteousness, and hence the only evil which essentially threatens to undermine the foundations of God's throne."—*Society the Redeemed Form of Man*, pp. 200–203.

"Subjective or personal consciousness, then: the feeling we all of us have that our natural selfhood is our own absolutely, and without reference to any grander natural objectivity, such for example as SOCIETY: is the brimming spiritual death wrapped up in every man by virtue of his finite generation. . . . There is no evil at all comparable with this either for comprehensiveness or intensity, if it be allowed to go uncorrected; for it is altogether fatal to man's spiritual life, which consists in his loving his neighbor as himself. Now the only possible way for a man to do this is to feel that he is *not*

"Deism," as I have already said, was Mr. James's name for the doctrine that represents God as external to a plurality of absolute and substantial subject beings.

"If the church . . . *could* have sincerely felt to be true what she always formally professed, viz. that God was the sole real and active life of our nature, she *might* perhaps have put herself at the head of human affairs, and victoriously led man's forlorn hope against the sullen and sodden deity that everywhere affects of right to bestride the world. . . .

"The sincere uncommitted mass of men are spiritually and intellectually incompetent to recognize any 'slough of despond' half so fatal or frightful to them, as that of deism, which is the conception of God as a power essentially outside of man, and therefore both inimical and hateful to him. Deism is out and out the only doctrine that has power logically to fill the human heart with despair toward God, *in making man's person a reality*. But this vile deistic doctrine is the very most cherished doctrine of the church itself, without which indeed to inspire it, it would be ready to confess itself a mere lunatic organization, without further business upon the earth. And there is no chance consequently of the church's again leading the human mind, in ministering to men's higher in-

---

self-centred, that his life is *not* his own personally, but belongs to him in strict community with his neighbor; thus that he and his neighbor are both alike dependent at every moment for every breath of life they draw upon one and the same merciful and impartial source. In other words a man loves his neighbor as himself only by virtue of his first loving God above himself, or supremely. And the only way this supreme love becomes developed or educated in him, is through his moral experience, or his obedience to law. Whenever, and so long as, man is tempted to commit false or malicious speaking, theft, adultery, murder, or covetousness, and yet abstains from doing it out of a sincere inward regard for the Divine name, his self-love, so far as it is harmful, is spiritually slain, and the Divine love infallibly replaces it. These formal vices express the whole substantial evil known to the human heart, and when man, therefore, in the exercise of a felt freedom and rationality deposes them or any of them from their habitual control over his action, not because they conflict with his outward welfare, or expose him to the contempt of men, but simply because they wound his inward reverence for the Divine name, he becomes spiritually regenerate or new-born. Falsehood, theft, adultery, murder, and covetousness are, in other words, only signs or symbols of a deeper and altogether latent spiritual evil fatally separating man from God: the evil of a supreme self-love. Grave as these evils unquestionably are in themselves, or absolutely, they have yet only a superficial moral quality, that is, grow out of men's still unreconciled or inharmonic relations *inter se*, or their frank insubjection to the social sentiment, and do not by any means necessarily imply any permanent spiritual or individual estrangement between them and God."—*Society the Redeemed Form of Man*, pp. 270, 268–269.

terests, unless she at once renounces the very doctrine by which she lives, and returns *ex animo* to the early faith which was once *literally* her only possession, namely: that God, the only true God, the only God worthy to inspire the devotion of the human heart, is not any God of the nations, or foreign supernatural deity at all, but is all simply the lord, that is, God-*man*, figuratively made known to us in the Christ, thus a most domestic deity, partaker of our own nature to the very brim, making the very grave a farce by virtue of it, essential source and purveyor in fact of the nature, and constant spiritual redeemer of it from the defilement and limitations imposed upon it by our own most absurd and dishonest personality.

"But it is idle and worse than idle to expect any revival of the church. The bible would have to be written over again, before that stale mother of harlots could ever presume again to put on the dew of her infancy, and aspire to head human hope in its patient, ever enduring battle against deistic oppression and tyranny. The church is absolutely identified with the deistic name and fame throughout history, so that no honest human cause, nor any sincere zeal for humanity has ever been ecclesiastically born or ecclesiastically propagated. The visible church is altogether dead in fact, *sans* teeth, *sans* eyes, *sans* taste, *sans* everything. Unknown to, and even unfelt by, itself consequently, it has providentially been replaced by a new and subtler, because living or invisible, church, which will neither itself be, nor of itself breed, any hindrance to human hope and aspiration."[36]

The treacherous part played by "professional religion" is thus described:—

"The only danger to the spirit of religion . . . comes from the effort of the soul to assume and cherish a devout *self*-consciousness; or so to *abound* in a religious sense, as to incur the imputation of religiosity or superstition. This is the inalienable vice of professional religion, the only sincere fruit it is capable of bringing forth. The evil spirit which religion is primarily intended to exorcise in us is the spirit of selfhood, based upon a most inadequate apprehension of its strictly *provisional* uses to our spiritual nurture. The gradual conquest or slaying of this unholy spirit of self in man is the sole function which religion proposes to itself during his natural life;

[36] *The New Church Independent*, August, 1881, pp. 374, 373.

and without taxing our co-operation too severely, it yet gives us enough to do before its benignant mission is fully wrought out. Such being the invariable office of the religious instinct, *professional* religion steps in to simulate its sway, and with an air all the while of even canting deference, proceeds to build again the things which were destroyed, by reorganizing man's selfhood on a more specious or consecrated basis, and so authenticating all its unslain lusts in a way of devotion to the conventicle, at least, if not to the open, undisguised world.

"Professional religion thus stamps itself the devil's subtlest device for keeping the human soul in bondage. Religion says death—*inward or spiritual death*—to the selfhood in man. Professional religion says: 'Nay, not death, above all not inward or spiritual—because this would be *living*—death, and obviously the selfhood must live in order to be vivified of God. By no means therefore let us say an *inward* or *living* death to selfhood, but an outward or *quasi* death, *professionally or ritually enacted*, and so operating a change of base for the selfhood. Selfhood doubtless has been hitherto based upon a most unrighteous enmity on the part of the world to God, and has of itself shared the enmity. Let man then only acknowledge, professionally or ritually, this wicked enmity of the world to God, and he may keep his selfhood unimpaired and unchallenged, to expand and flourish *in secula seculorum*.'

"Professional religion, I repeat, is the devil's masterpiece for ensnaring silly, selfish men. The ugly beast has two heads: one called Ritualism, intended to devour a finer and fastidious style of men, men of sentiment and decorum, cherishing scrupulously moderate views of the difference between man and God; the other called Revivalism, with a great red mouth intended to gobble up a coarser sort of men, men for the most part of a fierce carnality, of ungovernable appetite and passion, susceptible at best only of the most selfish hopes, and the most selfish fears, towards God. I must say, we are not greatly devastated here in Boston—though occasionally vexed—by either head of the beast; on the contrary, it is amusing enough to observe how afraid the great beast himself is of being pecked to pieces on our streets by a little indigenous bantam-cock which calls itself Radicalism, and which struts, and crows, and scratches gravel in a manner so bumptious and peremptory, that I defy any ordinary barnyard chanticleer to imitate it." [37]

[37] *Society the Redeemed Form of Man*, pp. 40–42.

Even the possession of the Bible has been unavailing to us, since its official interpreters have reversed its spiritual sense:—

"The letter of Revelation has doubtless proved inestimably advantageous to our civilization; but the most orderly citizenship is as remote from spontaneous or spiritual manhood, as baked apples are from ripe ones. Compared with heathen nations we are indeed as baked apples to green; but I do not see that apples plucked green from the tree and assiduously cooked, as we have been, are near so likely to ripen in the long run, as those which are still left hanging upon the boughs, exposed to God's unstinted sun and air. We manage to maintain our egregious self-complacency unperturbed by vehemently compassionating the heathen, and sending out missionaries to convert them to our foolish ecclesiastical habits: precisely as if a baked apple should grudge its fellows their natural ripening, and beg them also to come and sputter their indignant life away under the burning summer of the oven, under the blackening autumn of the bake-pan. In fact the heathen I suspect find it difficult to regard us yet even as baked fruit. Our ungenerous overbearing and polluting intercourse with them fits them rather to regard us only as very rotten fruit. Whether baked or rotten, however, we are in either case, so far as our ecclesiastical and political manners are concerned, past the chance of any inward or spiritual ripening. So far as our ecclesiastical conscience is concerned especially, there doesn't seem one drop of honest native unsophisticated juice left in us. If there were, could we be so content year in and year out to see our clergy, heterodox and orthodox, alternately cuff and clout God's sacred word—which is inwardly all alive and leaping with spiritual or universal meaning—as if it were some puny brat of man's begetting, some sickly old-wives' tale, some vapid and senile tradition, destitute even of a fabulous grace and tenderness?"[38]

As one of the appendices to *Substance and Shadow*, Mr. James gives us an apologue and its moral,—both of them too good sense and too good literature not to be copied here:—

"I knew a gentleman some years ago of exemplary religiosity and politeness, but of a seasoned inward duplicity, who failed in

[38] *Substance and Shadow*, pp. 503–504.

business as was supposed fraudulently. He was in the habit of meeting one of the largest of his creditors every Sunday on his way to church, where his own voice was always among the most melodious to confess any amount of abstract sins and iniquities; and he never failed to raise his hat from his head as he passed, and testify by every demonstrative flourish how much he would still do for the bare forms of friendship, when its life or substance was fled. The creditor was long impatient, but at last grew frantic under this remorseless courtesy, and stopping his debtor one day told him that he would cheerfully abandon to him the ten thousand dollars he had robbed him of, provided he would forego the exhibition of so much nauseous politeness. Sir, replied the imperturbable scamp, I would not forego the expression of my duty to you when we meet, for twice ten thousand dollars! This is very much our case religiously. Whereas if we would only give over our eternal grimacing and posturing, only leave off our affable but odious ducking and bowing to our great creditor, long enough to see the real truth of the case, and frankly acknowledge bankruptcy utter and fraudulent, nothing could be so hopeful. The supreme powers are infinitely above reckoning with us for our shortcomings, if we would only have the manliness to confess spiritual insolvency, and not seek any longer to hide it from their eyes and our own, under these transparent monkey-shines of a mock devotion; under this perpetual promise to pay which never comes to maturity, but gets renewed from Sunday to Sunday *in secula seculorum*. God does not need our labored civility, and must long ere this have sickened of our vapid doffing of the hat to him as we pass. He seeks our solid advantage, not our ridiculous patronage. He desires our living not our professional humility; and He desires it only for our sakes not His own. He would fashion us into the similitude of His perfect love, only that we might enjoy the unspeakable delights of His sympathetic fellowship. If He once saw us to be thus spontaneously disposed towards Him, thus genuinely qualified for the immortal participation of His power and blessedness, He would I am sure be more than content never to get a genuflexion from us again while the world lasted, nor hear another of our dreary litanies while sheep bleat and calves bellow."[39]

On the principle of *corruptio optimorum pessima*, it was natural that if the churches in general should in Mr. James's eyes have

[39] *Substance and Shadow*, pp. 520–521.

sold themselves to the devil, the arch-sinners in this respect should be the Swedenborgian congregations, who, if any, might be expected to know better. He accordingly never fails to lash them with his heartiest invective,—with what degree of justice or injustice, it is beyond my power to say. In the larger work in the present volume they have a chapter devoted to themselves. And here is a shorter extract, which will show the writer in his best denunciatory vein:—

"The swedenborgian sect assumes to be the New Jerusalem, which is the figurative name used in the Apocalypse to denote God's perfected spiritual work in human nature; and under this tremendous designation it is content to employ itself in doing—what? why in pouring new wine into old bottles with such a preternatural solicitude for the tenacity of the bottles, as necessitates an altogether comical indifference to the quality of the wine. New wine cannot safely go into old bottles but upon one condition, which is, that the wine had previously become swipes, or was originally very small beer. In fact, the swedenborgian sect, viewed as to its essential aims, though of course not as to its professed ones, is only on the part of its movers a strike for higher wages, that is, for higher ecclesiastical consideration than the older sects enjoy at the popular hands. And like all strikes, it will probably succumb at last to the immense stores of fat (or popular respect) traditionally accumulated under the ribs of the old organizations, and enabling them to hybernate through any stress of cold weather, merely by sucking their thumbs, or without assimilating any new material. No doubt the insurgents impoverish the older sects to the extent of their own bulk; but they do not substantially affect them in popular regard, because the people, as a rule, care little for truth, but much for the good that animates it; very little for dogmas, but very much for that undeniably human substance which underlies all dogmas, and makes them savory, whether technically sound or unsound. And here the new sect is at a striking disadvantage with all its more ancient competitors; for these are getting ashamed of their old narrowness, and are gradually expanding into some show of sympathy with human want. The sect of the *soi-disant* New Jerusalem, on the other hand, deliberately empties itself of all interest in the hallowed struggle which society is everywhere making for her very existence against established injustice and sanctified imposture, in order to concentrate its energy and prudence upon the washing and dressing, upon the larding and stuffing, upon the embalming and perfuming, of its own invincibly squalid little *corpus*. This pharisaic spirit, the spirit of separatism or sect, is the identical spirit of hell; and to attempt compassing any consideration for one's self at the divine hands, by making one's self to differ from other people, or claiming a higher divine sanctity than they enjoy, is to encounter the only sure damnation. . . . Let the reader, whatever else he may fairly or foolishly conclude against Swedenborg, acquit him point-blank of countenancing this abject ecclesiastical drivel."[40]

Thus did the sentiment of God's impartial indwelling in all humanity harden Mr. James's heart against all places where the "foolish babble of individual moralism" is preached, and make him unforgiving to whatever bore the name of Church. In setting forth his philosophy up to this point, I have made no reference to Christianity at all. Yet a Christian he was, and a most devout one, after his own fashion,—an *abject* Christian, as a clergyman in Boston called him at the time of his death. I confess, though, that I am myself unable to see any radical and essential necessity for the mission of Christ in his scheme of the universe. A "fall" there is, and a redemption; but with his view of the solidarity of man, we are *all* redeemers of the total order so far as we open ourselves each in his little measure to the spirit of God. Our state reverberates through the whole spiritual world, and helps the construction of that "society" which is the race's redeemed form. All the accounts he gives of Christ do but represent him in this function, in which in lesser degree all may share. I cannot help thinking that if my father had been born outside the pale of Christendom, he might perfectly well have brought together all the other elements of his system, much as it stands now, yet laid comparatively little stress on Christ. Still, the point is an obscure one, and I will let the author speak for himself.

He speaks of Christ in a great many places,—always with the following tenor:—

"To suppose that the universal Father of mankind cared for the Jew one jot more than for the Gentile, and that He cared for one

40 *Secret of Swedenborg,* pp. 209–210.

Jew also more than for another, actually intending to give both the former and the latter an endless earthly dominion, was manifestly to blacken the Divine character, and pervert it to the inflammation of every diabolic ambition. And yet this was that literal form of the Jewish hope to which Christ was born. The innocent babe opened his eyes upon mother and father, brother and sister, neighbour and friend, ruler and priest, stupidly agape at the marvels which heralded his birth,[41] and no doubt as his intelligence dawned he lent a naturally complacent ear to the promises of personal advancement and glory they showered upon him. He sucked in the subtlest spiritual poison with every swallow of his mother's milk, and his very religion bound him, so far as human probabilities went, to become an unmitigated devil. I find no trace of any man in history being subject to the temptations that beset this truest of men. I find no trace of any other man who felt himself called upon by the tenderest human love to loathe and disavow the proud and yearning bosom

[41] A word about Mr. James's attitude towards Biblical criticism is here not out of place. With the education he had, and with the tenacity of his feelings, it was quite impossible he should ever have ceased to regard the Scriptures as inspired books. And yet the atmosphere of *Aufklärung* in which he lived forbade him to keep unaltered that simple mode of regarding these writings which had satisfied his youth. He finally drifted into a state of mind on the subject which was neither credulous nor rationalistic, and not easy for another person to defend. There is a chapter *ad hoc* in the work to which this is an introduction; and this quotation will meanwhile stop the gap:—

"I confess for my part that I should as soon think of spitting upon my mother's grave, or offering any other offence to her stainless memory, as of questioning any of the Gospel facts. And this, not because I regard them as literally or absolutely true— for the whole realm of fact is as far beneath that of truth, as earth is beneath heaven— but simply because they furnish the indispensable WORD, or master-key, to our interpretation of God's majestic revelation of Himself in human nature. When accordingly I am asked whether I believe in the literal facts of Christ's birth from a virgin, his resurrection from death, his ascension into heaven, and so forth, I feel constrained to reply: That I neither believe in them nor disbelieve, because the sphere of fact is the sphere of men's knowledge, exclusively, and therefore invites neither belief nor disbelief; but that I have a most profound, even a heartfelt, conviction of the truth which they, and they alone, reveal, namely, *the truth of God's essentially human perfection, and,* as implied in that, *the amazing truth of His natural or adventitious manhood*: which conviction keeps me blessedly indifferent to, and utterly unvexed by, the cheap and frivolous scepticism with which so many of our learned modern pundits assail them. I have not the least reverence nor even respect for the facts in question, save as basing or ultimating this grand creative or spiritual truth; and while the truth stands to my apprehension, I shall be serenely obdurate to the learned reasonings of any of my contemporaries in regard to the facts, whether *pro* or *con*."— *Society the Redeemed Form of Man,* pp. 294–295.

that bore him. I find no other man in history whose profound reverence for infinite goodness and truth drove him to renounce the religion of his fathers, simply because that religion contemplated as its issue his own supreme aggrandizement; and whose profound love to man drove him to renounce every obligation of patriotism, simply because these obligations were plainly coincident with the supremest and subtlest inspirations of his own self-love. No doubt many a man has renounced his traditional creed because it associated him with the obloquy and contempt of his nation, or stood in the way of his personal ambition; and so no doubt many a man has abjured his country, because it disclaimed his title and ability to rule. In short, a thousand men can be found every day who do both of these things from the instinct of self-love. But the eternal peculiarity of the Christian fact is, that Christ did them utterly without the aid of that tremendous lever, actually while it was undermining his force, and subjecting him to ceaseless death. He discredited his paternal gods simply because they were bent upon doing him unlimited honour; and shrank from kindred and countrymen, only because they were intent upon rendering him unparalleled gratitude and benediction. What a mere obscenity every great name in history confesses itself beside this spotless Judean youth, who in the thickest night of time,—unhelped by priest or ruler, by friend or neighbour, by father or mother, by brother or sister, helped, in fact, if we may so consider it, only by the dim expectant sympathy of that hungry rabble of harlots and outcasts who furnished His inglorious retinue, and still further drew upon Him the ferocious scorn of all that was devout, and honourable and powerful in His nation,—yet let in eternal daylight upon the soul, by steadfastly expanding in his private spirit to the dimensions of universal humanity, so bringing, for the first time in history, the finite human bosom into perfect experimental accord with the infinite Divine Love. For my part I am free to declare that I find the conception of any Divinity superior to this radiant human form, inexpressibly treasonable to my own manhood. In fact, I do not hesitate to say that I find the orthodox and popular conception of Deity to be in the comparison a mere odious stench in the nostrils, against which I here indite my exuberant and eternal protest. I shall always cherish the most hearty and cheerful atheism towards every deity but him who has illustrated my own nature with such resplendent power, as to make me feel that man henceforth is the only name of honour, and that any God out of the strictest human proportions, any God with essentially disproportionate aims and ends to man, is an unmixed superfluity and nuisance."[42]

The reader ought now to be able to judge for himself whether the works of Henry James deserve further study on his part. For myself, nothing could be so agreeable as to believe that this unpretending introduction might lead a larger public to open the writings of which it treats. Although their author, as will have been noted, gives such ample credit to Swedenborg as the source of his opinions, I have all along spoken of him as an original thinker, whose philosophy was underived. Many disciples of Swedenborg, wielding high authority, say there is no warrant in the master's pages for Mr. James's views. It is certain, to say the very least, that Mr. James has given to the various elements in Swedenborg's teaching an extremely different accentuation and perspective relation to each other, from anything other readers have been able to find. In Swedenborg, as in other writers, much must count for *slag*, and the question "what is the *real* Swedenborg," will naturally be solved by different students in different ways. Such being the case, and I being personally entitled to no opinion, I have thought it best to ignore the name of Swedenborg altogether in the previous pages;

[42] *Christianity the Logic of Creation*, pp. 214–217. The *Angel*, Mr. James says in another place, could not do the work Christ did,—the work of reconciling man's self-love with God's pure love,—"because his entire vitality proceeds not upon the reconciliation of self-love with higher loves, but upon its forcible expulsion, and even, if that were possible, its extinction. But in the bosom of Jesus, exposed through the letter of His national hope to the boundless influx of every selfish lust, and yet persistently subjugating such lust to the inspirations of universal love, the requisite basis of union was at last found, and infinite Wisdom compassed at length a direct and adequate access to the most finite of intelligences. . . . In this sublime and steadfast soul, I say, the marriage of the Divine and Human was at last perfectly consummated, so that thenceforth the infinite and eternal expansion of our nature became, not merely possible, but most strictly inevitable. Accordingly, ever since that period, husband and father, lover and friend, patriot and citizen, priest and king, have been gradually assuming more human dimensions, have been gradually putting on glorified lineaments; or what is the same thing, the universal heart of man has been learning to despise and disown all *absolute* sanctities: not merely our threadbare human sanctities, sacerdotal and regal, conjugal and paternal, but also every the most renowned Divine sanctity itself, whose bosom is not the abode of the widest, tenderest, most patient and unswerving human love."—*Christianity the Logic of Creation*, pp. 200–201.

not meaning by this to prejudge the question, or attribute to my father an originality he would have disclaimed, but wishing merely to keep the exposition as short and uncomplicated as I could.

A word of comment after so much exposition may not be out of place. Common-sense theism, the popular religion of our European race, has, through all its apparent variations, remained essentially faithful to pluralism, one might almost say to polytheism. Neither Judaism nor Christianity could tend to alter this result, or make us generally see the world in any other light than as a collection of beings which, however they might have arisen, are now severally and substantively there, and the important thing about whom is their practical relations with each other. God, the Devil, Christ, the Saints, and we, are some of these beings. Whatever monistic and pantheistic metaphysics may have crept into the history of Christianity has been confined to epochs, sects, and individuals. For the great mass of men, the practical fact of pluralism has been a sufficient basis for the religious life, and the ultra-phenomenal unity has been nothing more than a lip-formula.

And naive as in the eyes of metaphysics such a view may seem, finite and short of vision and lacking dignity from the intellectual point of view, no philosopher, however subtle, can afford to treat it with disdain; unless, perhaps, he be ready to say that the spirit of Europe is all wrong, and that of Asia right. God, treated as a principle among others,—*primus inter pares*,—has warmth and blood and personality; is a concrete being whom it does not take a scholar to love and make sacrifices and die for, as history shows. Being almost like a personage in a drama, the lightning of dramatic interest can play from him and about him, and rivet human regard.

The "One and Only Being," however, the Universal Substance, the Soul and Spirit of Things, the First Principle of monistic metaphysics, call it by names as theological and reverential as we will, always seems, it must be confessed, a pale, abstract, and impersonal conception compared with that of the eternal living God, worshipped by the incalculable majority of our race. Such a monistic principle never can be worshipped by a majority of our race until the race's mental constitution change.

Now, the great peculiarity of Mr. James's conception of God is, that it is monistic enough to satisfy the philosopher, and yet warm and living and dramatic enough to speak to the heart of the common pluralistic man. This double character seems to make of this conception an entirely fresh and original contribution to religious thought. I call it monistic enough to satisfy the metaphysician, for although Mr. James's system is anything but a *bald* monism, yet it makes of God the one and only *active* principle; and that is practically all that monism demands. Our experience makes us, it is true, acquainted with an *other* of God, in our own selfhood; but for Mr. James, that other, that selfhood, has no positive existence, being really *naught*, a provisional phantom-soul breathed by God's love into mere logical negation. And that a monism, thus mitigated, can speak to the common heart, a perusal of those pages in which Mr. James portrays creation on God's part as an infinite passion of self-surrender to his opposite, will convince any reader. Anthropomorphism and metaphysics seem for the first time in these pages to go harmoniously hand in hand. The same sun that lights up the frozen summits of abstraction, lights up life's teeming plain,—and no chasm, but an open highway lies between.

The extraordinary power and richness of this conception of the Deity ought, one would say, to make Mr. James's writings indispensable to students of religious thought. Within their compass, each old element receives a fresh expression, each old issue a startling turn. It is hard to believe, that, when they are better known, they will not come to be counted among the few truly original theological works which our language owns. So that even those who think that no theological thought can be *conclusive* will, for this reason, perhaps, not refuse to them a lasting place in literature.

Their most serious enemy will be the *philosophic* pluralist. The naïf practical pluralism of popular religion ought, as I have said, to have no quarrel with the monism they teach. There is however a pluralism hardened by reflection, and deliberate; a pluralism which, in face of the old mystery of the One and the Many, has vainly sought peace in identification, and ended by taking sides against the One. It seems to me that the deepest of all philosophic differences is that between this pluralism and all forms of monism whatever. Apart from analytic and intellectual arguments, pluralism is a view to which we all practically incline when in the full and successful exercise of our moral energy. The life we then feel tingling through us vouches sufficiently for itself, and nothing tempts us to refer it to a higher source. Being, as we are, a match for whatever evils actually confront us, we rather prefer to think of them as en-

dowed with reality, and as being absolutely alien, but, we hope, subjugable powers. Of the day of our possible impotency we take no
thought; and we care not to make such a synthesis of our weakness
and our strength, and of the good and evil fortunes of the world, as
will reduce them all to fractions, with a common denominator, of
some less fluctuating Unity, enclosing some less partial and more
certain form of Good. The feeling of *action*, in short, makes us
turn a deaf ear to the thought of *being*; and this deafness and insensibility may be said to form an integral part of what in popular
phrase is known as "healthy-mindedness." Any absolute moralism
must needs be such a healthy-minded pluralism; and in a pluralistic
philosophy the healthy-minded moralist will always feel himself
at home.

But healthy-mindedness is not the whole of life; and the *morbid*
view, as one by contrast may call it, asks for a philosophy very different from that of absolute moralism. To suggest personal will and
effort to one "all sicklied o'er" with the sense of weakness, of helpless failure, and of fear, is to suggest the most horrible of things to
him. What he craves is to be consoled in his very impotence, to feel
that the Powers of the Universe recognize and secure him, all pas-
sive and failing as he is. Well, we are all *potentially* such sick men.
The sanest and best of us are of one clay with lunatics and prison-
inmates. And whenever we feel this, such a sense of the vanity of our
voluntary career comes over us, that all our morality appears but
as a plaster hiding a sore it can never cure, and all our well-doing
as the hollowest substitute for that well-*being* that our lives ought
to be grounded in, but, alas! are not. This well-being is the object
of the *religious* demand,—a demand so penetrating and unassuage-
able that no consciousness of such occasional and outward well-
doing as befalls the human lot can ever give it satisfaction. On the
other hand, to satisfy the religious demand is to deny the demands
of the moralist. The latter wishes to feel the empirical goods and
evils, on the recognition of which his activity proceeds, to be *real*
goods and evils, with their distinction absolutely preserved. So that
of religion and moralism, the morbid and the healthy view, it may
be said that what is meat to the one is the other's poison. Any absolute moralism is a pluralism; any absolute religion is a monism. It
shows the depth of Mr. James's religious insight that he first and
last and always made moralism the target of his hottest attack, and
pitted religion and it against each other as enemies, of whom one

must die utterly, if the other is to live in genuine form. The accord of moralism and religion is superficial, their discord radical. Only the deepest thinkers on both sides see that one must go. Popular opinion gets over the difficulty by compromise and contradiction, and the shifting, according to its convenience, of its point of view. Such inconsistency cannot be called a solution of the matter, though it practically seems to work with most men well enough. Must not the more radical ways of thinking, after all, appeal to the same umpire of practice for corroboration of their more consistent views? Is the religious tendency or the moralistic tendency on the whole the most serviceable to man's life, taking the latter in the largest way? By their fruits ye shall know them. *Solvitur ambulando*; for the *decision* we must perhaps await the day of judgment. Meanwhile, the battle is about us, and we are its combatants, steadfast or vacillating, as the case may be. It will be a hot fight indeed if the friends of philosophic moralism should bring to the service of their ideal, so different from that of my father, a spirit even remotely resembling the life-long devotion of his faithful heart.

Robert Gould Shaw:
Oration by Professor William James

Your Excellency, your Honor, Soldiers and Friends: In these un-veiling exercises the duty falls to me of expressing in simple words some of the feelings which have actuated the givers of St. Gaudens' noble work of bronze, and of briefly recalling the history of Robert Shaw and of his regiment to the memory of this possibly too forget-ful generation.

The men who do brave deeds are usually unconscious of their picturesqueness. For two nights previous to the assault upon Fort Wagner the Fifty-fourth Massachusetts Regiment had been afoot, making forced marches in the rain; and on the day of the battle the men had had no food since early morning. As they lay there in the evening twilight, hungry and wet, against the cold sands of Morris Island, with the sea-fog drifting over them, their eyes fixed on the huge bulk of the fortress looming darkly three quarters of a mile ahead against the sky, and their hearts beating in expectation of the word that was to bring them to their feet and launch them on their desperate charge, neither officers nor men could have been in any holiday mood of contemplation. Many and different must have been the thoughts that came and went in them during that hour of bodeful revery; but however free the flights of fancy of some of them may have been, it is improbable that anyone who lay there had so wild and whirling an imagination as to foresee in prophetic vision this morning of a future May when we, the people of a richer and more splendid Boston, with Mayor and Governor and troops from other States, and every circumstance of ceremony, should meet together to celebrate their conduct on that evening, and do their memory this conspicuous honor.

How, indeed, comes it that out of all the great engagements of the war, engagements in many of which the troops of Massachusetts had borne the most distinguished part, this officer, only a young Colonel, this regiment of black men and its maiden battle—a battle, moreover, which was lost—should be picked out for such unusual commemoration?

The historic significance of an event is measured neither by its material magnitude, nor by its immediate success. Thermopylæ was a defeat; but to the Greek imagination Leonidas and his few Spartans stood for the whole worth of grecian life. Bunker Hill was a defeat; but for our people the fight over that breastwork has always seemed to show as well as any victory that our forefathers were men of a temper not to be finally overcome. And so here. The war for our Union, with all the constitutional questions which it settled, and all the military lessons which it gathered in, has throughout its dilatory length but one meaning in the eye of history. And nowhere was that meaning better symbolized and embodied than in the constitution of this first Northern negro regiment.

Look at that monument and read the story—see the mingling of elements which the sculptor's genius has brought so vividly before the eye. There on foot go the dark outcasts, so true to nature that one can almost hear them breathing as they march. State after State by its laws had denied them to be human persons. The Southern leaders in congressional debates, insolent in their security, loved most to designate them by the contemptuous collective epithet of "this peculiar kind of property." There they march, warm-blooded champions of a better day for man. There on horseback, among them, in his very habit as he lived, sits the blue-eyed child of fortune upon whose happy youth every divinity had smiled. Onward they move together, a single resolution kindled in their eyes, and animating their otherwise so different frames. The bronze that makes their memory eternal betrays the very soul and secret of those awful years.

Since the 'thirties the slavery question had been the only question, and by the end of the 'fifties our land lay sick and shaking with it like a traveller who has thrown himself down at night beside a pestilential swamp and in the morning finds the fever through the marrow of his bones. "Only muzzle the Abolition fanatics," said the South, "and all will be well again!" But the Abolitionists could not be muzzled—they were the voice of the world's conscience, they were a part of destiny. Weak as they were, they drove the South to madness. "Every step she takes in her blindness," said Wendell Phillips, "is one more step towards ruin." And when South Carolina took the final step in battering down Fort Sumter, it was the fanatics of slavery themselves who called upon their idolized institution ruin swift and complete. What law and reason were unable to accomplish, had now to be done by that uncertain and dreadful dispenser of God's judgments, War—War, with its abominably casual inaccurate methods, destroying good and bad together, but at last able to hew a way out of intolerable situations when through man's delusion or perversity every better way is blocked.

Our great western republic had from its very origin been a singular anomaly. A land of freedom, boastfully so called, with human slavery enthroned at the heart of it, and at last dictating terms of unconditional surrender to every other organ of its life, what was it but a thing of falsehood and horrible self-contradiction? For three quarters of a century it had nevertheless endured, kept together by policy, compromise, and concession. But at last that republic was torn in two; and truth was to be possible under the flag. Truth, thank God, truth! even though for the moment it must be truth written in hell-fire.

And this, fellow-citizens, is why, after the great generals have had their monuments, and long after the abstract soldier's monuments have been reared on every village green, we have chosen to take Robert Shaw and his regiment as the subjects of the first soldier's monument to be raised to a particular set of comparatively undistinguished men. The very lack of external complication in the history of these soldiers is what makes them represent with such typical purity the profounder meaning of the Union cause.

Our nation had been founded in what we may call our American religion, baptized and reared in the faith that a man requires no master to take care of him, and that common people can work out their salvation well enough together if left free to try. But the founders had not dared to touch the great intractable exception; and slavery had wrought until at last the only alternative for the nation was to fight or die. What Shaw and his comrades stand for and show us is that in such an emergency Americans of all complexions and conditions can go forth like brothers, and meet death cheerfully if need be, in order that this religion of our native land shall not become a failure on the earth.

We of this Commonwealth believe in that religion; and it is not at all because Robert Shaw was an exceptional genius, but simply because he was faithful to it as we all may hope to be faithful in our measure when the times demand, that we wish his beautiful image to stand here for all time, an inciter to similarly unselfish public deeds.

Shaw thought but little of himself, yet he had a personal charm which, as we look back on him, makes us repeat: "None knew thee but to love thee, nor named thee but to praise." This grace of nature was united in him in the happiest way with a filial heart, a cheerful will, and a judgment that was true and fair. And when the war came, and great things were doing of the kind that he could help in, he went as a matter of course to the front. What country under heaven has not thousands of such youths to rejoice in, youths on whom the safety of the human race depends? Whether or not they leave memorials behind them, whether their names are writ in water or in marble, depends mostly on the opportunities which the accidents of history throw into their path. Shaw recognized the vital opportunity: he saw that the time had come when the colored people must put the country in their debt.

Colonel Lee has just told us something about the obstacles with which this idea had to contend. For a large party of us this was still exclusively a white man's war; and should colored troops be tried and not succeed, confusion would grow worse confounded. Shaw was a Captain in the Massachusetts Second when Governor Andrew invited him to take the lead in the experiment. He was very modest, and doubted for a moment his own capacity for so responsible a post. We may also imagine human motives whispering other doubts. Shaw loved the Second Regiment, illustrious already, and was sure of promotion where he stood. In this new negro-soldier venture, loneliness was inevitable, ridicule certain, failure possible; and Shaw was only twenty-five; and, although he had stood among the bullets at Cedar Mountain and Antietam, he had till then been walking socially on the sunny side of life. But whatever doubts may have beset him, they were over in a day, for he inclined naturally towards difficult resolves. He accepted the proffered command, and from that moment lived but for one object, to establish the honor of the Massachusetts Fifty-fourth.

I have had the privilege of reading his letters to his family from the day of April when, as a private in the New York Seventh, he obeyed the President's first call. Some day they must be published, for they form a veritable poem for serenity and simplicity of tone. He took to camp life as if it were his native element, and (like so many of our young soldiers) he was at first all eagerness to make arms his permanent profession. Drilling and disciplining; interminable marching and countermarching and picket duty on the upper Potomac as lieutenant in our Second Regiment, to which post he had soon been promoted; pride at the discipline attained by the Second, and horror at the bad discipline of other regiments; these are the staple matter of the earlier letters, and last for many months. These, and occasional more recreative incidents, visits to Virginian houses, the reading of books like Napier's *Peninsular War* or the *Idylls of the King*, Thanksgiving feasts and races amongst officers, that helped the weary weeks to glide away. Then the bloodier business opens, and the plot thickens till the end is reached. From first to last there is not a rancorous word against the enemy—often quite the reverse—and amid all the scenes of hardship, death, and devastation that his pen soon has to write of, there is unfailing cheerfulness and even a sort of innermost peace.

After he left it, Robert Shaw's heart still clung to the fortunes of the Second. Months later, when in South Carolina with the Fifty-fourth, he writes to his young wife: "I should have been Major of the Second now if I had remained there and lived through the battles. As regards my own pleasure, I had rather have that place than any other in the army. It would have been fine to go home a field officer in that regiment! Poor fellows, how they have been slaughtered!"

Meanwhile he had well taught his new command how to do their duty; for only three days after he wrote this he led them up the parapet of Fort Wagner, where he and nearly half of them were left upon the ground.

Robert Shaw quickly inspired others with his own love of discipline. There was something almost pathetic in the earnestness with which both the officers and men of the Fifty-fourth embraced their mission of showing that a black regiment could excel in every virtue known to man. They had good success, and the Fifty-fourth became a model in all possible respects. Almost the only trace of bitterness in Shaw's whole correspondence is over an incident in which he thought his men had been morally disgraced. It had become their duty, immediately after their arrival at the seat of war, to participate, in obedience to fanatical orders from the head of the department, in the sack and burning of the inoffensive little town of Darien on the Georgia coast. "I fear," he writes to his wife, "that such actions will hurt the reputation of black troops and of those connected with them. For myself I have gone through the war so far without dishonor, and I do not like to degenerate into a plunderer and a robber,—and the same applies to every officer in my regiment. After going through the hard campaigning and the hard fighting in Virginia, this makes me very much ashamed. There are two courses only for me to pursue: to obey orders and say nothing; or to refuse to go upon any more such expeditions, and be put under arrest and probably court-martialled, which is a very serious thing." Fortunately for Shaw, the general in command of that department was almost immediately relieved.

Four weeks of camp life and discipline on the Sea Islands, and the regiment had its baptism of fire. A small affair, but it proved the men to be staunch. Shaw again writes to his wife: "You don't know what a fortunate day this has been for me and for us all, excepting some poor fellows who were killed and wounded. We have fought at last alongside of white troops. Two hundred of my men on picket this morning were attacked by five regiments of infantry, some cavalry, and a battery of artillery. The Tenth Connecticut were on their left, and say they would have had a bad time if the Fifty-fourth men had not stood so well. The whole Division was under arms in fifteen minutes, and after coming up close in front of us, the enemy, finding us so strong, fell back. . . . General Terry sent me word he was highly gratified with the behavior of our men, and the officers and privates of other regiments praise us very much. All this is very gratifying to us personally, and a fine thing for the colored troops. I know this will give you pleasure, for it wipes out the remembrance of the Darien affair, which you could not but grieve over, though we were innocent participators."

The Adjutant of the Fifty-fourth, who made report of this skirmish to General Terry, well expresses the feelings of loneliness that still prevailed in that command:—

"The General's favorite regiment," writes the Adjutant,[1] "the Twenty-fourth Massachusetts Infantry, one of the best that had so far faced the rebel foe, largely officered by Boston men, was surrounding his headquarters. It had been a living breathing suspicion with us—perhaps not altogether justly—that all white troops abhorred our presence in the army, and that the Twenty-fourth would rather hear of us in some remote corner of the Confederacy than tolerate us in the advance of any battle in which they themselves were to act as reserves or lookers-on. Can you not then readily imagine the pleasure which I felt as I alighted from my horse, before General Terry and his staff—I was going to say his unfriendly staff, but of this I am not sure—to report to him, with Colonel Shaw's compliments, that we had repulsed the enemy without the loss of a single inch of ground. General Terry bade me mount again and tell Colonel Shaw that he was proud of the conduct of his men, and that he must still hold the ground against any future sortie of the enemy. You can even now share with me the sensation of that moment of soldierly satisfaction."

The next night but one after this episode was spent by the Fifty-fourth in disembarking on Morris Island in the rain, and at noon Colonel Shaw was able to report their arrival to General Strong, to whose brigade he was assigned. A terrific bombardment was playing on Fort Wagner, then the most formidable earthwork ever built, and the General, knowing Shaw's desire to place his men beside white troops, said to him: "Colonel, Fort Wagner is to be stormed this evening, and you may lead the column, if you say yes. Your men, I know, are worn out, but do as you choose." Shaw's face brightened. "Before answering the General, he instantly turned to me," writes the Adjutant, who reports the interview, "and said, 'Tell Colonel Hallowell to bring up the Fifty-fourth immediately.'"

This was done, and just before nightfall the attack was made. Shaw was serious, for he knew the assault was desperate, and had a premonition of his end. Walking up and down in front of the regiment, he briefly exhorted them to prove that they were men. Then he gave the order: "Move in quick time till within a hundred yards, then double quick and charge. Forward!" and the Fifty-fourth advanced to the storming, its Colonel and the colors at its head.

1 G. W. James: "The Assault upon Fort Wagner," in *War Papers Read before the Commandery of the State of Wisconsin, Military Order of the Loyal Legion of the U.S.* Milwaukee, 1891.

On over the sand, through a narrow defile which broke up the formation, double quick over the chevaux de frise, into the ditch and over it, as best they could, and up the rampart; with Fort Sumter, which had seen them, playing on them, and Fort Wagner, now one mighty mound of fire, tearing out their lives. Shaw led from first to last. Gaining successfully the parapet, he stood there for a moment with uplifted sword, shouting "Forward, Fifty-fourth!" and then fell headlong, with a bullet through his heart. The battle raged for nigh two hours. Regiment after regiment, following upon the Fifty-fourth, hurled themselves upon its ramparts, but Fort Wagner was nobly defended, and for that night stood safe. The Fifty-fourth withdrew after two thirds of its officers and five twelfths or nearly half its men had been shot down or bayoneted within the fortress or before its walls. It was good behavior for a regiment no one of whose soldiers had had a musket in his hands more than eighteen weeks, and which had seen the enemy for the first time only two days before.

"The negroes fought gallantly," wrote a Confederate officer, "and were headed by as brave a colonel as ever lived."

As for the Colonel, not a drum was heard nor a funeral note, not a soldier discharged his farewell shot, when the Confederates buried him, the morning after the engagement. His body, half stripped of its clothing, and the corpses of his dauntless negroes were flung into one common trench together, and the sand was shovelled over them, without a stake or stone to signalize the spot. In death as in life, then, the Fifty-fourth bore witness to the brotherhood of Man. The lover of heroic history could wish for no more fitting sepulchre for Shaw's magnanimous young heart. There let his body rest, united with the forms of his brave nameless comrades. There let the breezes of the Atlantic sigh, and its gales roar their requiem, while this bronze effigy and these inscriptions keep their fame alive long after you and I and all who meet here are forgotten.

How soon indeed are human things forgotten! As we meet here this morning, the Southern sun is shining on their place of burial, and the waves sparkling and the sea-gulls circling around Fort Wagner's ancient site. But the great earthworks and their thundering cannon, the commanders and their followers, the wild assault and repulse that for a brief space made night hideous on that far-off evening, have all sunk into the blue gulf of the past, and for the majority of this generation are hardly more than an abstract name, a picture, a tale that is told. Only when some yellow-bleached photograph of a soldier of the 'sixties comes into our hands, with that odd and vivid look of individuality due to the moment when it was taken, do we realize the concreteness of that bygone history, and feel how interminable to the actors in them were those leaden-footed hours and years. The photographs themselves erelong will fade utterly, and books of history and monuments like this alone will tell the tale. The great war for the Union will be like the siege of Troy, it will have taken its place amongst all other "old, unhappy, far-off things and battles long ago."

In all such events two things must be distinguished—the moral service of them from the fortitude which they display. War has been much praised and celebrated among us of late as a school of manly virtue; but it is easy to exaggerate upon this point. Ages ago, war was the gory cradle of mankind, the grim-featured nurse that alone could train our savage progenitors into some semblance of social virtue, teach them to be faithful one to another, and force them to sink their selfishness in wider tribal ends. War still excels in this prerogative; and whether it be paid in years of service, in treasure or in life-blood, the war-tax is still the only tax that men ungrudgingly will pay. How could it be otherwise, when the survivors of one successful massacre after another are the beings from whose loins we and all our contemporary races spring? Man is once for all a fighting animal; centuries of peaceful history could not breed the battle-instinct out of us; and our pugnacity is the virtue least in need of reinforcement by reflection, least in need of orator's or poet's help.

What we really need the poet's and orator's help to keep alive in us is not, then, the common and gregarious courage which Robert Shaw showed when he marched with you, men of the Seventh Regiment. It is that more lonely courage which he showed when he dropped his warm commission in the glorious Second to head your dubious fortunes, negroes of the Fifty-fourth. That lonely kind of courage (civic courage as we call it in peace-times) is the kind of valor to which the monuments of nations should most of all be reared, for the survival of the fittest has not bred it into the bone of human beings as it has bred military valor; and of five hundred of us who could storm a battery side by side with others, perhaps not one would be found ready to risk his worldly fortunes all alone in resisting an enthroned abuse. The deadliest enemies of nations are not their foreign foes; they always dwell within their borders. And from these internal enemies civilization is always in need of being saved. The nation blest above all nations is she in whom the civic genius of the people does the saving day by day, by acts without external picturesqueness; by speaking, writing, voting reasonably; by smiting corruption swiftly; by good temper between parties; by the people knowing true men when they see them, and preferring them as leaders to rabid partisans or empty quacks. Such nations have no need of wars to save them. Their accounts with righteousness are always even; and God's judgments do not have to overtake them fitfully in bloody spasms and convulsions of the race.

The lesson that our war ought most of all to teach us is the lesson that evils must be checked in time, before they grow so great. The Almighty cannot love such long-postponed accounts, or such tremendous settlements. And surely He hates all settlements that do such quantities of incidental devils' work. Our present situation, with its rancors and delusions, what is it but the direct outcome of the added powers of government, the corruptions and inflations of the war? Every war leaves such miserable legacies, fatal seeds of future war and revolution, unless the civic virtues of the people save the State in time.

Robert Shaw had both kinds of virtue. As he then led his regiment against Fort Wagner, so surely would he now be leading us against all lesser powers of darkness, had his sweet young life been spared. You think of many as I speak of one. For, North and South, how many lives as sweet, unmonumented for the most part, commemorated solely in the hearts of mourning mothers, widowed brides, or friends, did the inexorable war mow down! Instead of the full years of natural service from so many of her children, our country counts but their poor memories, "the tender grace of a day that is dead," lingering like echoes of past music on the vacant air.

But so and so only was it written that she should grow sound again. From that fatal earlier unsoundness those lives have bought for North and South together permanent release. The warfare is accomplished; the iniquity is pardoned. No future problem can be like that problem. No task laid on our children can compare in difficulty with the task with which their fathers had to deal. Yet as we face the future, tasks enough await us. The republic to which Robert Shaw and a quarter of a million like him were faithful unto death is no republic that can live at ease hereafter on the interest of

73

what they won. Democracy is still upon its trial. The civic genius of our people is its only bulwark, and neither laws nor monuments, neither battleships nor public libraries, nor great newspapers nor booming stocks; neither mechanical invention nor political adroitness, nor churches nor universities nor civil-service examinations can save us from degeneration if the inner mystery be lost. That mystery, at once the secret and the glory of our English-speaking race, consists in nothing but two common habits, two inveterate habits carried into public life—habits so homely that they lend themselves to no rhetorical expression, yet habits more precious, perhaps, than any that the human race has gained. They can never be too often pointed out or praised. One of them is the habit of trained and disciplined good temper towards the opposite party when it fairly wins its innings—it was by breaking from this habit the slave States nearly wrecked our Nation. The other is that of fierce and merciless resentment towards every man or set of men who break the public peace—it was by holding to this habit the free States saved her life.

O my countrymen, Southern and Northern, brothers hereafter, masters, slaves, and enemies no more, let us see to it that both of those heirlooms are preserved. So may our ransomed country, like the city of the promise, lie forever foursquare under Heaven, and the ways of all the nations be lit up by its light.

Human Immortality:
Two Supposed Objections to the Doctrine

PREFACE TO SECOND EDITION

So many critics have made one and the same objection to the doorway to immortality which my lecture claims to be left open by the 'transmission-theory' of cerebral action, that I feel tempted, as the book is again going to press, to add a word of explanation.

If our finite personality here below, the objectors say, be due to the transmission through the brain of portions of a preëxisting larger consciousness, all that can remain after the brain expires is the larger consciousness itself as such, with which we should thenceforth be perforce reconfounded, the only means of our existence in finite personal form having ceased.

But this, the critics continue, is the pantheistic idea of immortality, survival, namely, in the soul of the world; not the Christian idea of immortality, which means survival in strictly personal form.

In showing the possibility of a mental life after the brain's death, they conclude, the lecture has thus at the same time shown the impossibility of its identity with the personal life, which is the brain's function.

Now I am myself anything but a pantheist of the monistic pattern; yet for simplicity's sake I did in the lecture speak of the 'mother-sea' in terms that must have sounded pantheistic, and suggested that I thought of it myself as a unit. On page 30 [pp. 95–96], I even added that future lecturers might prove the loss of some of our personal limitations after death not to be matter for absolute regret. The interpretation of my critics was therefore not unnatural; and I ought to have been more careful to guard against its being made.

In note 5 on page 58 [p. 89] I partially guarded against it by saying that the 'mother-sea' from which the finite mind is supposed to be strained by the brain, need not be conceived of in pantheistic terms exclusively. There might be, I said, many minds behind the scenes as well as one. The plain truth is that *one may conceive the mental world behind the veil in as individualistic a form as one pleases, without any detriment to the general scheme by which the brain is represented as a transmissive organ.*

If the extreme individualistic view were taken, one's finite mundane consciousness would be an extract from one's larger, truer personality, the latter having even now some sort of reality behind the scenes. And in transmitting it—to keep to our extremely mechanical metaphor, which confessedly throws no light on the actual *modus operandi*—one's brain would also leave effects upon the part remaining behind the veil; for when a thing is torn, both fragments feel the operation.

And just as (to use a very coarse figure) the stubs remain in a check-book whenever a check is used, to register the transaction, so these impressions on the transcendent self might constitute so many vouchers of the finite experiences of which the brain had been the mediator; and ultimately they might form that collection within the larger self of memories of our earthly passage, which is all that, since Locke's day, the continuance of our personal identity beyond the grave has by psychology been recognized to mean.

It is true that all this would seem to have affinities rather with preëxistence and with possible re-incarnations than with the Christian notion of immortality. But my concern in the lecture was not to discuss immortality in general. It was confined to showing it to be *not incompatible* with the brain-function theory of our present mundane consciousness. I hold that it is so compatible, and compatible moreover in fully individualized form. The reader would be in accord with everything that the text of my lecture intended to say, were he to assert that every memory and affection of his present life is to be preserved, and that he shall never *in sæcula sæculorum* cease to be able to say to himself: "I am the same personal being who in old times upon the earth had those experiences."

Human Immortality

It is a matter unfortunately too often seen in history to call for much remark, that when a living want of mankind has got itself officially protected and organized in an institution, one of the things which the institution most surely tends to do is to stand in the way of the natural gratification of the want itself. We see this in laws and courts of justice; we see it in ecclesiasticisms; we see it in academies of the fine arts, in the medical and other professions, and we even see it in the universities themselves.

Too often do the place-holders of such institutions frustrate the spiritual purpose to which they were appointed to minister, by the technical light which soon becomes the only light in which they seem able to see the purpose, and the narrow way which is the only way in which they can work in its service.

I confess that I thought of this for a moment when the Corporation of our University invited me last spring to give this Ingersoll lecture. Immortality is one of the great spiritual needs of man. The churches have constituted themselves the official guardians of the need, with the result that some of them actually pretend to accord or to withhold it from the individual by their conventional sacraments,—withhold it at least in the only shape in which it can be an object of desire. And now comes the Ingersoll lectureship. Its high-minded founder evidently thought that our University might serve the cause he had at heart more liberally than the churches do, because a university is a body so much less trammeled by traditions and by impossibilities in regard to choice of persons. And yet one of the first things which the university does is to appoint a man like him who stands before you, certainly not because he is known as an enthusiastic messenger of the future life, burning to publish the good tidings to his fellow-men, but apparently because he is a university official.

Thinking in this way, I felt at first as if I ought to decline the appointment. The whole subject of immortal life has its prime roots in personal feeling. I have to confess that my own personal feeling about immortality has never been of the keenest order, and that, among the problems that give my mind solicitude, this one does not take the very foremost place. Yet there are individuals with a real passion for the matter, men and women for whom a life hereafter is a pungent craving, and the thought of it an obsession; and in whom keenness of interest has bred an insight into the relations of the subject that no one less penetrated with the mystery of it can attain. Some of these people are known to me. They are not official personages; they do not speak as the scribes, but as having direct authority. And surely, if anywhere a prophet clad in goatskins, and not a uniformed official, should be called to give inspiration, assurance, and instruction, it would seem to be here, on such a theme. Office, at any rate, ought not to displace spiritual calling.

And yet, in spite of these reflections, which I could not avoid making, I am here to-night, all uninspired and official as I am. I am sure that prophets clad in goatskins, or, to speak less figuratively, laymen inspired with emotional messages on the subject, will often enough be invited by our Corporation to give the Ingersoll lecture hereafter. Meanwhile, all negative and deadening as the remarks of a mere professional psychologist like myself may be in comparison with the vital lessons they will give, I am sure, upon mature reflection, that those who have the responsibility of administering the Ingersoll foundation are in duty bound to let the most various kinds of official personages take their turn as well. The subject is really an enormous subject. At the back of Mr. Alger's *Critical History of the Doctrine of a Future Life*, there is a bibliography of more than five thousand titles of books in which it is treated. Our Corporation cannot think only of the single lecture: it must think of the whole series of lectures *in futuro*. Single lectures, however emotionally inspired and inspiring they may be, will not be enough. The lectures must remedy each other, so that out of the series there shall emerge a collective literature worthy of the importance of the theme. This unquestionably was what the founder had in mind. He wished the subject to be turned over in all possible aspects, so that at last results might ponderate harmoniously in the true direction. Seen in this long perspective, the Ingersoll foundation calls for nothing so much as for minute division of labor. Orators must take their turn, and prophets; but narrow specialists as well. Theologians of every creed, metaphysicians, anthropologists, and psychologists must alternate with biologists and physicists and psychical researchers,—even with mathematicians. If any one of them presents a grain of truth, seen from his point of view, that will remain and accrete with truths brought by the others, his will have been a good appointment.

In the hour that lies before us, then, I shall seek to justify my appointment by offering what seem to me two such grains of truth, two points well fitted, if I am not mistaken, to combine with anything that other lecturers may bring.

These points are both of them in the nature of replies to objections, to difficulties which our modern culture finds in the old notion of a life hereafter,—difficulties that I am sure rob the notion of much of its old power to draw belief, in the scientifically cultivated circles to which this audience belong.

The first of these difficulties is relative to the absolute dependence of our spiritual life, as we know it here, upon the brain. One hears not only physiologists, but numbers of laymen who read the popular science books and magazines, saying all about us, How can we believe in life hereafter when Science has once for all attained to proving, beyond possibility of escape, that our inner life is a function of that famous material, the so-called 'gray matter' of our cerebral convolutions? How can the function possibly persist after its organ has undergone decay?

Thus physiological psychology is what is supposed to bar the way to the old faith. And it is now as a physiological psychologist that I ask you to look at the question with me a little more closely.

It is indeed true that physiological science has come to the conclusion cited; and we must confess that in so doing she has only carried out a little farther the common belief of mankind. Every one knows that arrests of brain development occasion imbecility, that blows on the head abolish memory or consciousness, and that brain-stimulants and poisons change the quality of our ideas. The anatomists, physiologists, and pathologists have only shown this generally admitted fact of a dependence to be detailed and minute. What the laboratories and hospitals have lately been teaching us is not only that thought in general is one of the brain's functions, but that the various special forms of thinking are functions of special portions of the brain. When we are thinking of things seen, it is our occipital convolutions that are active; when of things heard, it is a certain portion of our temporal lobes; when of things to be spoken, it is one of our frontal convolutions. Professor Flechsig of Leipzig (who perhaps more than any one may claim to have made the subject his own) considers that in other special convolutions those processes of association go on, which permit the more abstract processes of thought, to take place. I could easily show you these regions if I had here a picture of the brain.[1] Moreover, the diminished or exaggerated associations of what this author calls the *Körperfühlsphäre* with the other regions, accounts, according to him, for the complexion of our emotional life, and eventually decides whether one shall be a callous brute or criminal, an unbalanced sentimentalist, or a character accessible to feeling, and yet

[1] The gaps between the centres first recognized as motor and sensory—gaps which form in man two thirds of the surface of the hemispheres—are thus positively interpreted by Flechsig as intellectual centres strictly so called. [Compare his *Gehirn und Seele*, 2te Ausgabe, 1896, p. 23.] They have, he considers, a common type of microscopic structure; and the fibres connected with them are a month later in gaining their medullary sheath than are the fibres connected with the other centres. When disordered, they are the starting-point of the insanities, properly so called. Already Wernicke had defined insanity as disease of the organ of association, without so definitely pretending to circumscribe the latter—compare his *Grundriss der Psychiatrie*, 1894, p. 7. Flechsig goes so far as to say that he finds a difference of symptoms in general paralytics according as their frontal or their more posterior association-centres are diseased. Where it is the frontal centres, the patient's consciousness of self is more deranged than is his perception of purely objective relations. Where the posterior associative regions suffer, it is rather the patient's system of objective ideas that undergoes disintegration (*loc. cit.* pp. 89–91). In rodents Flechsig thinks there is a complete absence of association-centres,—the sensory centres touch each other. In carnivora and the lower monkeys the latter centres still exceed the association-centres in volume. Only in the katarhinal apes do we begin to find anything like the human type (p. 84).

In his little pamphlet, *Die Grenzen geistiger Gesundheit und Krankheit*, Leipzig, 1896, Flechsig ascribes the moral insensibility which is found in certain criminals to a diminution of internal pain-feeling due to degeneration of the 'Körperfühlsphäre,' that extensive anterior region first so named by Munk, in which he lays the seat of all the emotions and of the consciousness of self [*Gehirn und Seele*, pp. 62–68; *Die Grenzen*, etc., pp. 31–39, 48].—I give these references to Flechsig for concreteness' sake, not because his views are irreversibly made out.

well poised. Such special opinions may have to be corrected; yet so firmly established do the main positions worked out by the anatomists, physiologists, and pathologists of the brain appear, that the youth of our medical schools are everywhere taught unhesitatingly to believe them. The assurance that observation will go on to establish them ever more and more minutely is the inspirer of all contemporary research. And almost any of our young psychologists will tell you that only a few belated scholastics, or possibly some crack-brained theosophist or psychical researcher, can be found holding back, and still talking as if mental phenomena might exist as independent variables in the world.

For the purposes of my argument, now, I wish to adopt this general doctrine as if it were established absolutely, with no possibility of restriction. During this hour I wish you also to accept it as a postulate, whether you think it incontrovertibly established or not; so I beg you to agree with me to-day in subscribing to the great psycho-physiological formula: *Thought is a function of the brain.*

The question is, then, Does this doctrine logically compel us to disbelieve in immortality? Ought it to force every truly consistent thinker to sacrifice his hopes of an hereafter to what he takes to be his duty of accepting all the consequences of a scientific truth?

Most persons imbued with what one may call the puritanism of science would feel themselves bound to answer this question with a yes. If any medically or psychologically bred young scientists feel otherwise, it is probably in consequence of that incoherency of mind of which the majority of mankind happily enjoy the privilege. At one hour scientists, at another they are Christians or common men, with the will to live burning hot in their breasts; and, holding thus the two ends of the chain, they are careless of the intermediate connection. But the more radical and uncompromising disciple of science makes the sacrifice, and, sorrowfully or not, according to his temperament, submits to giving up his hopes of heaven.[2]

---

[2] So widespread is this conclusion in positivistic circles, so abundantly is it expressed in conversation, and so frequently implied in things that are written, that I confess that my surprise was great when I came to look into books for a passage explicitly denying immortality on physiological grounds, which I might quote to make my text more concrete. I was unable to find anything blunt and distinct enough to serve. I looked through all the books that would naturally suggest themselves, with no effect; and I vainly asked various psychological colleagues. And yet I should almost have been ready to take oath that I had read several such passages of the most categoric sort

This, then, is the objection to immortality; and the next thing in order for me is to try to make plain to you why I believe that it has in strict logic no deterrent power. I must show you that the fatal consequence is not coercive, as is commonly imagined; and that, even though our soul's life (as here below it is revealed to us) may be in literal strictness the function of a brain that perishes, yet it is not at all impossible, but on the contrary quite possible, that the life may still continue when the brain itself is dead.

The supposed impossibility of its continuing comes from too superficial a look at the admitted fact of functional dependence. The moment we inquire more closely into the notion of functional dependence, and ask ourselves, for example, how many kinds of functional dependence there may be, we immediately perceive that there is one kind at least that does not exclude a life hereafter at all. The fatal conclusion of the physiologist flows from his assuming offhand another kind of functional dependence, and treating it as the only imaginable kind.[3]

---

within the last decade. Very likely this is a false impression, and it may be with this opinion as with many others. The atmosphere is full of them; many a writer's pages logically presuppose and involve them; yet, if you wish to refer a student to an express and radical statement that he may employ as a text to comment on, you find almost nothing that will do. In the present case there are plenty of passages in which, in a general way, mind is said to be conterminous with brain-function, but hardly one in which the author thereupon explicitly denies the possibility of immortality. The best one I have found is perhaps this: "Not only consciousness, but every stirring of life, depends on functions that go out like a flame when nourishment is cut off. . . . The phenomena of consciousness correspond, element for element, to the operations of special parts of the brain. . . . The destruction of any piece of the apparatus involves the loss of some one or other of the vital operations; and the consequence is that, as far as life extends, we have before us only an organic function, not a *Ding-an-sich*, or an expression of that imaginary entity the Soul. This fundamental proposition . . . carries with it the denial of the immortality of the soul, since, where no soul exists, its mortality or immortality cannot be raised as a question. . . . The function fills its time,—the flame illuminates and therein gives out its whole being. That is all; and verily that is enough. . . . Sensation has its definite organic conditions, and, as these decay with the natural decay of life, it is quite impossible for a mind accustomed to deal with realities to suppose any capacity of sensation as surviving when the machinery of our natural existence has stopped." [E. Dühring: *Der Werth des Lebens*, 3d edition, pp. 48, 169.]

[3] The philosophically instructed reader will notice that I have all along been placing myself at the ordinary dualistic point of view of natural science and of common sense. From this point of view mental facts like feelings are made of one kind of stuff or substance, physical facts of another. An absolute phenomenism, not believing such a dualism to be ultimate, may possibly end by solving some of the prob-

lems that are insoluble when propounded in dualistic terms. Meanwhile, since the physiological objection to immortality has arisen on the ordinary dualistic plane of thought, and since absolute phenomenism has as yet said nothing articulate enough to count about the matter, it is proper that my reply to the objection should be expressed in dualistic terms—leaving me free, of course, on any later occasion to make an attempt, if I wish, to transcend them and use different categories.

Now, on the dualistic assumption, one cannot see more than two really different sorts of dependence of our mind on our brain: Either

(1) The brain brings into being the very stuff of consciousness of which our mind consists; or else

(2) Consciousness pre-exists as an entity, and the various brains give to it its various special forms.

If supposition 2 be the true one, and the stuff of mind pre-exists, there are, again, only two ways of conceiving that our brain confers upon it the specifically human form. It may exist

(a) In disseminated particles; and then our brains are organs of concentration, organs for combining and massing these into resultant minds of personal form. Or it may exist

(b) In vaster unities (absolute 'world-soul,' or something less); and then our brains are organs for separating it into parts and giving them finite form.

There are thus three possible theories of the brain's function, and no more. We may name them, severally,—

1. The theory of production;

2a. The theory of combination;

2b. The theory of separation.

In the text of the lecture, theory number 2b (specified more particularly as the transmission-theory) is defended against theory number 1. Theory 2a, otherwise known as the mind-dust or mind-stuff theory, is left entirely unnoticed for lack of time. I also leave it uncriticised in these notes, having already considered it, as fully as the so-far published forms of it may seem to call for, in my work, *The Principles of Psychology*, New York, Holt & Co., 1892, chapter VI. I may say here, however, that Professor W. K. Clifford, one of the ablest champions of the combination-theory, and originator of the useful term 'mind-stuff,' considers that theory incompatible with individual immortality, and in his review of Stewart's and Tait's book, *The Unseen Universe*, thus expresses his conviction:—

"The laws connecting consciousness with changes in the brain are very definite and precise, and their necessary consequences are not to be evaded .... Consciousness is a complex thing made up of elements, a stream of feelings. The action of the brain is also a complex thing made up of elements, a stream of nerve-messages. For every feeling in consciousness there is at the same time a nerve-message in the brain. ... Consciousness is not a simple thing, but a complex; it is the combination of feelings into a stream. It exists at the same time with the combination of nerve-messages into a stream. If individual feeling always goes with individual nerve-message, if combination or stream of feelings always goes with stream of nerve-messages, does it not follow that when the stream of nerve-messages is broken up, the stream of feelings will be broken up also, will no longer form a consciousness? does it not follow that when the messages themselves are broken up, the individual feelings will be resolved into still simpler elements? The force of this evidence is not to be weakened by any number of spiritual bodies. Inexorable facts connect our consciousness with this body that we know; and that not merely as a whole, but the parts of it are connected

When the physiologist who thinks that his science cuts off all hope of immortality pronounces the phrase, "Thought is a function of the brain," he thinks of the matter just as he thinks when he says, "Steam is a function of the tea-kettle," "Light is a function of the electric circuit," "Power is a function of the moving waterfall." In these latter cases the several material objects have the function of inwardly creating or engendering their effects, and their function must be called *productive* function. Just so, he thinks, it must be with the brain. Engendering consciousness in its interior, much as it engenders cholesterin and creatin and carbonic acid, its relation to our soul's life must also be called productive function. Of course, if such production be the function, then when the organ perishes, since the production can no longer continue, the soul must surely die. Such a conclusion as this is indeed inevitable from that particular conception of the facts.[4]

---

severally with parts of our brain-action. If there is any similar connexion with a spiritual body, it only follows that the spiritual body must die at the same time with the natural one." [*Lectures and Essays*, vol. i. pp. 247–249. Compare also passages of similar purport in vol. ii. pp. 65–70.]

[4] The theory of production, or materialistic theory, seldom ventures to formulate itself very distinctly. Perhaps the following passage from Cabanis is as explicit as anything one can find:—

"To acquire a just idea of the operations from which thought results, we must consider the brain as a particular organ specially destined to produce it; just as the stomach and intestines are destined to operate digestion, the liver to filter bile, the parotid and maxillary glands to prepare the salivary juices. The impressions, arriving in the brain, force it to enter into activity; just as the alimentary materials, falling into the stomach, excite it to a more abundant secretion of gastric juice, and to the movements which result in their own solution. The function proper to the first organ is that of receiving [*percevoir*] each particular impression, of attaching signs to it, of combining the different impressions, of comparing them with each other, of drawing from them judgments and resolves; just as the function of the other organ is to act upon the nutritive substances whose presence excites it, to dissolve them, and to assimilate their juices to our nature.

"Do you say that the organic movements by which the brain exercises these functions are unknown? I reply that the action by which the nerves of the stomach determine the different operations which constitute digestion, and the manner in which they confer so active a solvent power upon the gastric juice, are equally hidden from our scrutiny. We see the food-materials fall into this viscus with their own proper qualities; we see them emerge with new qualities, and we infer that the stomach is really the author of this alteration. Similarly we see the impressions reaching the brain by the intermediation of the nerves; they then are isolated and without coherence. The viscus enters into action; it acts upon them, and soon it emits [*renvoie*] them metamorphosed into ideas, to which the language of physiognomy or gesture, or the signs of speech and writing, give an outward expression. We conclude, then, with an equal certitude, that the brain digests, as it were, the impressions; that it

But in the world of physical nature productive function of this sort is not the only kind of function with which we are familiar. We have also releasing or permissive function; and we have transmissive function.

The trigger of a crossbow has a releasing function: it removes the obstacle that holds the string, and lets the bow fly back to its natural shape. So when the hammer falls upon a detonating compound. By knocking out the inner molecular obstructions, it lets the

---

performs organically the secretion of thought." [*Rapports du physique et du moral*, 8th edition, 1844, p. 137.]

It is to the ambiguity of the word 'impression' that such an account owes whatever plausibility it may seem to have. More recent forms of the production-theory have shown a tendency to liken thought to a 'force' which the brain exerts, or to a 'state' into which it passes. Herbert Spencer, for instance, writes:—

"The law of metamorphosis, which holds among the physical forces, holds equally between them and the mental forces. . . . How this metamorphosis takes place—how a force existing as motion, heat, or light, can become a mode of consciousness—how it is possible for aerial vibrations to generate the sensation we call sound, or for the forces liberated by chemical changes in the brain to give rise to emotion—these are mysteries which it is impossible to fathom. But they are not profounder mysteries than the transformations of the physical forces into each other." [*First Principles*, 2nd Edition, p. 217.]

So Büchner says: "Thinking must be regarded as a special mode of general natural motion, which is as characteristic of the substance of the central nervous elements as the motion of contraction is of the muscle-substance, or the motion of light is of the universal ether. . . . That thinking is and must be a mode of motion is not merely a postulate of logic, but a proposition which has of late been demonstrated experimentally. . . . Various ingenious experiments have proved that the swiftest thought that we are able to evolve occupies at least the eighth or tenth part of a second." [*Force and Matter*, New York, 1891, p. 242.]

Heat and light, being modes of motion, 'phosphorescence' and 'incandescence' are phenomena to which consciousness has been likened by the production-theory: "As one sees a metallic rod, placed in a glowing furnace, gradually heat itself, and—as the undulations of the caloric grow more and more frequent—pass successively from the shades of bright red to dark red (*sic*), to red-white, and develope, as its temperature rises, heat and light,—so the living sensitive cells, in presence of the incitations that solicit them, exalt themselves progressively as to their most interior sensibility, enter into a phase of erethism, and at a certain number of vibrations, set free (*dégagent*) pain as a physiological expression of this same sensibility superheated to a red-white." [J. Luys: *Le Cerveau*, p. 91.]

In a similar vein Mr. Percival Lowell writes: "When we have, as we say, an idea, what happens inside us is probably something like this: the neural current of molecular change passes up the nerves, and through the ganglia reaches at last the cortical cells . . . . When it reaches the cortical cells, it finds a set of molecules which are not so accustomed to this special change. The current encounters resistance, and in overcoming this resistance it causes the cells to glow. This white-heating of the cells we call consciousness. Consciousness, in short, is probably nerve-glow." [*Occult Japan*, Boston, 1895, p. 311.]

constituent gases resume their normal bulk, and so permits the explosion to take place.

In the case of a colored glass, a prism, or a refracting lens, we have transmissive function. The energy of light, no matter how produced, is by the glass sifted and limited in color, and by the lens or prism determined to a certain path and shape. Similarly, the keys of an organ have only a transmissive function. They open successively the various pipes and let the wind in the air-chest escape in various ways. The voices of the various pipes are constituted by the columns of air trembling as they emerge. But the air is not engendered in the organ. The organ proper, as distinguished from its air-chest, is only an apparatus for letting portions of it loose upon the world in these peculiarly limited shapes.

My thesis now is this: that, when we think of the law that thought is a function of the brain, we are not required to think of productive function only; *we are entitled also to consider permissive or transmissive function.* And this the ordinary psycho-physiologist leaves out of his account.

Suppose, for example, that the whole universe of material things —the furniture of earth and choir of heaven—should turn out to be a mere surface-veil of phenomena, hiding and keeping back the world of genuine realities. Such a supposition is foreign neither to common sense nor to philosophy. Common sense believes in realities behind the veil even too superstitiously; and idealistic philosophy declares the whole world of natural experience, as we get it, to be but a time-mask, shattering or refracting the one infinite Thought which is the sole reality into those millions of finite streams of consciousness known to us as our private selves.

> "Life, like a dome of many-colored glass,
> Stains the white radiance of Eternity."

Suppose, now, that this were really so, and suppose, moreover, that the dome, opaque enough at all times to the full super-solar blaze, could at certain times and places grow less so, and let certain beams pierce through into this sublunary world. These beams would be so many finite rays, so to speak, of consciousness, and they would vary in quantity and quality as the opacity varied in degree. Only at particular times and places would it seem that, as a matter of fact, the veil of nature can grow thin and rupturable enough for such effects to occur. But in those places gleams, however finite and unsatisfying, of the absolute life of the universe, are from time to time vouchsafed. Glows of feeling, glimpses of insight, and streams of knowledge and perception float into our finite world.

Admit now that *our brains* are such thin and half-transparent places in the veil. What will happen? Why, as the white radiance comes through the dome, with all sorts of staining and distortion imprinted on it by the glass, or as the air now comes through my glottis determined and limited in its force and quality of its vibrations by the peculiarities of those vocal chords which form its gate of egress and shape it into my personal voice, even so the genuine matter of reality, the life of souls as it is in its fullness, will break through our several brains into this world in all sorts of restricted forms, and with all the imperfections and queernesses that characterize our finite individualities here below.

According to the state in which the brain finds itself, the barrier of its obstructiveness may also be supposed to rise or fall. It sinks so low, when the brain is in full activity, that a comparative flood of spiritual energy pours over. At other times, only such occasional waves of thought as heavy sleep permits get by. And when finally a brain stops acting altogether, or decays, that special stream of consciousness which it subserved will vanish entirely from this natural world. But the sphere of being that supplied the consciousness would still be intact; and in that more real world with which, even whilst here, it was continuous, the consciousness might, in ways unknown to us, continue still.

You see that, on all these suppositions, our soul's life, as we here know it, would none the less in literal strictness be the function of the brain. The brain would be the independent variable, the mind would vary dependently on it. But such dependence on the brain for this natural life would in no wise make immortal life impossible,—it might be quite compatible with supernatural life behind the veil hereafter.

As I said, then, the fatal consequence is not coercive, the conclusion which materialism draws being due solely to its one-sided way of taking the word 'function.' And, whether we care or not for immortality in itself, we ought, as mere critics doing police duty among the vagaries of mankind, to insist on the illogicality of a denial based on the flat ignoring of a palpable alternative. How much more ought we to insist, as lovers of truth, when the denial is that of such a vital hope of mankind!

In strict logic, then, the fangs of cerebralistic materialism are drawn. My words ought consequently already to exert a releasing function on your hopes. You *may* believe henceforward, whether you care to profit by the permission or not. But, as this is a very abstract argument, I think it will help its effect to say a word or two about the more concrete conditions of the case.

All abstract hypotheses sound unreal; and the abstract notion that our brains are colored lenses in the wall of nature, admitting light from the super-solar source, but at the same time tingeing and restricting it, has a thoroughly fantastic sound. What is it, you may ask, but a foolish metaphor? And how can such a function be imagined? Isn't the common materialistic notion vastly simpler? Is not consciousness really more comparable to a sort of steam, or perfume, or electricity, or nerve-glow, generated on the spot in its own peculiar vessel? Is it not more rigorously scientific to treat the brain's function as function of production?

The immediate reply is, that, if we are talking of science positively understood, function can mean nothing more than bare concomitant variation. When the brain-activities change in one way, consciousness changes in another; when the currents pour through the occipital lobes, consciousness *sees* things; when through the lower frontal region, consciousness *says* things to itself; when they stop, she goes to sleep, etc. In strict science, we can only write down the bare fact of concomitance; and all talk about either production or transmission, as the mode of taking place, is pure super-added hypothesis, and metaphysical hypothesis at that, for we can frame no more notion of the details on the one alternative than on the other. Ask for any indication of the exact process either of transmission or of production, and Science confesses her imagination to be bankrupt. She has, so far, not the least glimmer of a conjecture or suggestion,—not even a bad verbal metaphor or pun to offer. *Ignoramus, ignorabimus,* is what most physiologists, in the words of one of their number, will say here. The production of such a thing as consciousness in the brain, they will reply with the late Berlin professor of physiology, is the absolute world-enigma,— something so paradoxical and abnormal as to be a stumbling block to Nature, and almost a self-contradiction. Into the mode of production of steam in a tea-kettle we have conjectural insight, for the terms that change are physically homogeneous one with another, and we can easily imagine the case to consist of nothing but alterations of molecular motion. But in the production of consciousness by the brain, the terms are heterogeneous natures altogether; and as far as our understanding goes, it is as great a miracle as if we said, Thought is 'spontaneously generated,' or 'created out of nothing.'

The theory of production is therefore not a jot more simple or credible in itself than any other conceivable theory. It is only a little more popular. All that one need do, therefore, if the ordinary materialist should challenge one to explain how the brain *can* be an organ for limiting and determining to a certain form a consciousness elsewhere produced, is to retort with a *tu quoque*, asking him in turn to explain how it can be an organ for producing consciousness out of whole cloth. For polemic purposes, the two theories are thus exactly on a par.

But if we consider the theory of transmission in a wider way, we see that it has certain positive superiorities, quite apart from its connection with the immortality question.

Just how the process of transmission may be carried on, is indeed unimaginable; but the outer relations, so to speak, of the process, encourage our belief. Consciousness in this process does not have to be generated *de novo* in a vast number of places. It exists already, behind the scenes, coeval with the world. The transmission-theory not only avoids in this way multiplying miracles, but it puts itself in touch with general idealistic philosophy better than the production-theory does. It should always be reckoned a good thing when science and philosophy thus meet.[5]

It puts itself also in touch with the conception of a 'threshold,'—a word with which, since Fechner wrote his book called *Psychophysik*, the so-called 'new Psychology' has rung. Fechner imagines as the condition of consciousness a certain kind of psycho-physical

[5]The transmission-theory connects itself very naturally with that whole tendency of thought known as transcendentalism. Emerson, for example, writes: "We lie in the lap of immense intelligence, which makes us receivers of its truth and organs of its activity. When we discern justice, when we discern truth, we do nothing of ourselves, but allow a passage to its beams." [*Self-Reliance*, p. 56.] But it is not necessary to identify the consciousness postulated in the lecture, as pre-existing behind the scenes, with the Absolute Mind of transcendental Idealism, although, indeed, the notion of it might lead in that direction. The absolute Mind of transcendental Idealism is one integral Unit, one single World-mind. For the purposes of my lecture, however, there might be many minds behind the scenes as well as one. All that the transmission-theory absolutely requires is that they should transcend *our* minds,—which thus come from *something* mental that pre-exists, and is larger than themselves.

movement, as he terms it. Before consciousness can come, a certain degree of activity in the movement must be reached. This requisite degree is called the 'threshold'; but the height of the threshold varies under different circumstances: it may rise or fall. Whẹn it falls, as in states of great lucidity, we grow conscious of things of which we should be unconscious at other times; when it rises, as in drowsiness, consciousness sinks in amount. This rising and lowering of a psycho-physical threshold exactly conforms to our notion of a permanent obstruction to the transmission of consciousness, which obstruction may, in our brains, grow alternately greater or less.[6]

---

[6] Fechner's conception of a 'psycho-physical threshold' as connected with his 'wave-scheme' is little known to English readers. I accordingly subjoin it, in his own words, abridged:—

"The psychically one is connected with a physically many; the physically many contract psychically into a one, a simple, or at least a more simple. Otherwise expressed: the psychically unified and simple are resultants of physical multiplicity; the physically manifold gives unified or simple results. . . .

"The facts which are grouped together under these expressions, and which give them their meaning, are as follows: . . . With our two hemispheres we think singly; with the identical parts of our two retinæ we see singly. . . . The simplest sensation of light or sound in us is connected with processes which, since they are started and kept up by outer oscillations, must themselves be somehow of an oscillatory nature, although we are wholly unaware of the separate phases and oscillations. . . .

"It is certain, then, that some unified or simple psychic resultants depend on physical multiplicity. But, on the other hand, it is equally certain that the multiplicities of the physical world do not always combine into a simple psychical resultant,—no, not even when they are compounded in a single bodily system. Whether they may not nevertheless combine into a *unified* resultant is a matter for opinion, since one is always free to ask whether the entire world, as such, may not have some unified psychic resultant. But of any such resultant we at least have no consciousness. . . .

"For brevity's sake, let us distinguish *psycho-physical continuity* and *discontinuity* from each other. Continuity, let us say, takes place so far as a physical manifold gives a unified or simple psychic resultant; discontinuity, so far as it gives a distinguishable multiplicity of such resultants. Inasmuch, however, as, within the unity of a more general consciousness or phenomenon of consciousness, there still may be a multiplicity distinguished, the continuity of a more general consciousness does not exclude the discontinuity of particular phenomena.

"One of the most important problems and tasks of Psycho-physics now is this: to determine the conditions (*Gesichtspunkte*) under which the cases of continuity and of discontinuity occur.

"Whence comes it that different organisms have separate consciousnesses, although their bodies are just as much connected by general Nature as the parts of a single organism are with each other, and these latter give a single conscious resultant? Of course we can say that the connection is more intimate between the parts of an organism than between the organisms of Nature. But what do we mean by a more intimate connection? Can an absolute difference of result depend on anything so relative? And does not Nature as a whole show as strict a connection as any organism does,—yea, one even more indissoluble? And the same questions come up within each organism. How comes it that, with different nerve-fibres of touch and sight, we distinguish different space-points, but with one fibre distinguish nothing, although the different fibres are connected in the brain just as much as the parts are in the single fibre? We may again call the latter connection the more *intimate*, but then the same sort of question will arise again.

"Unquestionably the problem which here lies before Psycho-physics cannot be *sharply* answered; but we may establish a general point of view for its treatment, consistently with what we laid down in a former chapter on the relations of more general with more particular phenomena of consciousness."

[The earlier passage is here inserted:] "The essential principle is this: That human psycho-physical activity must exceed a certain intensity for any waking consciousness at all to occur, and that during the waking state any particular specification of the said activity (whether spontaneous or due to stimulation), which is capable of occasioning a particular specification of consciousness, must exceed in its turn a certain further degree of intensity for the consciousness actually to arise. . . .

"This state of things (in itself a mere fact needing no picture) may be made clearer by an image or scheme, and also more concisely spoken of. Imagine the whole psycho-physical activity of man to be a wave, and the degree of this activity to be symbolized by the height of the wave above a horizontal basal line or surface, to which every psycho-physically active point contributes an ordinate. . . . The whole form and evolution of the consciousness will then depend on the rising and falling of this wave; the intensity of the consciousness at any time on the wave's height at that time; and the height must always *somewhere* exceed a certain limit, which we will call a *threshold*, if waking consciousness is to exit at all.

"Let us call this wave the *total wave*, and the threshold in question the *principal threshold*."

[Since our various states of consciousness recur, some in long, some in short periods], "we may represent such a long period as that of the slowly fluctuating condition of our general wakefulness and the general direction of our attention as a wave that slowly changes the place of its summit. If we call this the *under-wave*, then the movements of shorter period, on which the more special conscious states depend, can be symbolized by wavelets superposed upon the under-wave, and we can call these *over-waves*. They will cause all sorts of modifications of the under-wave's surface, and the total wave will be the resultant of both sets of waves.

"The greater, now, the strength of the movements of short period, the amplitude of the oscillations of the psycho-physical activity, the higher will the crests of the wavelets that represent them rise above, and the lower will their valleys sink below the surface of the under-wave that bears them. And these heights and depressions must exceed a certain limit of quantity which we may call the *upper threshold*, before the special mental state which is correlated with them can appear in consciousness" [pp. 454–456].

"So far now as we symbolize any system of psycho-physical activity, to which a generally unified or principal consciousness corresponds, by the image of a total wave rising with its crest above a certain 'threshold,' we have a means of schematizing in a single diagram the physical solidarity of all these psycho-physical systems throughout Nature, together with their psycho-physical discontinuity. For we need only draw all the waves so that they run into each other below the threshold, whilst above it they appear distinct, as in the figure below.

The transmission-theory also puts itself in touch with a whole class of experiences that are with difficulty explained by the production-theory. I refer to those obscure and exceptional phenomena reported at all times throughout human history, which the 'psychical-researchers,' with Mr. Frederic Myers at their head, are doing so much to rehabilitate;[7] such phenomena, namely, as religious

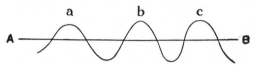

"In this figure *a, b, c* stand for three organisms, or rather for the total waves of psycho-physical activity of three organisms, whilst A B represents the threshold. In each wave the part that rises above the threshold is an integrated thing, and is connected with a single consciousness. Whatever lies below the threshold, being unconscious, separates the conscious crests, although it is still the means of physical connection.

"In general terms: wherever a psycho-physical total wave is continuous with itself above the threshold, there we find the unity or identity of a consciousness, inasmuch as the connection of the psychical phenomena which correspond to the parts of the wave also appears in consciousness. Whenever, on the contrary, total waves are disconnected, or connected only underneath the threshold, the corresponding consciousness is broken, and no connection between its several parts appears. More briefly: consciousness is continuous or discontinuous, unified or discrete, according as the psycho-physical total waves that subserve it are themselves continuous or discontinuous above the threshold. . . .

"If, in the diagram, we should raise the entire line of waves so that not only the crests but the valleys appeared above the threshold, then these latter would appear only as depressions in one great continuous wave above the threshold, and the discontinuity of the consciousness would be converted into continuity. We of course cannot bring this about. We might also squeeze the wave together so that the valleys should be pressed up, and the crests above the threshold flow into a line; then the discretely-feeling organisms would have become a singly-feeling organism. This, again, Man cannot voluntarily bring about, but it is brought about in Man's nature. His two halves, the right one and the left one, are thus united; and the number of segments of radiates and articulates show that more than two parts can be thus psychophysically conjoined. One need only cut them asunder, *i. e.* interpolate another part of nature between them under the threshold, and they break into two separately conscious beings." . . . [*Elemente der Psychophysik,* 1860, vol. ii. pp. 526–530.]

One sees easily how, on Fechner's wave-scheme, a world-soul may be expressed. All psycho-physical activity being continuous 'below the threshold,' the consciousness might also become continuous if the threshold sank low enough to uncover all the waves. The threshold throughout nature in general is, however, very high, so the consciousness that gets over it is of the discontinuous form.

[7] See the long series of articles by Mr. Myers in the *Proceedings of the Society for Psychical Research,* beginning in the third volume with automatic writing, and ending in the latest volumes with the higher manifestations of knowledge by mediums. Mr. Myers's theory of the whole range of phenomena is, that our normal consciousness is in continuous connection with a greater consciousness of which we do not know

conversions, providential leadings in answer to prayer, instantaneous healings, premonitions, apparitions at time of death, clairvoyant visions or impressions, and the whole range of mediumistic capacities, to say nothing of still more exceptional and incomprehensible things. If all our human thought be a function of the brain, then of course, if any of these things are facts,—and to my own mind some of them are facts,—we may not suppose that they can occur without preliminary brain-action. But the ordinary production-theory of consciousness is knit up with a peculiar notion of how brain-action *can* occur,—that notion being that all brain-action, without exception, is due to a prior action, immediate or remote, of the bodily sense-organs *on* the brain. Such action makes the brain produce sensations and mental images, and out of the sensations and images the higher forms of thought and knowledge in their turn are framed. As transmissionists, we also must admit this to be the condition of all our usual thought. Sense-action is what lowers the brain-barrier. My voice and aspect, for instance, strike upon your ears and eyes; your brain thereupon becomes more pervious, and an awareness on your part of what I say and who I am slips into this world from the world behind the veil. But, in the mysterious phenomena to which I allude, it is often hard to see where the sense-organs can come in. A medium, for example, will show knowledge of his sitter's private affairs which it seems impossible he should have acquired through sight or hearing, or inference therefrom. Or you will have an apparition of some one who is now dying hundreds of miles away. On the production-theory one does not see from what sensations such odd bits of knowledge are produced. On the transmission-theory, they don't have to be 'produced,'—they exist ready-made in the transcendental world, and all that is needed is an abnormal lowering of the brain-threshold to let them through. In cases of conversion, in providential leadings, sudden mental healings, etc., it seems to the subjects themselves of the experience as if a power from without, quite different from the ordinary action of the senses or of the sense-led mind, came into their life, as if the latter suddenly opened into that greater life in which it has its source. The word 'influx,' used in Swedenborgian circles, well describes this impression of new insight, or new willingness, sweeping over

---

the extent, and to which he gives, in its relation to the particular person, the not very felicitous name—though no better one has been proposed—of his or her 'subliminal' self.

us like a tide. All such experiences, quite paradoxical and meaningless on the production-theory, fall very naturally into place on the
other theory. We need only suppose the continuity of our consciousness with a mother-sea, to allow for exceptional waves occasionally
pouring over the dam. Of course the causes of these odd lowerings of
the brain's threshold still remain a mystery on any terms.

Add, then, this advantage to the transmission-theory,—an advantage which I am well aware that some of you will not rate very high,
—and also add the advantage of not conflicting with a life hereafter,
and I hope you will agree with me that it has many points of superiority to the more familiar theory. It is a theory which, in the history
of opinion on such matters, has never been wholly left out of account, though never developed at any great length. In the great
orthodox philosophic tradition, the body is treated as an essential
condition to the soul's life in this world of sense; but after death,
it is said, the soul is set free, and becomes a purely intellectual and
non-appetitive being. Kant expresses this idea in terms that come
singularly close to those of our transmission-theory. The death of
the body, he says, may indeed be the end of the sensational use of
our mind, but only the beginning of the intellectual use. "The
body," he continues, "would thus be, not the cause of our thinking, but merely a condition restrictive thereof, and, although essential to our sensuous and animal consciousness, it may be regarded
as an impeder of our pure spiritual life."[8] And in a recent book of
great suggestiveness and power, less well-known as yet than it deserves,—I mean *Riddles of the Sphinx*, by Mr. F. C. S. Schiller of
Oxford, late of Cornell University,—the transmission-theory is defended at some length.[9]

---

[8] See *Kritik der reinen Vernunft*, second edition, p. 809.

[9] I subjoin a few extracts from Mr. Schiller's work: "Matter is an admirably calcu-
lated machinery for regulating, limiting, and restraining the consciousness which it
encases. . . . If the material encasement be coarse and simple, as in the lower organisms, it permits only a little intelligence to permeate through it; if it is delicate
and complex, it leaves more pores and exits, as it were, for the manifestations of
consciousness. . . . On this analogy, then, we may say that the lower animals are
still entranced in the lower stage of brute *lethargy*, while we have passed into the
higher phase of *somnambulism*, which already permits us strange glimpses of a lucidity
that divines the realities of a transcendent world. And this gives the final answer to
Materialism: it consists in showing in detail . . . that Materialism is a hysteron prote-
ron, a putting of the cart before the horse, which may be rectified by just inverting
the connection between Matter and Consciousness. Matter is not that which *produces*
Consciousness, but that which *limits* it and confines its intensity within certain

94

But still, you will ask, in what positive way does this theory help us to realize our immortality in imagination? What we all wish to keep is just these individual restrictions, these selfsame tendencies and peculiarities that define us to ourselves and others, and constitute our identity, so called. Our finitenesses and limitations seem to be our personal essence; and when the finiting organ drops away, and our several spirits revert to their original source and resume their unrestricted condition, will they then be anything like those sweet streams of feeling which we know, and which even now our brains are sifting out from the great reservoir for our enjoyment here below? Such questions are truly living questions, and surely they must be seriously discussed by future lecturers upon this Ingersoll foundation. I hope, for my part, that more than one such lecturer will penetratingly discuss the conditions of our immortality, and tell us how much we may lose, and how much we may possibly

---

limits: material organization does not construct consciousness out of arrangements of atoms, but contracts its manifestation within the sphere which it permits. This explanation . . . admits the connection of Matter and Consciousness, but contends that the course of interpretation must proceed in the contrary direction. Thus it will fit the facts alleged in favour of Materialism equally well, besides enabling us to understand facts which Materialism rejected as 'supernatural.' It explains the lower by the higher, Matter by Spirit, instead of *vice versa*, and thereby attains to an explanation which is ultimately tenable instead of one which is ultimately absurd. And it is an explanation the possibility of which no evidence in favour of Materialism can possibly affect. For if, *e. g.*, a man loses consciousness as soon as his brain is injured, it is clearly as good an explanation to say the injury to the brain destroyed the mechanism by which the manifestation of consciousness was rendered possible, as to say that it destroyed the seat of consciousness. On the other hand, there are facts which the former theory suits far better. If, *e. g.*, as sometimes happens, the man after a time more or less recovers the faculties of which the injury to his brain had deprived him, and that not in consequence of a renewal of the injured part, but in consequence of the inhibited functions being performed by the vicarious action of other parts, the easiest explanation certainly is that after a time consciousness constitutes the remaining parts into a mechanism capable of acting as a substitute for the lost parts. And again, if the body is a mechanism for inhibiting consciousness, for preventing the full powers of the Ego from being prematurely actualized, it will be necessary to invert also our ordinary ideas on the subject of memory, and to account for forgetfulness instead of for memory. It will be during life that we drink the bitter cup of Lethe, it will be with our brain that we are enabled to forget. And this will serve to explain not only the extraordinary memories of the drowning and the dying generally, but also the curious hints which experimental psychology occasionally affords us that nothing is ever forgotten wholly and beyond recall." [*Riddles of the Sphinx*, London, Swan Sonnenschein, 1891, p. 293 ff.]

Mr. Schiller's conception is much more complex in its relations than the simple 'theory of transmission' postulated in my lecture, and to do justice to it the reader should consult the original work.

gain, if its finiting outlines should be changed? If all determination is negation, as the philosophers say, it might well prove that the loss of some of the particular determinations which the brain imposes would not appear a matter for such absolute regret.

But into these higher and more transcendental matters I refuse to enter upon this occasion; and I proceed, during the remainder of the hour, to treat of my second point. Fragmentary and negative it is, as my first one has been. Yet, between them, they do give to our belief in immortality a freer wing.

My second point is relative to the incredible and intolerable number of beings which, with our modern imagination, we must believe to be immortal, if immortality be true. I cannot but suspect that this, too, is a stumbling-block to many of my present audience. And it is a stumbling-block which I should thoroughly like to clear away.

It is, I fancy, a stumbling-block of altogether modern origin, due to the strain upon the quantitative imagination which recent scientific theories, and the moral feelings consequent upon them, have brought in their train.

For our ancestors the world was a small, and—compared with our modern sense of it—a comparatively snug affair. Six thousand years at most it had lasted. In its history a few particular human heroes, kings, ecclesiarchs, and saints stood forth very prominent, overshadowing the imagination with their claims and merits, so that not only they, but all who were associated familiarly with them, shone with a glamour which even the Almighty, it was supposed, must recognize and respect. These prominent personages and their associates were the nucleus of the immortal group; the minor heroes and saints of minor sects came next, and people without distinction formed a sort of background and filling in. The whole scene of eternity (so far, at least, as Heaven and not the nether place was concerned in it) never struck to the believer's fancy as an overwhelmingly large or inconveniently crowded stage. One might call this an aristocratic view of immortality; the immortals—I speak of Heaven exclusively, for an immortality of torment need not now concern us—were always an élite, a select and manageable number.

But, with our own generation, an entirely new quantitative imagination has swept over our western world. The theory of evolution now requires us to suppose a far vaster scale of times, spaces, and numbers than our forefathers ever dreamed the cosmic process to involve. Human history grows continuously out of animal history, and goes back possibly even to the tertiary epoch. From this there has emerged insensibly a democratic view, instead of the old aristocratic view, of immortality. For our minds, though in one sense they may have grown a little cynical, in another they have been made sympathetic by the evolutionary perspective. Bone of our bone and flesh of our flesh are these half-brutish prehistoric brothers. Girdled about with the immense darkness of this mysterious universe even as we are, they were born and died, suffered and struggled. Given over to fearful crime and passion, plunged in the blackest ignorance, preyed upon by hideous and grotesque delusions, yet steadfastly serving the profoundest of ideals in their fixed faith that existence in any form is better than non-existence, they ever rescued triumphantly from the jaws of ever-imminent destruction the torch of life, which, thanks to them, now lights the world for us. How small indeed seem individual distinctions when we look back on these overwhelming numbers of human beings panting and straining under the pressure of that vital want! And how inessential in the eyes of God must be the small surplus of the individual's merit, swamped as it is in the vast ocean of the common merit of mankind, dumbly and undauntedly doing the fundamental duty and living the heroic life! We grow humble and reverent as we contemplate the prodigious spectacle. Not our differences and distinctions,—we feel—no, but our common animal essence of patience under suffering and enduring effort must be what redeems us in the Deity's sight. An immense compassion and kinship fill the heart. An immortality from which these inconceivable billions of fellow-strivers should be excluded becomes an irrational idea for us. That our superiority in personal refinement or in religious creed should constitute a difference between ourselves and our messmates at life's banquet, fit to entail such a consequential difference of destiny as eternal life for us, and for them torment hereafter, or death with the beasts that perish, is a notion too absurd to be considered serious. Nay, more, the very beasts themselves— the wild ones at any rate—are leading the heroic life at all times. And a modern mind, expanded as some minds are by cosmic emotion, by the great evolutionist vision of universal continuity, hesitates to draw the line even at man. If any creature lives forever, why not all?—why not the patient brutes? So that a faith in immortality, if we are to indulge it, demands of us nowadays a scale of representation so stupendous that our imagination faints before it, and our personal feelings refuse to rise up and face the task. The supposition we are swept along to is too vast, and, rather than face the conclusion, we abandon the premise from which it starts. We give up our own immortality sooner than believe that all the hosts of Hottentots and Australians that have been, and shall ever be, should share it with us *in sæcula sæculorum*. Life is a good thing on a reasonably copious scale; but the very heavens themselves, and the cosmic times and spaces, would stand aghast, we think, at the notion of preserving eternally such an ever-swelling plethora and glut of it.

Having myself, as a recipient of modern scientific culture, gone through a subjective experience like this, I feel sure that it must also have been the experience of many, perhaps of most, of you who listen to my words. But I have also come to see that it harbors a tremendous fallacy; and, since the noting of the fallacy has set my own mind free again, I have felt that one service I might render to my listeners to-night would be to point out where it lies.

It is the most obvious fallacy in the world, and the only wonder is that all the world should not see through it. It is the result of nothing but an invincible blindness from which we suffer, an insensibility to the inner significance of alien lives, and a conceit that would project our own incapacity into the vast cosmos, and measure the wants of the Absolute by our own puny needs. Our christian ancestors dealt with the problem more easily than we do. We, indeed, lack sympathy; but they had a positive antipathy for these alien human creatures, and they naïvely supposed the Deity to have the antipathy, too. Being, as they were, 'heathen,' our forefathers felt a certain sort of joy in thinking that their Creator made them as so much mere fuel for the fires of hell. Our culture has humanized us beyond that point, but we cannot yet conceive them as our comrades in the fields of heaven. We have, as the phrase goes, *no use for them*, and it oppresses us to think of their survival. Take, for instance, all the Chinamen. Which of you here, my friends, sees any fitness in their eternal perpetuation unreduced in numbers? Surely not one of you. At most, you might deem it well to keep a few chosen specimens alive to represent an interesting and peculiar variety of humanity; but as for the rest, what comes in such surpassing numbers, and what you can only imagine in this abstract summary collective manner, must be something of which the units, you are sure, can have no individual preciousness. God himself, you think, can have no use for them. An immortality of every separate specimen must be to him and to the universe as indigestible a load to carry as it is to you. So, engulfing the whole subject in a sort of mental giddiness and nausea, you drift along, first doubting that the mass can be immortal, then losing all assurance in the immortality of your own particular person, precious as you all the while feel and realize the latter to be. This, I am sure, is the attitude of mind of some of you before me.

But is not such an attitude due to the veriest lack and dearth of your imagination? You take these swarms of alien kinsmen as they are *for you*: an external picture painted on your retina, representing a crowd oppressive by its vastness and confusion. As they are for you, so you think they positively and absolutely are. *I* feel no call for them, you say; therefore there *is* no call for them. But all the while, beyond this externality which is your way of realizing them, they realize themselves with the acutest internality, with the most violent thrills of life. 'Tis you who are dead, stone-dead and blind and senseless, in your way of looking on. You open your eyes upon a scene of which you miss the whole significance. Each of these grotesque or even repulsive aliens is animated by an inner joy of living as hot or hotter than that which you feel beating in your private breast. The sun rises and beauty beams to light his path. To miss the inner joy of him, as Stevenson says, is to miss the whole of him.[10] Not a being of the countless throng is there whose continued life is not called for, and called for intensely, by the consciousness that animates the being's form. That *you* neither realize nor understand nor call for it, that you have no use for it, is an absolutely irrelevant circumstance. That you have a saturation-point of interest tells us nothing of the interests that absolutely are. The Universe, with every living entity which her resources create, creates at the same time a call for that entity, and an appetite for its continuance,—creates it, if nowhere else, at least within the heart of the entity itself. It is absurd to suppose, simply because

---

10 I beg the reader to peruse R. L. Stevenson's magnificent little essay entitled 'The Lantern Bearers,' reprinted in the collection entitled *Across the Plains*. The truth is that we are doomed, by the fact that we are practical beings with very limited tasks to attend to, and special ideals to look after, to be absolutely blind and insensible to the inner feelings, and to the whole inner significance of lives that are different from our own. Our opinion of the worth of such lives is absolutely wide of the mark, and unfit to be counted at all.

our private power of sympathetic vibration with other lives gives out so soon, that in the heart of infinite being itself there can be such a thing as plethora, or glut, or supersaturation. It is not as if there were a bounded room where the minds in possession had to move up or make place and crowd together to accommodate new occupants. Each new mind brings its own edition of the universe of space along with it, its own room to inhabit; and these spaces never crowd each other,—the space of my imagination, for example, in no way interferes with yours. The amount of possible consciousness seems to be governed by no law analogous to that of the so-called conservation of energy in the material world. When one man wakes up, or one is born, another does not have to go to sleep, or die, in order to keep the consciousness of the universe a constant quantity. Professor Wundt, in fact, in his *System of Philosophy,* has formulated a law of the universe which he calls the law of increase of spiritual energy, and which he expressly opposes to the law of conservation of energy in physical things.[11] There seems no formal limit to the positive increase of being in spiritual respects; and since spiritual being, whenever it comes, affirms itself, expands and craves continuance, we may justly and literally say, regardless of the defects of our own private sympathy, that the supply of individual life in the universe can never possibly, however immeasurable it may become, exceed the demand. The demand for that supply is there the moment the supply itself comes into being, for the beings supplied demand their own continuance.

I speak, you see, from the point of view of all the other individual beings, realizing and enjoying inwardly their own existence. If we are pantheists, we can stop there. We need, then, only say that through them, as through so many diversified channels of expression, the eternal Spirit of the Universe affirms and realizes its own infinite life. But if we are theists, we can go farther without altering the result. God, we can then say, has so inexhaustible a capacity for love that his call and need is for a literally endless accumulation of created lives. He can never faint or grow weary, as we should, under the increasing supply. His scale is infinite in all things. His sympathy can never know satiety or glut.

I hope now that you agree with me that the tiresomeness of an over-peopled Heaven is a purely subjective and illusory notion, a sign of human incapacity, a remnant of the old narrow-hearted aris-

11 W. Wundt: *System der Philosophie,* Leipzig, Engelmann, 1889, p. 315.

tocratic creed. "Revere the Maker, lift thine eye up to his style and manners of the sky," and you will believe that this is indeed a democratic universe, in which your paltry exclusions play no regulative part. Was your taste consulted in the peopling of this globe? How, then, should it be consulted as to the peopling of the vast City of God? Let us put our hand over our mouth, like Job, and be thankful that in our personal littleness we ourselves are here at all. The Deity that suffers us, we may be sure, can suffer many another queer and wondrous and only half-delightful thing.

For my own part, then, so far as logic goes, I am willing that every leaf that ever grew in this world's forests and rustled in the breeze should become immortal. It is purely a question of fact: are the leaves so, or not? Abstract quantity, and the abstract needlessness in our eyes of so much reduplication of things so much alike, have no connection with the subject. For bigness and number and generic similarity are only manners of our finite way of thinking; and, considered in itself and apart from our imagination, one scale of dimensions and of numbers for the Universe is no more miraculous or inconceivable than another, the moment you grant to a universe the liberty to be at all, in place of the Non-entity that might conceivably have reigned.

The heart of being can have no exclusions akin to those which our poor little hearts set up. The inner significance of other lives exceeds all our powers of sympathy and insight. If we feel a significance in our own life which would lead us spontaneously to claim its perpetuity, let us be at least tolerant of like claims made by other lives, however numerous, however unideal they may seem to us to be. Let us at any rate not decide adversely on our own claim, whose grounds we feel directly, because we cannot decide favorably on the alien claims, whose grounds we cannot feel at all. That would be letting blindness lay down the law to sight.

Preface to Starbuck's *Psychology of Religion*

The author of the following pages has thought in his modesty that, since his name is as yet unknown to fame, his book might gain a prompter recognition if it were prefaced by a word of recommendation from some more hardened writer. Believing the book to be valuable, I am glad to be able to write such a preface.

Many years ago Dr. Starbuck, then a student in Harvard University, tried to enlist my sympathies in his statistical inquiry into the religious ideas and experiences of the circumambient population. I fear that to his mind I rather damned the whole project with my words of faint praise. The question-circular method of collecting information had already, in America, reached the proportions of an incipient nuisance in psychological and pedagogical matters. Dr. Starbuck's questions were of a peculiarly searching and intimate nature, to which it seemed possible that an undue number of answers from egotists lacking in sincerity might come. Moreover, so few minds have the least spark of originality that answers to questions scattered broadcast would be likely to show a purely conventional content. The writers' ideas, as well as their phraseology, would be the stock-in-trade of the Protestant Volksgeist, historically and not psychologically based; and, being in it one's self, one might as well cipher it all out *a priori* as seek to collect it in this burdensome, inductive fashion. I think I said to Dr. Starbuck that I expected the chief result of his circulars would be a certain number of individual answers relating peculiar experiences and ideas in a way that might be held as typical. The sorting and extracting of percentages and reducing to averages, I thought, would give results of comparatively little significance.

But Dr. Starbuck kept all the more resolutely at his task, which has involved an almost incredible amount of drudging labour. I have handled and read a large proportion of his raw material, and I have just finished reading the revised proofs of the book. I must say that the results amply justify his own confidence in his methods, and that I feel somewhat ashamed at present of the littleness of my own faith.

The material, quite apart from the many acutely interesting individual confessions which it contains, is evidently sincere in its general mass. The Volksgeist of course dictates its special phraseology and most of its conceptions, which are almost without exception Protestant, and predominantly of the Evangelical sort; and for comparative purposes similar collections ought yet to be made from Catholic, Jewish, Mohammedan, Buddhist and Hindoo sources.

But it has been Dr. Starbuck's express aim to disengage the general from the specific and local in his critical discussion, and to reduce the reports to their most universal psychological value. It seems to me that here the statistical method has held its own, and that its percentages and averages have proved to possess genuine significance. Dr. Starbuck's conclusion, for example, that 'conversion' is not a unique experience, but has its correspondences in the common events of moral and religious development, emerges from the general parallelism of ages, sexes, and symptoms shown by statistical comparison of different types of personal evolution, in some of which conversion, technically so called, was present, whilst it was absent in others. Such statistical arguments are not mathematical proofs, but they support presumptions and establish probabilities, and in spite of the lack of precision in many of their data, they yield results not to be got at in any less clumsy way.

Rightly interpreted, the whole tendency of Dr. Starbuck's patient labour is to bring compromise and conciliation into the long standing feud of Science and Religion. Your 'evangelical' extremist will have it that conversion is an absolutely supernatural event, with nothing cognate to it in ordinary psychology. Your 'scientist' sectary, on the other hand, sees nothing in it but hysterics and emotionalism, an absolutely pernicious pathological disturbance. For

Dr. Starbuck, it is not necessarily either of these things. It may in countless cases be a perfectly normal psychologic crisis, marking the transition from the child's world to the wider world of youth, or from that of youth to that of maturity—a crisis which the evangelical machinery only methodically emphasises, abridges and regulates.

But I must not in this preface forestall the results of the pages that follow it. They group together a mass of hitherto unpublished facts, forming a most interesting contribution both to individual and to collective psychology. They interpret these facts with rare discriminatingness and liberality—broad-mindedness being indeed their most striking characteristic. They explain two extremes of opinion to each other in so sympathetic a way that, although either may think the last word has yet to be said, neither will be left with that sense of irremediable misunderstanding which is so common after disputes between scientific and religious persons. And, finally, they draw sagacious educational inferences. On the whole, then, Christians and Scientists alike must find in them matter for edification and improvement.

Dr. Starbuck, in short, has made a weighty addition to that great process of taking account of psychological and sociological stock, with which our generation has come to occupy itself so busily. He has broken ground in a new place, his only predecessor (so far as I am aware) being Dr. Leuba, in his similar but less elaborate investigation in Volume VII of the *American Journal of Psychology*. The examples ought to find imitators, and the inquiry ought to be extended to other lands, and to populations of other faiths.

I have no hesitation in recommending the volume, both for its religious and for its psychological interest. I am sure it will obtain the prompt recognition which its importance as a documentary study of human nature deserves.

Preface to Lutoslawski's *World of Souls*

The author of the book to which I write this preface has shown by that weighty english work, *The Logic of Plato*, that he is an accomplished philosopher in the technical and scholarly sense of that much abused term. That he is versatile as well as scholarly would seem to follow from the fact that his previous writings, numerous, if not voluminous, embrace essays in six other languages, latin, polish, russian, german, spanish, and french, and range in subject from chemistry to politics. In the present work—if the term "work" can be applied to what is so free an outpouring of the writer's heart—the cosmopolitan, the speaker of many languages and lover of human nature, takes the bit in his teeth and almost entirely "gets away" from the technical philosopher. *The Soul's Power* is in fact the simple confession of faith of a peculiarly sympathetic and generous-minded human being nourished, it is true, on philosophy, but now expressing all the idealities that are in him in direct affirmative form; and refusing (for this time at least) to be hindered by any of those technical cobwebs and possible objections, which so haunt the minds of professors of philosophy speaking *ex cathedrâ*, that to affirm a thing naively and on their own responsibility is a risk that they hardly ever take.

Professor Lutoslawski honours philosophy; he even adores it, along its platonizing traditions; but he finds little use for its sceptical scruples and inhibitions. He is a genuine transcendentalist, in the Emersonian sense. To many he will assuredly be as a prophet, speaking not as the scribes, but with authority, and communicating confidence and cheer.

Our general attitudes towards life, our faiths that things ought to be and must be thus and so, usually lie deeper than our articulate reasonings. For the most part these latter are but masquerades for social purposes. They confirm convictions but rarely create them, and they almost never bear them in upon the unwilling minds of others. Personal example, the contagion of an attitude, is, in every sphere save that of the plainest facts of sense, the great opinion-confirming and communicating power. Of course the personal example must have communicability, impressiveness, authority. If it work through writing, the writer must have literary magic, charm, the demonic quality. Whether our present author have this infectious quality in a high degree, or in any degree, is a question that can be answered only by the success or non-success of his book.

To the writer of this preface he seems to have it; though he would probably have it far more strikingly were he writing in his native tongue. He who has it can afford to express himself affirmatively and non-ratiocinatively, and Professor Lutoslawski reasons less than he affirms. This is the more natural, since his beliefs are after all in the line of great human traditions. He is a spiritualist to the core; that is, he believes in individual souls as ultimate and irreducible facts. He calls them "substances"; but prejudice against that scholastic term ought not to stand between the english reader and the author's practical meaning, which is that each of us, in his inner individuality, is a permanently receptive and permanently active part of the universe. The universe is a great hierarchic system of such individual souls. In other words Professor Lutoslawski is no monist, either in the materialistic or the idealistic sense, but a pluralist, a monadologist. The world has only the unity of a collection, the immense collection of living souls of all orders, from those most numerous ones at the bottom which animate the particles of matter, to the single leading soul whom we call God, at the top. But this God is not "the Creator" in the theological sense; he is only a leader, a worker upon forces that are often refractory. Between him and us there are intermediary spirits; and our author, if classed under cut-and-dried rubrics, must be distinctly called a polytheist rather than a theist.

Monadism and polytheism, always the real instinctive belief of the people, but long repressed in philosophic circles, are slowly beginning to show their faces aggressively again in the philosophic literature of our time. Our author may be considered an efficient ally of this movement.

Of course it carries with it the belief that the immediate influence of one soul upon another is the universal and elementary type of causation; also that freedom must exist, and along with it the possibility of non-uniformity of behavior; so that the uniformities of Nature on which science leans would appear rather to be practical statistical results of the enormous number of elementary agents at play in the lower ranges of Nature, than consequences of a transcendental principle which Nature has to obey *a priori*.

All these points are still more compendiously set forth in a smaller treatise by Professor Lutoslawski: *Ueber die Grundvoraussetzungen und Consequenzen der individualistischen Weltanschauung.* (Helsingfors, 1898.) To the reader who may wish a dryer and more purely objective treatment of the subject, I can strongly recommend that charmingly executed piece of work.

Such, in meagerest terms, is the abstract metaphysical frame within which Professor Lutoslawski takes up his attitude towards life. And surely few philosophers have so livingly expressed the consequences of their theoretic view of the world. Most men, outside of philosophic class-rooms, think they believe what this writer believes: they assent to freedom and immortality, to souls and the intercourse of souls. But what a difference between such dead-and-alive assent and such a faculty of belief as that which animates our polish friend! He believes vitally and practically. For him this universe is *really* made up of souls and their relations. A perfect passion of friendship, love, brotherhood and loyalty sings throughout his pages. These things are the absolute things in his universe. With them, with freedom, with immortality, all good things are possible; the best is *really* possible, for the organs of its possibility are really here. We live in a genuinely spiritual republic, slowly but surely evolving into what men have dreamed of as the kingdom of Heaven.

Of course in the concrete filling out of this part of his program, Professor Lutoslawski is utopian and romantic, and deliberately so. But utopias and romances are also forces as the world goes, so that is no radical reproach.—I leave all other details to the reader. Such books, such "livres de bonne foy," are sure to find their level in the end without the aid of publishers, critics, or preface-writers. Those whom they help, speak of them to others; and they finally gain their natural sympathetic constituency. Surely if passionate humanity and generosity can win a sympathetic hearing for a writer, Professor Lutoslawski is sure of his audience in advance.

Emerson

The pathos of death is this, that when the days of one's life are ended, those days that were so crowded with business and felt so heavy in their passing, what remains of one in memory should usually be so slight a thing. The phantom of an attitude, the echo of a certain mode of thought, a few pages of print, some invention, or some victory we gained in a brief critical hour, are all that can survive the best of us. It is as if the whole of a man's significance had now shrunk into a mere musical note or phrase, suggestive of his singularity— happy are those whose singularity gives a note so clear as to be victorious over the inevitable pity of such a diminution and abridgment.

An ideal wraith like this, of Emerson's singularity, hovers over all Concord today, taking in the minds of those of you who were his neighbors and intimates a somewhat fuller shape, remaining more abstract in the younger generation, but bringing home to all of us the notion of a spirit indescribably precious. The form that so lately moved upon these streets and country roads, or awaited in these fields and woods the beloved Muse's visits, is now dust; but the soul's note, the spiritual voice, rises strong and clear above the uproar of the times, and seems securely destined to exert an ennobling influence over future generations.

What gave a flavor so matchless to Emerson's individuality was, even more than his rich mental gifts, their combination. Rarely has a man so known the limits of his genius or so unfailingly kept within them. "Stand by your order," he used to say to youthful students; and perhaps the paramount impression one gets of his life is of his loyalty to his own type and mission. The type was that of what he liked to call the scholar, the perceiver of pure truth, and the mission was that of the reporter in worthy form of each perception. The day is good, he said, in which we have the most perceptions. There are times when the cawing of a crow, a weed, a snow-flake, or a farmer planting in his field, become symbols to the intellect of truths equal to those which the most majestic phenomena can open. Let me mind my own charge, then, walk alone, consult the sky, the field and forest, sedulously waiting every morning for the news concerning the structure of the universe which the good Spirit will give me.

This was the first half of Emerson, but only half; for his genius was insatiate for expression, and his truth had to be clad in the right verbal garment. The form of the garment was so vital with Emerson that it is impossible to separate it from the matter. They form a chemical combination,—thoughts which would be trivial expressed otherwise are important through the nouns and verbs to which he married them. The style is the man, it has been said; the man Emerson's mission culminated in his style, and if we must define him in one word, we have to call him Artist. He was an artist whose medium was verbal and who wrought in spiritual material.

This duty of spiritual seeing and reporting determined the whole tenor of his life. It was to shield it from invasion and distraction that he dwelt in the country, and that he consistently declined to entangle himself with associations or to encumber himself with functions which, however he might believe in them, he felt were duties for other men and not for him. Even the care of his garden, "with its stoopings and fingerings in a few yards of space," he found "narrowing and poisoning," and took to long free walks and saunterings instead, without apology. "Causes" innumerable sought to enlist him as their "worker"—all got his smile and word of sympathy, but none entrapped him into service. The struggle against slavery itself, deeply as it appealed to him, found him firm: "God must govern his own world, and knows his way out of this pit without my desertion of my post, which has none to guard it but me. I have quite other slaves to free than those negroes, to wit, imprisoned thoughts far back in the brain of man, and which have no watchman or lover or defender but me." This in reply to the possible questions of his conscience. To hot-blooded moralists with more objective ideas of duty, such a fidelity to the limits of his genius must often have made him seem provokingly remote and unavailable; but we who can see things in more liberal perspective must unqualifiedly approve the results. The faultless tact with which he kept his safe limits while he so dauntlessly asserted himself within them is an example fitted to give heart to other theorists and artists the world over.

The insight and creed from which Emerson's life followed can be best summed up in his own verse:—

> "So nigh is grandeur to our dust,
> So near is God to man!"

Through the individual fact there ever shone for him the effulgence of the Universal Reason. The great Cosmic Intellect terminates and houses itself in mortal men and passing hours. Each of us is an angle of its eternal vision, and the only way to be true to our Maker is to be loyal to ourselves. "O rich and various Man!" he cries, "thou palace of sight and sound, carrying in thy senses the morning and the night and the unfathomable galaxy; in thy brain, the geometry of the City of God; in thy heart, the bower of love and the realms of right and wrong."

If the individual open thus directly into the Absolute, it follows that there is something in each and all of us, even the lowliest, that ought not to consent to borrowing traditions and living at second hand. "If John was perfect, why are you and I alive?" writes Emerson. "As long as any man exists, there is some need of him; let him fight for his own." This faith that in a life at first hand there is something sacred is perhaps the most characteristic note in Emerson's writings. The hottest side of him is this non-conformist persuasion, and if his temper could ever verge on common irascibility, it would be by reason of the passionate character of his feelings on this point. The world is still new and untried. In seeing freshly, and not in hearing of what others saw, shall a man find what truth is. "Each one of us can bask in the great morning which rises out of the eastern sea, and be himself one of the children of the light." "Trust thyself: every heart vibrates to that iron string. . . . There is a time in every man's education when he arrives at the conviction that ... imitation is suicide; that he must take himself for better or worse as his portion; and know that though the wide universe is full of good, no kernel of nourishing corn can come to him but through his toil bestowed on that plot of ground which is given to him to till."

The matchless eloquence with which Emerson proclaimed the sovereignty of the living individual electrified and emancipated his generation, and this bugle-blast will doubtless be regarded by future critics as the soul of his message. The present man is the aboriginal reality, the Institution is derivative, and the past man is irrelevant and obliterate for present issues. If anyone would lay an axe to your tree with a text from 1 John, v. 7, or a sentence from Saint Paul, say to him, Emerson wrote, " 'My tree is Ygdrasil—the tree of life.' . . . Let him know by your security that your conviction is clear and sufficient, and if he were Paul himself, that you also are here, and with your Creator." "Cleave ever to God," he insisted, "against the name of God";—and so, in spite of the intensely religious character of his total thought, when he began his career it seemed to many of his brethren in the clerical profession that he was little more than an iconoclast and desecrator.

Emerson's belief that the individual must in reason be adequate to the vocation for which the Spirit of the world has called him into being is the source of those sublime pages, hearteners and sustainers of our youth, in which he urges his hearers to be incorruptibly true to their own private conscience. Nothing can harm the man who rests in his appointed place and character. Such a man is invulnerable; he balances the universe, balances it as much by keeping small when he is small as by being great and spreading when he is great. "I love and honor Epaminondas," said Emerson, "but I do not wish to be Epaminondas. I hold it more just to love the world of this hour, than the world of his hour. Nor can you, if I am true, excite me to the least uneasiness by saying, 'He acted, and thou sittest still.' I see action to be good, when the need is, and sitting still to be also good. Epaminondas, if he was the man I take him for, would have sat still with joy and peace, if his lot had been mine. Heaven is large, and affords space for all modes of love and fortitude." "The fact that I am here certainly shows me that the soul had need of an organ here. Shall I not assume the post?"

The vanity of all super-serviceableness and pretense was never more happily set forth than by Emerson in the many passages in which he develops this aspect of his philosophy. Character infallibly proclaims itself. "Hide your thoughts! Hide the sun and moon. They publish themselves to the universe. They will speak through you though you were dumb. They will flow out of your actions, your manners, and your face. . . . Don't *say* things. What you *are* stands over you the while, and thunders so that I cannot hear what you say to the contrary. . . . What a man *is* engraves itself upon him in letters of light. Concealment avails him nothing; boasting nothing. There is confession in the glances of our eyes; in our smiles; in salutations; and the grasp of hands. His sin bedaubs him, mars all his good impression. Men know not why they do not trust him; but they do not trust him. His vice glasses his eye, cuts lines of mean expression in his cheek, pinches the nose, sets the mark of the beast on the back of the head, and writes O fool! fool! on the forehead of a king. If you would not be known to do any thing, never do it. A man may play the fool in the drifts of a desert, but every grain of sand shall seem to see. . . . How can a man be concealed! How can a man be concealed!"

On the other hand, never was a sincere word or a sincere thought utterly lost. "Never a magnanimity fell to the ground, but there is some heart to greet and accept it unexpectedly. . . . The hero fears not, that, if he withhold the avowal of a just and brave act, it will go unwitnessed and unloved. One knows it,— himself,—and is pledged by it to sweetness of peace, and to nobleness of aim, which will prove in the end a better proclamation than the relating of the incident."

The same indefeasible right to be exactly what one is, provided one only be authentic, spreads itself, in Emerson's way of thinking, from persons to things and to times and places. No date, no position is insignificant, if the life that fills it out be only genuine:—

"In solitude, in a remote village, the ardent youth loiters and mourns. With inflamed eye, in this sleeping wilderness, he has read the story of the Emperor Charles the Fifth, until his fancy has brought home to the surrounding woods, the faint roar of cannonades in the Milanese, and marches in Germany. He is curious concerning that man's day. What filled it? the crowded orders, the stern decisions, the foreign despatches, the Castilian etiquette? The soul answers—Behold his day here! In the sighing of these woods, in the quiet of these gray fields, in the cool breeze that sings out of these northern mountains; in the work-men, the boys, the maidens you meet,—in the hopes of the morn-ing, the ennui of noon, and sauntering of the afternoon; in the disquieting comparisons; in the regrets at want of vigor; in the great idea, and the puny execution;—behold Charles the Fifth's day; another, yet the same; behold Chatham's, Hampden's, Bay-ard's, Alfred's, Scipio's, Pericles's day,—day of all that are born of women. The difference of circumstance is merely costume. I am tasting the self-same life,—its sweetness, its greatness, its pain, which I so admire in other men. Do not foolishly ask of the in-scrutable, obliterated past, what it cannot tell,—the details of that nature, of that day, called Byron, or Burke;—but ask it of the enveloping Now . . . . Be lord of a day, and you can put up your history books."

Thus does "the deep today which all men scorn" receive from Emerson superb revindication. "Other world! there is no other world." All God's life opens into the individual particular, and here and now, or nowhere, is reality. The present hour is the de-cisive hour, and every day is doomsday.

Such a conviction that Divinity is everywhere may easily make of one an optimist of the sentimental type that refuses to speak ill of anything. Emerson's drastic perception of differences kept him at the opposite pole from this weakness. After you have seen men a few times, he could say, you find most of them as alike as their barns and pantries, and soon as musty and as dreary. Never was such a fastidious lover of significance and distinction, and never an eye so keen for their discovery. His optimism had nothing in common with that indiscriminate hurrahing for the Universe with which Walt Whitman has made us familiar. For Emerson, the individual fact and moment were indeed suffused with absolute radiance, but it was upon a condition that saved the situation—they must be worthy specimens,—sincere, authentic, archetypal; they must have made connection with what he calls the Moral Sentiment, they must in some way act as symbolic mouthpieces of the Universe's meaning. To know just which thing does act in this way, and which thing fails to make the true connection, is the secret (somewhat in-communicable, it must be confessed) of seership, and doubtless we must not expect of the seer too rigorous a consistency. Emerson himself was a real seer. He could perceive the full squalor of the individual fact, but he could also see the transfiguration. He might easily have found himself saying of some present-day agitator against our Philippine conquest what he said of this or that reformer of his own time. He might have called him, as a private person, a tedious bore and canter. But he would infallibly have added what he then added: "It is strange and horrible to say this, . . . for I feel that under him and his partiality and exclusiveness is the earth and the sea and all that in them is, and the axis around which the universe revolves passes through his body where he stands."

Be it how it may, then, this is Emerson's revelation:—The point of any pen can be an epitome of reality; the commonest person's act, if genuinely actuated, can lay hold on eternity. This vision is the head-spring of all his outpourings; and it is for this truth, given to no previous literary artist to express in such penetratingly persuasive tones, that posterity will reckon him a prophet, and, perhaps neglecting other pages, piously turn to those that convey this message. His life was one long conversation with the invisible divine, expressing itself through individuals and particulars:—"So nigh is grandeur to our dust, so near is God to man!"

I spoke of how shrunken the wraith, how thin the echo, of men is after they are departed. Emerson's wraith comes to me now as if it were but the very voice of this victorious argument. His words to this effect are certain to be quoted and extracted more and more as time goes on, and to take their place among the Scriptures of humanity. " 'Gainst death and all oblivious enmity shall you pace forth," beloved Master. As long as our English language lasts, men's hearts will be cheered and their souls strengthened and liberated by the noble and musical pages with which you have enriched it.

Introduction to Fechner's *Life After Death*

I gladly accept the translator's invitation to furnish a few words of introduction to Fechner's *Büchlein vom Leben nach dem Tode*, the more so as its somewhat oracularly uttered sentences require, for their proper understanding, a certain acquaintance with their relations to his general system.

Fechner's name lives in physics as that of one of the earliest and best determiners of electrical constants, also as that of the best systematic defender of the atomic theory. In psychology it is a commonplace to glorify him as the first user of experimental methods, and the first aimer at exactitude in facts. In cosmology he is known as the author of a system of evolution which, while taking great account of physical details and mechanical conceptions, makes consciousness correlative to and coeval with the whole physical world. In literature he has made his mark by certain half-humoristic, half-philosophic essays published under the name of Dr. Mises —indeed the present booklet originally appeared under that name. In æsthetics he may lay claim to be the earliest systematically empirical student. In metaphysics he is not only the author of an independently reasoned ethical system, but of a theological theory worked out in great detail. His mind, in short, was one of those multitudinously organized cross-roads of truth, which are occupied only at rare intervals by children of men, and from which nothing is either too far or too near to be seen in due perspective. Patient observation and daring imagination dwelt hand in hand in Fechner; and perception, reasoning, and feeling all flourished on the largest scale without interfering either with the other's function.

Fechner was, in fact, a philosopher in the "great" sense of the term, although he cared so much less than most philosophers do for purely logical abstractions. For him the abstract lived in the concrete; and although he worked as definitely and technically as the narrowest specialist works in each of the many lines of scientific inquiry which he successively followed, he followed each and all of them for the sake of his one overmastering general purpose, the purpose namely of elaborating what he called the "daylight-view" of the world into greater and greater system and completeness.

By the daylight-view, as contrasted with the night-view, Fechner meant the anti-materialistic view,—the view that the entire material universe, instead of being dead, is inwardly alive and consciously animated. There is hardly a page of his writing that was not probably connected in his mind with this most general of his interests.

Little by little the materialistic generation that called his speculations fantastic has been replaced by one with greater liberty of imagination. Leaders of thought, a Paulsen, a Wundt, a Preyer, a Lasswitz, treat Fechner's pan-psychism as plausible, and write of its author with veneration. Younger men chime in, and Fechner's philosophy promises to become scientifically fashionable. Imagine a Herbert Spencer who, to the unity of his system and its unceasing touch with facts, should have added a positively religious philosophy instead of Spencer's dry agnosticism; who should have mingled humor and lightness (even though it were germanic lightness) with his heavier ratiocinations; who should have been no less encyclopedic and far more subtle; who should have shown a personal life as simple and as consecrated to the one pursuit of truth,—imagine this, I say, if you can, and you may form some idea of what the name of Fechner is more and more coming to stand for, and of the esteem in which it is more and more held by the studious youth of his native Germany. His belief that the whole material universe is conscious in divers spans and wave-lengths, inclusions and envelopments, seems assuredly destined to found a school that will grow more systematic and solidified as time goes on.

The general background of the present dogmatically written little treatise is to be found in the *Tagesansicht*, in the *Zend-Avesta*, and in various other works of Fechner's. Once grasp the idealistic notion that inner experience is the reality, and that matter is but a form in which inner experiences may appear to one another when they affect each other from the outside; and it is easy to believe that consciousness or inner experience never originated, or developed, out of the unconscious, but that it and the physical universe are co-eternal aspects of one self-same reality, much as concave and convex are aspects of one curve. "Psychophysical movement," as Fechner calls it, is the most pregnant name for all the reality that is. As "movement" it has a "direction"; as "psychical" the direction can be felt as a "tendency" and as all that lies connected in the way of inner experience with tendencies,—desire, effort, success, for example; while as "physical" the direction can be defined in spatial terms and formulated mathematically or otherwise in the shape of a descriptive "law."

But movements can be superimposed and compounded, the smaller on the greater, as wavelets upon waves. This is as true in the mental as in the physical sphere. Speaking psychologically, we may say that a general wave of consciousness rises out of a subconscious background, and that certain portions of it catch the emphasis, as wavelets catch the light. The whole process is conscious, but the emphatic wave-tips of the consciousness are of such contracted span that they are momentarily insulated from the rest. They realize themselves apart, as a twig might realize itself, and forget the parent tree. Such an insulated bit of experience leaves, however, when it passes away, a memory of itself. The residual and subsequent consciousness becomes different for its having occurred. On the physical side we say that the brain-process that corresponded to it altered permanently the future mode of action of the brain.

Now, according to Fechner, our bodies are just wavelets on the surface of the earth. We grow upon the earth as leaves grow upon a tree, and our consciousness arises out of the whole earth-consciousness,—which it forgets to thank,—just as within our consciousness an emphatic experience arises, and makes us forget the whole background of experience without which it could not have come. But as it sinks again into that background it is not forgotten. On the contrary, it is remembered and, as remembered, leads a freer life, for it now combines, itself a conscious idea, with the innumerable, equally conscious ideas of other remembered things. Even so is it, when we die, with the whole system of our outlived experiences.

During the life of our body, although they were always elements in the more general enveloping earth-consciousness, yet they themselves were unmindful of the fact. Now, impressed on the whole earth-mind as memories, they lead the life of ideas there, and realize themselves no longer in isolation, but along with all the similar vestiges left by other human lives, entering with these into new combinations, affected anew by experiences of the living, and affecting the living in their turn, enjoying, in short, that "third stage" of existence with the definition of which the text of the present work begins.

God, for Fechner, is the totalized consciousness of the whole universe, of which the Earth's consciousness forms an element, just as in turn my human consciousness and yours form elements of the whole earth's consciousness. As I apprehend Fechner (though I am not sure), the whole Universe—God therefore also—evolves in time: that is, God has a genuine history. Through us as its human organs of experience the earth enriches its inner life, until it also "geht zu grunde" and becomes immortal in the form of those still wider elements of inner experience which its history is even now weaving into the total cosmic life of God.

The whole scheme, as the reader sees, is got from the fact that the span of our own inner life alternately contracts and expands. You cannot say where the exact outline of any present state of consciousness lies. It shades into a more general background in which even now other states lie ready to be known. This background is the inner aspect of what physically appear, first, as our residual and only partially excited neural elements, and then more remotely as the whole organism which we call our own.

This indetermination of the partition, this fact of a changing threshold, is the analogy which Fechner generalizes, that is all.

There are many difficulties attaching to his theory. The complexity with which he himself realizes them, and the subtlety with which he meets them are admirable. It is interesting to see how closely his speculations, due to such different motives, and supported by such different arguments, agree with those of some of our own philosophers. Royce's Gifford lectures, *The World and the Individual*, Bradley's *Appearance and Reality*, and A. E. Taylor's *Elements of Metaphysics*, present themselves immediately to one's mind.

Remarks at the Peace Banquet[1]

I am only a philosopher, and there is only one thing that a philosopher can be relied on to do. You know that the function of statistics has been ingeniously described as being the refutation of other statistics. Well, a philosopher can always contradict other philosophers. In ancient times philosophers defined man as the rational animal; and philosophers since then have always found much more to say about the rational than about the animal part of the definition. But looked at candidly, reason bears about the same proportion to the rest of human nature that we in this hall bear to the rest of America, Europe, Asia, Africa and Polynesia. Reason is one of the very feeblest of Nature's forces, if you take it at any one spot and moment. It is only in the very long run that its effects become perceptible. Reason assumes to settle things by weighing them against one another without prejudice, partiality or excitement; but what affairs in the concrete are settled by is and always will be just prejudices, partialities, cupidities and excitements. Appealing to reason as we do, we are in a sort of a forlorn-hope situation, like a small sand-bank in the midst of a hungry sea ready to wash it out of existence. But sand-banks grow when the conditions favor; and weak as reason is, it has the unique advantage over its antagonists that its activity never lets up and that it presses always in one

[1] This banquet was given in Boston on the closing day of the World's Peace Congress, October 7, 1904.

direction, while men's prejudices vary, their passions ebb and flow, and their excitements are intermittent. Our sand-bank, I absolutely believe, is bound to grow,—bit by bit it will get dyked and breakwatered. But sitting as we do in this warm room, with music and lights and the flowing bowl and smiling faces, it is easy to get too sanguine about our task, and since I am called to speak, I feel as if it might not be out of place to say a word about the strength of our enemy.

Our permanent enemy is the noted bellicosity of human nature. Man, biologically considered, and whatever else he may be in the bargain, is simply the most formidable of all beasts of prey, and, indeed, the only one that preys systematically on its own species. We are once for all adapted to the military *status*. A millennium of peace would not breed the fighting disposition out of our bone and marrow, and a function so ingrained and vital will never consent to die without resistance, and will always find impassioned apologists and idealizers.

Not only men born to be soldiers, but non-combatants by trade and nature, historians in their studies, and clergymen in their pulpits, have been war's idealizers. They have talked of war as of God's court of justice. And, indeed, if we think how many things beside the frontiers of states the wars of history have decided, we must feel some respectful awe, in spite of all the horrors. Our actual civilization, good and bad alike, has had past wars for its determining condition. Great-mindedness among the tribes of men has always meant the will to prevail, and all the more so if prevailing included slaughtering and being slaughtered. Rome, Paris, England, Brandenburg, Piedmont,—soon, let us hope, Japan,—along with their arms have made their traits of character and habits of thought prevail among their conquered neighbors. The blessings we actually enjoy, such as they are, have grown up in the shadow of the wars of antiquity. The various ideals were backed by fighting wills, and where neither would give way, the God of battles had to be the arbiter. A shallow view, this, truly; for who can say what might have prevailed if man had ever been a reasoning and not a fighting animal? Like dead men, dead causes tell no tales, and the ideals that went under in the past, along with all the tribes that represented them, find to-day no recorder, no explainer, no defender.

But apart from theoretic defenders, and apart from every soldierly individual straining at the leash, and clamoring for opportunity, war has an omnipotent support in the form of our imagination. Man lives *by* habits, indeed, but what he lives *for* is thrills and excitements. The only relief from Habit's tediousness is periodical excitement. From time immemorial wars have been, especially for non-combatants, the supremely thrilling excitement. Heavy and dragging at its end, at its outset every war means an explosion of imaginative energy. The dams of routine burst, and boundless prospects open. The remotest spectators share the fascination. With that awful struggle now in progress on the confines of the world, there is not a man in this room, I suppose, who doesn't buy both an evening and a morning paper, and first of all pounce on the war column.

A deadly listlessness would come over most men's imagination of the future if they could seriously be brought to believe that never again *in saecula saeculorum* would a war trouble human history. In such a stagnant summer afternoon of a world, where would be the zest or interest?

This is the constitution of human nature which we have to work against. The plain truth is that people *want* war. They want it anyhow; for itself; and apart from each and every possible consequence. It is the final bouquet of life's fireworks. The born soldiers want it hot and actual. The non-combatants want it in the background, and always as an open possibility, to feed imagination on and keep excitement going. Its clerical and historical defenders fool themselves when they talk as they do about it. What moves them is not the blessings it has won for us, but a vague religious exaltation. War, they feel, is human nature at its uttermost. We are here to do our uttermost. It is a sacrament. Society would rot, they think, without the mystical blood-payment.

We do ill, I fancy, to talk much of universal peace or of a general disarmament. We must go in for preventive medicine, not for radical cure. We must cheat our foe, politically circumvent his action, not try to change his nature. In one respect war is like love, though in no other. Both leave us intervals of rest; and in the intervals life goes on perfectly well without them, though the imagination still dallies with their possibility. Equally insane when once aroused and under headway, whether they shall be aroused or not depends on accidental circumstances. How are old maids and old bachelors made? Not by deliberate vows of celibacy, but by sliding on from year to year with no sufficient matrimonial provocation. So of the nations with their wars. Let the general possibility of war be left open, in Heaven's name, for the imagination to dally with. Let the soldiers dream of killing, as the old maids dream of marrying. But organize in every conceivable way the practical machinery for making each successive chance of war abortive. Put peace-men in power; educate the editors and statesmen to responsibility;—how beautifully did their trained responsibility in England make the Venezuela incident abortive! Seize every pretext, however small, for arbitration methods, and multiply the precedents; foster rival excitements and invent new outlets for heroic energy; and from one generation to another, the chances are that irritations will grow less acute and states of strain less dangerous among the nations. Armies and navies will continue, of course, and will fire the minds of populations with their potentialities of greatness. But their officers will find that somehow or other, with no deliberate intention on anyone's part, each successive "incident" has managed to evaporate and to lead nowhere, and that the thought of what might have been remains their only consolation.

The last weak runnings of the war spirit will be "punitive expeditions." A country that turns its arms only against uncivilized foes is, I think, wrongly taunted as degenerate. Of course it has ceased to be heroic in the old grand style. But I verily believe that this is because it now sees something better. It has a conscience. It knows that between civilized countries a war is a crime against civilization. It will still perpetrate peccadillos, to be sure. But it is afraid, afraid in the good sense of the word, to engage in absolute crimes against civilization.

Reason and Faith

I am asked to discuss Faith and Reason, but no definite question concerning them is proposed. It is also announced in print that Professor Howison and I will probably oppose each other, but I sincerely hope that this may not be the case. If we do, it will very likely be over the question of Reason's all-sufficiency to reach religious conclusions without the aid of faith, so I will, with your permission, begin by speaking of that point.

Whether Reason be deemed all-sufficient or not will depend on what you mean by Reason. Strictly and technically, Reason is a faculty not of facts but of principles and relations. Out of her own resources she cannot say what facts exist; but if one fact be given her, she can infer another fact; and she is supposed to be able, by certain principles that she possesses, to lay down in advance what relations facts must stand in to each other, that causes, for example, must precede, not follow their effects, and the like.

The religious question is altogether one of facts. Does a God *exist* or not? Is the world *actually run* by its higher or by its lower forces? To feel things to be higher and lower, but to confess the higher things impotent, would be an irreligious conclusion. *If* there be a God, Reason can be theistic and say that we exist alongside of him, or pantheistic and say that we are parts of him; but *that* there is a God, Reason can only infer from the facts of experience, from their character as needing a cause, or from the purpose they display.

If we take Reason in this strict sense of a faculty of inference, nothing is more notorious than her insufficiency to put religious conclusions on a solid base. To say nothing of pantheism and theism and their squabbles, atheism itself has always appealed to Reason for support. The most deeply atheistic book I have seen of late is that *Life of Reason*, by my colleague Santayana, which I recommend you all to read. For my colleague Royce, on the other hand, as you all know, God's existence is the one fact that Reason makes secure. Which of these thinkers does genuine Reason actuate? Speaking after the manner of men, and judging by other tests than the religious one, Reason in both of them is far superior to what it is in most of us. Neither can claim a monopoly of it; neither can say that his colleague doesn't use it, but reaches his conclusions by blind Faith.

Men of the world would probably say that Faith has a finger in the conclusions of both men. Their Reason indicates the opening and their Faith jumps in. Faith uses a logic altogether different from Reason's logic. Reason claims certainty and finality for her conclusions. Faith is satisfied if hers seem probable and practically wise.

Faith's form of argument is something like this: Considering a view of the world: "It is *fit* to be true," she feels; "it would be well if it *were* true; it *might* be true; it *may* be true; it *ought* to be true," she says; "it *must* be true," she continues; "it *shall* be true," she concludes, "*for me*; that is, I will treat it as if it *were* true so far as my advocacy and actions are concerned."

Obviously this is no intellectual chain of inferences, like the *sorites* of the logic-books. You may call it the 'faith-ladder,' if you like; but, whatever you call it, it is the sort of slope on which we all habitually live. In no complex matter can our conclusions be more than *probable*. We use our feelings, our good-will, in judging where the greater probability lies, and when our judgment is made, we practically turn our back on the lesser probabilities as if they were not there. Probability, as you know, is mathematically expressed by a fraction. But seldom can we *act* fractionally—half-action is no action (what is the use of only half-killing your enemy? —better not touch him at all); so for purposes of action we equate the most probable view to 1 (or certainty) and other views we treat as naught.

Now the advocates of Reason's all-sufficiency can follow either of two courses, but not both.

They can approve of the faith-ladder and adopt it, but at the same time call it an exercise of Reason. In this case they close the controversy by a verbal definition, which amounts to a material surrender to the opposite side.

Or they can stick to Reason's more customary definition, and forbid us the faith-ladder, as something liable only to mislead. "Brace yourself against its fatal slope," they can say; "wait for full evidence; Reason and facts must alone decide; rule good-will out; don't move until you're sure." But this advice is so obviously impossible to follow in any considerable practical or theoretical affair, and the rationalists themselves follow it so very little in their books and practice, fornicating as they do habitually with the unclean thing which they denounce, that I do not see how it can be seriously taken. Virtually it amounts to forbidding us to *live*.

I conclude, then, that there is nothing left to dispute about. If the word Reason be taken to cover the faith-process, then Reason is indeed all-sufficient. But if it be taken to exclude the faith-process, then its insufficiency to found a man's religion solidly seems to me too obvious for any further discussion to be carried on.

But perhaps I have mistaken your meaning altogether. Perhaps you had Reason versus Experience rather than Reason versus Faith in view. In that case I think that there is something more to be said.

The religious question, we agreed, is a question about facts. From the facts of finite experience, religious rationalism thinks, Reason can infer the Infinite, from the visible she can infer the invisible world.

Now, historically the pretension of religious rationalism has been that *all* the facts of experience, rightly interpreted, physical facts and moral facts, lead to religious conclusions, and that specifically religious facts, such as conversions, mystical insights, or providential leadings, though they may confirm our religion, are not needed to establish it in the first instance. Common natural facts will do.

But here I have to repeat what I said at the outset. *Do* the facts of natural experience force men's Reason, as it concretely exists, to religious conclusions? Certainly men having every *other* appearance of possessing Reason have been led to irreligious conclusions by the facts of the world. Men will probably always conclude diversely in this matter, as they have concluded diversely up to this hour. Some will see in moral facts a power that makes for righteousness, and in physical facts a power that geometrizes and is intellectual, that creates order and loves beauty. But alongside of all such facts there are contrary facts in abundance; and he who seeks *them* can equally well infer a power that defies righteousness, creates disorder, loves ugliness, and aims at death. It depends on which kind of fact you single out as the more essential. If your Reason tries to be impartial, if she resorts to statistical comparison, and asks which class of facts tip the balance, and which way tends the drift, she must, it seems to me, conclude for irreligion, unless we give her more specific religious experiences to go by; for the *last* word everywhere, according to purely naturalistic science, is the word of Death, the death-sentence passed by Nature on plant and beast, and man and tribe, and earth and sun, and everything that she has made.

But religious experience, strictly and narrowly so-called, gives Reason an additional set of facts to use. They show another possibility to Reason, and Faith then can jump in.

Briefly, the facts I mean can be described as experiences of an unexpected life succeeding upon death. By this I don't mean immortality, or the death of the body. I mean the death and termination of certain mental processes within the individual's experience, processes that run to failure, and in some individuals, at least, eventuate in despair. Just as romantic love seems a comparatively recent literary invention, so these experiences of a life that supervenes upon despair seem to have played no great part in official theology till Luther's time; and the best way to indicate their character will possibly be to draw a contrast between the inner life of ourselves and of the ancient Greeks and Romans.

The Greeks and Romans, in all that concerned their moral life, were an extraordinarily solemn set of folks. The Athenians thought that the very gods must admire the rectitude of Phocion and Aristides; and those gentlemen themselves were apparently of much the same opinion. Cato's veracity was so impeccable that the extremest incredulity a Roman could express of anything was to say "I wouldn't believe it even if Cato told me." Good was good and bad was bad, for these people. Hypocrisy, which Church-Christianity brought in, hardly existed; the naturalistic system held firm; its values showed no hollowness and brooked no irony. The individual, if virtuous enough, could meet all possible requirements. The pagan pride had never crumbled.

Luther broke through the crust of all this naturalistic self-sufficiency. He thought (and possibly he was right) that Saint Paul had done it already. Religious experience of the Lutheran type brings all our naturalistic standards to bankruptcy. You are strong only by being weak, it shows. You cannot live on pride or self-sufficingness. There is a light in which all the naturally founded and currently accepted distinctions, excellences, and safeguards of our characters appear as absolute childishness. To give up one's conceit of being good, is the only door to the Universe's deeper reaches.

These deeper reaches are familiar enough to evangelical Christianity and to what is now-a-days known as 'Mind-cure' religion or 'New-Thought.' The phenomenon is that of new ranges of life succeeding on our most despairing moments. There are resources in us that naturalism, with its literal virtues, never recks of, possibilities that take our breath away, and show a world wider than either physics or philistine ethics can imagine. Here is a world in which all is well, *in spite* of certain forms of death, indeed *because* of certain forms of death, death of hope, death of strength, death of responsibility, of fear and worry, death of everything that paganism, naturalism and legalism pin their trust on.

Reason, operating on our other experiences, even our psychological experiences, would never have inferred these specifically religious experiences in advance of their actual coming. She could not suspect their existence, for they are discontinuous with 'natural' experience, and invert its values. But as they come and are given, Creation widens to our view. They suggest that our 'natural' experience, so-called, may only be a fragment of reality. They soften Nature's outlines and open out the strangest possibilities and perspectives.

This is why it seems to me that Reason, working in abstraction from specifically religious experiences, will always omit something, and fail to reach completely adequate conclusions. This is why 'religious experience,' peculiarly so-called, needs, in my opinion, to be carefully considered and interpreted by everyone who aspires to reason out a true religious philosophy.

The Energies of Men[1]

We habitually hear much nowadays of the difference between structural and functional psychology. I am not sure that I understand the difference, but it probably has something to do with what I have privately been accustomed to distinguish as the analytical and the clinical points of view in psychological observation. Professor Sanford, in a recently published "Sketch of a Beginner's Course in Psychology," recommended "the physician's attitude" in that subject as the thing the teacher should first of all try to impart to the pupil. I fancy that few of you can have read Professor Pierre Janet's masterly works in mental pathology without being struck by the little use he makes of the machinery usually relied on by psychologists, and by his own reliance on conceptions which in the laboratories and in scientific publications we never hear of at all.

Discriminations and associations, the rise and fall of thresholds, impulses and inhibitions, fatigue,—these are the terms into which our inner life is analyzed by psychologists who are not doctors, and in which, by hook or crook, its aberrations from normality have to be expressed. They can indeed be described, after the fact, in such terms, but always lamely; and everyone must feel how much is unaccounted for, how much left out.

When we turn to Janet's pages, we find entirely other forms of

[1] Delivered as the Presidential Address before the American Philosophical Association at Columbia University, December 28, 1906.

thought employed. Oscillations of the level of mental energy, differences of tension, splittings of consciousness, sentiments of insufficiency and of unreality, substitutions, agitations and anxieties, depersonalizations—such are the elementary conceptions which the total view of his patient's life imposes on this clinical observer. They have little or nothing to do with the usual laboratory categories. Ask a scientific psychologist to predict what symptoms a patient must have when his 'supply of mental energy' diminishes, and he can utter only the word 'fatigue.' He could never predict such consequences as Janet subsumes under his one term 'psychasthenia'—the most bizarre obsessions and agitations, the most complete distortions of the relation between the self and the world.

I do not vouch for Janet's conceptions being valid, and I do not say that the two ways of looking at the mind contradict each other or are mutually incongruous; I simply say that they are incongru-*ent*. Each covers so little of our total mental life that they do not even interfere or jostle. Meanwhile the clinical conceptions, though they may be vaguer than the analytic ones, are certainly more adequate, give the concreter picture of the way the whole mind works, and are of far more urgent practical importance. So the 'physician's attitude,' the 'functional psychology,' is assuredly the thing most worthy of general study to-day.

I wish to spend this hour on one conception of functional psychology, a conception never once mentioned or heard of in laboratory circles, but used perhaps more than any other by common, practical men—I mean the conception of the *amount of energy available* for running one's mental and moral operations by. Practically everyone knows in his own person the difference between the days when the tide of this energy is high in him and those when it is low, though no one knows exactly what reality the term energy covers when used here, or what its tides, tensions, and levels are in themselves. This vagueness is probably the reason why our scientific psychologists ignore the conception altogether. It undoubtedly connects itself with the energies of the nervous system, but it presents fluctuations that cannot easily be translated into neural terms. It offers itself as the notion of a quantity, but its ebbs and floods produce extraordinary qualitative results. To have its level raised is the most important thing that can happen to a man, yet in all my reading I know of no single page or paragraph of a scientific psychology book in which it receives mention—the psychologists have left it to be treated by the moralists and mind-curers and doctors exclusively.

Everyone is familiar with the phenomenon of feeling more or less alive on different days. Everyone knows on any given day that there are energies slumbering in him which the incitements of that day do not call forth, but which he might display if these were greater. Most of us feel as if we lived habitually with a sort of cloud weighing on us, below our highest notch of clearness in discernment, sureness in reasoning, or firmness in deciding. Compared with what we ought to be, we are only half-awake. Our fires are damped, our drafts are checked. We are making use of only a small part of our possible mental and physical resources. In some persons this sense of being cut off from their rightful resources is extreme, and we then get the formidable neurasthenic and psychasthenic conditions, with life grown into one tissue of impossibilities, that the medical books describe.

Part of the imperfect vitality under which we labor can be explained by scientific psychology. It is the result of the inhibition exerted by one part of our ideas on other parts. Conscience makes cowards of us all. Social conventions prevent us from telling the truth after the fashion of the heroes and heroines of Bernard Shaw. Our scientific respectability keeps us from exercising the mystical portions of our nature freely. If we are doctors, our mind-cure sympathies, if we are mind-curists, our medical sympathies, are tied up. We all know persons who are models of excellence, but who belong to the extreme philistine type of mind. So deadly is their intellectual respectability that we can't converse about certain subjects at all, can't let our minds play over them, can't even mention them in their presence. I have numbered among my dearest friends persons thus inhibited intellectually, with whom I would gladly have been able to talk freely about certain interests of mine, certain authors, say, as Bernard Shaw, Chesterton, Edward Carpenter, H. G. Wells, but it wouldn't do, it made them too uncomfortable, they wouldn't play, I had to be silent. An intellect thus tied down by literality and decorum makes on one the same sort of impression that an able-bodied man would who should habituate himself to do his work with only one of his fingers, locking up the rest of his organism and leaving it unused.

In few of us are functions not tied-up by the exercise of other functions. G. T. Fechner is an extraordinary exception that proves the rule. He could use his mystical faculties while being scientific. He could be both critically keen and devout. Few scientific men can pray, I imagine. Few can carry on any living commerce with 'God.' Yet many of us are well aware how much freer in many directions and abler our lives would be, were such important forms of energizing not sealed up. There are in everyone potential forms of activity that actually are shunted out from use.

The existence of reservoirs of energy that habitually are not tapped is most familiar to us in the phenomenon of 'second wind.' Ordinarily we stop when we meet the first effective layer, so to call it, of fatigue. We have then walked, played, or worked 'enough,' and desist. That amount of fatigue is an efficacious obstruction, on this side of which our usual life is cast. But if an unusual necessity forces us to press onward, a surprising thing occurs. The fatigue gets worse up to a certain critical point, when gradually or suddenly it passes away, and we are fresher than before. We have evidently tapped a level of new energy, masked until then by the fatigue-obstacle usually obeyed. There may be layer after layer of this experience. A third and a fourth 'wind' may supervene. Mental activity shows the phenomenon as well as physical, and in exceptional cases we may find, beyond the very extremity of fatigue-distress, amounts of ease and power that we never dreamed ourselves to own, sources of strength habitually not taxed at all, because habitually we never push through the obstruction, never pass those early critical points.

When we do pass, what makes us do so?

Either some unusual stimulus fills us with emotional excitement, or some unusual idea of necessity induces us to make an extra effort of will. *Excitements, ideas, and efforts,* in a word, are what carry us over the dam.

In those hyperesthetic conditions which chronic invalidism so often brings in its train, the dam has changed its normal place. The pain-threshold is abnormally near. The slightest functional exercise gives a distress which the patient yields to and stops. In such cases of 'habit-neurosis' a new range of power often comes in consequence of the bullying-treatment, of efforts which the doctor obliges the patient, against his will, to make. First comes the very extremity of distress, then follows unexpected relief. There seems no doubt that we are each and all of us to some extent victims of habit-neurosis. We have to admit the wider potential range and the habitually narrow actual use. We live subject to inhibition by degrees of fatigue which we have come only from habit to obey. Most of us may learn to push the barrier farther off, and to live in perfect comfort on much higher levels of power.

Country people and city people, as a class, illustrate this difference. The rapid rate of life, the number of decisions in an hour, the many things to keep account of, in a busy city-man's or woman's life, seem monstrous to a country-brother. He doesn't see how we live at all. But settle him in town; and in a year or two, if not too old, he will have trained himself to keep the pace as well as any of us, getting more out of himself in any week than he ever did in ten weeks at home. The physiologists show how one can be in nutritive equilibrium, neither losing nor gaining weight, on astonishingly different quantities of food. So one can be in what I might call 'efficiency-equilibrium' (neither gaining nor losing power when once the equilibrium is reached), on astonishingly different quantities of work, no matter in what dimension the work may be measured. It may be physical work, intellectual work, moral work, or spiritual work.

Of course there are limits: the trees don't grow into the sky. But the plain fact remains that men the world over possess amounts of resource, which only very exceptional individuals push to their extremes of use.

The excitements that carry us over the usually effective dam are most often the classic emotional ones, love, anger, crowd-contagion, or despair. Life's vicissitudes bring them in abundance. A new position of responsibility, if it do not crush a man, will often, nay, one may say, will usually, show him to be a far stronger creature than was supposed. Even here we are witnessing (some of us admiring, some deploring—I must class myself as admiring) the dynamogenic effects of a very exalted political office upon the energies of an individual who had already manifested a healthy amount of energy before the office came.

Mr. Sydney Olivier has given us a fine fable of the dynamogenic effects of love in a fine story called "The Empire Builder," in the *Contemporary Review* for May, 1905. A young naval officer falls in love at sight with a missionary's daughter on a lost island, which his ship accidentally touches. From that day onward he must see her again; and he so moves Heaven and earth and the Colonial Office and the Admiralty to get sent there once more, that the island finally is annexed to the empire in consequence of the various fusses he is led to make. People must have been appalled lately in San Francisco to find the stores of bottled up energy and endurance they possessed.

Wars, of course, and shipwrecks, are the great revealers of what men and women are able to do and bear. Cromwell's and Grant's careers are the stock examples of how war will wake a man up. I owe to Professor Norton's kindness the permission to read to you part of a letter from Colonel Baird Smith, written shortly after the six weeks' siege of Delhi in 1857, for the victorious issue of which that excellent officer was chiefly to be thanked. He writes as follows:—

... "My poor wife had some reason to think that war and disease between them had left very little of a husband to take under nursing when she got him again. An attack of Camp Scurvy had filled my mouth with sores, shaken every joint in my body and covered me all over with livid spots so that I was marvellously unlovely to look upon. A smart knock on the ancle joint from the splinter of a shell that burst in my face, in itself a mere bagatelle of a wound, had been of necessity neglected under the pressing and incessant calls upon me and had grown worse and worse till the whole foot below the ancle became a black mass and seemed to threaten mortification. I insisted however on being allowed to use it till the place was taken, mortification or no, and tho' the pain was sometimes horrible I carried my point and kept up to the last. On the day after the assault I had an unlucky fall on some bad ground and it was an open question for a day or two whether I hadn't broken my arm at the elbow. Fortunately it turned out to be only a very severe sprain but I am still conscious of the wrench it gave me. To crown the whole pleasant catalogue I was worn to a shadow by a constant diarrhœa and consumed as much opium as would have done credit to my father-in-law.[2] However, thank God I have a good share of Tapleyism in me and come out strong under difficulties. I think I may confidently say that no man ever saw me out of heart or ever heard one croaking word from me even when our prospects were gloomiest. We were sadly scourged by the cholera and it was almost appalling to me to find that out of twenty-seven officers present I could muster

[2] Thomas De Quincey.

only fifteen for the operations of the attack. However, it was done and after it was done came the collapse. Don't be horrified when I tell you that for the whole of the actual Siege and in truth for some little time before, I almost lived on Brandy. Appetite for food I had none but I forced myself to eat just sufficient to sustain life and I had an incessant craving for brandy as the strongest stimulant I could get. Strange to say I was quite unconscious of its affecting me in the slightest degree. *The excitement of the work was so great that no lesser one seemed to have any chance against it and I certainly never found my intellect clearer or my nerves stronger in my life.* It was only my wretched body that was weak and the moment the real work was done by our becoming complete masters of Delhi I broke down without delay and discovered that if I wished to live I must continue no longer the system that had kept me up, till the crisis was past. With it passed away as if in a moment all desire to stimulate and a perfect loathing of my late staff of life took possession of me."

Such experiences show how profound is the alteration in the manner in which, under excitement, our organism will sometimes perform its physiological work. The metabolisms become different when the reserves have to be used, and for weeks and months the deeper use may go on.

Morbid cases, here as elsewhere, lay the normal machinery bare. In the first number of Dr. Morton Prince's *Journal of Abnormal Psychology*, Dr. Janet has discussed five cases of morbid impulse, with an explanation that is precious for my present point of view. One is a girl who eats, eats, eats, all day. Another walks, walks, walks, and gets her food from an automobile that escorts her. Another is a dipsomaniac. A fourth pulls out her hair. A fifth wounds her flesh and burns her skin. Hitherto such freaks of impulse have received Greek names (as bulimia, dromomania, etc.) and been scientifically disposed of as "episodic syndromata of hereditary degeneration." But it turns out that Janet's cases are all what he calls psychasthenics, or victims of a chronic sense of weakness, torpor, lethargy, fatigue, insufficiency, impossibility, unreality, and powerlessness of will; and that in each and all of them the particular activity pursued, deleterious though it be, has the temporary result of raising the sense of vitality and making the patient feel alive again. These things reanimate; they would reanimate *us*; but it happens that in each patient the particular freak-activity chosen is the only thing that does reanimate; and therein lies the morbid state. The way to treat such persons is to discover to them more usual and useful ways of throwing their stores of vital energy into gear.

Colonel Baird Smith, needing to draw on altogether extraordinary stores of energy, found that brandy and opium were ways of throwing them into gear.

Such cases are humanly typical. We are all to some degree oppressed, unfree. We don't come to our own. It is there, but we don't get at it. The threshold must be made to shift. Then many of us find that an excentric activity—a 'spree,' say—relieves. There is no doubt that to some men sprees and excesses of almost any kind are medicinal, temporarily at any rate, in spite of what the moralists and doctors say.

But when the normal tasks and stimulations of life don't put a man's deeper levels of energy on tap, and he requires distinctly deleterious excitements, his constitution verges on the abnormal. The normal opener of deeper and deeper levels of energy is the will. The difficulty is to use it; to make the effort which the word volition implies. But if we *do* make it (or if a god, though he were only the god Chance, makes it through us), it will act dynamogenically on us for a month. It is notorious that a single successful effort of moral volition, such as saying 'no' to some habitual temptation, or performing some courageous act, will launch a man on a higher level of energy for days and weeks, will give him a new range of power.

The emotions and excitements due to usual situations are the usual inciters of the will. But these act discontinuously; and in the intervals the shallower levels of life tend to close in and shut us off. Accordingly the best practical knowers of the human soul have invented the thing known as methodical ascetic discipline to keep the deeper levels constantly in reach. Beginning with easy tasks, passing to harder ones, and exercising day by day, it is, I believe, admitted that disciples of asceticism can reach very high levels of freedom and power of will.

Ignatius Loyola's spiritual exercises must have produced this result in innumerable devotees. But the most venerable ascetic system, and the one whose results have the most voluminous experimental corroboration, is undoubtedly the Yoga system in Hindostan. From time immemorial, by Hatha Yoga, Raja Yoga, Karma Yoga, or whatever code of practice it might be, Hindu aspirants to perfection have trained themselves, month in and out, for years. The result claimed, and certainly in many cases accorded by impartial judges, is strength of character, personal power, unshakability of soul. But it is not easy to disentangle fact from tradition in Hindu affairs. So I am glad to have a European friend who has submitted to Hatha Yoga training, and whose account of the results I am privileged to quote. I think you will appreciate the light it throws on the question of our unused reservoirs of power.

My friend is an extraordinarily gifted man, both morally and intellectually, but has an instable nervous system, and for many years has lived in a circular process of alternate lethargy and over-animation: something like three weeks of extreme activity, and then a week of prostration in bed. An unpromising condition, which the best specialists in Europe had failed to relieve; so he tried Hatha Yoga, partly out of curiosity, and partly with a sort of desperate hope. What follows is a short extract from a letter sixty pages long which he addressed me a year ago.

"Thus I decided to follow Vivekananda's advice: 'Practice hard: whether you live or die by it doesn't matter.' My improvised chela and I began with starvation. I do not know whether you did try it ever . . . but voluntary starvation is very different from involuntary, and implies more temptations. We reduced first our meals to twice a day and then to once a day. The best authorities agree that in order to control the body fasting is essential, and even in the Gospel the worst spirits are said to obey only those who fast and pray. We reduced very much the amount of food, disregarding chemical theories about the need of albumen, sometimes living on olive oil and bread; or on fruits alone; or on milk and rice; in very small quantities—much less than I formerly ate at one meal. I began to get lighter every day, and lost 20 pounds in a few weeks; but this could not stop such a desperate undertaking . . . rather starve than live as a slave! Then besides we practised *asana* or postures, breaking almost our limbs. Try to sit down on the floor and to kiss your knees without bending them, or to join your hands on the usually unapproachable upper part of your back, or to bring the toe of your right foot to your left ear without bending the knees . . . these are easy samples of posture for a Yogi.

"All the time also breathing exercises: keeping the breath in and out up to two minutes, breathing in different rhythms and positions. Also very much prayer and Roman Catholic practices combined with the Yoga, in order to leave nothing untried and to be protected against the tricks of Hindu devils! Then concentration of thought on different parts of the body, and on the processes going on within them. Exclusion of all emotions, dry logical reading, as intellectual diet, and working out logical problems. . . . I wrote a Handbook of Logic as a *Nebenprodukt* of the whole experiment.[3]

"After a few weeks I broke down and had to interrupt everything, in a worse state of prostration than ever. . . . My younger chela went on unshaken by my fate; and as soon as I arose from bed I tried again, decided to fight it out, even feeling a kind of determination such as I had never felt before, a certain absolute will of victory at any price and faith in it. Whether it is my own merit or a divine grace, I cannot judge for certain, but I prefer to admit the latter. I had been ill for seven years, and some people say this is a term for many punishments. However base and vile a sinner I had been, perhaps my sins were about to be forgiven, and Yoga was only an exterior opportunity, an object for concentration of will. I do not yet pretend to explain much of what I have gone through, but the fact is that since I arose from bed on August 20, no new crisis of prostration came again, and I have now the strongest conviction that no crisis will ever return. If you consider that for the past years there has been not a single month without this lethargy, you will grant that even to an outside observer four successive months of increasing health are an objective test. In this time I underwent very severe penances, reducing sleep and food and increasing the task of work and exercise. My intuition was developed by these practices: there came a sense of certainty, never known before, as to the things needed by the body and the mind, and the body came to obey like a wild horse tamed. Also the mind learned to obey, and the current of thought and feeling was shaped according to my will. I mastered sleep and hunger, and the flights of thought, and came to know a peace never known before, an inner rhythm of unison with a deeper rhythm above or beyond. Personal wishes ceased, and the consciousness of being the instrument of a superior power arose. A calm certainty of indubitable success in every undertaking imparts great and real power. I often guessed the thoughts of my companion . . . we observed generally the greatest isolation and silence. We both felt an unspeakable joy in the simplest natural impressions, light, air, landscape, any kind of simplest food; and

---

[3] This handbook was published last March.

above everything in rhythmical respiration, which produces a state of mind without thought or feeling, and still very intense, indescribable.

"These results began to be more evident in the fourth month of uninterrupted training. We felt quite happy, never tired, sleeping only from 8 P.M. to midnight, and rising with joy from our sleep to another day's work of study and exercise. . . .

"I am now in Palermo, and have had to neglect the exercises in the last few days, but I feel as fresh as if I were in full training and see the sunny side of all things. I am not in a hurry, rushing to complete ———."

And here my friend mentions a certain life-work of his own about which I had better be silent. He goes on to analyze the exercises and their effects in an extremely practical way, but at too great length for me to entertain you with. Repetition, alteration, periodicity, parallelism (or the association of the idea of some desirable vital or spiritual effect with each movement), etc., are laws which he deems highly important. "I am sure," he continues, "that everybody who is able to concentrate thought and will, and to eliminate superfluous emotions, sooner or later becomes a master of his body and can overcome every kind of illness. This is the truth at the bottom of all mind-cures. Our thoughts have a plastic power over the body."

You will be relieved, I doubt not, to hear my excentric correspondent here make connection at last with something you know by heart, namely, 'suggestive therapeutics.' Call his whole performance, if you like, an experiment in methodical self-suggestion. That only makes it more valuable as an illustration of what I wish to impress in as many ways as possible upon your minds, that we habitually live inside our limits of power. Suggestion, especially under hypnosis, is now universally recognized as a means, exceptionally successful in certain persons, of concentrating consciousness, and, in others, of influencing their bodies' states. It throws into gear energies of imagination, of will, and of mental influence over physiological processes, that usually lie dormant, and that can only be thrown into gear at all in chosen subjects. It is, in short, dynamogenic; and the cheapest terms in which to deal with our amateur Yogi's experience is to call it auto-suggestive.

I wrote to him that I couldn't possibly attribute any sacramental value to the particular Hatha Yoga processes, the postures, breathings, fastings, and the like, and that they seemed to me but so many manners, available in his case and his chela's, but not for everybody, of breaking through the barriers which life's routine had concreted round the deeper strata of the will, and gradually bringing its unused energies into action.

He replied as follows: "You are quite right that the Yoga exercises are nothing else than a methodical way of increasing our will. Because we are unable to will at once the most difficult things, we must imagine steps leading to them. Breathing being the easiest of the bodily activities, it is very natural that it offers a good scope for exercise of will. The control of thought could be gained without breathing-discipline, but it is simply easier to control thought simultaneously with the control of breath. Anyone who can think clearly and persistently of one thing needs not breathing exercises. You are quite right that we are not using all our power and that we often learn how much we *can* only when we *must*. . . . The power that we do not use up completely can be brought [more and more] into use by what we call *faith*. Faith is like the manometer of the will, registering its pressure. If I could believe that I can levitate, I could do it. But I cannot believe, and therefore I am clumsily sticking to earth. . . . Now this faith, this power of credulity, can be educated by small efforts. I can breathe at the rate of say twelve times a minute. I can easily believe that I can breathe ten times a minute. When I have accustomed myself to breathe ten times a minute, I learn to believe it will be easy to breathe six times a minute. Thus I have actually learned to breathe at the rate of once a minute. How far I shall progress I do not know. . . . The Yogi goes on in his activity in an even way, without fits of too much or too little, and he is eliminating more and more every unrest, every worry—growing into the infinite by regular training, by small additions to a task which has grown familiar. . . . But you are quite right that religious-crises, love-crises, indignation-crises, may awaken in a very short time powers similar to those reached by years of patient Yoga practice. . . . The Hindus themselves admit that Samadhi can be reached in many ways and with complete disregard of every physical training."

Allowance made for every enthusiasm and exaggeration, there can be no doubt of my friend's regeneration—relatively, at any rate. The second letter, written six months later than the first (ten months after beginning Yoga practice, therefore), says the improvement holds good. He has undergone material trials with indifference, travelled third class on Mediterranean steamers, and fourth class on African trains, living with the poorest Arabs and sharing their unaccustomed food, all with equanimity. His devotion to certain interests has been put to heavy strain, and nothing is more remarkable to me than the changed moral tone with which he reports the situation. Compared with certain earlier letters, these read as if written by a different man, patient and reasonable instead of vehement, self-subordinating instead of imperious. The new tone persists in a communication received only a fortnight ago (fourteen months after beginning training)—there is, in fact, no doubt that profound modification has occurred in the running of his mental machinery. The gearing has changed, and his will is available otherwise than it was. Available without any new ideas, beliefs, or emotions, so far as I can make out, having been implanted in him. He is simply more balanced where he was more unbalanced.

You will remember that he speaks of faith, calling it a 'manometer' of the will. It sounds more natural to call our will the manometer of our faiths. Ideas set free beliefs, and the beliefs set free our wills (I use these terms with no pretension to be 'psychological'), so the will-acts register the faith-pressure within. Therefore, having considered the liberation of our stored-up energy by emotional excitements and by efforts, whether methodical or unmethodical, I must now say a word about *ideas* as our third great dynamogenic agent. Ideas contradict other ideas and keep us from believing them. An idea that thus negates a first idea may itself in turn be negated by a third idea, and the first idea may thus regain its natural influence over our belief and determine our behavior. Our philosophic and religious development proceeds thus by credulities, negations, and the negating of negations.

But whether for arousing or for stopping belief, ideas may fail to be efficacious, just as a wire at one time alive with electricity, may at another time be dead. Here our insight into causes fails us, and we can only note results in general terms. In general, whether a given idea shall be a live idea, depends more on the person into whose mind it is injected than on the idea itself. The whole history of 'suggestion' opens out here. Which are the suggestive ideas for this person, and which for that? Beside the susceptibilities determined by one's education and by one's original peculiarities of character, there are lines along which men simply as men tend to be inflammable by ideas. As certain objects naturally awaken love, anger, or cupidity, so certain ideas naturally awaken the energies of loyalty, courage, endurance, or devotion. When these ideas are effective in an individual's life, their effect is often very great indeed. They may transfigure it, unlocking innumerable powers which, but for the idea, would never have come into play. 'Fatherland,' 'The Union,' 'Holy Church,' the 'Monroe Doctrine,' 'Truth,' 'Science,' 'Liberty,' Garibaldi's phrase 'Rome or Death,' etc., are so many examples of energy-releasing abstract ideas. The *social* nature of all such phrases is an essential factor of their dynamic power. They are forces of detent in situations in which no other force produces equivalent effects, and each is a force of detent only in a specific group of men.

The memory that an oath or vow has been made will nerve one to abstinences and efforts otherwise impossible: witness the 'pledge' in the history of the temperance movement. A mere promise to his sweetheart will clean up a youth's life all over—at any rate for a time. For such effects an educated susceptibility is required. The idea of one's 'honour,' for example, unlocks energy only in those who have had the education of a gentleman, so called.

That delightful being, Prince Pückler-Muskau, writes to his wife from England that he has invented "a sort of artificial resolution respecting things which are difficult of performance." "My device," he says, "is this:—I give my word of honour most solemnly to myself, to do, or to leave undone, this or that. I am of course extremely cautious in the use of this expedient . . . but when once the word is given, even if I afterwards think I have been precipitate or mistaken, I hold it to be perfectly irrevocable, whatever inconveniences I foresee likely to result. . . . If I were capable of breaking my word after such mature consideration, I should lose all respect for myself;—and what man of sense would not prefer death to such an alternative? . . . [When the mysterious formula is pronounced,] no alteration in my own views—nothing short of physical impossibility—must, for the welfare of my soul, alter my will. . . . I find something very satisfactory in the thought, that man has the power of framing such props and weapons out of the most trivial materials, indeed out of nothing, merely by the force of his will, which thereby truly deserves the name of omnipotent."[4]

4 *Tour in England, Ireland, and France*, Philadelphia, 1833, p. 435.

Conversions, whether they be political, scientific, philosophic, or religious, form another way in which bound energies are let loose. They unify, and put a stop to ancient mental interferences. The result is freedom, and often a great enlargement of power. A belief that thus settles upon an individual always acts as a challenge to his will. But, for the particular challenge to operate, he must be the right challeng*ee*. In religious conversions we have so fine an adjustment that the idea may be in the mind of the challengee for years before it exerts effects; and why it should do so then is often so far from obvious that the event is taken for a miracle of grace, and not a natural occurrence. Whatever it is, it may be a highwater mark of energy, in which 'noes,' once impossible, are easy, and in which a new range of 'yeses' gain the right of way.

We are just now witnessing—but our scientific education has unfitted most of us for comprehending the phenomenon—a very copious unlocking of energies by ideas, in the persons of those converts to 'New Thought,' 'Christian Science,' 'Metaphysical Healing,' or other forms of spiritual philosophy, who are so numerous among us to-day. The ideas here are healthy-minded and optimistic; and it is quite obvious that a wave of religious activity, analogous in some respects to the spread of early Christianity, Buddhism, and Mohammedanism is passing over our American world. The common feature of these optimistic faiths is that they all tend to the suppression of what Mr. Horace Fletcher has termed "fearthought." Fearthought he defines as "the self-suggestion of inferiority"; so that one may say that these systems all operate by the suggestion of power. And the power, small or great, comes in various shapes to the individual, power, as he will tell you, not to 'mind' things that used to vex him, power to concentrate his mind, good cheer, good temper; in short, to put it mildly, a firmer, more elastic moral tone. The most genuinely saintly person I have ever known is a friend of mine now suffering from cancer of the breast. I do not assume to judge of the wisdom or unwisdom of her disobedience to the doctors, and I cite her here solely as an example of what ideas can do. Her ideas have kept her a practically well woman for months after she should have given up and gone to bed. They have annulled all pain and weakness and given her a cheerful active life, unusually beneficent to others to whom she has afforded help.

How far the mind-cure movement is destined to extend its influence, or what intellectual modifications it may yet undergo, no one can foretell. Being a religious movement, it will certainly outstrip the purviews of its rationalist critics, such as we here may be supposed to be.

I have thus brought a pretty wide induction to bear upon my thesis, and it appears to hold good. The human individual lives usually far within his limits; he possesses powers of various sorts which he habitually fails to use. He energizes below his maximum, and he behaves below his optimum. In elementary faculty, in coördination, in power of inhibition and control, in every conceivable way, his life is contracted like the field of vision of an hysteric subject—but with less excuse, for the poor hysteric is diseased, while in the rest of us it is only an inveterate *habit*—the habit of inferiority to our full self—that is bad.

Expressed in this vague manner, everyone must admit my thesis to be true. The terms have to remain vague; for though every man of woman born knows what is meant by such phrases as having a good vital tone, a high tide of spirits, an elastic temper, as living energetically, working easily, deciding firmly, and the like, we should all be put to our trumps if asked to explain in terms of scientific psychology just what such expressions mean. We can draw some child-like psychophysical diagrams, and that is all. In physics the conception of 'energy' is perfectly defined. It is correlated with the conception of 'work.' But mental work and moral work, although we cannot live without talking about them, are terms as yet hardly analyzed, and doubtless mean several heterogeneous elementary things. Our muscular work is a voluminous physical quantity, but our ideas and volitions are minute forces of release, and by 'work' here we mean the substitution of higher *kinds* for lower *kinds* of detent. Higher and lower here are qualitative terms, not translatable immediately into quantities, unless indeed they should prove to mean newer or older forms of cerebral organization, and unless newer should then prove to mean cortically more superficial, older, cortically more deep. Some anatomists, as you know, have pretended this; but it is obvious that the intuitive or popular idea of mental work, fundamental and absolutely indispensable as it is in our lives, possesses no degree whatever of scientific clearness to-day.

Here, then, is the first problem that emerges from our study. Can any one of us refine upon the conceptions of mental work and mental energy, so as later to be able to throw some definitely analytic light on what we mean by 'having a more elastic moral tone,' or by 'using higher levels of power and will'? I imagine that we may have to wait long before progress in this direction is made. The problem is too homely; one doesn't see just how to get in the electric keys and revolving drums that alone make psychology scientific to-day.

My fellow-pragmatist in Florence, G. Papini, has adopted a new conception of philosophy. He calls it the *doctrine of action* in the widest sense, the study of all human powers and means (among which latter, *truths* of every kind whatsoever figure, of course, in the first rank). From this point of view philosophy is a *pragmatic*, comprehending, as tributary departments of itself, the old disciplines of logic, metaphysic, physic, and ethic.

And here, after our first problem, two other problems burst upon our view. My belief that these two problems form a program of work well worthy of the attention of a body as learned and earnest as this audience, is, in fact, what has determined me to choose this subject, and to drag you through so many familiar facts during the hour that has sped.

The first of the two problems is *that of our powers*, the second *that of our means of unlocking them or getting at them*. We ought somehow to get a topographic survey made of the limits of human power in every conceivable direction, something like an ophthalmologist's chart of the limits of the human field of vision; and we ought then to construct a methodical inventory of the paths of access, or keys, differing with the diverse types of individual, to the different kinds of power. This would be an absolutely concrete study, to be carried on by using historical and biographical material mainly. The limits of power must be limits that have been realized in actual persons, and the various ways of unlocking the reserves of power must have been exemplified in individual lives. Laboratory experimentation can play but a small part. Your psychologist's *Versuchsthier*, outside of hypnosis, can never be called on to tax his energies in ways as extreme as those which the emergencies of life will force on him.

So here is a program of concrete individual psychology, at which anyone in some measure may work. It is replete with interesting facts, and points to practical issues superior in importance to anything we know. I urge it therefore upon your consideration. In some shape we have all worked at it in a more or less blind and fragmentary way; yet before Papini mentioned it I had never thought of it, or heard it broached by anyone, in the generalized form of a program such as I now suggest, a program that might with proper care be made to cover the whole field of psychology, and might show us parts of it in a very fresh light.

It is just the generalizing of the problem that seems to me to make so strong an appeal. I hope that in some of you the conception may unlock unused reservoirs of investigating power.

The Powers of Men

Everyone knows what it is to start a piece of work, either intellectual or muscular, feeling stale—or *oold*, as an Adirondack guide once put it to me. And everybody knows what it is to "warm up" to his job. The process of warming up gets particularly striking in the phenomenon known as "second wind." On usual occasions we make a practice of stopping an occupation as soon as we meet the first effective layer (so to call it) of fatigue. We have then walked, played, or worked "enough," so we desist. That amount of fatigue is an efficacious obstruction on this side of which our usual life is cast. But if an unusual necessity forces us to press onward, a surprising thing occurs. The fatigue gets worse up to a certain critical point, when gradually or suddenly it passes away, and we are fresher than before. We have evidently tapped a level of new energy, masked until then by the fatigue-obstacle usually obeyed. There may be layer after layer of this experience. A third and a fourth "wind" may supervene. Mental activity shows the phenomenon as well as physical, and in exceptional cases we may find, beyond the very extremity of fatigue-distress, amounts of ease and power that we never dreamed ourselves to own, sources of strength habitually not taxed at all, because habitually we never push through the obstruction, never pass those early critical points.

For many years I have mused on the phenomenon of second wind, trying to find a physiological theory. It is evident that our organism has stored-up reserves of energy that are ordinarily not called upon, but that may be called upon: deeper and deeper strata of combustible or explosible material, discontinuously arranged, but ready for use by anyone who probes so deep, and repairing themselves by rest as well as do the superficial strata. Most of us continue living unnecessarily near our surface. Our energy-budget is like our nutritive budget. Physiologists say that a man is in "nutritive equilibrium" when day after day he neither gains nor loses weight. But the odd thing is that this condition may obtain on astonishingly different amounts of food. Take a man in nutritive equilibrium, and systematically increase or lessen his rations. In the first case he will begin to gain weight, in the second case to lose it. The change will be greatest on the first day, less on the second, less still on the third; and so on, till he has gained all that he will gain, or lost all that he will lose, on that altered diet. He is now in nutritive equilibrium again, but with a new weight; and this neither lessens nor increases because his various combustion-processes have adjusted themselves to the changed dietary. He gets rid, in one way or another, of just as much N, C, H, etc., as he takes in *per diem*.

Just so one can be in what I might call "efficiency-equilibrium" (neither gaining nor losing power when once the equilibrium is reached), on astonishingly different quantities of work, no matter in what direction the work may be measured. It may be physical work, intellectual work, moral work, or spiritual work.

Of course there are limits: the trees don't grow into the sky. But the plain fact remains that men the world over possess amounts of resource, which only very exceptional individuals push to their extremes of use. But the very same individual, pushing his energies to their extreme, may in a vast number of cases keep the pace up day after day, and find no "reaction" of a bad sort, so long as decent hygienic conditions are preserved. His more active rate of energizing does not wreck him; for the organism adapts itself, and as the rate of waste augments, augments correspondingly the rate of repair.

I say the *rate* and not the *time* of repair. The busiest man needs no more hours of rest than the idler. Some years ago Professor Patrick, of the Iowa State University, kept three young men awake for four days and nights. When his observations on them were finished, the subjects were permitted to sleep themselves out. All awoke from this sleep completely refreshed, but the one who took longest to restore himself from his long vigil only slept one-third more time than was regular with him.

If my reader will put together these two conceptions, first, that few men live at their maximum of energy, and second, that anyone may be in vital equilibrium at very different rates of energizing, he will find, I think, that a very pretty practical problem of national economy, as well as of individual ethics, opens upon his view. In rough terms, we may say that a man who energizes below his normal maximum fails by just so much to profit by his chance at life; and that a nation filled with such men is inferior to a nation run at higher pressure. The problem is, then, how can men be trained up to their most useful pitch of energy? And how can nations make such training most accessible to all their sons and daughters. This, after all, is only the general problem of education, formulated in slightly different terms.

"Rough" terms, I said just now, because the words "energy" and "maximum" may easily suggest only *quantity* to the reader's mind, whereas in measuring the human energies of which I speak, qualities as well as quantities have to be taken into account. Everyone feels that his total *power* rises when he passes to a higher *qualitative* level of life.

Writing is higher than walking, thinking is higher than writing, deciding higher than thinking, deciding "no" higher than deciding "yes"—at least the man who passes from one of these activities to another will usually say that each later one involves a greater element of *inner work* than the earlier ones, even though the total heat given out or the foot-pounds expended by the organism, may be less. Just how to conceive this inner work physiologically is as yet impossible, but psychologically we all know what the word means. We need a particular spur or effort to start us upon inner work; it tires us to sustain it; and when long sustained, we know how easily we lapse. When I speak of "energizing," and its rates and levels and sources, I mean therefore our inner as well as our outer work.

Let no one think, then, that our problem of individual and national economy is solely that of the maximum of pounds raisable against gravity, the maximum of locomotion, or of agitation of any sort, that human beings can accomplish. That might signify little more than hurrying and jumping about in inco-ordinated ways;

whereas inner work, though it so often reinforces outer work, quite as often means its arrest. To relax, to say to ourselves (with the "new thoughters") "Peace! be still!" is sometimes a great achievement of inner work. When I speak of human energizing in general, the reader must therefore understand that sum-total of activities, some outer and some inner, some muscular, some emotional, some moral, some spiritual, of whose waxing and waning in himself he is at all times so well aware. How to keep it at an appreciable maximum? How not to let the level lapse? That is the great problem. But the work of men and women is of innumerable kinds, each kind being, as we say, carried on by a particular faculty; so the great problem splits into two subproblems, thus:

(1.) What are the limits of human faculty in various directions?

(2.) By what diversity of means, in the differing types of human beings, may the faculties be stimulated to their best results?

Read in one way, these two questions sound both trivial and familiar: there is a sense in which we have all asked them ever since we were born. Yet *as a methodical programme of scientific inquiry,* I doubt whether they have ever been seriously taken up. If answered fully, almost the whole of mental science and of the science of conduct would find a place under them. I propose, in what follows, to press them on the reader's attention in an informal way.

The first point to agree upon in this enterprise is that *as a rule men habitually use only a small part of the powers which they actually possess and which they might use under appropriate conditions.*

Everyone is familiar with the phenomenon of feeling more or less alive on different days. Everyone knows on any given day that there are energies slumbering in him which the incitements of that day do not call forth, but which he might display if these were greater. Most of us feel as if a sort of cloud weighed upon us, keeping us below our highest notch of clearness in discernment, sureness in reasoning, or firmness in deciding. Compared with what we ought to be, we are only half awake. Our fires are damped, our drafts are checked. We are making use of only a small part of our possible mental and physical resources. In some persons this sense of being cut off from their rightful resources is extreme, and we then get the formidable neurasthenic and psychasthenic conditions, with life grown into one tissue of impossibilities, that so many medical books describe.

Stating the thing broadly, the human individual thus lives usually far within his limits; he possesses powers of various sorts which he habitually fails to use. He energizes below his *maximum*, and he behaves below his *optimum*. In elementary faculty, in co-ordination, in power of *inhibition* and control, in every conceivable way, his life is contracted like the field of vision of an hysteric subject—but with less excuse, for the poor hysteric is diseased, while in the rest of us it is only an inveterate *habit*—the habit of inferiority to our full self—that is bad.

Admit so much, then, and admit also that the charge of being inferior to their full self is far truer of some men than of others; then the practical question ensues: *to what do the better men owe their escape? and, in the fluctuations which all men feel in their own degree of energizing, to what are the improvements due, when they occur?*

In general terms the answer is plain:

Either some unusual stimulus fills them with emotional excitement, or some unusual idea of necessity induces them to make an extra effort of will. *Excitements, ideas, and efforts,* in a word, are what carry us over the dam.

In those "hyperesthetic" conditions which chronic invalidism so often brings in its train, the dam has changed its normal place. The slightest functional exercise gives a distress which the patient yields to and stops. In such cases of "habit-neurosis" a new range of power often comes in consequence of the "bullying-treatment," of efforts which the doctor obliges the patient, much against his will, to make. First comes the very extremity of distress, then follows unexpected relief. There seems no doubt that *we are each and all of us to some extent victims of habit-neurosis.* We have to admit the wider potential range and the habitually narrow actual use. We live subject to arrest by degrees of fatigue which we have come only from habit to obey. Most of us may learn to push the barrier farther off, and to live in perfect comfort on much higher levels of power.

Country people and city people, as a class, illustrate this difference. The rapid rate of life, the number of decisions in an hour, the many things to keep account of, in a busy city man's or woman's life, seem monstrous to a country brother. He doesn't see how we live at all. A day in New York or Chicago fills him with terror. The danger and noise make it appear like a permanent earthquake.

But *settle* him there, and in a year or two he will have caught the pulse-beat. He will vibrate to the city's rhythms; and if he only succeeds in his avocation, whatever that may be, he will find a joy in all the hurry and the tension, he will keep the pace as well as any of us, and get as much out of himself in any week than he ever did in ten weeks in the country.

The stimuli of those who successfully respond and undergo the transformation here, are duty, the example of others, and crowd-pressure and contagion. The transformation moreover is a chronic one: the new level of energy becomes permanent. The duties of new offices of trust are constantly producing this effect on the human beings appointed to them. The physiologists call a stimulus "dynamogenic" when it increases the muscular contractions of men to whom it is applied; but appeals can be dynamogenic morally as well as muscularly. We are witnessing here in America to-day the dynamogenic effect of a very exalted political office upon the energies of an individual who had already manifested a healthy amount of energy before the office came.

Humbler examples show perhaps still better what chronic effects duty's appeal may produce in chosen individuals. John Stuart Mill somewhere says that women excel men in the power of keeping up sustained moral excitement. Every case of illness nursed by wife or mother is a proof of this; and where can one find greater examples of sustained endurance than in those thousands of poor homes, where the woman successfully holds the family together and keeps it going by taking all the thought and doing all the work—nursing, teaching, cooking, washing, sewing, scrubbing, saving, helping neighbors, "choring" outside—where does the catalogue end? If she does a bit of scolding now and then who can blame her? But often she does just the reverse; keeping the children clean and the man good tempered, and soothing and smoothing the whole neighborhood into finer shape.

Eighty years ago a certain Montyon left to the Académie française a sum of money to be given, in small prizes, to the best examples of "virtue" of the year. The Academy's committees, with great good sense, have shown a partiality to virtue's simple and chronic, rather than to her spasmodic and dramatic flights; and the exemplary housewives reported on have been wonderful and admirable enough. In Paul Bourget's report for this year we find numerous cases, of which this is a type: Jeanne Chaix, eldest of six children, mother

152

insane, father chronically ill. Jeanne, with no money but her wages at a pasteboard-box factory, directs the household, brings up the children, and successfully maintains the family of eight, which thus subsists, morally as well as materially, by the sole force of her valiant will. In some of these French cases charity to outsiders is added to the inner family burden; or helpless relatives, young or old, are adopted, as if the strength were inexhaustible and ample for every appeal. Details are too long to quote here; but human nature, responding to the call of duty, appears nowhere sublimer than in the person of these humble heroines of family life.

Turning from more chronic to acuter proofs of human nature's reserves of power, we find that the stimuli that carry us over the usually effective dam are most often the classic emotional ones, love, anger, crowd-contagion or despair. Despair lames most people, but it wakes others fully up. Every siege or shipwreck or polar expedition brings out some hero who keeps the whole company in heart. Last year there was a terrible colliery explosion at Courrières in France. Two hundred corpses, if I remember rightly, were exhumed. After twenty days of excavation, the rescuers heard a voice. "Me voici," said the first man unearthed. He proved to be a collier named Némy, who had taken command of thirteen others in the darkness, disciplined them and cheered them, and brought them out alive. Hardly any of them could see or speak or walk when brought into the day. Five days later, a different type of vital endurance was unexpectedly unburied in the person of one Berton who, isolated from any but dead companions, had been able to sleep away most of his time.

A new position of responsibility will usually show a man to be a far stronger creature than was supposed. Cromwell's and Grant's careers are the stock examples of how war will wake a man up. I owe to Professor C. E. Norton, my colleague, the permission to print part of a private letter from Colonel Baird Smith, written shortly after the six weeks' siege of Delhi in 1857, for the victorious issue of which that excellent officer was chiefly to be thanked. He writes as follows:

. . . My poor wife had some reason to think that war and disease between them had left very little of a husband to take under nursing when she got him again. An attack of camp-scurvy had filled my mouth with sores, shaken every joint in my body, and covered me all over with sores and livid spots, so that I was marvelously unlovely to look upon.

A smart knock on the ankle-joint from the splinter of a shell that burst in my face, in itself a mere bagatelle of a wound, had been of necessity neglected under the pressing and incessant calls upon me, and had grown worse and worse till the whole foot below the ankle became a black mass and seemed to threaten mortification. I insisted, however, on being allowed to use it till the place was taken, mortification or no; and though the pain was sometimes horrible, I carried my point and kept up to the last. On the day after the assault I had an unlucky fall on some bad ground, and it was an open question for a day or two whether I hadn't broken my arm at the elbow. Fortunately it turned out to be only a severe sprain, but I am still conscious of the wrench it gave me. To crown the whole pleasant catalogue, I was worn to a shadow by a constant diarrhœa, and consumed as much opium as would have done credit to my father-in-law [Thomas De Quincey]. However, thank God I have a good share of Tapleyism in me and come out strong under difficulties. I think I may confidently say that no man ever saw me out of heart, or ever heard one croaking word from me even when our prospects were gloomiest. We were sadly scourged by the cholera, and it was almost appalling to me to find that out of twenty-seven officers present, I could only muster fifteen for the operations of the attack. However, it was done, and after it was done came the collapse. Don't be horrified when I tell you that for the whole of the actual siege, and in truth for some little time before, I almost lived on brandy. Appetite for food I had none, but I forced myself to eat just sufficient to sustain life, and I had an incessant craving for brandy as the strongest stimulant I could get. Strange to say, I was quite unconscious of its affecting me in the slightest degree. *The excitement of the work was so great that no lesser one seemed to have any chance against it, and I certainly never found my intellect clearer or my nerves stronger in my life.* It was only my wretched body that was weak, and the moment the real work was done by our becoming complete masters of Delhi, I broke down without delay and discovered that if I wished to live I must continue no longer the system that had kept me up until the crisis was past. With it passed away as if in a moment all desire to stimulate, and a perfect loathing of my late staff of life took possession of me.

Such experiences show how profound is the alteration in the manner in which, under excitement, our organism will sometimes perform its physiological work. The processes of repair become different when the reserves have to be used, and for weeks and months the deeper use may go on.

Morbid cases, here as elsewhere, lay the normal machinery bare. In the first number of Dr. Morton Prince's *Journal of Abnormal*

Psychology, Dr. Janet has discussed five cases of morbid impulse, with an explanation that is precious for my present point of view. One is a girl who eats, eats, eats, all day. Another walks, walks, walks, and gets her food from an automobile that escorts her. Another is a dipsomaniac. A fourth pulls out her hair. A fifth wounds her flesh and burns her skin. Hitherto such freaks of impulse have received Greek names (as bulimia, dromomania, etc.) and been scientifically disposed of as "episodic syndromata of hereditary degeneration." But it turns out that Janet's cases are all what he calls psychasthenics, or victims of a chronic sense of weakness, torpor, lethargy, fatigue, insufficiency, impossibility, unreality, and powerlessness of will; and that in each and all of them the particular activity pursued, deleterious though it be, has the temporary result of raising the sense of vitality and making the patient feel alive again. These things reanimate; they would reanimate *us*; but it happens that in each patient the particular freak-activity chosen is the only thing that does reanimate; and therein lies the morbid state. The way to treat such persons is to discover to them more usual and useful ways of throwing their stores of vital energy into gear.

Colonel Baird Smith, needing to draw on altogether extraordinary stores of energy, found that brandy and opium were ways of throwing them into gear.

Such cases are humanly typical. We are all to some degree oppressed, unfree. We don't come to our own. It is there, but we don't get at it. The threshold must be made to shift. Then many of us find that an excentric activity—a "spree," say—relieves. There is no doubt that to some men sprees and excesses of almost any kind are medicinal, temporarily at any rate, in spite of what the moralists and doctors say.

But when the normal tasks and stimulations of life don't put a man's deeper levels of energy on tap, and he requires distinctly deleterious excitements, his constitution verges on the abnormal. The normal opener of deeper and deeper levels of energy is the will. The difficulty is to use it, to make the effort which the word volition implies. But if we *do* make it (or if a god, though he were only the god Chance, makes it through us), it will act dynamogenically on us for a month. It is notorious that a single successful effort of moral volition, such as saying "no" to some habitual temptation, or performing some courageous act, will launch a man on a higher level of energy for days and weeks, will give him a new range of power. "In the act of uncorking the whiskey bottle which I had brought home to get drunk upon," said a man to me, "I suddenly found myself running out into the garden, where I smashed it on the ground. I felt so happy and uplifted after this act, that for two months I wasn't tempted to touch a drop."

The emotions and excitements due to usual situations are the usual inciters of the will. But these act discontinuously; and in the intervals the shallower levels of life tend to close in and shut us off. Accordingly the best practical knowers of the human soul have invented the thing known as methodical ascetic discipline to keep the deeper levels constantly in reach. Beginning with easy tasks, passing to harder ones, and exercising day by day, it is, I believe, admitted that disciples of asceticism can reach very high levels of freedom and power of will.

Ignatius Loyola's spiritual exercises must have produced this result in innumerable devotees. But the most venerable ascetic system, and the one whose results have the most voluminous experimental corroboration is undoubtedly the Yoga system in Hindostan. From time immemorial, by Hatha Yoga, Raja Yoga, Karma Yoga, or whatever code of practice it might be, Hindu aspirants to perfection have trained themselves, month in and out, for years. The result claimed, and certainly in many cases accorded by impartial judges, is strength of character, personal power, unshakeability of soul. In an article in the *Philosophical Review* for January last, from which I am largely copying here, I have quoted at great length the experience with "Hatha Yoga" of a very gifted European friend of mine, who by persistently carrying out for several months its methods of fasting from food and sleep, its exercises in breathing and thought-concentration, and its fantastic posture-gymnastics, seems to have succeeded in waking up deeper and deeper levels of will and moral and intellectual power in himself, and to have escaped from a decidedly menacing brain-condition of the "circular" type, from which he had suffered for years.

Judging by my friend's letters, of which the last I have is written fourteen months after the Yoga training began, there can be no doubt of his relative regeneration. He has undergone material trials with indifference, traveled third-class on Mediterranean steamers, and fourth-class on African trains, living with the poorest Arabs and sharing their unaccustomed food, all with equanimity. His devotion to certain interests has been put to heavy strain, and nothing is more remarkable to me than the changed moral tone with which he reports the situation. Compared with certain earlier letters, these read as if written by a different man, patient and reasonable instead of vehement, self-subordinating instead of imperious. A profound modification has unquestionably occurred in the running of his mental machinery. The gearing has changed, and his will is available otherwise than it was.

My friend is a man of very peculiar temperament. Few of us would have had the will to start upon the Yoga training, which, once started, seemed to conjure the further will-power needed out of itself. And not all of those who could launch themselves would have reached the same results. The Hindus themselves admit that in some men the results may come without call or bell. My friend writes to me: "You are quite right in thinking that religious crises, love-crises, indignation-crises may awaken in a very short time powers similar to those reached by years of patient Yoga-practice."

Probably most medical men would treat this individual's case as one of what it is fashionable now to call by the name of "self-suggestion," or "expectant attention"—as if those phrases were explanatory, or meant more than the fact that certain men can be influenced, while others cannot be influenced, by certain sorts of *ideas*. This leads me to say a word about ideas considered as dynamogenic agents, or stimuli for unlocking what would otherwise be unused reservoirs of individual power.

One thing that ideas do is to contradict other ideas and keep us from believing them. An idea that thus negates a first idea may itself in turn be negated by a third idea, and the first idea may thus regain its natural influence over our belief and determine our behavior. Our philosophic and religious development proceeds thus by credulities, negations and the negating of negations.

But whether for arousing or for stopping belief, ideas may fail to be efficacious, just as a wire at one time alive with electricity, may at another time be dead. Here our insight into causes fails us, and we can only note results in general terms. In general, whether a given idea shall be a live idea, depends more on the person into whose mind it is injected than on the idea itself. Which is the suggestive idea for this person, and which for that one? Mr. Fletcher's disciples regenerate themselves by the idea (and the fact) that they are chewing, and re-chewing, and super-chewing their food. Dr.

Dewey's pupils regenerate themselves by going without their break-fast—a fact, but also an ascetic idea. Not everyone can use *these* ideas with the same success.

But apart from such individually varying susceptibilities, there are common lines along which men simply as men tend to be in-flammable by ideas. As certain objects naturally awaken love, anger, or cupidity, so certain ideas naturally awaken the energies of loyalty, courage, endurance, or devotion. When these ideas are effective in an individual's life, their effect is often very great indeed. They may transfigure it, unlocking innumerable powers which, but for the idea, would never have come into play. "Fatherland," "the Flag," "the Union," "Holy Church," "the Monroe Doctrine," "Truth," "Science," "Liberty," Garibaldi's phrase "Rome or Death," etc., are so many examples of energy-releasing ideas. The social nature of such phrases is an essential factor of their dynamic power. They are forces of detent in situations in which no other force produces equivalent effects, and each is a force of detent only in a specific group of men.

The memory that an oath or vow has been made will nerve one to abstinences and efforts otherwise impossible; witness the "pledge" in the history of the temperance movement. A mere promise to his sweetheart will clean up a youth's life all over—at any rate for a time. For such effects an educated susceptibility is required. The idea of one's "honor," for example, unlocks energy only in those of us who have had the education of a "gentleman," so called.

That delightful being, Prince Pückler-Muskau, writes to his wife from England that he has invented "a sort of artificial resolu-tion respecting things that are difficult of performance. My device," he continues, "is this: *I give my word of honour most solemnly to myself* to do or to leave undone this or that. I am of course ex-tremely cautious in the use of this expedient, but when once the word is given, even though I afterwards think I have been precipi-tate or mistaken, I hold it to be perfectly irrevocable, whatever in-conveniences I foresee likely to result. If I were capable of breaking my word after such mature consideration, I should lose all respect for myself—and what man of sense would not prefer death to such an alternative? . . . When the mysterious formula is pronounced, no alteration in my own views, nothing short of physical impossibili-ties, must, for the welfare of my soul, alter my will. . . . I find something very satisfactory in the thought that man has the power of framing such props and weapons out of the most trivial materials, indeed out of nothing, merely by the force of his will, which thereby truly deserves the name of omnipotent."[1]

Conversions, whether they be political, scientific, philosophic, or religious, form another way in which bound energies are let loose. They unify us, and put a stop to ancient mental interferences. The result is freedom, and often a great enlargement of power. A belief that thus settles upon an individual always acts as a challenge to his will. But, for the particular challenge to operate, he must be the right challeng*ee*. In religious conversions we have so fine an adjustment that the idea may be in the mind of the challengee for years before it exerts effects; and why it should do so then is often so far from obvious that the event is taken for a miracle of grace, and not a natural occurrence. Whatever it is, it may be a highwater mark of energy, in which "noes," once impossible, are easy, and in which a new range of "yeses" gains the right of way.

We are just now witnessing a very copious unlocking of energies by ideas, in the persons of those converts to "New Thought," "Christian Science," "Metaphysical Healing," or other forms of spiritual philosophy, who are so numerous among us to-day. The ideas here are healthy-minded and optimistic; and it is quite obvious that a wave of religious activity, analogous in some respects to the spread of early Christianity, Buddhism, and Mohammedanism is passing over our American world. The common feature of these optimistic faiths is that they all tend to the suppression of what Mr. Horace Fletcher calls "fearthought." Fearthought he defines as the "self-suggestion of inferiority"; so that one may say that these systems all operate by the suggestion of power. And the power, small or great, comes in various shapes to the individual,—power, as he will tell you, not to "mind" things that used to vex him, power to concentrate his mind, good cheer, good temper—in short, to put it mildly, a firmer, more elastic moral tone.

The most genuinely saintly person I have ever known is a friend of mine now suffering from cancer of the breast—I hope that she may pardon my citing her here as an example of what ideas can do. Her ideas have kept her a practically well woman for months after she should have given up and gone to bed. They have annulled all pain and weakness and given her a cheerful active life, unusually beneficent to others to whom she has afforded help. Her doctors, ac-

---

[1] *Tour in England, Ireland, and France,* Philadelphia, 1833, p. 435.

quiescing in results they could not understand, have had the good sense to let her go her own way.

How far the mind-cure movement is destined to extend its influence, or what intellectual modifications it may yet undergo, no one can foretell. It is essentially a religious movement, and to academically nurtured minds its utterances are tasteless and often grotesque enough. It also incurs the natural enmity of medical politicians, and of the whole trades-union wing of that profession. But no unprejudiced observer can fail to recognize its importance as a social phenomenon to-day, and the higher medical minds are already trying to interpret it fairly, and make its power available for their own therapeutic ends.

Dr. Theophilus Hyslop of the great West Riding Asylum in England said last year to the British medical association that the best sleep-producing agent which his practice had revealed to him was *prayer*. I say this, he added [I am sorry here that I must quote from memory], purely as a medical man. The exercise of prayer, in those who habitually exert it, must be regarded by us doctors as the most adequate and normal of all the pacifiers of the mind and calmers of the nerves.

But in few of us are functions not tied up by the exercise of other functions. Relatively few medical men and scientific men, I fancy, can pray. Few can carry on any living commerce with "God." Yet many of us are well aware of how much freer and abler our lives would be, were such important forms of energizing not sealed up by the critical atmosphere in which we have been reared. There are in everyone potential forms of activity that actually are shunted out from use. Part of the imperfect vitality under which we labor can thus be easily explained. One part of our mind dams up—even *damns* up!—the other parts.

Conscience makes cowards of us all. Social conventions prevent us from telling the truth after the fashion of the heroes and heroines of Bernard Shaw. We all know persons who are models of excellence, but who belong to the extreme philistine type of mind. So deadly is their intellectual respectability that we can't converse about certain subjects at all, can't let our minds play over them, can't even mention them in their presence. I have numbered among my dearest friends persons thus inhibited intellectually, with whom I would gladly have been able to talk freely about certain interests of mine, certain authors, say, as Bernard Shaw, Chesterton, Edward

Carpenter, H. G. Wells, but it wouldn't do, it made them too uncomfortable, they wouldn't play, I had to be silent. An intellect thus tied down by literality and decorum makes on one the same sort of impression that an able-bodied man would who should habituate himself to do his work with only one of his fingers, locking up the rest of his organism and leaving it unused.

I trust that by this time I have said enough to convince the reader both of the truth and of the importance of my thesis. The two questions, first, that of the possible extent of our powers; and, second, that of the various avenues of approach to them, the various keys for unlocking them in diverse individuals, dominate the whole problem of individual and national education. We need a topography of the limits of human power, similar to the chart which oculists use of the field of human vision. We need also a study of the various types of human being, with reference to the different ways in which their energy-reserves may be appealed to and set loose. Biographies and individual experiences of every kind may be drawn upon for evidence here.

The Moral Equivalent of War

The war against war is going to be no holiday excursion or camping party. The military feelings are too deeply grounded to abdicate their place among our ideals until better substitutes are offered than the glory and shame that come to nations as well as to individuals from the ups and downs of politics and the vicissitudes of trade. There is something highly paradoxical in the modern man's relation to war. Ask all our millions, north and south, whether they would vote now (were such a thing possible) to have our war for the Union expunged from history, and the record of a peaceful transition to the present time substituted for that of its marches and battles, and probably hardly a handful of excentrics would say yes. Those ancestors, those efforts, those memories and legends, are the most ideal part of what we now own together, a sacred spiritual possession worth more than all the blood poured out. Yet ask those same people whether they would be willing in cold blood to start another civil war now to gain another similar possession, and not one man or woman would vote for the proposition. In modern eyes, precious tho' wars may be, they must not be waged solely for the sake of the ideal harvest. Only when forced upon one, only when an enemy's injustice leaves us no alternative, is a war now thought permissible.

It was not thus in ancient times. The earlier men were hunting men; and to hunt a neighboring tribe, kill the males, loot the village and possess the females, was the most profitable, as well as the most exciting, way of living. Thus were the more martial tribes selected, and in chiefs and peoples a pure pugnacity and love of glory came to mingle with the more fundamental appetite for plunder.

Modern war is so expensive that we feel trade to be a better avenue to plunder; but modern man inherits all the innate pugnacity and all the love of glory of his ancestors. To show war's irrationality and horror has no effect upon him. The horrors make the fascination. War is the *strong* life; it is life *in extremis*. War-taxes are the only ones men never hesitate to pay, as the budgets of all nations show.

History is a bath of blood. The Iliad is one long recital of how Diomedes and Ajax, Sarpedon and Hector *killed*. No detail of the wounds they made is spared us, and the greek mind fed upon the story. Greek history is a panorama of jingoism and imperialism— war for war's sake, all the citizens being warriors. It is horrible reading, because of the irrationality of it all—save for the purpose of making 'history'—and the history is that of the utter ruin of a civilization which in intellectual respects was perhaps the highest the earth has ever seen.

Those wars were purely piratical. Pride, gold, women, slaves, excitement, were their only motives. In the Peloponnesian war, for example, the Athenians ask the inhabitants of Melos (the island where the 'Venus of Melos' was found), hitherto neutral, to acknowledge their lordship. The envoys meet, and hold a debate which Thucydides gives in full, and which, for sweet reasonableness of form, would have satisfied a Matthew Arnold. "The powerful exact what they can," said the Athenians, "and the weak grant what they must." When the Meleans say that sooner than be slaves they will appeal to the gods, the Athenians reply: "Of the gods we believe, and of men we know, that by a law of their nature wherever they can rule they will. This law was not made by us, and we are not the first who have acted upon it; we did but inherit it, . . . and we know that you and all mankind, if you were as strong as we are, would do as we do. So much for the gods; we have told you why we expect to stand as high in their good opinion as you." Well, the Meleans still refused, and their town was taken. "The Athenians," Thucydides quietly says, "thereupon put to death all who were of military age, and made slaves of the women and children. They then colonised the island, sending thither five hundred settlers of their own."

Alexander's career was piracy pure and simple, nothing but an orgy of power and plunder, made romantic by the character of the hero. There was no rational principle in it, and the moment he died his generals and governors attacked one another. The cruelty of those times is incredible. When Rome finally conquered Greece, Paulus Aemilius was told by the Roman Senate to reward his soldiers for their toil by 'giving' them the old kingdom of Epirus. They sacked seventy cities and carried off a hundred and fifty thousand inhabitants as slaves. How many they killed I know not; but in Aetolia they killed all the senators, five hundred and fifty in number. Brutus was 'the noblest Roman of them all,' yet to reanimate his soldiers on the eve of Philippi he promises to give them the cities of Sparta and Thessalonica to ravage, if they win the fight.

Such was the gory nurse that trained societies to cohesiveness. We inherit the warlike type; and for most of the capacity of heroism of which the human race is full we have to thank this cruel history. Dead men tell no tales, and if there were tribes of other type than this, they have left no survivors. Our ancestors have bred pugnacity into our bone and marrow, and thousands of years of peace won't breed it out of us. The popular imagination fairly fattens on the thought of wars. Let public opinion once reach a certain fighting pitch, and no ruler can withstand it. In the Boer war both governments began with bluff; but they couldn't stay there—the military tension was too much for them. In 1898 our people had read the word WAR in letters three inches high in every newspaper for three months. The pliant politician McKinley was swept away by their eagerness, and our squalid war with Spain became a necessity.

At the present day, civilized opinion is a curious mental mixture. The military instincts and ideals are as strong as ever, but they are confronted by reflective criticisms which sorely curb their ancient freedom. Innumerable writers are showing up the bestial side of military service. Pure loot and mastery seem no longer morally avowable motives, and pretexts must be found for attributing them solely to the enemy. England and we, our army and navy authorities repeat without ceasing, arm solely for 'peace'; Germany and Japan it is who are bent on loot and glory. 'Peace' in military mouths to day is a synonym for 'war expected.' The word has become a pure provocative, and no government sincerely wishing peace should allow it ever to be printed in a newspaper. Every up-to-date Dictionary should say that 'peace' and 'war' mean the same thing, now *in posse*, now *in actu*. It may even reasonably be said that the intensely sharp competitive *preparation* for war by the nations is the *real war*, permanent, unceasing; and that the battles are only a sort of public verification of the military mastery gained during the 'peace'-interval.

It is plain that on this subject civilized man has developed a sort of double personality. If we take european nations, no legitimate interest of any one of them would seem to justify the tremendous destructions which a war (to compass it) would necessarily entail. It would seem as tho' common sense and reason ought to find a way to reach agreement in every conflict of honest interests. I myself think it our bounden duty to believe in international rationality as far as possible. But, as things stand, I see how desperately hard it is to bring the peace-party and the war-party together. I believe that the difficulty is due to certain deficiencies in the program of pacificism which set the militarist imagination strongly, and to a certain extent justifiably, against it. In the whole discussion both sides are on imaginative and sentimental ground. It is but one utopia against another, and everything one says must be abstract and hypothetical. Subject to this criticism and caution, I shall try to characterize in abstract strokes the opposite imaginative forces, and point out what to my own very fallible mind seems the best utopian hypothesis, the most promising line of conciliation.

In my remarks, pacificist tho' I am, I shall refuse to speak of the bestial side of the war-régime (already done justice to by so many writers) and consider only the higher aspects of militaristic sentiment. Patriotism no one thinks discreditable; nor does anyone deny that war is the romance of history. But inordinate ambitions are the soul of all patriotism, and the possibility of violent death the soul of all romance. The militarily patriotic and romantic-minded, and especially the professional military class, refuse to admit for a moment that war may be a transitory phenomenon in social evolution. The notion of a sheep's paradise like that revolts, they say, our higher imagination. Where then would be the steeps of life? If war had ever stopped, we should have to re-invent it, in their view, to redeem life from flat degeneration.

All reflective apologists for war at the present day take it religiously. It is to them a sort of sacrament; its profits are to the vanquished as well as to the victor; and quite apart from any question of profit, it is an absolute good, we are told, for it is human nature at its highest dynamic. Its 'horrors' are a cheap price to pay for rescue from the only alternative supposed, of a world of clerks and teachers, of co-education and zoophily, of 'consumers' leagues' and 'associated charities,' of industrialism unlimited, and feminism unabashed. No scorn, no hardness, no valor any more! Fie upon such a cattleyard of a planet!

So far as the central essence of this feeling goes, no healthy-minded person, it seems to me, can help partaking of it to some degree. Militarism is the great preserver of our ideals of hardihood, and human life without hardihood would be contemptible. Without risks or prizes for the darer, history would be insipid indeed; and there is a type of military character which everyone feels that the race should never cease to breed, for everyone is sensitive to its superiority. The duty is incumbent on mankind, of keeping military characters in stock—of keeping them, if not for use, then as ends in themselves and as pure pieces of perfection—so that Roosevelt's weaklings and mollycoddles may not end by making everything else disappear from the face of nature.

This natural feeling forms, I think, the innermost soul of army-writings. Without any exception known to me, militarist authors take a highly mystical view of their subject, and regard war as a biological or sociological necessity, uncontrolled by ordinary psychological checks and motives. When the time of development is ripe the war must come, reason or no reason, for the justifications pleaded are invariably fictitious. War is, in short, a permanent human *obligation*. General Homer Lea, in his recent book *The Valor of Ignorance*, plants himself squarely on this ground. Readiness for war is for him the essence of nationality, and ability in it the supreme measure of the health of nations.

Nations, General Lea says, are never stationary—they must necessarily expand or shrink, according to their vitality or decrepitude. Japan now is culminating; and by the fatal law in question it is impossible that her statesmen should not long since have entered, with extraordinary foresight, upon a vast policy of conquest—the game in which the first moves were her wars with China and Russia and her treaty with England, and of which the final objective is the capture of the Philippines, the Hawaiian Islands, Alaska, and the whole of our Coast west of the Sierra Passes. This will give Japan what her ineluctable vocation as a state absolutely forces her to claim, the possession of the entire Pacific Ocean; and to oppose these deep designs we Americans have, according to our author, nothing but our conceit, our ignorance, our commercialism, our corruption, and our feminism. General Lea makes a minute technical comparison of the military strength that we at present could oppose to the strength of Japan, and concludes that the Islands, Alaska, Oregon and Southern California would fall almost without resistance, that San Francisco must surrender in a fortnight to a japanese investment, and that in three or four months the war would be over, and our republic, unable to regain what it had heedlessly neglected to protect sufficiently, would then 'disintegrate,' until perhaps some Caesar should arise to weld us again into a nation.

A dismal forecast indeed! Yet not absolutely unplausible, if the mentality of Japan's statesmen be of the Caesarian type of which history shows so many examples, and which is all that General Lea seems able to imagine. There is no reason to think, after all, that women can no longer be the mothers of Napoleonic or Alexandrian characters; and if these characters should appear in Japan and find their opportunity, just such surprises as *The Valor of Ignorance* paints may lurk in ambush for us. Ignorant as we still are of the innermost recesses of japanese mentality, we may be foolhardy in disregarding such possibilities.

Other militarists are more complex and more moral in their considerations. The *Philosophie des Krieges* by S. R. Steinmetz is a good example. War, according to this author, is an ordeal instituted by God, who weighs the nations in its balance. It is the essential form of the State, and the only function in which peoples can employ all their powers at once and convergently. No victory is possible save as the resultant of a totality of virtues, no defeat for which some vice or weakness is not responsible. Fidelity, cohesiveness, tenacity, heroism, conscience, education, inventiveness, economy, wealth, physical health and vigor—there isn't a moral or intellectual point of superiority that doesn't tell, when God holds his assizes and hurls the peoples upon one another. *Die Weltgeschichte ist das Weltgericht*; and Dr. Steinmetz does not believe that in the long run chance and luck play any part in apportioning the issues.

The virtues that prevail, it must be noted, are virtues anyhow, superiorities that count in peaceful as well as in military competition; but the strain on them, being infinitely intenser in the latter case, makes war infinitely more searching as a trial. No ordeal, according to this author, can be comparable to its winnowings. Its dread hammer is the welder of men into cohesive states, and nowhere but in such states can human nature adequately develope its capacity. The only alternative is 'degeneration.'

Dr. Steinmetz is a conscientious thinker, and his book, short as it is, takes much into account. Its upshot, it seems to me, can be summed up in Simon Patten's word, that mankind was nursed in pain and fear, and that the transition to a 'pleasure-economy' may be fatal to a being untrained to powers of defense against its disintegrative influences. If we speak of *the fear of emancipation from the fear-régime,* we put the militarist attitude into a single phrase: fear regarding ourselves now taking the place of the ancient fear of the enemy.

Turn the fear over in my mind as I will, it all seems to lead back to two unwillingnesses of the imagination, one esthetic, and the other moral: unwillingness, first, to envisage a future in which army-life, with its many elements of charm, shall be forever impossible, and in which the destinies of peoples shall nevermore be decided quickly, thrillingly, and tragically by force, but only gradually and insipidly by 'evolution'; and, secondly, unwillingness to see the supreme theatre of human strenuousness closed, and the splendid military aptitudes of men doomed to remain always in a state of latency and never to show themselves in action. These insistent unwillingnesses, no less than other esthetic and ethical insistencies, have, it seems to me, to be listened to and respected. One cannot meet them effectively by mere counter-insistency on war's expensiveness and horror. The horror makes the thrill; and when it is a question of getting the extremest and supremest out of human nature, talk of expense sounds ignominious. The weakness of so much merely negative criticism is evident—pacificism makes no converts from the military party. The military party denies neither the bestiality nor the horror, nor the expense; it only says that these things tell but half the story. It only says that war is *worth* these things; that, taking human nature as a whole, wars are its best protection against its weaker and more cowardly self, and that mankind cannot afford to adopt a peace-economy.

Pacificists ought to enter more deeply into the esthetical and ethical point of view of their opponents. Do that first in any controversy, says J. J. Chapman, *then move the point,* and your opponent will follow. So long as anti-militarists propose no substitutes for the disciplinary function of war, no *moral equivalent* of war, analogous, as one might say, to the mechanical equivalent of heat, so long they fail to realize the full inwardness of the situation. And as a rule they do fail. The duties, penalties and sanctions pictured in the utopias they paint are all too weak and tame to touch the military-minded. Tolstoy's pacificism is the only exception to this rule, for it is profoundly pessimistic as regards all this world's values, and makes the fear of the Lord furnish the moral spur provided elsewhere by the fear of the enemy. But our socialistic peace-advocates all believe absolutely in this world's values; and instead of the fear of the Lord and the fear of the enemy, the only fear they reckon with is the fear of poverty if one be lazy. This weakness pervades all the socialistic literature with which I am acquainted. Even in Lowes Dickinson's exquisite dialogue,[1] high wages and short hours are the only forces invoked for overcoming man's distaste for repulsive kinds of labor. Meanwhile men at large still live as they always have lived, under a pain-and-fear economy—for those of us who live in an ease-economy are but an island in the stormy ocean—and the whole atmosphere of present-day utopian literature tastes mawkish and dishwatery to people who still keep a sense for life's more bitter flavors. It suggests, in truth, ubiquitous inferiority.

Inferiority is always with us, and merciless scorn of it is the keynote of the military temper. "Hounds, would you live forever?" shouted Frederick the Great. "Yes," say our utopians, "let us live forever, and raise our level gradually." The best thing about our 'inferiors' to day is that they are as tough as nails, and physically and morally almost as insensitive. Utopianism would see them soft and squeamish, while militarism would keep their callousness, but transfigure it into a meritorious characteristic, needed by 'the service,' and redeemed by that from the suspicion of inferiority. All the qualities of a man acquire dignity when he knows that the service of the collectivity that owns him needs them. If proud of the collectivity, his own pride rises in proportion. No collectivity is like an army for nourishing such pride; but it has to be confessed that the only sentiment that the image of pacific cosmopolitan industrialism is capable of arousing in countless worthy breasts is shame at the idea of belonging to *such* a collectivity. It is obvious that the United States of America as they exist to day impress a mind like General

[1] *Justice and Liberty*, N. Y., 1909.

Lea's as so much human blubber. Where is the sharpness and precipitousness, the contempt for life, whether one's own, or another's?
Where is the savage 'yes' and 'no,' the unconditional duty? Where
is the conscription? Where is the blood-tax? Where is anything that
one feels honoured by belonging to?

Having said thus much in preparation, and by way of conciliating the side I don't belong to, I will now confess my own utopia.
I devoutly believe in the ultimate reign of peace and in the gradual
advent of some sort of a socialistic equilibrium. The fatalistic view
of the war-function is to me nonsense, for I know that war-making
is due to definite motives and subject to prudential checks and reasonable criticisms, just like any other form of enterprise. And
when whole nations are the armies, and the science of destruction
vies in intellectual refinement with the sciences of production, I
see that war becomes absurd and impossible from its own monstrosity. Extravagant ambitions will have to be replaced by reasonable claims, and nations must make common cause against them.
I see no reason why all this should not apply to yellow as well as
to white nations, and I look forward to a future when acts of war
shall be formally outlawed among civilized peoples.

All these beliefs of mine put me squarely into the anti-militarist
party. But I do not believe that peace either ought to be or will be
permanent on this globe, unless the states pacifically organized preserve some of the old elements of army-discipline. A permanently
successful peace-economy cannot be a simple pleasure-economy. In
the more or less socialistic future towards which mankind seems to
be drifting we must still subject ourselves collectively to those severities that answer to our real position upon this only partly
hospitable globe. We must make new energies and hardihoods
continue the manliness to which the military mind so faithfully
clings. Martial virtues must be the enduring cement; intrepidity,
contempt of softness, surrender of private interest, obedience to
command, must still remain the rock upon which states are built—
unless, indeed, we wish for dangerous reactions against commonwealths fit only for contempt, and liable to invite attack whenever
a centre of crystallization for military-minded enterprise is formed
anywhere in their neighborhood.

The war-party is assuredly right in affirming and reaffirming that
the martial virtues, altho' originally gained by the race through
war, are absolute and permanent human goods. Patriotic pride and

ambition in their military form are, after all, only specifications of a more universal and enduring competitive passion. They are its first form, but that is no reason for supposing them to be its last form. Men now are proud of belonging to a conquering nation, and without a murmur they lay down their persons and their wealth, if by so doing they may fend off subjection. But who can be sure that *other aspects of one's country* may not, with time and education and suggestion enough, come to be regarded with similarly effective feelings of pride and shame? Why should men not some day feel that it is worth a blood-tax to belong to a collectivity superior in *any* ideal respect? Why should they not blush with indignant shame if the community that owns them is vile in any way whatsoever? Individuals, daily more numerous, now feel this civic passion. It is only a question of blowing on the spark till the whole population gets incandescent, and on the ruins of the old morals of military honour, a stable system of morals of civic honour builds itself up. What the whole community comes to believe in grasps the individual as in a vise. The war-function has graspt us so far; but constructive interests may some day seem no less imperative, and impose on the individual a hardly lighter burden.

Let me illustrate my idea more concretely. There is nothing to make one indignant in the mere fact that life is hard, that men should toil and suffer pain. The planetary conditions once for all are such, and we can stand it. But that so many men, by mere accidents of birth and opportunity, should have a life of *nothing else* but toil and pain and hardness and inferiority imposed upon them, should have *no* vacation, while others natively no more deserving get no taste of this campaigning life at all—*this* is capable of arousing indignation in reflective minds. It may end by seeming shameful to all of us that some of us have nothing but campaigning, and others have nothing but unmanly ease. If now—and this is my idea —there were, instead of military conscription a conscription of the whole youthful population to form for a certain number of years a part of the army enlisted against *nature*, the injustice would tend to be evened out, and numerous other benefits to the commonwealth would follow. The military ideals of hardihood and discipline would be wrought into the growing fibre of the people; no one would remain blind, as the luxurious classes now are blind, to man's real relations to the globe he lives on, and to the permanently solid and hard foundations of his higher life. To coal and iron mines, to freight trains, to fishing fleets in December, to dish-washing, clothes-washing, and window-washing, to road-building and tunnel-making, to foundries and stoke-holes, and to the frames of skyscrapers, would our gilded youths be drafted off, according to their choice, to get the childishness knocked out of them, and to come back into society with healthier sympathies and soberer ideas. They would have paid their blood-tax, done their own part in im-memorial human warfare against nature, they would tread the earth more proudly, the women would value them more highly, they would be better fathers and teachers of the following generation.

Such a conscription, with the state of public opinion that would have required it, and the moral fruits it would bear, would pre-serve in the midst of a pacific civilization the manly virtues which the military party is so afraid of seeing disappear in peace. We should get toughness without callousness, authority with as little criminal cruelty as possible, and painful work done cheerily because the duty is temporary, and threatens not, as now, to degrade the whole re-mainder of one's life. I spoke of the 'moral equivalent' of war. So far, war has been the only force that can discipline a whole com-munity, and until an equivalent discipline is organized, I believe that war must have its way. But I have no serious doubt that the ordinary prides and shames of social man, once developed to a cer-tain intensity, are capable of organizing such a moral equivalent as I have sketched, or some other just as effective for preserving man-liness of type. Tho' an infinitely remote utopia just now, in the end it is but a question of time, of skilful propagandism, and of opinion-making men seizing historic opportunities.

The martial type of character can be bred without war. Strenu-ous honour and disinterestedness abound elsewhere. Priests and medical men are in a fashion educated to it, and we should all feel some degree of it imperative if we were conscious of our work as an obligatory service to the state. We should be *owned*, as soldiers are by the army, and our pride would rise accordingly. We could be poor, then, without humiliation, as army officers now are. The only thing needed henceforward is to inflame the civic temper as past history has inflamed the military temper.

"In many ways," says H. G. Wells, "military organisation is the most peaceful of activities. When the contemporary man steps from the street of clamorous insincere advertisement, push, adulteration, underselling and intermittent employment, into the barrack-yard, he steps on to a higher social plane, into an atmosphere of service and co-operation and of infinitely more honourable emulations. Here at least men are not flung out of employment to degenerate because there is no immediate work for them to do. They are fed and drilled and trained for better services. Here at least a man is supposed to win promotion by self-forgetfulness and not by self-seeking."[2] Bad as barrack life may be, it is very congruous with ancestral human nature, and it has the higher aspects which Wells thus emphasizes. Wells adds[3] that he thinks that the conceptions of order and discipline, the tradition of service and devotion, of physical fitness, unstinted exertion, and universal responsibility, which universal military duty is now teaching european nations, will remain a permanent acquisition, when the last ammunition has been used in the fireworks that celebrate the final peace. I believe as he does. It would be simply preposterous if the only force that could work ideals of honour and standards of efficiency into english or american natures should be the fear of being killed by the Germans or the Japanese. Great indeed is Fear; but it is not, as our military enthusiasts believe and try to make us believe, the only stimulus known for awakening the higher ranges of men's spiritual energy. The amount of alteration in public opinion that my utopia postulates is vastly less than the difference between the mentality of those black warriors who pursued Stanley's party on the Congo with their cannibal war-cry of 'Meat! meat!' and that of the 'general-staff' of any civilized nation. History has seen the latter interval bridged over: the former one can be bridged over much more easily.

[2] *First and Last Things*, 1908, p. 215.
[3] *Ibid.*, p. 226.

Notes

Notes

The William James Collection is housed in the Houghton Library of Harvard University. It can be identified by the call number 'MS Am 1092', with, sometimes, either 'b' or 'f' as a prefix and a decimal following the numeral '2'. Many books from James's library are also preserved there; many of these are sufficiently identified by their call numbers which begin either with 'WJ' or 'AC'. Other books from his library are in Harvard's Widener Library and elsewhere, and in such cases their location is stated. Still others were sold and have not been located. However, Ralph Barton Perry made a list, noting markings and annotations; this unpublished list can be consulted at Houghton.

Since work on this edition began, the Houghton Library has reclassified the manuscripts and many letters in the James Collection. A new and more detailed guide was prepared. The new call numbers are used in the present notes. Apparently, in time, the 'WJ' class will be eliminated, but thus far only a few books have been affected. Some books have been transferred recently from Widener to Houghton, while others, reported by Perry as sold or not listed at all, have turned up in the Widener stacks and other collections. The concluding volumes of this edition will contain a complete account of James's library and will give the then current call numbers and locations. Since the same volumes will contain James's annotations, extensively indexed, only those annotations are noted in the present volume which appear to have a direct bearing upon the text at hand.

James was a very active reader who filled his books with annotations and markings. The term 'markings' refers to underlining, vertical lines in margins, exclamation points, question marks, the notation 'N.B.', and 'Qu' for 'quote'. James's style of marking is distinctive: the N.B.'s are such that the same vertical stroke serves for both the 'N' and the 'B', while his underlining often has a peculiar waver. Furthermore, James habitually filled the flyleaves of his books with indexes, in some cases simply jotting down a page number or two, in others, noting numerous subjects and marking passages for attention or quotation. Pages singled out in this fashion usually have markings. Thus, for books protected in Houghton, the risk of error in attributing a given marking to James is slight. The risk is greater for materials in open stacks such as those in Widener, where the only claim made is that the book was owned or used by James and that there are markings. Where the books have been sold, we are totally dependent upon Perry's reports.

Works by James published in the present edition are cited in this edition, identified as WORKS, while others are cited in the original editions.

3.1 longer] Henry James (1811-1882), *Spiritual Creation: And the Necessary Implication of Nature in It. An Essay towards Ascertaining the Rôle of Evil in Divine Housekeeping*. The relations between William James and his father are discussed by Ralph Barton Perry, *The Thought and Character of William James*, 2 vols. (Boston: Little, Brown, 1935), I, 125-166; Austin Warren, *The Elder Henry James* (New York: Macmillan, 1934); Frederic Harold Young, *The Philosophy of Henry James, Sr.* (New York: Bookman Associates, ^c1951), Clinton Hartley Grattan, *The Three Jameses* (London: Longmans, Green, 1932). A trunk containing Henry James's Swedenborg materials, with some indications of use by William James, can be found in the library of the Swedenborg School of Religion, Newton, Mass.

3.5 autobiographic] *Immortal Life: Illustrated in a Brief Autobiographic Sketch of the Late Stephen Dewhurst*; published in part as "Stephen Dewhurst's Autobiography," *Atlantic Monthly*, 54 (November 1884), 649-662; reprinted in part in *Henry James, Senior: A Selection of His Writings*, ed. Giles Gunn (Chicago: American Library Association, 1974). The *Atlantic Monthly* version appeared with a brief introductory note probably by William James. This note can be found in Professor Bowers's textual Introduction.

3.11 *Society*] *Society the Redeemed Form of Man, and the Earnest of God's Omnipotence in Human Nature: Affirmed in Letters to a Friend* (Boston: Houghton, Osgood, 1879).

4.4 manuscript] An unpublished *General Index and Briefs of Letters* (J233) at Houghton provides an incomplete guide to the Henry James manuscripts and letters in that library.

4.5 periodical] An incomplete list of the writings of Henry James is included in the *Literary Remains*. More complete lists are found in Young and in Dwight W. Hoover, *Henry James, Sr. and the Religion of Community* (Grand Rapids, Mich.: William B. Eerdmans, ^c1969).

4.6 Carlyle] "Some Personal Recollections of Carlyle," *Atlantic Monthly*, 47 (May 1881), 593-609. Henry James met Thomas Carlyle (1795-1881), Scottish essayist and historian, while in England in 1843-1844 and was a frequent visitor at the Carlyle house then and again in 1855. Emerson provided the letter of introduction. In his essay, Henry James quotes extensively from a notebook in which he had recorded the conversations of Carlyle and other visitors. James's enthusiasm for Carlyle cooled and in his essay he voices some harsh judgments.

5.33 disciples] Warren, pp. 254-255, mentions the following as disciples of Henry James: Julia A. Kellogg (1830-1914), American educator and writer, author of a book about Henry James (see p. 6n); Charles Holbrook Mann (1839-1918), American clergyman and writer; Samuel Clarence Eby, a Swedenborgian clergyman and writer. Among James's English Swedenborgian correspondents, Warren lists William White (c.1831-1890), author of *Emanuel Swedenborg: His Life and Writings* (1867); James John Garth Wilkinson (1812-1899), physician and Swedenborgian writer; Horace Field, religious writer. William James's correspondence with Wilkinson and members of Wilkinson's family is at Houghton (bMS Am 1092, letters 1170-1174; bMS Am 1237.18).

6.40 Milsand] Joseph Antoine Milsand (1817-1886), French critic, *Luther et le serf-arbitre* (Paris: Fischbacher, 1884). James's copy is in Widener (C

1282.104). A letter from William James to Milsand on *The Literary Remains* was published by D. G. Charlton, "An Unpublished Letter of William James," *Philosophical Quarterly* (St. Andrews), 1 (October 1951), 439-443. Charlton provides notes on the relations between James and Milsand.

8.16 Hegel] References to Hegel are frequent in William James's writings. More sustained discussions can be found in "On Some Hegelisms," reprinted in *The Will to Believe*, WORKS, and in "Hegel and His Method," *A Pluralistic Universe*, WORKS. For works by Hegel from James's library see *The Will to Believe*, WORKS, note to 196.12.

8.44 *Christianity*] *Christianity the Logic of Creation* (New York: D. Appleton, 1857), pp. 132-134. Originally written as a series of letters to Wilkinson.

9.8 "abysmal] *The Secret of Swedenborg: Being an Elucidation of His Doctrine of the Divine Natural Humanity* (Boston: Fields, Osgood, 1869), p. 169. "Abysmal destitution" and similar expressions are frequently used by Henry James.

11.8 "the] *Society the Redeemed Form of Man*, p. 326: "I can conceive of some intolerable goose of a man, inflated past all bounds of sanity by a conceit of his own personal consequence, posing to attract or compel my homage. But the great and sincere creator of men, never! He is infinitely free from such posturing and trickery."

11.12 "I] Source not found.

12.6 Divine-Natural] 'Divine-natural humanity' is one of the more characteristic of Henry James's expressions and appears in most of his writings.

12.32 "This] Source not found.

12.39 "Just] "Letter from Henry James," *New Church Independent*, 27 (September 1879), 409-414. This is a rejoinder, dated August 7, 1879, to W. H. G., an unidentified reviewer of *Society the Redeemed Form of Man* in the *Independent*, 27 (May 1879), 229-235.

13.17 Swedenborg] For Henry James's account of his conversion to Swedenborgianism see the text, 30.15-37.24. His conversion took place in 1844 in England at about the time when there was considerable interest in the teachings of Emanuel Swedenborg (1688-1772), Swedish scientist and religious writer, among New England intellectuals. Attempts to organize Swedenborgian churches were viewed by James as revivals of ecclesiasticism.

13.19 Fourier] François Marie Charles Fourier (1772-1837), French socialist writer. Warren, pp. 87-126, gives 1845 as the date when James's interest in Fourier began. Warren discusses the spread of Fourier's ideas among Henry James's friends, especially Swedenborgians.

13.19 first] According to the bibliography appended to *The Literary Remains*, Henry James's first two works were *What Constitutes the State?* (New York, 1846) and *Tracts for the New Times. No 1. Letter to a Swedenborgian* (New York, 1847). An earlier work, *Remarks on the Apostolic Gospel* (1840), is listed by other bibliographers.

14.1 "Nothing] *The Secret of Swedenborg*, pp. 47-48. The quoted passage is introduced as follows: "If any two notions are radically opposed on their subjective side, it is those of creator and creature. Objectively, or in creation, creator and creature are one and undistinguishable. But in their subjective aspect nothing can be . . ." (p. 47).

14.17 "Swedenborg's] *Secret*, p. 22.

14.21 "In] *Secret*, pp. 27-29.

15.35 "The] *Secret*, p. 30.

16.28 "a] "Representative Character of the Sexes," *New Church Independent*, 29 (April 1881), 161-169; the quotation is on p. 167.

16.31 "In] *Substance and Shadow: Or Morality and Religion in Their Relation to Life: An Essay upon the Physics of Creation* (Boston: Ticknor and Fields, 1863), pp. 82-84. Page numbers of what is described as the second edition, revised (Boston: Ticknor and Fields, 1866), are the same as those of the first. It is reported that William James suggested that he design a cut for the title page showing a man flogging a dead horse (*The Letters of Henry James*, ed. Percy Lubbock, 2 vols. [New York: Charles Scribner's Sons, 1920], I, 6-9).

18.12 "There] *The Secret of Swedenborg*, p. 132.

18.17 "This] *Secret*, p. 52.

18.23 "necessitates] *Secret*, p. 185.

21.1 "I] *Substance and Shadow*, pp. 73-74.

23.34 "sensibly] *Christianity the Logic of Creation*, pp. 23-24: "Did we *sensibly* perceive God to be the sole life of the universe: were this truth no less a dictate of *feeling* than of reason, we should be most unhappy. For as in that case we should not *feel* life to be in ourselves, of course we should fail to appropriate it, or make it our own, and consequently should fail to realise that selfhood, or *proprium*, which is the condition of all our bliss, because it is the source of all the characteristic activity that separates man from brute. We should sit like stocks and stones, leaving Him who *obviously* was life, to the exclusive appropriation and enjoyment of it."

24.29 "By] *Substance and Shadow*, p. 5.

24.36 Adam] *Christianity the Logic of Creation*, pp. 120-121: "For Eve, according to Swedenborg, symbolizes the Divinely vivified selfhood of man. The Adamic dough, heavy and disheartening before, becomes lively enough now in all conscience, becomes instinct and leaping with vitality, although that vitality has no more positive form than a protest against death, a struggle against mortality. Thus had we had Adam, 'male and female,' alone for a progenitor, we should never have emerged from our Edenic or infantine gristle: we should have remained for ever in a state of Paradisiac childishness and imbecility: in a word, we should have been destitute of our most human characteristic, which is history or progress."

25.4 "Every] *Substance and Shadow*, p. 75. William James reverses the order of passages and inserts the words "the depths of the essential dearth in which its subject's roots are plunged." Their source has not been found.

26.6 The] *The Secret of Swedenborg*, pp. 161-165.

28.33 "Self-conceit] *Christianity the Logic of Creation*, p. 38.

37.38 headed] Instead of a running title, Henry James used subject headings. For the pages quoted, these are "My Moral Death and Burial," "Profound Moral Illusion under Which I Had Been Living," and "My Relief from It Equivalent to My Belief in the Incarnation."

38.21 "When] *Society the Redeemed Form of Man*, p. 131: "Swedenborg makes nature the realm of *uncreation*: and by that unexpected word sends a breath of health to the deepest heart of hell. It is what neither *is* nor *exists* in itself, but only *seems* to be and exist to a subject intelligence. But its use as such seeming is incomparably great."

40.1 "He] Source not found.

40.14 "What] "Redemption, Natural Not Personal," *New Church Independent*, 29 (July 1881), 315-324; the quotation is from p. 316.

42.20 "The] In *Christianity the Logic of Creation*, the quoted passage is preceded by "Christ overcomes hell by His own proper power or manhood, whereas the angel would be . . ." (p. 17).

46.35 essay] "The Old and the New Theology," a lecture in two parts, in *Lectures and Miscellanies* (New York: Redfield, 1852).

46.36 *Church*] *The Church of Christ Not an Ecclesiasticism. A Letter to a Sectarian* (New York: Redfield, 1854); 2nd ed., enlarged (London: W. White, 1856). According to Young (p. 322), the work originated as a letter to Wilkinson.

50.4 "If] "What Is Personality?" *New Church Independent*, 29 (August 1881), 367-377. This is a letter dated August 23, 1881.

56.12-13 "foolish] Source not found.

59.12 disciples] Julia Kellogg found James's philosophy to be independent of Swedenborg and "profoundly original" (pp. 5-6). A reviewer of *The Secret of Swedenborg* concluded that Swedenborg is much narrower than the "generous and broad estimate Mr. James makes of his theology" (*Nation*, 9 [November 18, 1869], 436-437).

61.34 pluralism] For similar remarks about the contrast between monism and pluralism see *Pragmatism*, WORKS, p. 64, and *A Pluralistic Universe*, WORKS, p. 147.

64.3 St. Gaudens'] Augustus Saint-Gaudens (1848-1907), sculptor of the monument to Robert Gould Shaw on the Boston Common, dedicated on May 31, 1897.

64.5 Shaw] Robert Gould Shaw (1837-1863), colonel in the Union army during the Civil War. Shaw was in command of the Fifty-Fourth Regiment of Massachusetts Volunteer Infantry, the first regiment of black soldiers organized in the north, and was killed in action during the assault on Fort Wagner, near Charleston, S.C., on July 18, 1863. For histories of the regiment see Luis F. Emilio, *A Brave Black Regiment: History of the Fifty-Fourth Regiment of Massachusetts Volunteer Infantry* (1894; rpt. New York: Arno Press, 1969) and Peter Burchard, *One Gallant Rush: Robert Gould Shaw and His Brave Black Regiment* (New York: St. Martin's Press, c1965). Excerpts from letters by Henry James to Sarah Blake Sturgis Shaw, Robert Gould Shaw's mother, are given by Perry.

66.6-7 Phillips] Wendell Phillips (1811-1884), American orator and abolitionist.

67.12 "None] From the poem by Fitz-Greene Halleck (1790-1867), American poet, "On the Death of Joseph Rodman Drake, of New York, Sept. 1820," *Alnwick Castle, with Other Poems* (New York: G. & C. Carvill, 1827), p. 29.

67.25 Lee] Henry Lee (1817-1898) served on the staff of Governor Andrew while the regiment was being organized. Lee was a member of the committee which erected the Shaw monument. His report, delivered during the ceremony, appears in *Exercises at the Dedication of the Monument to Colonel Robert Gould Shaw* (Boston: Municipal Printing Office, 1897).

67.29 Andrew] John Albion Andrew (1818-1867), governor of Massachusetts in 1861-1866, a leading advocate of organizing blacks for military service.

67.33 Second] Shaw served as a commissioned officer in the Second Massachusetts Infantry Regiment from May 1861 to March 1863 when he accepted command of the Fifty-Fourth. With the Second Regiment, he saw service in Maryland and northern Virginia.

68.4 April] Shaw served as a private in the Seventh Regiment, New York State Militia, in April and May 1861.

68.16 Napier's] William Francis Patrick Napier (1785-1860), British military historian and general, *History of the War in the Peninsula and in the South of France, from the Year 1807 to the Year 1814* (1828-1840).

68.26 writes] On May 2, 1863, in New York City, Shaw married Anna Haggerty. Shaw's letters to Anna and others were printed privately, *Letters* (Cambridge, Mass.: University Press, 1864). The copy in Houghton (*AC 85.Sh284.864l) was consulted for the present notes. Some of these letters appeared in another private edition, *Letters to Parents* (1876) (*AC 85.Sh284.876l). The location of the originals is unknown and it is unknown whether James used the originals or the printed versions. James is quoting from the letter of July 13, 1863 (*Letters*, p. 325).

69.7 "I] Letter of June 12, 1863 (*Letters*, pp. 297-299). James is piecing together various passages. The looting and burning of Darien on June 11 was ordered by James Montgomery (1814-1871), who was in command of the raid.

69.21 "You] Letter of July 15, 1863 (*Letters*, pp. 325-326).

69.30 Terry] Alfred Howe Terry (1827-1890).

70.1 Adjutant] Garth Wilkinson James (1845-1883), James's brother, served as adjutant of the Fifty-Fourth and was wounded in the assault on Fort Wagner. His account is found in "The Assault on Fort Wagner," *War Papers Read before the Commandery of the State of Wisconsin, Military Order of the Loyal Legion of the United States*, I (Milwaukee: Burdick, Armitage & Allen, 1891), 19-20.

70.21 Strong] George Crockett Strong (1832-1863), American general, in command of the assault on Fort Wagner, himself mortally wounded in the attack.

70.29 Adjutant] The conversation between Strong and Shaw is not found in Garth Wilkinson James's account. It is reported by Emilio (p. 72), a captain in the Fifty-Fourth and a participant in the assault. The command to move in quick time is reported by Emilio on p. 79.

70.30 Hallowell] Edward Needles Hallowell (1836-1871), officer in the Fifty-Fourth Regiment.

71.1 On] James's account of the assault could be based on Emilio, pp. 79-82. Shaw's last command is on p. 82. In a table on p. 392, Emilio summarizes the casualty figures: three officers killed, eleven wounded, and about 250 enlisted men killed, wounded, or missing, out of a total of about 600 who took part in the assault.

71.18 Confederate] From a letter by Lieutenant Iredell Jones, quoted by Emilio, p. 95.

71.24 trench] For an account of Shaw's burial see Emilio, pp. 98-103. On pp. 102-103, Emilio quotes Francis George Shaw's letter of August 24, 1863, requesting that no efforts be made to locate and remove his son's body from the common trench.

72.9 "old] William Wordsworth, "The Solitary Reaper," lines 19-20, *The Poetical Works of William Wordsworth*, ed. E. de Selincourt and Helen Darbishire, III (Oxford: Clarendon, 1946), 77.

73.30 "the] From Tennyson's "To E. L., on His Travels in Greece," *The Works of Alfred Lord Tennyson* (London: Macmillan, 1905), p. 124.

75.2 critics] George Holmes Howison (1834-1916), American philosopher, on November 18, 1898, while thanking James for a copy of *Human Immortality*, wrote: "And yet, noble as the essay is, & truly beautiful & helpful, I think it shows the unsatisfactory limitations of empirical philosophy in a way that the human spirit interested in the question of immortality cannot be satisfied with. The one weak point in your exposition, as it appears to me, is your failure to connect your argument *securely* with the possibility of *individual* immortality. Especially in your note 5, to p. 23, does this gap show. There you do not make the possible 'many minds behind the scenes' identical with *our* minds; for you unfortunately say, that 'all the transmission theory requires is that they should transcend *our* minds,—which thus come from *something* mental that pre-exists, & is larger than themselves.' But if these transcendent minds are not *ours*, of what earthly avail is their survival of the death of the brain to us?" To this James replied on November 27: "I never caught, till I read it, the idea that my supposition about the brain could be worked by the ordinary spiritualistic philosophy by simply making the 'mother sea' consist of the collection of individual spirits, each in a completer and truer form than what filters through into this phenomenal life. I wish I had tho't of that when I wrote the note on p. 58, to which you refer" (bMS Am 1092.9 [259, 1053]). Howison repeated this criticism in a paper before the Berkeley Club of Oakland in April 1899, published as "Human Immortality: Its Positive Argument with Reference to the Ingersoll Lecture of Professor James," *The Limits of Evolution and Other Essays* (New York: Macmillan, 1901) (WJ 439.94). However, Howison's paper came too late to influence James's Preface. On June 17, 1901, James wrote Howison: "You have treated me *most* handsome in your book. I have already warded off the accusation you (very naturally) make against my suggestion of the *modus operandi* of immortality, in a preface to the second edition" (#1057). The correspondence between James and Howison is at Houghton (bMS Am 1092.9 [247-268, 1024-1065]) and in the Bancroft Library of the University of California. Perry, I, 762-777, discusses their relations and provides excerpts from letters.

Thomas Davidson (1840-1900), Scottish-born writer and James's close friend, reviewed *Human Immortality* in the *International Journal of Ethics*, 9 (January 1899), 256-259 and asked "What comfort is there for those who long for individual immortality, in the surmise that, after the decay of the brain, and the withdrawal of the consciousness individuated by it, 'the consciousness might, in ways unknown to us, continue still'?" (p. 259). Most of the correspondence between James and Davidson is at Houghton (bMS Am 1092.9 [115-127, 830-883]). Three letters from James are in the Sterling Memorial Library of Yale University. Perry, I, 731-761, discusses their relations. Houghton has James's copy of *The Philosophical System of Antonio Rosmini-Serbati*, trans. and ed. Thomas Davidson (London: Kegan Paul, Trench, 1882) (WJ 841.77). James's memorial essay "Thomas Davidson: A Knight-Errant of the Intellectual Life" is reprinted in *Memories and Studies* (New York: Longmans, Green, 1911).

C. W. Hodge, in a review in the *Psychological Review*, 6 (July 1899), 424-426, offered similar criticisms.

76.27 Locke's] See *The Principles of Psychology*, WORKS, pp. 331, 368.

77.14-15 Corporation] James was voted Ingersoll lecturer at the February 15, 1897 meeting of the Harvard Corporation (*Harvard Graduates' Magazine*, 5 [June 1897], 625).

77.22 founder] The Ingersoll Lectureship was established in the bequest of Caroline Haskell Ingersoll who died on January 26, 1893, and was carrying out the wishes of her father, George Goldthwait Ingersoll. It is named the "Ingersoll Lecture on the Immortality of Man."

78.12 problems] James's personal attitude towards immortality is discussed by Perry, II, 355-359; see also James's response to the questionnaire on religion distributed by James Bissett Pratt, *The Letters of William James*, ed. Henry James, 2 vols. (Boston: Little, Brown, 1920), II, 212-215.

78.35 Alger's] William Rounseville Alger (1822-1905), American clergyman, *A Critical History of the Doctrine of a Future Life*, 4th ed. (New York: W. J. Widdleton, 1861). In some later editions, the bibliography was published as a separate volume.

80.10 Flechsig] Paul Emil Flechsig (1847-1929), German physiologist and psychologist, *Gehirn und Seele*, 2nd ed. (Leipzig: Veit, 1896). In James's annotated copy in Widener (Phil 6115.6.7) on p. 23, there are cross-references to pp. 656, 85.

80.27-28 Wernicke] Carl Wernicke (1848-1905), German psychologist, *Grundriss der Psychiatrie in klinischen Vorlesungen*, 2 vols. (Leipzig: Thieme, 1894), p. 7: "Die Geisteskrankheit erscheint uns so als Krankheit des Associationsorganes." James's copy is in Widener (Phil 6972.2.10). For other works by Wernicke from James's library see *The Principles of Psychology*, WORKS, note to 49.25.

80.39 pamphlet] Paul Flechsig, *Die Grenzen geistiger Gesundheit und Krankheit* (Leipzig: Veit, 1896). On the cover of his copy of *Gehirn und*

Seele, James has: "Flechsig: Die Grenzen geistiger Gesundheit u. Krankheit, ibid '96. pp. 48. Moral insensibility comes from dim.^{n} of Schmerzgefühl. Alcohol and opium produce it. So does hypnotism. It comes from the degeneration of the Körpergefühlsphäre, which is the seat of character, p. 31-39."

80.42 Munk] Hermann Munk (1839-1912), German physiologist. For Munk's work on localization of functions in the brain see *The Principles of Psychology*, WORKS, note to 42.5.

82.25 "Not] Eugen Karl Dühring (1833-1921), German philosopher, *Der Werth des Lebens populär dargestellt*, 3rd ed. (Leipzig: Fues, 1881), pp. 47-48, 169.

83.30 *Principles*] Chapter 6 (WORKS, pp. 148-182) is titled "The Mind-Stuff Theory."

83.32 Clifford] William Kingdon Clifford (1845-1879), British mathematician and philosopher. Clifford discusses mind-stuff in "On the Nature of Things-in-Themselves," *Lectures and Essays*, ed. Leslie Stephen and Frederick Pollock, 2 vols. (London: Macmillan, 1879), II, 71-88. Both volumes of this edition were sold from James's library. Clifford's review of *The Unseen Universe* appears in *Lectures and Essays*, I, 228-253. *The Unseen Universe or Physical Speculations on a Future State* (New York: Macmillan, 1875) was published anonymously, but is attributed to Peter Guthrie Tait (1831-1901), Scottish mathematician and physicist, and Balfour Stewart (1828-1887), Scottish physicist. James reviewed the work in the *Nation*, 20 (May 27, 1875), 366-367.

84.21 Cabanis] Pierre Jean Georges Cabanis (1757-1808), French philosopher, *Rapports du physique et du moral de l'homme*, 2nd ed., 2 vols. (Paris: Crapelet, 1805), I, 152-154. Perry reports that a copy of the 8th edition with "thought is a brain secretion 137-138" on the flyleaf was sold.

85.14 Spencer] Herbert Spencer (1820-1903), *First Principles of a New System of Philosophy* (London: Williams and Norgate, 1862; 2nd rev. ed., 1867). James's very heavily annotated copy is a reprint of the revised edition (New York: D. Appleton, 1877) (WJ 582.24.4). The quotation is found on p. 217 (sec. 71).

85.23 Büchner] Ludwig Büchner (1824-1899), German philosopher. Perry, I, 470 states that James read Büchner's *Kraft und Stoff* in 1863. Numerous German and English editions were published. James seems to be quoting from *Force and Matter or Principles of the Natural Order of the Universe. With a System of Morality Based Thereon*, translated from the fifteenth German edition (New York: Peter Eckler, 1891), p. 242.

85.32 "As] Jules Luys (1828-1897), French anatomist and physician, *Le Cerveau et ses fonctions* (Paris: Baillière, 1876), pp. 91-92. James's copy in Widener (Phil 6121.7.3) is dated January 1877. The following list appears in the back: "! 48, 72, 82,-4, 91-2, 115, 172, 204, 208." For other works by Luys from James's library see *The Principles of Psychology*, WORKS, note to 72.23.

85.41 Lowell] Percival Lowell (1855-1916), American astronomer, *Occult Japan or the Way of the Gods: An Esoteric Study of Japanese Personality and Possession* (Boston: Houghton, Mifflin, 1895), pp. 311-312. James's copy is in Houghton (Jap 1308.94.75.13*).

86.29 "Life] Percy Bysshe Shelley, "Adonais," stanza LII: "The One remains, the many change and pass; | Heaven's light forever shines, Earth's shadows fly; | Life, like a dome of many-colored glass, | Stains the white radiance of Eternity, | Until Death tramples it to fragments.—Die . . ." (*The Complete Poetical Works of Percy Bysshe Shelley* [Boston: Houghton, Mifflin, 1901], p. 316).

88.35 Berlin] A reference to Emil Du Bois-Reymond (1818–1896), German physiologist, *Die sieben Welträthsel* (1882). For a similar remark see *Essays in Philosophy*, WORKS, p. 91. The words *"ignoramus"* and *"ignoribus"* appear in the concluding paragraph of Du Bois-Reymond's *Über die Grenzen des Naturerkennens* (1872).

89.28 Fechner] Gustav Theodor Fechner (1801–1887), German psychologist, physicist, and philosopher. James discusses Fechner in "Concerning Fechner" in *A Pluralistic Universe*, WORKS; for discussions of the threshold and psychophysics see *A Pluralistic Universe*, WORKS, notes to 69.31 and 104.11. In *The Principles of Psychology*, James based his account of the threshold primarily upon Wundt.

89.32 Emerson] From the essay "Self-Reliance," in *Essays*, first series (Boston: Fields, Osgood, 1869) (*AC 85.J2376.Zz869e), p. 56 (*Emerson's Complete Works* [1884], II, 65). For an explanation of the Emerson reference see note to 109.11. James's index to *Essays* contains "We lie in the lap of immense intelligence, 56."

92.5 Myers] Frederic William Henry Myers (1843–1901), English writer and psychical researcher. In "Frederic Myers' Services to Psychology," *Memories and Studies*, pp. 146–147, James states that Myers turned from literature to psychical research in order to seek evidence for immortality. Houghton preserves James's copy of *Science and a Future Life* (London: Macmillan, 1893) (*AC 85.J2376.Zz893m[A]) as well as other works by Myers. James discusses Myers's work on the subliminal consciousness in *The Varieties of Religious Experience* (New York: Longmans, Green, 1902), p. 511 and elsewhere. For the articles on automatic writing in the *Proceedings of the Society for Psychical Research* (English), see *The Principles of Psychology*, WORKS, note to 378.13; for those on "The Subliminal Consciousness," *The Will to Believe*, WORKS, note to 233.24.

92.34 *Elemente*] Gustav Theodor Fechner, *Elemente der Psychophysik*, 2 vols. (Leipzig: Breitkopf und Härtel, 1860) (WJ 727.13), II, 526–530. James's copy is dated Berlin, December 1867.

93.36 'influx,'] The following from Swedenborg's *The True Christian Religion; Containing the Universal Theology of the New Church* (New York: American Swedenborg Printing and Publishing Society, 1912), p. 8, can be cited: "This influx is into the souls of men, by reason that the soul is the inmost and supreme part of man; and the influx from God enters therein, and descends from thence into the inferior parts, which it quickens and enlivens in proportion to its reception."

94.17 Kant] *Critique of Pure Reason*, A778-779=B806-807. For James's copies of Kant, see *Some Problems of Philosophy*, WORKS, note to 14.6.

94.26 Schiller] Ferdinand Canning Scott Schiller (1864–1937), British philosopher, *Riddles of the Sphinx* (London: Swan Sonnenschein, 1891), pp.

293-296. This book, published under the pseudonym A. Troglodyte, was offered unsuccessfully to Cornell as a doctoral thesis. A copy was sold from James's library, with "matter as restrictive etc. 293" on the flyleaf. For the relations between James and Schiller see *Some Problems of Philosophy*, WORKS, note to 24.35. Schiller reviewed *Human Immortality* in the *Nation*, 67 (December 1, 1898), 416-417.

99.24 Stevenson] Robert Louis Stevenson, "The Lantern-Bearers," in *Across the Plains* (New York: Charles Scribner's Sons, 1892), p. 226.

100.14 Wundt] Wilhelm Wundt (1832-1920), German psychologist and philosopher, *System der Philosophie* (Leipzig: W. Engelmann, 1889) (WJ 796.59.6), p. 315.

101.1 "Revere] From Emerson's "Threnody," *Poems* (Boston: Houghton, Mifflin, 1885), p. 138 (vol. IX of *Emerson's Complete Works*).

102.6 Starbuck] Edwin Diller Starbuck (1866-1947), American psychologist, attended Harvard College in 1893-1894, the Harvard Divinity School in 1894-1895, received the M.A. degree in 1895. Preserved are five letters from Starbuck to James (bMS Am 1092, letters 1023-1027), and copies of two from James to Starbuck (bMS Am 1092.1). Also preserved are *The Psychology of Religion: An Empirical Study of the Growth of Religious Consciousness* (London: Walter Scott, 1899) (WJ 350.83) and several pamphlets. James made extensive use of the responses collected by Starbuck in *Varieties*.

103.24 Starbuck's] A view developed in ch. 9 (pp. 135-144) on "Conversion as a Normal Human Experience."

104.23 Leuba] James Henry Leuba (1868-1946), Swiss-born psychologist, "A Study in the Psychology of Religious Phenomena," *American Journal of Psychology*, 7 (April 1896), 309-385. James's copy of the offprint is in Houghton (Phil 5627.20.10*). Copies of two letters from James to Leuba are at Houghton (bMS Am 1092.1).

105.1 author] Wincenty Lutoslawski (1863-1954), Polish philosopher and writer. The bulk of the correspondence between James and Lutoslawski is in the Beinecke Rare Book and Manuscript Library of Yale University. Houghton has fourteen letters from Lutoslawski to James (bMS Am 1092, letters 522-535) and copies of twenty letters to Lutoslawski from James (bMS Am 1092.1). Houghton preserves James's unmarked copy of *O Logice Platona* (Warsaw: E. Wende, 1892) (WJ 871.52.2), James's copy of *Über die Grundvoraussetzungen und Consequenzen der individualistischen Weltanschauung* (Helsinki 1898) (WJ 871.52.4), and annotated and bound proofs of about half of *Seelenmacht* (WJ 871.52). The Widener copy of *Seelenmacht: Abriss einer zeitgemässen Weltanschauung* (Leipzig: W. Engelmann, 1899) (Phil 665.7) was given by James on July 10, 1899. Perry, II, 213-217, discusses the relations between James and Lutoslawski.

105.2 *Logic*] *The Origin and Growth of Plato's Logic* (London: Longmans, Green, 1897).

109.11 Emerson's] For the relations between the James family and Ralph Waldo Emerson see Perry, I, 39-103. Perry, I, 247-248, quotes Emerson's letter to Herman Grimm (1828-1901), German essayist and art historian, introducing William James, and Grimm's reply to Emerson following James's arrival. Houghton preserves James's notes on Emerson (bMS Am 1092.9

[4514]). These seem to be connected with readings from Emerson given by James several times; see the *Harvard Crimson* (November 6, 1905), p. 3, for an announcement of one such reading. In Houghton are nine annotated works by Emerson from James's library. Some account of the annotations is given by Frederic I. Carpenter, "William James and Emerson," *American Literature* (March 1939), 39–57. Since most of James's copies were of the Riverside Edition of *Emerson's Complete Works*, references to appropriate volumes in the Riverside Edition are added in parentheses when a different edition is cited.

110.1 "Stand] *Lectures and Biographical Sketches* (Boston: Houghton, Mifflin, 1884) (WJ 424.25.8), p. 240 (vol. X of *Emerson's Complete Works*). James's copy is identified as being from his wife and is dated June 1879, impossible as that may seem.

110.4 scholar] *Lectures and Biographical Sketches* includes an essay on "The Scholar" with some markings by James. However, "The American Scholar" and "Literary Ethics" in *Miscellanies; Embracing Nature, Addresses, and Lectures* (Boston: Ticknor and Fields, 1868) (WJ 424.25.12) are much more heavily marked. James's copy of the *Miscellanies* is dated Scarboro, July 1871. The same essays were published as vol. I of *Emerson's Complete Works*, under the title *Nature, Addresses, and Lectures* (Boston: Houghton, Mifflin, ᶜ1883).

110.6 day] "Inspiration," *Letters and Social Aims* (Boston: Houghton, Mifflin, ᶜ1883) (*AC 85.J2376.Zz903e), p. 280 (vol. VIII of *Emerson's Complete Works*). James's index contains "R W. E *280, 294,* 258-9."

110.14 genius] "Natural History of Intellect," *Natural History of Intellect and Other Papers* (Boston: Houghton, Mifflin, ᶜ1893) (*AC 85.J2376.Zz893e), p. 40 (vol. XII of *Emerson's Complete Works*): "Genius is not a lazy angel contemplating itself and things. It is insatiable for expression. Thought must take the stupendous step of passing into realization." James marked part of this passage "R. W. E."

110.20 style] Georges Louis Leclerc de Buffon (1707–1788), French naturalist, in the conclusion of his *Discours sur le style*.

110.29 garden] Similar passages can be found in "Wealth," *The Conduct of Life*, new and rev. ed. (Boston: Houghton, Mifflin, 1889) (*AC 85.J2376.Zz889e), p. 113 (vol. VI of *Emerson's Complete Works*) and in Edward Waldo Emerson, *Emerson in Concord: A Memoir* (Boston: Houghton, Mifflin, 1889) (WJ 424.25.18), p. 126, quoting from Emerson's journal for 1847.

110.35 "God] *Emerson in Concord*, p. 78, quoting from Emerson's journal for 1852.

111.11 "So] From Emerson's "Voluntaries," *Poems*, p. 180.

111.14 Cosmic] See p. 89n.

111.17 "O] "The Method of Nature," *Miscellanies*, p. 197 (I, 196).

111.25 "If] "Nominalist and Realist," *Essays*, second series, new and rev. ed. (Boston: Houghton, Mifflin, 1889) (*AC 85.J2376.Zz889e), pp. 228–229 (vol. III of *Emerson's Complete Works*); also in vol. III of the Centenary Edition of the *Complete Works of Ralph Waldo Emerson* (Boston: Houghton, Mifflin, 1904) (*AC 85.J2376.Zz904e), p. 240.

111.34 "Each] "The Method of Nature," *Miscellanies*, pp. 211-212 (I, 210).

111.36 "Trust] "Self-Reliance," *Essays*, first series, p. 41 (II, 49).

111.36 There] *Essays*, first series, p. 40 (II, 48).

112.8 past] "Self-Reliance," *Essays*, first series, p. 58 (II, 66): "Whence, then, this worship of the past? The centuries are conspirators against the sanity and authority of the soul." In James's copy, part of this passage is marked.

112.9 If] "The Sovereignity of Ethics," *Lectures*, p. 193.

112.14 "Cleave] "Natural History of Intellect," *Natural History of Intellect*, p. 6.

112.27 "I] "Spiritual Laws," *Essays*, first series, p. 145 (II, 153). James's index contains "Be yourself, 145+ Dont be, 247—Cf. 267." James could have in mind Emerson's claim in "The Over-Soul" that "the weakness of the will begins, when the individual would be something of himself" (p. 247 [II, 255]). The apparent conflict can be reconciled by reference to Emerson's view that in order to hear the voice of God, the God who dwells in man, a man must "listen to himself, withdrawing himself from all the accents of other men's devotion" (p. 267 [II, 276]).

112.35 "The] "Spiritual Laws," *Essays*, first series, p. 146 (II, 154).

113.1 "Hide] "Literary Ethics," *Miscellanies*, p. 180 (I, 180).

113.4 Don't] "Social Aims," *Letters and Social Aims*, p. 95.

113.6 What] "Spiritual Laws," *Essays*, first series, pp. 142-143 (II, 150-151).

113.20 "Never] *Essays*, first series, p. 142 (II, 150).

113.22 hero] *Essays*, first series, p. 143 (II, 151).

113.32 "In] *Miscellanies*, pp. 156-157 (I, 157-159).

114.15 "the] "Works and Days," *Society and Solitude* (Boston: Houghton, Mifflin, 1884), p. 167 (vol. VII of *Emerson's Complete Works*).

114.16 "Other] *Lectures*, p. 192: "When I talked with an ardent missionary, and pointed out to him that his creed found no support in my experience, he replied, 'It is not so in your experience, but is so in the other world.' I answer: Other World! there is no other world. God is one and omnipresent; here or nowhere is the whole fact."

114.18 The] "Works and Days," *Society and Solitude*, p. 168: "No man has learned anything rightly until he knows that every day is Doomsday."

114.33 Moral] "The Preacher," *Lectures*, pp. 216-217: The moral sentiment is "that, which being in all sound natures, and strongest in the best and most gifted men, we know to be implanted by the Creator of Men. It is a commandment at every moment and in every condition of life to do the duty of that moment and to abstain from doing the wrong." In James's copy, this passage is marked.

115.5 "It] James Elliot Cabot, *A Memoir of Ralph Waldo Emerson*, 2 vols.

(Boston: Houghton, Mifflin, 1887), II, 427, quoted by Cabot without a source.

116.2 Fechner's] Gustav Theodor Fechner, *Das Büchlein vom Leben nach dem Tode* (Dresden: C. F. Grimmer, 1836), was translated by Mary C. Wadsworth as *The Little Book of Life after Death* (Boston: Little, Brown, 1904). James's copy of an 1887 German edition was sold.

116.11 evolution] Gustav Theodor Fechner, *Einige Ideen zur Schöpfungs- und Entwickelungsgeschichte der Organismen* (Leipzig: Breitkopf und Härtel, 1873).

116.15 Mises] The satirical writings published under the Dr. Mises pseudonym were later collected in a single volume, *Kleine Schriften von Dr. Mises* (Leipzig: Breitkopf und Härtel, 1875). They are listed in *A Pluralistic Universe*, WORKS, note to 69.9.

117.11 "daylight-] Gustav Theodor Fechner, *Die Tagesansicht gegenüber die Nachtansicht* (Leipzig: Breitkopf und Härtel, 1879) (WJ 727.13.2).

117.20 Paulsen] Friedrich Paulsen (1846–1908), German philospher. Paulsen's *Introduction to Philosophy*, published in an English translation by Frank Thilly with a preface by James (New York: Holt, 1895) (WJ 350.68), contains numerous references to Fechner. James's Preface is reprinted in *Essays in Philosophy*, WORKS.

117.20 Wundt] Wilhelm Wundt, *Gustav Theodor Fechner* (Leipzig: W. Engelmann, 1901).

117.20 Preyer] Wilhelm Thierry Preyer (1842–1897), German physiologist and psychologist. His correspondence with Fechner has been published, *Wissenschaftliche Briefe von Gustav Theodor Fechner und W. Preyer* (Hamburg: Voss, 1890).

117.21 Lasswitz] Kurd Lasswitz (1848–1910), German philosopher, *Gustav Theodor Fechner* (Stuttgart: Fr. Frommann, 1896) (WJ 748.83.2).

117.39 *Zend-Avesta*] Gustav Theodor Fechner, *Zend-Avesta oder über die Dinge des Himmels und des Jenseits*, 2 vols. (Leipzig: Voss, 1851). James's annotated copy is of the second edition, 2 vols. (Hamburg and Leipzig: Voss, 1901) (WJ 727.13.4). It is dated Chocorua, September 1907.

119.36 Royce's] Josiah Royce (1855–1916), American philosopher, James's colleague at Harvard, *The World and the Individual*, 2 vols. (New York: Macmillan, 1899–1901) (WJ 477.98.6). James's index to the first volume of *Zend-Avesta* has "Royce—165, 170." There are other indications of agreement between Fechner and Royce.

119.37 Bradley's] Francis Herbert Bradley (1846–1924), English philosopher, *Appearance and Reality* (London: Swan Sonnenschein, 1893) (WJ 510.2). James's writings on Bradley are reprinted in *Essays in Philosophy*, WORKS; for notes on their correspondence and an additional work from James's library see *Essays in Philosophy*, WORKS, notes to 65.1, 66.28.

119.37-38 Taylor's] Alfred Edward Taylor (1869–1945), British philosopher, *Elements of Metaphysics* (London: Methuen, 1903) (WJ 584.98). One letter from Taylor to James is at Houghton (bMS Am 1092, letter 1134).

120.1 I] For a note on the development of James's interest in the psychology of war see Perry, II, 272. Nineteen works on the psychology of war were given to Harvard; an unpublished list can be found at Houghton (bMS Am 1092.9 [4579], fols. 80-81). A complete list will appear in the volume of manuscript remains. For an earlier indication of interest in war see *Varieties*, pp. 366-367.

120.22 World's] The thirteenth international congress of peace societies was held in Boston, October 3-8, 1904. The proceedings were published as the *Official Report of the Thirteenth Universal Peace Congress* (Boston: Peace Congress Committee, 1904). James's remarks appear in the *Official Report*, pp. 266-269.

121.28 Brandenburg] A province of the kingdom of Prussia, often considered the nucleus of the Prussian state.

121.28 Piedmont] A region of northern Italy, center of the movement for Italian unification.

121.28 Japan] The Russo-Japanese war was fought in 1904-1905.

123.7-8 Venezuela] The protracted dispute between Great Britain and Venezuela over the boundaries of British Guiana was brought to a crisis by President Grover Cleveland's message to Congress of December 17, 1895. The message was widely interpreted as a threat of war should Britain refuse to settle the dispute by arbitration. Both in private letters and in public, James was harshly critical. According to Perry, who quotes from several of James's letters on the issue (II, 304-307), this incident marks the beginning of James's public opposition to American imperialism.

124.1 discuss] While James was teaching at Stanford in 1906, he took part, on February 5, in a discussion before the Unitarian Club of California, together with John W. Buckham, of the Pacific Theological Seminary, George W. Stone, and Howison (see a brief report of the meeting in the *Pacific Unitarian*, 14 [March 1906], 146). The club intended to print the proceedings in full, but the earthquake on April 18 forced a change of plan. On January 23, 1906, James wrote Howison: "Do you know that I am to be joined with you as one speech maker at the Unitarian Club dinner Feb. 5th? I have accepted, with fear and trembling, as always when speech-making is involved." On February 7, again writing to Howison, James remarked: "You were in great heart that night; and the way you poured damnation and endearment over *me* in your speech, so blended that I couldnt tell which was stock and which was flavoring, was a unique experience." In his letter of February 14, James develops their differences: "But as for the 'real person,' why should all that *intellectual* abstraction belong to it more than the more concrete life of personal *affection* which common sense considers more intimately there" (bMS Am 1092.9 [1059-1061]).

125.8 Santayana] George Santayana (1863-1952), American philosopher, James's colleague at Harvard, *The Life of Reason or the Phases of Human Progress*, 5 vols. (New York: Charles Scribner's Sons, 1905-1906). Houghton preserves all but the second volume from James's library (WJ 479.62). For a note on the relations between James and Santayana see *Some Problems of Philosophy*, WORKS, note to 34.33.

125.23 argument] In his notes for his course given at Stanford University in 1906, under the heading "Faith," James writes: "Its natural logic is the sorites: fit to be, ought to be, may be, must be, shall be, is, etc. . . ." (bMS Am 1092.9 [4516], fol. 100). The faith-ladder is used in *A Pluralistic Universe*, WORKS, p. 148, and in *Some Problems of Philosophy*, WORKS, p. 113.

126.35 mystical] For a more detailed treatment of the evidential value of mystical states see *Varieties* (1902), pp. 422-423.

127.6 power] The notion of God as a power "which makes for righteousness" can be found in Matthew Arnold (1822-1888), English poet and critic, *Literature and Dogma*, ch. 1, sec. 5 (Matthew Arnold, *Dissent and Dogma*, ed. R. H. Super [Ann Arbor: University of Michigan Press, c1968], p. 200).

127.34 Greeks] In copying portions of "Reason and Faith" for *A Pluralistic Universe*, WORKS, p. 137, James attributes this view to Gilbert Keith Chesterton (1874-1936), English writer, but does not cite a source. In his *Heretics* (New York: John Lane, 1905), pp. 153-154, Chesterton describes pagans as "above all things reasonable and respectable." According to James's diary for January 6, 1906, James read *Heretics* while on his way to California to teach at Stanford.

128.16 'Mind-cure'] James's interest in the mind-cure movement can be best estimated from his use of the mind-cure literature in *Varieties*. See also *A Pluralistic Universe*, WORKS, note to 138.16.

129.1 We] One of James's notebooks at Houghton (bMS Am 1092.9 4516]) contains an outline of "The Energies of Men," with the indication that it was delivered before the Psychology Club at Harvard on May 18, 1906. The outline appears as an appendix to the present volume.

129.2 structural] Structural psychology in the United States is associated primarily with Edward Bradford Titchener (1867-1927); functional psychology, with John Dewey (1859-1952) and James Rowland Angell (1869-1949). Both tendencies had close ties with James's *Principles*.

129.6 Sanford] Edmund Clark Sanford (1859-1924), American psychologist, "A Sketch of a Beginner's Course in Psychology," *Pedagogical Seminary*, 13 (March 1906), 118-124. Sanford writes: "I call it the 'physician's attitude' because it is easy to understand that the physician . . . is accustomed to put off the personal relation . . . and look at each person as a case, as an organism whose behavior is definitely determined by fixed laws—in whose body cause and effect follow in inevitable sequence" (p. 120).

129.10 Janet's] Pierre Janet (1859-1947), French psychologist. In the *Principles*, James often quotes Janet's *L'Automatisme psychologique* (Paris: Alcan, 1889) (WJ 642.59). Works by Janet from James's library will be listed in the volume of manuscript remains.

130.10 Janet] Pierre Janet, *Les Obsessions et la psychasthénie*, 2 vols. (Paris: Alcan, 1903). James's annotated copy of vol. I, inscribed to him by Janet, is in Widener (Phil 6959.1.9 [B]).

131.21 Shaw] For James's view of George Bernard Shaw (1856-1950), see Perry, II, 467 and *Letters*, II, 263.

131.32 Chesterton] H. G. Wells's account of James climbing a ladder in order to see Chesterton over a garden wall is quoted by Gay Wilson Allen, *William James: A Biography* (New York: Viking Press, 1967), p. 464.

131.32 Carpenter] Edward Carpenter (1844-1929), English poet and essayist. One letter from Carpenter to James is at Houghton (bMS Am 1092, letter 68).

131.33 Wells] Herbert George Wells (1866-1946), English novelist and sociologist. The correspondence between James and Wells is at Houghton (bMS Am 1092.9 [666-669, 3881-3889]); a selection appears in *Letters*.

133.36 Olivier] Sydney Haldane Olivier (1859-1943), British statesman, "An Empire Builder," *Contemporary Review*, 87 (May 1905), 692-704. Four letters from Olivier to James are at Houghton (bMS Am 1092, letters 635-638), while four letters from James to Olivier appear in *Sydney Olivier: Letters and Selected Writings*, ed. Margaret Olivier (London: George Allen & Unwin, 1948), pp. 123-127. Olivier sent James the manuscript of the story. James replied: "That love can be a gate of access to 'cosmic emotion' or 'mystic experience,' or 'conversion' must be true. Your own experience of it as purged of egotistic elements is very striking indeed, magnificent, in fact. How come you never to have published the little tale?" (*Sydney Olivier*, p. 124 [letter of June 1, 1903]).

134.4 People] James is referring to the San Francisco earthquake of April 18, 1906. See his "On Some Mental Effects of the Earthquake," *Youth's Companion*, 80 (June 7, 1906), pp. 283-284, reprinted in *Essays in Psychology*, WORKS.

134.10 Norton's] Charles Eliot Norton (1827-1908), American art historian. Norton met Baird Smith while traveling in India (Sara Norton, *Letters of Charles Eliot Norton*, 2 vols. [Boston: Houghton, Mifflin, 1913], I, 86n).

134.11 Baird Smith] Richard Baird Smith (1818-1861), served in the British army during the Indian Mutiny. His letter to Norton, dated November 1, 1857, is at Houghton (bMS Am 1088 [6780]).

134.34 Tapleyism] Perhaps a reference to Mark Tapley, a character in Dickens' *Martin Chuzzlewit*, who remains merry even under adverse circumstances.

134.40 De Quincey] Thomas De Quincey (1785-1859), English essayist, author of *Confessions of an English Opium-Eater*.

135.25 Janet] Pierre Janet, "On the Pathogenesis of Some Impulsions," *Journal of Abnormal Psychology*, 1 (April 1906), 1-17.

137.5 friend] The friend is Wincenty Lutoslawski.

137.18 Vivekananda's] Swami Vivekananda (1863-1902), Indian religious leader. James met Vivekananda while the latter was lecturing in the United States in 1896. For a note on their relations see *A Pluralistic Universe*, WORKS, note to 18.15.

138.6 Handbook] Wincenty Lutoslawski, *Logika ogolna czyli teorja poznania i logika formalna* (1906).

139.39 wrote] James's letter of May 6, 1906 (bMS Am 1092 for copy in Houghton).

142.9 Garibaldi's] Giuseppe Garibaldi (1807-1882), Italian patriot.

142.22 Pückler-Muskau] Hermann Ludwig Heinrich von Pückler-Muskau

(1785–1871), German traveler and writer, *Tour in England, Ireland, and France, in the Years 1826, 1827, 1828, and 1829* (Philadelphia: Carey, Lea & Blanchard, 1833), pp. 434–435. The account is based in part on letters written by Pückler-Muskau to his former wife while he was touring England in search of a rich wife to retrieve the family fortunes.

143.1 *Conversions*] James discusses conversion at length in *Varieties* (1902), pp. 189–258.

143.24 Fletcher] Horace Fletcher (1849–1919), American writer and lecturer on health and dietetics, *Happiness As Found in Forethought Minus Fearthought* (Chicago: Herbert S. Stone, 1897). Four letters from Fletcher to James (bMS Am 1092, letters 197–200), and copies of fourteen letters from James to Fletcher (bMS Am 1092.1) are in Houghton. The *Harvard Crimson*, November 7, 1905, p. 1, published a letter from James urging students to attend a lecture by Fletcher. Quotations from James were sometimes used in Fletcher's advertising. James for a time tried Fletcherism, the very thorough chewing of every bite of food, but without much success. James's copy of Fletcher's *Menticulture* (Chicago: Herbert S. Stone, 1898) is in Widener (Phil 6115.18.7).

145.10 Papini] Giovanni Papini (1881–1956), Italian writer. James's "G. Papini and the Pragmatist Movement in Italy" is reprinted in *Essays in Philosophy*, WORKS. For a note on the letters between James and Papini see *Essays in Philosophy*, WORKS, note to 144.18. Papini sketches out his program in "Licenzio la filosofia," *Il crepuscolo dei filosofi (Kant, Hegel, Schopenhauer, Comte, Spencer, Nietzsche)* (Milan: Lombarda, 1906), pp. 265–280.

148.35–36 Patrick] George Thomas White Patrick (b. 1857), American philosopher and psychologist, and J. Allen Gilbert, "On the Effects of Loss of Sleep," *Psychological Review*, 3 (September 1896), 469–483.

150.2 relax] James discusses the subject of relaxation at length in "The Gospel of Relaxation," *Talks to Teachers on Psychology: And to Students on Some of Life's Ideals* (New York: Henry Holt, 1899), pp. 199–228.

152.17 individual] In the *American Magazine* text (p. 59), this section is given the heading "The Energies of Roosevelt." Theodore Roosevelt became president in 1901. For James's attitude towards Roosevelt, see Perry, II, 311–315.

152.20 Mill] James could be referring to John Stuart Mill, *The Subjection of Women* (London: Longmans, Green, Reader, and Dyer, 1869), pp. 112–115.

152.33 Montyon] Jean Baptiste Antoine Robert Auget, baron de Montyon (1733–1820), French philanthropist.

152.39 Bourget's] Paul Bourget (1852–1935), French writer, "Discours de M. Paul Bourget," *Recueil des Discours, Rapports et Pièces Diverses Lus dans les Séances Publiques et Particulières de l'Académie Française 1900–1909*, pt. 2 (Paris: Firmin-Didot, 1910), pp. 941–970. Bourget delivered his address on November 29, 1906. His account of Jeanne Chaix is on pp. 956–957.

153.17–18 Courrières] The explosion in the coal mines of Courrières, in northern France, took place on March 10, 1906. Some 1,100 miners were killed. The rescue of the miner Némy and his companions is described in the *Times* (London), March 31, 1906, p. 7.

153.31 Norton] See notes to 134.10–134.40.

155.1 Janet] See note to 135.25.

156.28 friend] See note to 137.5.

157.38 Fletcher's] See note to 143.24.

158.1 Dewey's] Edward Hooker Dewey (c. 1837–1904), advocate of the "No Breakfast Plan" and other fasting cures.

158.26 Pückler-Muskau] See note to 142.22.

160.13 Hyslop] Theophilus Bulkeley Hyslop (1863–1933), British psychiatrist, "A Discussion of Occupation and Environment As Causative Factors of Insanity," *British Medical Journal*, vol. 2 for 1905 (October 14), pp. 941–944 (remark on p. 944). The paper was read on July 27, 1905 at the annual meeting of the British Medical Association.

162.1 [1]war] Gay Wilson Allen, p. 451, states that "The Moral Equivalent of War" was delivered as an address at Stanford on February 25, 1906. In his diary for February 21, 1906, James notes that he "addresst 'Assembly' on War & Arbitration" (bMS Am 1092.9 [4555]). This date is confirmed by the Stanford student paper, the *Daily Palo Alto*, which on February 20 announced that James, described as the acting head of the Philosophy Department, and Dean Hodges, special preacher at the Memorial Church, would tomorrow morning address "the second student body Assembly of the semester" on the general topic of "Arbitration and Its Relations to War and Peace." On February 21 the *Daily Palo Alto* reported James's address but made no mention of what is perhaps the distinctive feature of "The Moral Equivalent of War," James's proposal that the military virtues should be cultivated in other ways. In a collection of notes (bMS Am 1092.9 [4476]), there is a phrase outline of a lecture on war written on Hotel St. Francis, San Francisco, stationery. James refers to the "moral equivalent of war," but the outline seems to have no direct connection with "The Moral Equivalent." For additional details Professor Bowers's textual introduction should be consulted. See also note to 169.2.

163.25 Thucydides] *Thucydides*, trans. Benjamin Jowett, 2 vols. (Oxford: Clarendon, 1881), I, 399, 403, 407 (ch. 5, secs. 89, 105, 116).

164.6 Aemilius] Aemilius Paulus, Roman general, pillaged Epirus in 167 B.C.

164.27 Spain] James was a member of the Anti-Imperialist League which opposed American policy in the Philippines. Especially in 1899, he wrote a number of letters to editors on the Philippine question.

166.27 Lea] Homer Lea (1879–1912), American adventurer and writer, *The Valor of Ignorance* (New York: Harper & Brothers, 1909), pp. 13, 160–161, and elsewhere. In 1904, Lea was made a general in China, and throughout defended China's interests. This work was reprinted in 1942. In his diary, James notes that he finished reading this work on November 26, 1909.

167.25 Steinmetz] Sebald Rudolf Steinmetz (1862–1940), Dutch social philosopher, *Die Philosophie des Krieges* (Leipzig: Barth, 1907). James's copy is in Houghton (Int 6909.07B*).

167.35 *Die*] Friedrich Schiller, from the poem "Resignation," *Sämtliche Werke*, I (Munich: Hanser, 1958), 133.

168.8 Patten's] Simon Nelson Patten (1852-1933), American political economist. Patten's *Heredity and Social Progress* (1903) was sold from James's library.

168.40 Chapman] John Jay Chapman (1862-1933), American lawyer and essayist. The correspondence between James and Chapman is at Houghton (bMS Am 1092, letters 122-137) (bMS Am 1854 [877-882, 5312-5330]) (bMS Am 1854.1 [373]).

169.2 *moral*] The words "the moral equivalent of war," coupled with "the mechanical equivalent of heat," appear in *Varieties* (1902), p. 367. In his phrase outline (see note to 162.1), James originally wrote "Find mechanical equivalent for war." The 'mechanical' was then deleted in favor of 'moral'.

169.7 Tolstoy's] For James's view of Tolstoy see Perry, I, 709.

169.15 Dickinson's] Goldsworthy Lowes Dickinson (1862-1932), English writer, *Justice and Liberty: A Political Dialogue* (New York: Doubleday, Page, 1909), first published in 1908. In Houghton is *Religion, a Criticism and a Forecast* (New York: McClure, Phillips, 1905) (WJ 518.13).

172.37 Wells] Herbert George Wells, *First and Last Things: A Confession of Faith and a Rule of Life* (New York: G. P. Putnam's Sons, 1908), pp. 214-215.

173.23 Stanley's] James uses the same anecdote in *The Will to Believe*, WORKS, p. 192. He is referring to Henry Morton Stanley (1841-1904), British explorer, *Through the Dark Continent*, II (New York: Harper & Brothers, 1879), 201.

I. K. S.

Appendixes

I. Notes for "The Energies of Men"

II. Notes for an Unidentified Lecture

Appendix I
Notes for "The Energies of Men"

Folios 116^v–119 of bMS Am 1092.9 (4516), a Partridge and Cooper bound notebook of white leaves 220 × 176 mm., ruled in blue. The text has been deleted by a vertical stroke on each page. These notes for a talk to the Psychology Club at Harvard on May 18, 1906, probably constitute a preliminary version of the later "Energies of Men" address to the American Philosophical Association at Columbia University on December 28, 1906.

[*fol.* 116^v]
Talk to Psychology-Club at Harvard, May 18 '06

When a student of Psychol. I always regarded it as but a part of the larger
    science of ['human nature' *del.*] living beings.
Anthropology.   (Comp psychol. a germ)
Official psychology a very *small* part! (even if one do *not* limit it à la M-g)
What does it do? Study elementary processes like discrimination & associa-
    tion.
Janet's psych as théme.
Can't deduce Lutheran conversion—contrast with pagan pride etc.
Janet's cases in Prince's journal. *Sexual excess as relief [*insrtd. in right mrgn.*
    and extending into left mrgn. of fol. 117]
All have their root in a feeling of insufficiency, *fatigue* [*in left mrgn.*] "Psy-
    choleptic" crises," which the excentric [*fol.* 117] activity *relieves ['ie'
    ov. 'ea'] .
Let me ask you to look at the concrete human being in action, and you will
    see that these abnormal cases are *typical.*
His['s' *del.*] happiness or unhappiness is his most important fact. Oppressed,
    inhibited, or free!
Few of us entirely free.
But we occasionally get free—find we have *more resources than we thought.*
I wish to generalize this fact, and spend the hour in illustrating it.
Concrete psychology (functional?) also has its place.
Begin with "second wind."
[*fol.* 117^v] Critical point must be passed.
In many habit neuroses also. *Bully* them!
Reservoirs of energy not usually drawn on.
In great catastrophes & crises, folks astonish themselves
(Gen. Baird Smith.)

Falling in love (Olivier's tale.)

Revenge some great insult.

Indignation at injustice

Religious conversion.

Evidently there is *a threshold* which stands at diff.ᵗ heights in diff.ᵗ people, and shifts in the same person.

Some habitually *use* what in others is below [*fol.* 118] the threshold, except *when a [*ab. del.* 'by'] crisis *comes. [*ab. del.* 'it is to']

A good example is the religious difference

Some *can,* some *can't pray* or believe in God.

To him who *can,* it is a source of power.

"Conversion" may change a man's type

["Imitative!" do you say? What if it is?]

(Miss Webb)

Healings; Eddyism; "New Thought."

Great advantage to be open thus—

Ashburner type vs. my own.

This brings us into the *Intellect.*

Mystical experiences

Catholic vis[i]on

Mystical theology.

[*fol.* 118ᵛ] Yoga discipline.

"Power" claimed, and apparently shown.

Lutoslawski's letter.

My reply: —awake deeper levels of will.

A single successful effort of moral will, saying no to some habitual temptation, or performing some courageous act, will act dynamogenically for a month with any body.

Generalize: we are only half awake—like one who should use only his little finger.

Two problems:

    1. ['Who' *del.*] To measure the transmarginal resources. [*fol.* 119]

    2. To tap them.

Big task! but worthy.

It leads to a *real [*intrl.*] "Pragmatic."

Its first beginnings must be vague and groping, largely occupied with the study of ['those will-attitudes wh. M-g cuts off.' *del.*] states of will.

Laboratory psychology may be more accurate at present, but this program makes it look *small!*

[*short rule del. w. finer pen*]

*We must beware, if we are lab. psychologists, of professional inhibitions

———————————————— [*added w. finer pen*]

Appendix II
Notes for an Unidentified Lecture

In the James Collection, bMS Am 1092.9 (4476), is a sheet of St. Francis Hotel (San Francisco) blue stationery with notes or headings. Conjecturally, this sheet may date from February 5, 1906, when James attended the Pacific Coast Unitarian Club dinner at the hotel and spoke on "Reason and Faith." It is just possible that he seized some break in the occasion to jot down notes for future addresses on his schedule.* The shorter list of headings on the verso could have been written in contemplation of the February 21 Stanford student assembly at which James spoke on "The Psychology of the War Spirit." It must be remarked, however, that the brief summary of this speech printed by the *Daily Palo Alto* (see under the textual account of "The Moral Equivalent of War") does not repeat any of these headings. The longer list strongly suggests some different talk to students, with its exhortation to 'Read! Read! read!' The curious phrase 'My exam.' could be taken as suggesting a classroom, but in context a reference to an examination he was giving or would give in California is not appropriate. Nor is it probable that 'exam.' is shorthand for *example*. Just possibly, Professor Skrupskelis suggests, the reference is to the story about Oliver Wendell Holmes's "farcical" questioning of James during his medical examination, for which see G. W. Allen, *William James* (New York: Viking Press, 1967), pp. 157–158 and the note on p. 531. There would seem to be little possibility that the heading for H. G. Wells and the discovery of the future has any connection with the end of "The Moral Equivalent of War"; nor does the reference to Roosevelt seem to fit, so far as can be told from the context. In short, the larger list seems to preserve some unpublished and perhaps never written-out popular talk to students in James's hortatory vein.

[*recto*]
"Be yourself."—which self?
Old man talking to young ones. *sexagenarian centurion [*intrl.*]
Precipice.
['Chances & possib' *del.*]

---

*Of course, James could have stayed at the St. Francis on some other occasion. It is only the coincidence of notes on war and his address on the war spirit that suggests February 5, 1906. The headings in the longer list would not have been inappropriate for a talk to students during his 1898 visit to Berkeley to give the summer-school "Talks to Teachers" series; but the interest in war indicated by the verso headings makes an 1898 date less appropriate than his 1906 term at Stanford.

Si jeunesse savait
Immortality—erst know how to live
Changes here.
Changes in my time.
Educational state. My exam.
Diff^t *universe
What you will see here. 50 years hence.
H. G. Wells. Discovery of future.
Trust to become experts, my habit chapter.
Give up sloth, cowardice.
Mark Twain anecdote [*in mrgn. vert., continued*
    vert. at head of page]
Appreciate advantages   Jews
Associate with betters   Roosevelt
Read! Read! read!
[*rule*]
More expert *professionally* up to 70, less loose curiosity.
[*rule*]
Value of a civilization (once cruelties & degradations removed) is proportional
    to percentage of 1st class characters to population.
Athens ahead in this, but full of atrocities
[*verso*]
['Sexag' *del.*]
—Can't say courage, can't say effort
Makers of country
Democracy
flattening out
Soldier type
Fling life away like a flower
Greek life
Find *moral [*ab. del.* 'mechanical'] equivalent for war.
"Kickers" contrast of America with England
Only get inflamed—as well for righteousness as for anything else
Commerce—all the selfish interests are organized & combined. Shall not the
    ideal ones?
[*vert. to the left opposite the first* 5 *lines*]
Absence of historic background
[*vert. to the right*]
Preciousness of
[*vert. to the left of next* 4 *lines*]
In a democracy the country belongs to each of us. Its shame is his shame etc.
    no excuse

A Note on the Editorial Method

The Text of
Essays in Religion and Morality

Apparatus

Emendations
Textual Notes
Historical Collation
Alterations in the Manuscripts
Word-Division

A Note on the Editorial Method

These volumes of THE WORKS OF WILLIAM JAMES offer the critical text of a definitive edition of his published and unpublished writings (letters excepted). A text may be called 'critical' when an editor intervenes to correct the errors and aberrations of the copy-text[1] on his own responsibility or by reference to other authoritative documents, and also when he introduces authoritative revisions from such documents into the basic copy-text. An edition may be called 'definitive' (a) when the editor has exhaustively determined the authority, in whole or in part, of all preserved documents for the text; (b) when the text is based on the most authoritative documents produced during the work's formulation and execution and then during its publishing history; and (c) when the complete textual data of all authoritative documents are recorded, together with a full account of the edited text's divergences from the document chosen as copy-text, so that the user may reconstruct these sources in complete verbal detail as if they were before him. When backed by this data, a critical text in such a definitive edition may be called 'established' if from the fully recorded documentary evidence it attempts to reconstruct the author's true and fullest intention, even though in some details the restoration of intention from imperfect sources is conjectural and subject to differing opinion.

The most important editorial decision for any work edited without modernization[2] is the choice of its copy-text, that documen-

---

[1] The copy-text is that document, whether a manuscript or a printed edition, chosen by the editor as the most authoritative basis for his text, and therefore one which is reprinted in the present edition subject only to recorded editorial emendations, and to substitution or addition of readings from other authoritative documents, judged to be necessary or desirable for completing James's final intentions.

[2] By 'modernization' one means the silent substitution for the author's of an entirely new system of punctuation, spelling, capitalization, and word-division in order to bring these original old-fashioned 'accidentals' of the text thoroughly up to date for the benefit

tary form on which the edited text will be based. Textual theorists have long distinguished two kinds of authority: first, the authority of the words themselves—the *substantives*; second, the authority of the punctuation, spelling, capitalization, word-division, paragraphing, and devices of emphasis—the *accidentals* so-called—that is, the texture in which the substantives are placed but itself often a not unimportant source of meaning. In an unmodernized edition like the present, an attempt is made to print not only the substantives but also their 'accidental' texture, each in its most authoritative form. The most authoritative substantives are taken to be those that reflect most faithfully the author's final intentions as he revised to perfect the form and meaning of his work. The most authoritative accidentals are those which are preferential, and even idiosyncratic, in the author's usage even though not necessarily invariable in his manuscripts. These characteristic forms convey something of an author's flavor, but their importance goes beyond aesthetic or antiquarian appreciation since they may become important adjuncts to meaning. It is precisely these adjuncts, however, that are most susceptible to compositorial and editorial styling away from authorial characteristics and toward the uniformity of whatever contemporary system the printing or publishing house fancied. Since few authors are in every respect so firm in their 'accidental' intentions as to demand an exact reproduction of their copy, or to attempt systematically to restore their own system in proof from divergent compositorial styling, their 'acceptance' of printing-house styling is meaningless as an indication of intentions. Thus, advanced editorial theory agrees that in ordinary circumstances the best authority for the accidentals is that of a holograph manuscript or, when the manuscript is not preserved,

---

of a current reader. It is the theory of the present edition, however, that James's turn-of-the-century 'accidentals' offer no difficulty to a modern scholar or general reader and that to tamper with them by 'modernization' would not only destroy some of James's unique and vigorous flavor of presentation but would also risk distortion of his meaning. Since there is every evidence that, in his books at least, James was concerned to control the texture of presentation and made numerous nonverbal as well as verbal changes in preparing printer's copy, and later in proof, for an editor to interfere with James's specific, or even general, wishes by modernizing his system of 'accidentals' would upset on many occasions the designedly subtle balances of his meaning. Moreover, it would be pointless to change his various idiosyncrasies of presentation, such as his increasing use of 'reform' spellings and his liking for the reduction of the capitals in words like *darwinism*. Hence in the present edition considerable pains have been devoted to reprinting the authoritative accidentals of the copy-text and also by emendation to their purification, so far as documentary evidence extends, from the housestyling to which they were subjected in print, which was not entirely weeded out in proof. For a further discussion, see below under the question of copy-text and its treatment.

whatever typed or printed document is closest to it, so that the fewest intermediaries have had a chance to change the text and its forms. Into this copy-text—chosen on the basis of its most authoritative accidentals—are placed the latest revised substantives, with the result that each part of the resulting eclectic text is presented in its highest documentary form of authority.[3] It is recognized, however, that an author may be so scrupulous in supervising each stage of the production of a work that the accidentals of its final version join with the revised substantives in representing his latest intentions more faithfully than in earlier forms of the text. In such special cases a document removed by some stages from a preserved manuscript or from an early intermediary may in practical terms compose the best copy-text.[4]

Each work, then, must be judged on its merits. In general, experience shows that whereas James accepted some journal styling without much objection even though he read proof and had the chance to alter within reason what he wished, he was more seriously concerned with the forms of certain of his accidentals in the books, not only by his marking copy pasted up from journal articles for the printer but more particularly when he received the galley proofs. Indeed, it is not too much to state that James sometimes regarded the copy that he submitted for his books (especially when it was manuscript) as still somewhat in a draft state, to be shaped by proof-alterations to conform to his ultimate intentions. The choice of copy-texts in the WORKS, therefore, rests on the evidence available for each document, and the selection will vary according to the circumstances of 'accidental' authority as superior either in the early or in the late and revised forms of the text. In this connection, the earlier discussions in the textual analyses for the philosophical volumes of this edition give examples of the evidence and its application to the selection of copy-text that are pertinent to the present volume.

On the other hand, although James demonstrably made an effort

---

[3] The use of these terms, and the application to editorial principles of the divided authority between both parts of an author's text, was chiefly initiated by W. W. Greg, "The Rationale of Copy-Text," *Studies in Bibliography*, 3 (1950-51), 19-36. For extensions of the principle, see Fredson Bowers, "Current Theories of Copy-Text," *Modern Philology*, 68 (1950), 12-20; "Multiple Authority: New Concepts of Copy-Text," *The Library*, 5th ser., 27 (1972), 81-115; "Remarks on Eclectic Texts," *Proof*, 4 (1974), 31-76, all reprinted in *Essays in Bibliography, Text, and Editing* (Charlottesville: University Press of Virginia, 1975).

[4] An extensive analysis of specific problems in the mechanical application of traditional theories of copy-text to revised modern works may be found in Bowers, "Greg's 'Rationale of Copy-Text' Revisited," *Studies in Bibliography*, 31 (1978), 90-161.

to control the forms of certain of his accidentals in the proofs, even when he had been relatively careless about their consistency in his manuscript printer's copy, he was not always equally attentive to every detail of the housestyling that printers imposed on his work. In some cases he simply did not observe anomalies even in his own idiosyncratic practices; in others he may have been relatively indifferent when no real clash of principles was involved. Thus, when an editor is aware by reason of inconsistencies that certain 'accidental' printing-house stylings have been substituted for James's own practices as established in manuscripts and marked copy, or have been substituted for relatively neutral journal copy that seems to approximate James's usual practice, he may feel justified in emending to recover by the methods of textual criticism as much of the purity of the Jamesian accidentals as of the substantives—both ultimately contributing to the most complete and accurate expression of James's meaning.

Except for the small amount of silent alteration listed below, every editorial change in the copy-text has been recorded, with the identification of its immediate source and the record of the rejected copy-text reading. An asterisk prefixed to the page-line reference (always to this edition) indicates that the alteration is discussed in a Textual Note. The formulas for notation are described in the headnotes to the list of Emendations and to the Historical Collation, but it may be well to mention here the use of the term *stet* to call attention in special cases to the retention of the copy-text reading. Textual Notes discuss certain emendations or refusals to emend. The Historical Collation lists all readings in the collated authoritative documents that differ from the edited text except for those recorded in the list of Emendations, which are not repeated in the Historical Collation. The principles for the recording of variants are described in the headnote to this Collation, including the special notation for cross-reference to the list of Alterations in the Manuscripts.

When manuscripts are preserved in the textual transmission, their rejected variants will be recorded in the Historical Collation according to the finally inscribed readings of the text. In cases where the manuscript is copy-text and has been emended, rejected manuscript readings appear in the Emendations and are not repeated in the Historical Collation. James's manuscripts are likely to be much rewritten both during the course of composition and in the process of review, creating variants while he struggled to give shape to his thought that are of particular concern to the scholar. Since this edition is bound to the principle that its apparatus should substitute for all authoritative documents, special provision is made by a list of Alterations in the Manuscripts for the analysis and description of every difference between the initial inscription and the final revision. Alterations which are included in the Historical Collation or Emendations (set off by a special warning sign) as part of the final manuscript reading there recorded as a variant are not repeated in the list of Alterations in the Manuscripts.

A special section of the apparatus treats hyphenated word-compounds, listing the correct copy-text form of those broken between lines by the printer of the present edition and indicating those in the present text, with the form adopted, that were broken between lines in the copy-text and partake of the nature of emendations. Consultation of the first list will enable any user to quote from the present text with the correct hyphenation of the copy-text.

Manuscript material that is reproduced or is quoted in this edition is transcribed in diplomatic form,[5] without emendation, except for two features. As with many writers, James's placement of punctuation in relation to quotation marks was erratic, sometimes appearing within the marks as in the standard American system for commas and periods, sometimes outside according to the sense as in the British system, and sometimes carelessly placed immediately below the quotation mark. To attempt to determine the exact position of each mark would often be impossible; hence all such punctuation is placed as it would be by an American printer, the system that James in fact seems to have employed himself when he thought of it. Second, the spacing of ellipsis dots has been normalized. As part of this normalization the distinction is made (James's spacing usually being variable and ambiguous) between the closeup placement of the first of four dots when it represents the period directly after the last quoted word and the spaced placement (as in three dots) when the ellipsis begins in mid-sentence and the fourth dot thus represents the final period. According to convenience, manuscripts may be transcribed in their final, or clear-text, form, with all alteration variants recorded systematically in an apparatus list, or on occasion they may be transcribed with a record of their alteration variants placed within the text. An abstract of the major features of the formulaic system for

---

[5] A diplomatic transcript reproduces exactly the final form of the original, insofar as type can represent script, but with no attempt to follow the lining of the original or visually—by typographical devices—to reproduce deletions, interlineations, additions, or substitutions. It follows that no emendation is attempted in such a transcript and all errors in the text are allowed to stand without correction, although a sparing use of square brackets for addition or clarification has been permitted.

recording alterations, especially when they are described within the transcript of the text, may be found in the headnote to the Alterations in the Manuscripts.[6]

In this edition of THE WORKS OF WILLIAM JAMES an attempt has been made to identify the exact edition used by James for his quotations from other authors and ordinarily to emend his carelessnesses of transcription so that the quotation will reproduce exactly what the author wrote in every detail. All such changes are noted in the list of Emendations. On some occasions James altered quotations for his own purposes in such a manner that his version should be respected. Such readings are retained in the text but recorded in the list of Emendations (with the signal *stet*), and the original form is provided for the information of the consulting scholar. The general principles governing the treatment of emendations are as follows. As a rule, the author's accidentals are inserted from the original to replace variants created in the normal course of James's copying without particular attention to such features, or of compositorial styling. For substantives, James faced the usual problem of a quoter in getting at the meat of the quotation by judicious condensation. He was likely to mark major omissions by ellipsis dots. On the other hand, he was by no means invariably scrupulous in indicating a number of his alterations. Thus to condense a quotation he might silently omit material ranging from a phrase to several sentences. Major omissions that would require excessive space to transcribe in the list of Emendations are indicated in the text by editorially added dots, recorded as emendations. For minor condensing omissions, James's text is ordinarily allowed to stand without the distraction of ellipsis dots, and the omitted matter is recorded as part of a *stet* entry in the list of Emendations. However, James's treatment of quotations could be more cavalier. Sometimes to speed up the quotation, but occasionally to sharpen its application to his own ideas, he paraphrased a word or phrase, or a major part of a sentence. Since alteration of this nature was consciously engaged in for literary or philosophic purposes, James's text in such cases is allowed to stand but the original reading is given as part of a *stet* entry in the Emendations. (Rarely, he paraphrased a whole quotation although enclosing it within quotation marks, in which case the marks are editorially removed as an emendation.) More troublesome are the minor variants in wording that seem to have no purpose idealogically or as

[6] For full details of this system, see F. Bowers, "Transcription of Manuscripts: The Record of Variants," *Studies in Bibliography,* 29 (1976), 212-264.

condensations. When in the opinion of the editor these represent merely careless or inadvertent slips in copying, on a par with James's sometimes casual transcription of accidentals, the originals are restored as emendations. Within James's quotations, paragraphing that he did not observe in the original has not been recorded and final dots have not been added editorially when he ends a quotation short of the completion of a sentence. Variation from the original in James's choice whether to begin a quotation with a capital or lower-case letter has also not been recorded. Similarly, James's syntactical capitalization or use of lower case following ellipsis has been ignored whenever by necessity it differs from the original.

Although James's own footnotes are preserved in the text as he wrote them (the only footnotes allowed in the present edition), the citations have been expanded and corrected as necessary in Professor Skrupskelis' Notes to provide the full bibliographical detail required by a scholar, this ordinarily having been neglected in James's own sketchy notation. The Notes also provide full information about quotations in the text that James did not footnote.

References to McDermott (McD) are to the "Annotated Bibliography," *The Writings of William James,* ed. John J. McDermott (New York: Random House, 1967).

Silent alterations in the text of this work concern themselves chiefly with mechanical presentation. For instance, heading capitals are normalized in the first line of any chapter or section, headings may have their final periods removed, the headlines of the originals may be altered for the purposes of the present edition, anomalous typographical conventions or use of fonts may be normalized including roman or italic syntactical punctuation, which here has been made to conform to a logical system. The minutiae of the accidentals of footnote reference have not been recorded as emendations or as rejected readings. For example, in the footnotes book titles are silently italicized from whatever other form present in the copy-text, as within quotation marks; the use of roman or italic fonts is normalized as is the general system of punctuating bibliographical references. In short, such matters involving the reference system have been silently brought into conformity with the printing practice of the time, and usually conform to that found in the styling of the period. When unusual features call for unusual treatment, special notice is always given. Finally, such purely typographical matters as the use of an asterisk instead of a number for a footnote are not recorded.

All line numbers keyed to the text include section numbers and subheadings but do not include spaces after titles or subheadings or within the text itself. James's references to pages within the same essay are silently adjusted to the present edition; references to other volumes already published in the WORKS are added in brackets after James's original page numbers.

The intent of the editorial treatment both in large and in small matters, and in the recording of the textual information, has been to provide a clean reading text for the general user, with all specialized material isolated for the convenience of the scholar who wishes to consult it. The result has been to establish in the wording James's final intentions in their most authoritative form, divorced from verbal corruption whether in the copy-text or in subsequent printings or editions. To this crucial aim has been added the further attempt to present James's final verbal intentions within a logically contrived system of his own accidentals that in their texture are as close to their most authoritative form as controlled editorial theory can establish from the documentary evidence that has been preserved for each work.

The aid offered by this edition to serious scholars of William James's writings is not confined to the presentation of a trustworthy, purified, and established text. Of equal ultimate importance are the apparatuses devoted to the facts about the progress of James's thought from its earliest known beginnings to final publication in journal and book, and continuing to annotation in his private copies by the record of alterations that were usually never made public except when practicable in a few plate-changes. Most of the materials here made available for close study of the development and refinement of James's ideas—almost literally in the workshop—have not previously been seen by scholars except in the James Collection of the Houghton Library, and then they could not be studied in detail without tiresome collation (here fully recorded in the apparatus). Scholars may find fascinating and fruitful for study the record of the manuscripts which—as they can be reconstructed from its apparatus—offer material for scholarly analysis of the way in which James shaped the thought itself as well as its expression, if the two can indeed ever be separated. As this edition progresses, the entire collection of manuscripts and of annotated journals and books at Harvard will be brought to philosophers, wherever they may live, for analysis and research in the privacy and convenience of their own studies.

It is the belief of the editors of the WORKS, and the Advisory Board, that this living historical record of the development of James's philosophical and religious ideas and their expression, as found in the apparatus and appendixes, is as significant a part of the proposed 'definitive edition' for the purposes of scholarly research as is the establishment of texts closer to James's own intentions than is customarily represented by any single preserved document.

F. B.

The Text of *Essays in Religion and Morality*

INTRODUCTION TO *THE LITERARY REMAINS OF THE LATE HENRY JAMES* (1884).

Copy-text: (LR) *The Literary Remains of the Late Henry James,* edited with an Introduction by William James (Boston: Houghton Mifflin, [1884]), pp. 7-119 (McD 1884:5). The title page of the original printing reads: 'THE | LITERARY REMAINS | OF THE LATE | HENRY JAMES | 𝕰𝖉𝖎𝖙𝖊𝖉 𝖜𝖎𝖙𝖍 𝖆𝖓 𝕴𝖓𝖙𝖗𝖔𝖉𝖚𝖈𝖙𝖎𝖔𝖓 | BY WILLIAM JAMES | [device] | BOSTON | JAMES R. OSGOOD AND COMPANY | 1885'. On the verso is the notice: '*Copyright, 1884,* | BY WILLIAM JAMES. | [short rule] | *All rights reserved.* |𝖀𝖓𝖎𝖛𝖊𝖗𝖘𝖎𝖙𝖞 𝕻𝖗𝖊𝖘𝖘 : | JOHN WILSON AND SON, CAMBRIDGE.' When Osgood went bankrupt, Houghton Mifflin took over the stock and reissued the book with its own title, undated, but with a copyright notice of 1884. No volume in the James Collection is identifiable as James's private copy. The two catalogued as *AC85.J2334.8841 (A) and (B) are presentations. Osgood entered the book for copyright under no. 23373 on November 21, 1884; the Library of Congress received the two deposit copies on December 15.

Writing to his father from London on December 14, 1882, after receiving news of his serious illness by telegram, James offered characteristically stoic words of comfort, a moving tribute to the father's intellectual influence on him, and added:

You need be in no anxiety about your literary remains. I will see them well taken care of, and that your words shall not suffer for being concealed. At Paris I heard that Milsand, whose name you may remember in the "Revue des Deux Mondes" and elsewhere, was an admirer of the "Secret of Swedenborg," and Hodgson told me your last book had deeply impressed him. So will it be; especially, I think, if a collection of *extracts* from your various writings were published, after the manner of the extracts from Carlyle, Ruskin, & Co. I have long thought such a volume would be the best monument to you (bMS Am 1092.9 [2545]).

Further mention of the plan for *Literary Remains* appears to be a typed letter of January 9, 1883, sent to James's brother Henry from London:

> I must now make amends for my rather hard ['recep' *del.*] non-receptivity of his doctrines as he urged them so absolutely during his life, by trying to get a little more public justice done them now. As life closes, all a man has done seems like one cry or sentence. Father's cry was the single one that religion is real. The thing is so to "voice" it that other ears shall hear,—no easy task, but a worthy one, which in some shape I shall attempt (#2605).

A few months later, back in the United States, he was investigating his father's papers as indicated by a dictated letter of May 6, 1883, to Houghton Mifflin:

> Can you inform me how many stereotyped pages you have of my father, Henry James's Autobiography?—*My Spiritual Education* is its title, I think, although I find a manuscript title page called *Immortal Life.* The proofs I find among his papers go down to page 55, but as there is an odd page, 62, I think they must be incomplete. If you have anything beyond page 55 I wish you would send me proof of it.
>
> I intend to publish it with other remains of my father as soon as leisure permits (bMS Am 1925 [945]).

The next letter, of July 12 (without year date but probably in 1883), addressed to Parke Godwin indicates that James was still in the planning stage. The following quotation is reprinted from the catalogue *The Collector,* #842, p. 14, of approximately October 1975, issued by Walter R. Benjamin Autographs, Inc. of Hunter, N.Y.:

> "*The manuscript poor Father left of his new book, with a fragment beginning his autobiography, (about 70 pages of print) will be published as soon as I get opportunity to begin the work. I contemplate at the same time publishing (in the same volume) a selection of the best rhetorical passages to be found in his already published books. It seems to me that such extracts may lead many readers to the originals, and so prove the best way to keep his name from dying out of the memory of his fellowmen.*" He does not feel that what few letters he has found merit printing. He does recall his father writing to Godwin in a peculiarly humorous strain and he would appreciate receiving such letters as may have been preserved. He will, of course, return them when he has no further use for them.

On March 30, 1884, James remarked in a typed letter to Thomas Davidson, "This summer I am to edit my poor father's literary remains, 'with a sketch of his writings' which will largely consist of extracts, & no doubt help to the making him better known" (bMS

Am 1092.9 [855]). In a dictated letter to Katharine James Prince dated June 25 but clearly in 1884, he added, "We have brought [to Springfield Center, Otsego County, New York] plenty of books and among the things I hope to do here is the getting of poor father's literary remains into such shape that a part of them, at any rate, may be published in the fall" (Colby College). As late as October 18, 1884, James dictated a letter to his brother Henry: "You ask about fathers [*stet*] book. My introduction will be about 120 pages, more than ½ of it being extracts. I worked hard at it for two or three weeks during the summer and felt as if I had never been as intimate with father before. The Book ought to [be] out by middle of November" (#2614). Two days later, on October 20, he remarked in a dictated letter to Katharine Prince: "I succeeded during the summer in doing ['th' *del.*] my part of the work on fathers [*stet*] literary remains. The book will appear in two or three weeks. I made a lot of extracts from his previous writings some of which I think you will enjoy" (Colby College). To Karl Stumpf he wrote on November 15, 1884, complaining of his ill health, "besides having during the past few months to get through the press a volume of my father's literary remains" (#3780). Another letter to Katharine Prince on December 24 starts: "I mailed you yesterday a copy of poor dear old Father's 'Literary Remains,' which you are not bound to read if your head disagrees, but which I know you will like to see and possess. The Autobiography will, however[,] interest you, and perhaps parts of the Introduction, in the writing of which all alone here last summer, I seemed to sink into an intimacy with Father["'s mind' *del.*], which I had never before enjoyed. I trust he takes cognizance of it, somewhere" (Colby College).

The theme of atonement appears once more in a letter of February 20, 1885, addressed to Shadworth Hodgson, "For I fear he found *me* pretty unresponsive during *his [*ab. del.* 'my'] life time; and that through my means any post mortem response should come seems a sort of atonement" (#972).

James dipped into his own pocket but he was forced to call on family assistance to subsidize the volume. Writing to Henry on May 21, 1885, about the bankruptcy of Osgood, the original publisher, he explained: "I will gladly lend you anything you want. I owe you, as it is, $128.50 advanced on father's book. I am not likely to lose more than *25 [*ov.* '28'] dollars of what they owe me on that. Aunt Kate insisted on paying $150.00 of the publication expenses. I will send you the $128.00 tomorrow, & glad to get the debt off my hands so quickly" (#2618). Finances recur in a letter to Henry of September 17:

Introduction to The Literary Remains of the Late Henry James

In sending you the ['1000' *del.*] *£ [*insrtd.*] 200 ['lbs' *del.*] (less than 1000. I forget just how much) I told you part of it was repayment of 125 (or 128.50) I had borrowed from you to print Father's book. You had previously insisted that I should not consider that a loan. I am willing, (now that you turn out not to be a loser by Osgood) to treat it as you propose. I am a good deal out of pocket by the book, for which I have not yet received one cent, and of which the sale promises to be very slow. I hoped its publication would increase the demand for his other books. But Houghton's July semi annual account shows only six copies sold in six months, and me in their debt for bindings. Alas! poor Father! It is sad (#2624).

On October 23, 1885, James wrote to Henry: "You say no notice has been taken of father's book. *Doch*! in the Spectator, one of the last September numbers or 1st October ones, I think, was a page-long article, respectful enough, but completely commonplace, and not worth looking up" (#2625). Finally, in the September 19 continuation of a September 1, 1887, letter to Henry, he reported: "I got Ticknor's account last week—poor Father's literary remains *has [ab. del. 'only'] sold *only [*intrl.*] one copy in the past six months! It is pitiful, but there's nothing to be done about it" (#2634).

When he was searching through his father's papers James came upon a fragment of an autobiographical sketch that he reprinted as "Stephen Dewhurst's Autobiography" in the *Atlantic Monthly*, 54 (November 1884), 649-662, in the hope that it would attract attention to the newly published *Literary Remains*. He wrote Henry on October 18, 1884: "I let Scudder have the little autobiography for the Atlantic. I thought it would advertise somewhat the book and in this age of publication would on the whole be no sacrifice of dignity. I trust you feel so likewise" (#2614). Although the few notes are unsigned, they must represent James's writing. On page 649 the "Autobiography" is prefaced by the following bracketed note:

Among the papers left by Mr. Henry James, Sr., was one entitled "Immortal Life: illustrated in a brief autobiographic sketch of the late Stephen Dewhurst. Edited, with an introduction by Henry James." Under the slight disguise of a fictitious autobiography, Mr. James began a sketch of the growth of his mind upon a back-ground of personal history. The paper was left in a fragmentary form, and is here published, with two omissions and with the exception of the explanatory introduction.

James then glosses half a dozen of the fictitious references in the text: Somerset County he identifies on page 649 as County Cavan, Ireland; Baltimore as Albany, New York; a gun-shot wound in the arm is glossed as "At the age of thirteen, Mr. James had his right leg so severely burned while playing the then not usual game of fire-ball that he was confined to his bed for two years, and two thigh amputations had to be performed." On page 650 Dewhurst's mother's father, unnamed, is identified as "John Barber, of (then) Montgomery, Orange Co., N.Y. (near Newburgh)"; this grandfather's two brothers who fought in the Revolutionary War, Colonel F. B. and Major W. B., are identified as Francis Barber and William Barber, respectively. At the end on page 662 James adds the bracketed note "End of the manuscript" and subscribes *"Henry James."*

James's last act of piety was his publication in the *Atlantic Monthly,* 94 (December 1904), 740-745, of his father's essay "Emerson," presumably found among his papers after the publication of *Literary Remains.* To this essay James prefixed the following headnote (McD 1904:18), which refers to the essay entitled "Some Personal Recollections of Carlyle," in *Literary Remains,* pp. 421-468:

[NOTE.—The paper that follows was composed by the late Henry James in 1868, or thereabouts, and read a few times to private audiences. It forms a sort of *pendant* to a more elaborate paper on Carlyle, which had been written previously, and which, after Carlyle's death, appeared in the ATLANTIC (May, 1881), and subsequently in Henry James's *Literary Remains* (Boston, 1885). Whoso wishes to see a more unceremonious view of Emerson than that now printed, will find it in the latter book, pp. 292-302. My father was a theologian of the "twice-born" type, an out-and-out Lutheran, who believed that the moral law existed solely to fill us with loathing for the idea of our own merits, and to make us turn to God's grace as our only opportunity. But God's grace, in Mr. James's system, was not for the individual in isolation: the sphere of redemption was *Society.* In a Society organized divinely our *natures* will not be altered, but our spontaneities, because they then will work harmoniously, will all work innocently, and the Kingdom of Heaven will have come. With these ideas, Mr. James was both fascinated and baffled by his friend Emerson. The personal graces of the man seemed to prefigure the coming millennium, but the resolute individualism of his thought, and the way in which his imagination rested on superior personages, and on heroic anecdotes about them, as if these were creation's ultimates, set my father's philosophy at defiance. For him no man was superior to another in the final plan. Emerson would listen, I fancy, as if charmed, to James's talk of the "divine natural Humanity," but he would never *subscribe*; and this, from one whose native gifts were so suggestive of that same Humanity, was disappointing. Emerson, in short, was a "once-born" man; he lived in moral distinctions, and recognized no need of a redemptive process. My father worked off his mingled enchantment and irritation in the following pages, in which he pits Emerson's unconscious being against his conscious intellect, and treats the latter as symbolic of the natively innocent Humanity that is to be.—WILLIAM JAMES.]

For his introduction to *Literary Remains* James or an amanuensis copied the numerous quotations from his father's writings with no particular regard for the exact accidentals of the originals. The changes are chiefly in punctuation but occasionally in spelling and in capitalization. The present edition restores in most cases the Henry James, Sr., accidentals but gives William the usual leeway in substantives for his purposes of condensation and general presentation. The recording in the list of Emendations of some hundreds of these restored trifling accidentals would have consumed more space than could be justified for this particular text; hence the quotations have been silently corrected in their copy-text accidentals to bring them into conformity with the originals, and only the substantive variants have been recorded as emendations. However, the textual editor's alterations have been listed, and *stet* entries have been made for all variants, whether accidental or substantive, where the readings of the copy-text have been retained as against the original documents.

ROBERT GOULD SHAW: ORATION BY PROFESSOR WILLIAM JAMES (1897).

Copy-text: (M) *The Monument to Robert Gould Shaw* (Boston: Houghton Mifflin, 1897), pp. 71-87 (McD 1897:2), published simultaneously in the identical typesetting with *Exercises at the Dedication of the Monument to Colonel Robert Gould Shaw* (Boston: Municipal Printing Office, 1897), pp. 35-53.

A copy of the program laid in James's copy of the Houghton Mifflin volume (*AC85.J2376.A897m) reads: CEREMONIES | Incident to the | Unveiling of the | Colonel Robert G. Shaw Memorial | AT | MUSIC HALL, BOSTON, MONDAY, 31 MAY, 1897. | [orn. rule] | [outlined letters] *Order of Exercises.* | [orn. rule] | Music, [10 dots] Instrumental | Meeting called to order by the Chief Marshal, and the | Chairman of the Committee on the Memorial | called to preside. | Prayer, [4 dots] Rev. Edward H. Hall, Chaplain of the Day | Greeting to His Excellency the Governor, Roger | Wolcott, and Transfer of the Memorial to His Honor | the Mayor of Boston, by the Chairman of the | Committee. | Acceptance by His Honor, Mayor Quincy. | Chorus, [10 dots] "Our Heroes" | Oration, [4 dots] Prof. William James, of Harvard University | Chorus, [6 dots] "Battle Hymn of the Republic" | Address, [3 dots] Pres. Booker T. Washington, of Tuskegee Institute | Music, [10 dots] Instrumental.

The reason for James's selection as orator is provided in the introduction given him by Governor Wolcott: "In that splendid charge at Fort Wagner, side by side with those to whom was given the happy destiny of an heroic death, were others, white and black, who like them gladly held out their lives a willing offering to Fate.

Among these, wounded but not dead, fell Adjutant James [Garth W. James, died 1883]. It is fitting that the committee should have selected his brother, Professor William James of Harvard University, to tell the story that is commemorated in this monument."

On February 7, 1897, in a letter to his brother Henry, dictated to his wife Alice, James wrote:

> Honours have been cast in my path with unusual frequency since I wrote you. I have been invited, ['an' *del.*] to give the address at the unveiling of the St [*stet*] Gaudens monument to Robert Shaw Wilkie's Colonel, and have accepted. It's a strange freak of the whirligig of fortune that finds me haranguing the multitude on Boston Common, and I hesitated a good deal what to do. But one ought not to be too ready to funk an honour and the problem is really a very simple one, there being only three or four things which any possible orator would on that occasion have to say. It resolves itself really into the labor of making one's phrases impressive. It comes off on Decoration Day, the 31st of May. The monument is really a glorious work of art, simple and realistic, and worthy of comparison with the very best modern work. Don't bruit this abroad as it won't get into the papers, I hope, for some time (bMS Am 1092.9 [2776]).

In an undated letter to Harvard's William Roscoe Thayer, James declined to give an address in the Agassiz series: "I haven't got two Agassiz discourses [see McD 1897:1] inside of me; and even if I had I have all that I can do in the line of preparation for that sort of thing in the Address at the unveiling of the Shaw monument at the end of May. Compositions of that sort are excessively difficult tasks for my brain" (bMS Am 1631 [212]). On April 4 he announced to Henry that he had finished the speech but would need to revise it (bMS Am 1092.9 [2777]). On April 14 Booker T. Washington thanked James for the copy he had received of the oration (probably that of the first typescript) and promised to consult with him if duplication were to occur in his own address (bMS Am 1092 [1163]). On June 9 Washington wrote again to thank James for his praise of Washington's address and to respond in kind (bMS Am 1092 [1164]).

On May 31, the night of the event, James's wife Alice wrote to Henry her account of the occasion:

> It is late and the household is in bed but I cannot sleep till I have told you of how great a day we have lived through, and of how noble William's part in it has been. You will read his address and feel its beauty, but you cannot measure the full power of it unless you had been one of that great audience in Music Hall, listening with rapt attention from the first word to the last. When the Governor introduced William the cheering was *tremendous* and long continued. Speaking of it to me afterwards William said "Did you notice that applause, it looks as if I were popular"! He will never half know how many

people here care for him. Well! When the oration was over Mr Eliot, Col. Lee, and all the other men who have for years been watching & working for this day, came about us and each in his own way told me of their profound delight in, and appreciation of William's oration. He spoke it very simply—not as if he himself thought it very fine—but tired as he was he was heard perfectly even to the edge of the standing crowd.

Last evening when we were beating about that dreary Back Bay, the rain pouring down on us while we tried to find a throat specialist I had a great fear that William's dear voice would go utterly. It was a nervous symptom but a threatening form when we thought of today's strain. . . .

June 1st P.S. Every kind of congratulation has come to William today. He is very tired, but he is pleased with his success and next week we leave for dear, peaceful Chocorua (bMS Am 1092.11 [37]).

To this Henry replied on June 15 with praise for the address and the comment: "What a funk indeed—over the voice-question—you must have been in the night before! But now it all adds to the romance and the drama" (bMS Am 1094 [1621]). James's own account appears in a typed letter to Henry of June 5:

Alice wrote you *(I think) [*parens ink added*] a brief word after the crisis of last Monday. It took it out of me nervously a good deal, for it came at the end of the month of May, when I am always fagged to death; and for a week previous I had almost lost my voice with hoarseness. At nine o'clock the night before I ran in['to a' *ink del.*] *to a [*ink insrtd.*] laryngologist in Boston, who sprayed and cauterized and otherwise tuned up my throat, giving me *pellets [*ink* 1 'e' *ov.* 'i'] to suck all the morning. By a sort of miracle I spoke for three-quarters of an hour without becoming perceptibly hoarse. But it is a curious kind of physical effort to fill a hall as large as Boston Music Hall, unless you are trained to the work. You have to shout and bellow, and you seem to yourself wholly unnatural. The day was an extraordinary occasion for sentiment. The streets were thronged with people, and I was toted around for two hours in a barouche at the tail end of the procession. There were seven such carriages in all, and I had the great pleasure of being with St. Gaudens, who is a most charming and modest man. The weather was cool and the skies were weeping, but not enough to cause any serious discomfort. They simply formed a harmonious background to the pathetic sentiment that reigned over the day. It was very peculiar, and people have been speaking about it ever *since—[*ink dash ov. comma*] the last wave of the war breaking over Boston, everything softened and made poetic and unreal by distance, poor little Robert Shaw erected into a great symbol of deeper things than he ever realized himself—"the tender grace of a day that is *dead"—[*ink dash insrtd.*] etc. We shall never have anything like it again. The monument is really superb, certainly one of the finest things of this century. Read the darkey Washington's speech, a model of elevation and brevity. The thing that struck me most in the day was the faces of the old 54th soldiers, of which there were perhaps about thirty or forty present, with such respectable old darkey faces, the heavy animal look entirely absent, and in its place the wrinkled, patient, good old darkey citizen.

As for myself, I will never accept such a job again. It is entirely outside of my legitimate line of business, although my speech seems to have been a great success, if I can judge by the encomiums which are pouring in upon me on every hand. I brought in some mugwumpery at the end, but it was very difficult to manage it (bMS Am 1092.9 [2779]).

Later, on July 2, James thanked Professor George H. Howison for his comments on the Oration, and added: "It was a wonderful day for pathos, more so, I think, than any one was prepared for—the last wave of the war breaking over Boston, and stirring feelings that every one had more or less forgotten. The very skies were gently weeping, and the ['whole' *del.*] *material* of the celebration being purely romantic, the whole thing was ideal in the extreme. I groaned at the job, before it was over; but now I am very glad to have had the privilege of being associated with it" (#1044).

In the oration James refers to his having read Shaw's letters to his family from the day in April that he enlisted and adds, "Some day they must be published." It is odd that James did not know and was not referred to the edition of Shaw's letters that was privately printed by the University Press in Cambridge in 1864, but the differences in text between the letters as he quotes from them in the oration and the printed version are so marked as to suggest that he used the originals, though perhaps altering them for the purposes of public delivery. At any rate, under the circumstances it has not been thought necessary to provide in the Historical Collation the extensive listing of differences between the letters as utilized in the oration and as found in the privately printed 1864 book. Outside of Shaw's letters how widely James read in preparation for the oration is not altogether clear, but it is certain that he drew, perhaps exclusively, for the account of the attack on Fort Wagner on the *History of the Fifty-fourth Regiment of Massachusetts Volunteer Infantry 1863-1865* (Boston: Boston Book Co., 1894; offset reprint as *A Brave Black Regiment*, New York: Arno Press and the New York Times, 1969), by Luis F. Emilio, a captain in the regiment, who took part in the assault. A few passages are taken over almost verbatim. With *at noon . . . immediately.'"* (70.20-30) one may compare Emilio's account:

Upon arriving at Morris Island, Colonel Shaw and Adjutant James walked toward the front to report to General Strong, whom they at last found, and who announced that Fort Wagner was to be stormed that evening. Knowing Colonel Shaw's desire to place his men beside white troops, he said, "You may lead the column, if you say 'yes.' Your men, I know, are worn out, but do as you choose." Shaw's face brightened, and before replying, he requested Adjutant James to return and have Lieutenant-Colonel Hallowell bring up the Fifty-fourth (p. 72).

Similarly, *Walking . . . head.* (70.33-37) is drawn from:

Colonel Shaw walked along the front to the centre, and giving the command, "Attention!" the men sprang to their feet. Then came the admonition, "Move in quick time until within a hundred yards of the fort; then double quick, and charge!" A slight pause, followed by the sharp command, "Forward!" and the Fifty-fourth advanced to the storming (p. 79).

A detail in *with uplifted . . . heart.* (71.7-8) comes from: "with uplifted sword, shouting, 'Forward, Fifty-fourth!' and then fell dead, shot through the heart, besides other wounds" (p. 82). Finally, *"The . . . lived."* (71.18-19) comes from "The negroes fought gallantly, and were headed by as brave a colonel as ever lived" (p. 95).

The oration must first have been written out in longhand in a draft not now preserved, for the earliest text we have is TMs, a typescript (MS Am 1092.9 [4538]) now mounted, ending incomplete with a deleted passage after 'echoes of past music on the vacant air.' (73.31). The typescript is a professional one, the ribbon copy, typed on a wove paper 10½ x 8″ watermarked Merchants Pure Bond, the sheets numbered in the upper right corner. Pencil and ink revisions can only occasionally be placed in order. It would seem that there was an initial series of ink alterations on first reading over the typescript, followed by an extensive pencil revision, followed in turn by an equally extensive revision in ink, a few pencil alterations, and at least one further round in ink.[1] From time to time James added on extra sheets handwritten passages or substituted revisions for deleted typed text, either supplementing the typed pages or replacing typed sheets that were then discarded. The original typed sheets that are preserved are numbered [1] 2, 5-15, 19(16), 20(17), 21(18), 22(19), 23(20). Handwritten sheets appear as fols. 3, 3½, 4, 6½, 7½, 8½, 16-18, 21½.

The typed text on fol. 1 opens with a paragraph starting 'The death struggles of one generation become the material for the works of art of the next', but not utilized in the final printed ver-

---

[1] As noted in some Emendation and Historical Collation entries, a few pencil revisions were touched up or altered in ink, and typed passages altered in pencil (and in ink) may be deleted in ink. That some pencil alterations were later than some ink is demonstrated on fol. 15 in a typed passage now deleted in ink and then rewritten later in longhand, the typed text now represented by revised 71.14-17. The typescript had read 'regiment only eighteen weeks old which had smelt the enemy's powder'. In an ink revision James interlined 'which had been' over a caret between 'regiment' and 'only', and deleted 'old' in favor of the ink interlineation 'in existence, and'. Later, in pencil, he deleted these two ink revisions, substituting pencil 'whose first recruits had been mustered in' for the first and 'earlier' for 'in existence' of the second.

sion. Then at its end, following a thanks to the donors and the sculptor, James wrote-in and circled "Turn over" and on the verso of the sheet, headed "Insert" he wrote in ink what became the second sentence of the final opening paragraph, *In these unveiling exercises . . . Robert Shaw and of his regiment* (64.1-5). Folios 3-4 of TMs have been removed and replaced by three sheets of handwritten substitutes (65.9 *should be . . . casual inaccurate* 66.13), foliated 3, 3½, 4, the first two on Merchants Bond paper but fol. 4 on a laid paper 11 × 8½" watermarked in script Bankers Linen. Folio 3½ (65.20 [*om. in text; see Emendations entry* 65.20 *for original reading*] *which until then . . . march,* 65.30) is written on the reversed back of original typed fol. 21 (for which see later). The typed sheets resume with fol. 5 (66.13 *methods*) and continue to 6, after which is placed a sheet numbered 6½ (altered from 7) which holds the handwritten substitute (67.13 *This grace . . . kind* 67.16) for a deleted typed passage heading typed fol. 7, renumbered 7 in ink in the upper margin for clarity when a deleted ink interlined prefix to the first line of the typed text obscured the number. The preceding typed fol. 6 had ended with the text *he thought little* [M *Shaw thought but little*] *of himself* (67.11). In the lower margin, written vertically, James noted parenthetically in ink, later deleted, "I shall revise this characterization, which leaves the martial quality out too much." The following ink addition in the lower margin (67.11 *But he* [M *yet he*] *. . . praise."* 67.13) was written after this note to himself but does not emphasize Shaw the soldier, nor indeed does the handwritten addition on fol. 6½.

This addition foliated 6½ is written on the reversed back of a sheet that had originally begun, in James's hand, 'In *this [alt. fr. 'the'] unveiling ceremony the duty has fallen to me of expressing in simple *words, [*ab. del.* 'language,'] but in this *public ['p' *ov.* 'f'] fashion, [*ab. del.* 'manner,'] the ['feelings and' *del.*] thoughts and feelings which may have actuated the donors of the monument.' (This is the trial for the insertion found on the verso of fol. 1, *In these unveiling . . . regiment.*) Below, after a space, is a trial, now deleted: 'Think *for a moment [*intrl.*] of *the [*ov.* 'its'] ['antecedents of its' *del. intrl.*] Colonel and think of its rank and file. Think'. Below this is still another deleted trial, 'whose Colonel, reared in *luxury, [*comma insrtd. bef. del.* ''s lap,'] & educated in the best culture of two continents, casts in his lot with'. The two latter trials, of similar material, may have formed early jottings for the eventual continuation of the upper trial for the insertion of fol. 1 verso, but it is perhaps more likely that they lie in back of the text on handwritten fol. 3½ beginning *Look at the* [M *that*] *monument* (65.23 ff.). The present recto of fol. 6½ was written after the page had been turned upside down to put the deleted two words 'In this' at the foot, out of the way. Since these words begin the first trial found on the verso, it seems evident that the three verso trials were written on the back of a sheet which James had started with 'In this' before breaking off and beginning again on the verso. Thus the addition *This grace . . . kind* (67.13-16) comes later than the tinkering with the opening of the oration.

The typed text resumes with fol. 7 *that he could* (67.16) after a deletion and ends with *Fortune sends an opportunity, but the man's sense for what is vital in things must be alert to take it up.*, a sentence omitted from the print after *path.* (67.22). The lower half of fol. 7 contains a massive, much reworked deletion for which is then substituted a handwritten revision on fol. 7½, a sheet of wove paper watermarked Old Berkshire Mill 1897. This revised text (67.22 *Shaw . . . moment his* 67.31) is followed by typed fol. 8, ending *eagerness to* (68.8) after which is inserted another handwritten sheet, fol. 8½, on Berkshire Mill paper (68.8-9 *make arms . . . discipline of* 68.13) which revises a deleted passage heading typed fol. 9. From the start of undeleted text on fol. 9 (68.13 *other regiments*) to the end of the upper third of fol. 15 (71.8 *and then fell*) followed by a massive deletion, the typescript pages are in order. However, the deletion of the lower two-thirds of fol. 15 and of the upper third of original typed 16 is replaced by three sheets of handwritten substitute (71.8 *headlong . . . Fort* 71.35), the first on Merchants Bond paper originally numbered 15½ but altered to 16, the second on Berkshire Mill paper marked 17, and a half-page of inscription on Merchants Bond paper numbered 18. When after the upper deletion the typed text resumes (71.35-36 *Wagner's*), the numbering 16 is altered in ink to 19, and so on for the rest of the typed pages ending with 23(20). On fol. 21(18) after *enthroned abuse.* (72.40) five handwritten lines on Merchants Bond paper (72.40 *The deadliest . . . saved. The* 73.3) foliated 21½ replace a deleted sentence at the head of fol. 22(19) as well as a deleted handwritten first revisory attempt at the foot of 21(18). In turn this text on 21½ was written on the reversed back of an earlier attempt at the same passage written in pencil and marked 21½ but deleted in ink.

Typed text resumes on fol. 22(19) with *nation truly blest* [M *nation blest*] (73.3) and breaks off on fol. 23(20) with *vacant air.* (73.31) above seven deleted typed lines concluding the page, unrevised except for a prefixed *But* and ink commas after *So . . . only.* However, as remarked, handwritten fol. 3½ of an insertion had been written on the reversed back of what was originally the next fol. 21, the typed number and text undeleted, which in two lines concluded the original typescript after *had to deal. (fol. 23*[20] 73.37) with *Can we prize too highly, can* | [*fol.* 21] *we guard too zealously a treasure for which so dear a price was paid? No,.* Below the two typed lines in a following note, both later deleted with a single diagonal ink stroke, James wrote: "One page more of peroration inspiring to avert all future civil wars will close the thing. I shall write that page later on." Whether or not James's announcement to Henry on April 4 about the completion of the speech was written before or after the typescript had been made (very likely before), one might conjecture that this note could have been added sometime in the second week of April, perhaps. The undeleted state of its typed text and foliation indicates that it antedates the addition of handwritten fols. 16-18 which caused the typed foliation of 16-20 to be changed by hand to 19-23. It also must antedate, of course, the use of the back of the sheet for the insertion of fol. 3½. The later deletion of the typed text in the lower part of fol. 23(20) after only minor revises in ink is a little odd in that it does not differ markedly from the printed text, at least no more than could have been contrived by normal annotation of the typed lines. Thus James would have made a fresh start on the peroration with a new sheet[2] (now lost) that substantially repeated the deletion before continuing to the close. The evidence that the ink alteration of the deleted passage was unusually slight suggests that James did not write the note and later compose the peroration until he had looked over the typescript as a whole and made some preliminary revisions in ink, this probably on receipt of the sheets from the typist. If this is so, then there is further evidence that at least one stage of ink revision precedes the first of the two layers of pencil alteration. That the peroration was completed before the major revision that led to the insertion of the handwritten leaves is suggested by the use of discarded original fol. 21 for the inscription of added fol. 3½ as the second of two inserted leaves. We need not assume that James came to the conclusion before further revision of the whole than that which is represented in the now deleted text at the foot of fol. 23(20); but at least the really major layer(s) of revision found in the added sheets seems to have come later.[3]

---

[2] He could not utilize the space below the two typed lines on original fol. 21 to begin the peroration because the handwritten note took up too much space.

[3] The note on fol. 21 that he would write the peroration later may perhaps be addressed to himself, but its wording suggests, instead, the possibility that James wrote it for the information of the typist. Hence it may well have been added at the moment that

The numerous differences between the printed text and the final readings of the typescript indicate that for delivery another typescript, now lost, was made up from the preserved draft, this second typescript (in ribbon or carbon, and manifestly containing still further revision) serving as the printer's copy. The circumstances behind the duplicate printing of the speech from identical type as part of two separate publications recording the ceremony are unknown. The different contents of the two volumes, as well as their variant pagination, demonstrate that their production was not a simple case of overrun sheets but instead of reimposition and rearrangement of standing type. Since the type for James's oration is identical, without variation, in both printings, the question of priority has no textual significance, fortunately. Whether the type was set by the Boston Municipal Printing Office and was utilized by some arrangement by Houghton Mifflin, or vice versa, is not established. The H. O. Houghton Printing Orders for 1897, p. 255, in the Houghton Library, Harvard, record the Shaw volume as Item 659 entered on July 15 for 500 copies to be charged to the Committee of the Shaw Memorial. Thus the Houghton Mifflin edition was not a commercial but a subsidized production. The original order was noted as received on July 17, as given out on August 4, the book on press August 11 as order no. 358, the sheets sent to the drying room on August 19 and to the bindery on August 31.

The oration was reprinted in a different typesetting with other material from the ceremonies under the title "The Commemoration of Robert Gould Shaw," in P[13], the *Harvard Graduates' Magazine,* 6 (September 1897), the oration occupying pages 28-37. This text follows M very closely, with no signs that James had looked over the copy and made any alterations. The substantive variant *Virginia* for *Virginian* (68.16) is not supported by TMs. The several occasions when the punctuation in P[13] agrees with TMs against M are very likely fortuitous since it is improbable that James would have confined any reading-over of the M pages for the *Magazine* to the alteration of a few punctuation marks.

In the Houghton Library, catalogued as *AC85.J2376.A897m,

James finished reading the returned sheets and marking them occasionally as something caught his eye; but it could have come later after enough revision so that James was at least contemplating a second (purportedly final) typing of the first typed draft. If so, his original intention would have been to get the body of his speech into shape for retyping before he tackled the conclusion, an intention that he abandoned as the revision began to spread out and he saw the necessity to complete the oration and then revise it as a whole from the beginning to a known end. The final typescript, not preserved, would have been made up from the revised sheets of the present draft plus the handwritten sheets of the peroration.

is a copy of the Houghton Mifflin volume with various revisions in pencil and in ink in James's hand. Inserted in the volume is a slip "Corrected by W. J." in the hand of his son, Henry Jr. When Henry James, Jr., brought together seventeen of his father's pieces, including the oration in its revised form, under the title *Memories and Studies* (New York and London: Longmans, Green & Co., 1911), he asserted in the Prefatory Note that he was carrying out a plan for a collection that had been in his father's mind before his death. One could conjecture that James made the revisions for the proposed *Harvard Graduates' Magazine* reprint but by some mishap the copy was not given to the printer. On the other hand, the possibility must be admitted that they were made at a later time with collection in view.[4] No certainty is possible.

The editorial problem of James's Shaw oration chiefly concerns the choice of copy-text. Despite the closer relation of TMs to the lost original holograph, the great number of differences between the final text of TMs and that of M indicates that James devoted his usual scrupulous care to publication and that on the whole the printed text has the superior overall authority for the accidentals,[5] usually the governing factor in the choice of copy-text. This situation is found in other of James's texts when antecedent drafts have been preserved. It is simpler, therefore, to restore a limited number of TMs accidental readings[6] where M runs contrary to James's usual style and the difference may reasonably be imputed to the printer than to attempt to place the heavily revised substantives within the accidental texture of TMs. For this reason M has been selected as copy-text, altered chiefly by the introduction of

---

[4] If so, the annotated Houghton Mifflin volume would represent the only known example of copy marked for this rather vaguely planned collection. The casual correction of some offprints found in the James Collection does not seem to have been made with the same purpose in view, especially since various of these were further revised in other copies for collection in *The Meaning of Truth* and the proposed *Essays in Radical Empiricism*. The appearance in the marked copy of one necessary correction in Henry James, Jr.'s hand (the alteration in ink of *have* to *had* at 73.37, a reading made independently in P[13]) does not bear on the question of the purpose of William James's annotation of the copy.

[5] However, the variant shortening of a number of paragraphs made in M, although retained in the present edition, is more likely to have been added by the printer for typographical reasons and its authority is highly suspect. Nowhere else in a revision does James tinker with the paragraphing to this extent.

[6] The highest authority in TMs comes in the handwritten sections, whether inserted pages or revisions to the typed text. There is some indication, however, that the typist was relatively faithful to James's punctuation and capitalization. Hence some emendations may be drawn from typed readings, even though of lesser authority than those in James's autograph.

James's final intentions for publication as evidenced by the readings of the marked copy of the *Monument* volume in the James Collection. Although the text of P¹³, the *Harvard Graduates' Magazine,* has no ostensible authority, the textual editor has deemed it wisest to list in the Historical Collation its independent variation from M both for accidentals and substantives, and to record its readings, as appropriate, in the list of Emendations. On the other hand, although it reprints the text of James's revised copy (not always faithfully), *Memories and Studies* (M&S) has no independent authority. As an historical record, therefore, only its substantives are noticed in the list of Emendations (except for one correction drawn from it) and in the Historical Collation.

Although James placed between quotation marks the account by Adjutant Garth W. James of the Fifty-fourth's baptism under fire from *War Papers* cited in his footnote (70.1-18), the quotation is treated somewhat freely for the purposes of the oration and James, of course, never troubled to restore the exact text. Since the oration is not a scholarly essay in which James's quotations are usually corrected in this edition from his source, his own version has been allowed to stand in the present text. The actual quotation from *War Papers* is as follows:

His favorite regiment, the 24th Massachusetts Infantry, one of the best that had so far ever faced the rebel foe, recruited within the precincts of Boston, largely officered by Boston men, was surrounding his headquarters. It had become a living, breathing suspicion with us, and perhaps not altogether justly, that all white troops abhorred our presence in the army, that the 24th Massachusetts Infantry would rather hear of us in some remote corner of the Confederacy than tolerate us in the advance of any battle in which they were themselves called upon to act as reserves or lookers on. I appeal to you, then, comrades, can you not readily share with me that indescribable sensation which a youthful soldier feels, who, placed in a like situation, leading heroic negro soldiers on to victorious battle for the first time in the history of the war, as I alighted from my horse, before Gen. Terry, and his staff (I was going to say his unfriendly staff, but of this I am not sure), to report to him, with Col. Shaw's compliments, that we had repulsed the enemy without the loss of an inch of ground. Gen. Terry bade me mount again after a few words interchanged between us, and tell Col. Shaw that he was proud of the conduct of his men, and to still hold the ground against any future sortie of the enemy. I believe you can, comrades, even now, share with me the sensation of that moment of soldierly satisfaction! (pp. 19-20).

HUMAN IMMORTALITY: TWO SUPPOSED OBJECTIONS TO THE DOCTRINE (1898).

Copy-text: (HI) *Human Immortality* (Boston and New York: Houghton Mifflin, 1898) (McD 1898:5). The "Preface to Second Edition" uses as copy-text the printing of 1899 (McD 1899:11).

The first edition, first printing, may be described as follows:

HUMAN IMMORTALITY | TWO SUPPOSED OBJECTIONS | TO THE DOC-TRINE | BY | WILLIAM JAMES | PROFESSOR OF PHILOSOPHY AT HAR-VARD UNIVERSITY AND | INGERSOLL LECTURER FOR 1898 | [Riverside Press device] | BOSTON AND NEW YORK | HOUGHTON, MIFFLIN AND COMPANY | 𝕿𝖍𝖊 𝕽𝖎𝖛𝖊𝖗𝖘𝖎𝖉𝖊 𝕻𝖗𝖊𝖘𝖘, 𝕮𝖆𝖒𝖇𝖗𝖎𝖉𝖌𝖊 | 1898

Collation: unsigned $[1^4 \; 2\text{-}4^{12}]$, 40 leaves, pp. [i-vi] [1] 2-45 [46-47] 48-70 [71-74]

Contents: p. i: blank; p. ii: advertisements; p. iii: title; p. iv: 'COPYRIGHT, 1898, BY WILLIAM JAMES | ALL RIGHTS RESERVED'; p. v: 'THE INGERSOLL LECTURESHIP | [short rule] | *Extract from the will of Miss Caroline Haskell Ingersoll,* | *who died in Keene, County of Cheshire, New* | *Hampshire, Jan. 26, 1893.*'; p. vi: blank; p. 1: '[headpiece] | HUMAN IM-MORTALITY | [short rule] ', 'I'^{3} (orn.); p. 46: blank; p. 47: '[headpiece] | NOTES | [short rule] '; on p. 70: 'THE END.'; p. 71: ' 𝕿𝖍𝖊 𝕽𝖎𝖛𝖊𝖗𝖘𝖎𝖉𝖊 𝕻𝖗𝖊𝖘𝖘 | CAMBRIDGE, MASSACHUSETTS U.S.A. | ELECTROTYPED AND PRINT-ED BY | H. O. HOUGHTON AND CO.'; pp. 72-74: blank.

Paper and binding: laid paper, vertical chainlines, unwatermarked (179 X 120 mm.), top edge gilt; cream endpapers front and back, free leaf attached to leaf pasted down on cover. Blue cloth, spine in gold: 'HUMAN | IMMOR-TALITY | [short rule] | JAMES | HOUGHTON | MIFFLIN Cᵒ'.

Copies consulted: Harvard (*AC85.J2376.898h), University of Virginia (BT921.J2 1898).

The book was registered for copyright in the name of Houghton, Mifflin under no. 41266, on July 9, 1898; two copies were received by the Library of Congress on October 5, 1898. *Publishers' Weekly* announced publication in the issue of October 15, 1898.

An important letter of May 31, 1898, from James to Houghton Mifflin gives us the date for his return of the first proofs, and interestingly tells us that the title had been changed from *A Future Life* to *Human Immortality* during the correction of these proofs:

> I enclose the first instalment of proof, corrected. You will observe that I have changed the title to Human Immortality, partly to conform to the Ingersoll bequest more closely, partly because I think it will look much better on the title page, and also sound better in the mouth than "a future life." I have left the running titles unchanged, leaving it to you to decide whether *they [*ab. del.* 'it'] should be correspondingly altered.
>
> I trust that the notes, which have a substantive importance, will not be in a type much smaller than the text. I can myself see no reason why they should n't be in the same identical type (bMS Am 1925 [945]).

In the third printing, the date on the title page was altered to 1899, and in the fifth to 1900.

In the H. O. Houghton Printing Orders for 1898–1901 (fMS Am 1185.9[2]) preserved in the Houghton Library, Harvard, entries are found for the first five printings. Order no. 725 for the first printing of 1000 copies was received on August 15, 1898, the book was put to press on September 22, and the sheets sent to the bindery on October 1 (II, 84). For the second printing, order no. 1002 for 1000 copies was received on October 26, 1898, it was at press on November 3, and the sheets sent to the bindery on November 9 (p. 85). Order no. 44 for 500 copies of the third printing was received on January 24, 1899, it was at press on January 26, and sheets were sent to be bound on March 28; the change of the date to 1899 is specified under the instructions (p. 87). The fourth printing is found under order no. 326 for 1000 copies received on April 7, 1899, sent to the Riverside Press on April 13, printed on April 22, and the sheets sent to be bound on May 11 (p. 88). The last record is order no. 89, the fifth printing, for 500 copies received on January 18, 1900, sent to the Riverside Press and printing started on January 20, the sheets sent to the bindery on January 29 (p. 92). Instructions are given to change the title page date to 1900 and to remove the line '*SECOND EDITION*', adding the 5th impression on the copyright page.

Although no special instructions for the title page are found in the Order Book for the fourth printing received on April 7, 1899 (order no. 326, p. 88), the instructions for the paging indicate that the so-called 'second edition' may be identified as this printing. This impression adds '*SECOND EDITION*' above the device on the title, retains the date 1899 instituted in the third printing, and collates, for the preliminaries: pp. [2] [i-v] vi-ix [x] : p. $^\pi$1: blank; p. $^\pi$2: advertisements; p. i: title; p. ii: copyright notice; p. iii: Ingersoll Lectureship notice; p. iv: blank; p. v: '[headpiece] | PREFACE TO SECOND EDITION | [short rule] ', S^3 (orn.), ending on p. ix; p. x: blank. The paging for the first three printings is given in the Order Book as pages 78: b1 + ad + 4 + 70 + imp + bl, whereas that for the fourth printing takes account of the added preface by requiring pages 84: b1 + ad + 10 + 70 + imp + bl. Machine collation on the Hinman Collator of a University of Virginia copy of the first printing (BT921.J2 1898, copy 2) against the fourth or 'second edition' printing (BT921.J2 1899) discloses no plate changes, not even the correction of the misprint 'trimphantly' in line 23 of page 33.

The first English edition was published on October 8, 1898 (date stamp in British Library copy 4257.bb.32), the title page conjugate with the American sheets of 1898:

HUMAN IMMORTALITY | TWO SUPPOSED OBJECTIONS | TO THE DOC-TRINE | BY | WILLIAM JAMES | PROFESSOR OF PHILOSOPHY AT HARVARD UNIVERSITY AND | INGERSOLL LECTURER FOR 1898 | A. P. WATT & SON | 𝕳𝖆𝖘𝖙𝖎𝖓𝖌𝖘 𝕳𝖔𝖚𝖘𝖊 | NORFOLK STREET, STRAND | LONDON

The Houghton printing order no. 725 for the first impression had the note to run six copies with the imprint of A. P. Watt and Son. These special copies as received by the copyright libraries in Great Britain on October 8, 1898, represent a holding operation for copyright purposes, and the true English edition was the one that was reset throughout by Archibald Constable, in 1898, with the description:

HUMAN IMMORTALITY | TWO SUPPOSED OBJECTIONS | TO THE DOC-TRINE | BY | WILLIAM JAMES | Professor of Philosophy at Harvard University | and Ingersoll Lecturer for 1898 | WESTMINSTER | ARCHIBALD CONSTABLE & CO | 2 WHITEHALL GARDENS | 1898

Collation: [A]^8 B-H^8, 64 leaves, pp. [1-4] 5-87 [88] 89-126 [127-128]

Contents: pp. 1-2: blank; p. 3: title; p. 4: 'BUTLER & TANNER, | THE SELWOOD PRINTING WORKS, | FROME, AND LONDON.'; p. 5: 'THE INGERSOLL LECTURESHIP'; p. 7: text, headed 'HUMAN IMMORTALITY' ending on p. 87; p. 88: blank; p. 89: 'NOTES'; on p. 126: 'THE END. | [short rule] | Butler & Tanner, Frome and London.'; pp. 127-128: blank.

Copies of this first printing of what Constable regarded as the second English edition were not deposited in the statutory libraries of the British Museum or the Bodleian but one is found in the London Library. However, the second printing from these plates was deposited in the British Museum on February 13, 1899 (4257.a.29), and is identical with the 'second edition' (the first Constable printing) except for 'THIRD EDITION' on the title above the imprint, for press notices on *Human Immortality* printed on p. 1 (p. 2 remaining blank), and for Constable advertisements on pp. 127-128. The Bodleian Library has a copy of this 'edition' also, in its original binding (9215.f.2) whereas the British Museum copy has been rebound. The London Library has a copy dated 1903 and carrying the notice 'FIFTH EDITION' on the title. A sixth edition from Constable was published in 1906, the British Library copy (4256.eee.2) carrying the deposit date of October 13. The next edition—the last from Constable—was in 1917, in gray paper wrappers, with the title 'HUMAN IMMORTALITY | TWO SUPPOSED OBJECTIONS | TO THE DOCTRINE | BY | WILLIAM JAMES | LONDON | CONSTABLE & COMPANY | LIMITED'. On the verso of its title is the notice: 'This Address formed the Ingersoll Lecture at | Harvard University for 1898 and was First | Published December, 1898. Reprinted | 1899, 1903, 1906, 1917.'

(Bodleian 9215.f.24). Copyright was transferred to Dent in 1917, who published a new and reset edition deposited in the British Museum on July 23 (4255.ee.8): 'HUMAN IMMORTALITY | TWO SUPPOSED OBJECTIONS | TO THE DOCTRINE | BY | WILLIAM JAMES | INGERSOLL LECTURER FOR 1897-1898 | [device] | 1917 | LONDON AND TORONTO | J. M. DENT & SONS LTD.' The book collates 8°: [A]⁸ B-E⁸, 40 leaves, pp. [1-4] 5-80. On p. 80 is the colophon, 'THE TEMPLE PRESS, PRINTERS, LET-WORTH, ENGLAND'. In this edition the Preface to the Second Edition appeared for the first time in England.

The first reset Constable edition in England in 1898 was a faith-ful reprint of the 1898 first American sheets issued by Watt save for a misprint in 81.2. The Dent edition has not been collated. In the United States, Houghton Mifflin through the Riverside Press put out a number of printings from the original plates, usually un-dated and unidentifiable by inspection.

On October 23, 1897, James wrote to F. C. S. Schiller to thank him for a review and mentioned: "I wrote you a post-card re-cently . . . patting you on the back for your article on Immortality in the 'New World.' A staving good thing. I am myself to give the 'Ingersoll Lecture on Human Immortality' here in November—the second lecturer on the foundation. I treat the matter very inferi-orly to you, but use your conception of the brain as a sifting agency, which explains my question in the letter" (*Letters*, II, 66). Exactly one year later, after reading the essay, Schiller sent to James various comments on it (bMS Am 1092 [830]).

The Harvard Corporation voted James as Ingersoll Lecturer on February 15, 1897 (*Harvard Graduates' Magazine*, 5 [June 1897], 625); he gave the lecture in the Fogg Museum on Wednesday, No-vember 10, 1897. A brief announcement is found in the *Harvard Advocate,* 32 (November 6, 1897), followed by a short outline of the lecture in the same publication on November 11, the day after the address. On December 26, 1897, James repeated the lecture before the Society for Ethical Culture of Chicago, led by W. M. Salter, who had married the sister of James's wife Alice. James begins a letter of November 20, 1897, to Salter with "The ques-tion was raised last summer of my reading my lecture on immortal-ity to your society. It went off here well enough and Alice sees no reason why it should n't be the right sort of thing for your audi-ence." Possible dates are offered with December 27 (in error for the 26th) being the preferred (bMS Am 1092.9 [3680]). In a letter of November 25, James accepts the date of Sunday, December 26, and adds: "As for the lecture, ['it is' *del.*] I was appointed on a new foundation: the "Ingersoll lecture [*closing and opening db. qt. mks. del.*] on Human Immortality, which is to be yearly given and printed. My title is: 'On two supposed objections to the doctrine of a future life.' Don't announce it in any more general form, as I simply confine myself to *these [*poss.* 'those'] two points, one being the 'thought-a-function-of-the-brain' objection, the other the *incredibility of such an [*intrl.*] awful ['pop' *del.*] glut of population in the other world" (#3681). The reference in the first letter to a summer discussion does not necessarily mean that the lecture had been written at that time, but only that the appointment had been accepted and the subject known. According to George Holmes Howison (*The Limits of Evolution* [New York: Macmillan, 1901], p. 279n) James repeated the lecture in September 1898 before the Berkeley Club of Oakland, California.

There being no authority in the English editions, their variants have not been recorded in the Historical Collation.

PREFACE TO STARBUCK'S *PSYCHOLOGY OF RELIGION* (1899).

Copy-text: (S) *The Psychology of Religion,* by Edwin Diller Starbuck (London: Walter Scott, Ltd.; New York: Charles Scribner's Sons, 1899), pp. vii-x (McD 1899:5).

The title page reads: 'THE | PSYCHOLOGY OF RELIGION | An Empirical Study of the Growth of | Religious Consciousness | BY | EDWIN DILLER STARBUCK, PH.D. | ASSISTANT PROFESSOR OF EDUCATION AT LELAND STANFORD | JUNIOR UNIVERSITY | *With a Preface by* | WILLIAM JAMES | PROFESSOR OF PHILOSOPHY AT HARVARD UNIVERSITY | LONDON | WALTER SCOTT, LTD., PATERNOSTER SQUARE | CHARLES SCRIBNER'S SONS | 153-157 FIFTH AVENUE, NEW YORK | 1899'.

The correspondence in which Starbuck asked James to contribute a preface does not seem to have been preserved. A few dates may be gathered, however, from James's correspondence with Havelock Ellis, who was the editor of the Contemporary Science Series in which the book appeared. On August 11, 1899, James wrote to Ellis on a postcard from Bad-Nauheim, Germany: "I sent a card to you at Lelant the other day, explaining my situation here, and begging you to let me have any revises of Starbuck's proofs which may be ready," to which he added a postscript: "Your card of the 8th. has just arrived. Thanks for the information about S.'s proofs" (Havelock Ellis Collection, Yale University Library). From London he wrote to Ellis on September 10, 1899, again, "If there are any *duplicate [*intrl.*] proofs of Starbuck's volume available I should be happy to receive them—not of course for the sake of contributing to their correction, but in order to help me with the promised preface." Finally, on October 17 James again addressed Ellis from London: "Here goes the preface: valeat quantum! [¶] My illness and hard-pressed condition prevent me from copying it out. But I fancy that this pencil draft will be legible both to you & the printers. I should be thankful for any suggested amendments to the proof; and I still feel that a preface from me is rather impertinent." Obviously there are missing letters in this correspondence, but it seems clear that before August 8, 1899, James had been in touch with Ellis about the preface, that it was composed in early October and its original draft sent to Ellis on October 17. James wrote as if he expected proof, but no record of receipt and correction has been observed, nor is it known whether the printer set directly from James's pencil draft or whether Ellis had a typescript prepared as printer's copy. James signed the preface and subscribed it "Harvard University, October 1899" but the letters demonstrate that it was written in London.

PREFACE TO LUTOSLAWSKI'S *WORLD OF SOULS* (1899).

Copy-text: (MS) Holograph manuscript in the James Collection (bMS Am 1092.9 [4462]). Reference is also made to (L) Wincenty Lutoslawski, *A World of Souls* (George Allen & Unwin, 1924), pp. 5-8 (McD 1899:12), the preface subscribed 'William James. Harvard University, August 1899.'

The manuscript consists of eleven leaves of wove paper (250 × 203 mm.) watermarked AGAWAM BOND, foliated [1] 2-11 and headed 'Preface' triple underlined. The manuscript is signed on fol. 11; beneath the signature the sheet has been cut off to allow the attachment of a pasted-on slip of laid paper with rectangular wire-marks containing the direction in a strange hand, 'The above Ms. must be returned with 2 copies of revised proof to Prof. William James c/o Brown Shipley & Co London England'. Deleted false starts occur on the versos of fols. 3, 7, and 10.

The date on which James agreed to write the preface is not known, but it was before July 26, 1899, when Lutoslawski on a postcard wrote: "In looking at your last postcard I notice that you speak therein of that intended preface as if it were written and sent simultaneously—whatever has been my cowardice in begging this help from you, I should be extremely sorry if your Ms had been lost, for I did not receive it. Did you send it? An American friend in Philadelphia, who has undertaken to seek an American publisher for the Souls Power—writes me—after my imprudent communica-

tion of the news that a Preface by you might be added to the Ms—
that then a publisher will be found at once. But that is not in order
to trouble you—let it be as it is—if you have written something I
shall use it—if not—then do not waste your time on me" (bMS Am
1092 [527]).

It seems that this postcard crossed one from James, sent from
Cambridge on July 21, 1899:

> Yes! I will write a preface for your Seelenmachte, although many things in it
> "go agin" me—*e.g.* the use made of the Substanzbegriff. But no matter—here
> goes. Order *revise* proofs in duplicate to be sent me, c/o Brown, Shipley &
> Co., Bankers, London.—You will I hope, before now have received my recent
> letter. We sail on the 15th. for Hamburg, whence for a few weeks to Nauheim,
> and then to England (Yale).

From Bad-Nauheim on August 5 James wrote a joking postcard
declining, evidently, some invitation from Lutoslawski to visit him
and cure himself by nudity, which contains the sentence, "I propose that your english ['Sole' *del.*] S.P. should have your portrait
as a frontispiece, taken *in [*ov.* 'as'] this state of nature!—it would
harmonize most completely with the absolute candor and sincerity
with which your soul displays itself throughout the book" (Yale).
Again from Bad-Nauheim, on August 18, in a long letter answering
some emotional outburst from Lutoslawski, James added: "Now
as regards the preface, I thought I could write it better after
freshly reading the english proofs, particularly since you *said [*ab.
del.* 'say'] the English ed. would contain matter omitted from the
german. Therfore [*stet*] after reading the chapters in the german of
which I wrote you a word in the spring, I left the rest lying, preferring to finish the book in its english version. But I have it with me
in German, & shall immediately set to work at it. . . . So it will
take a few days to finish Seelen Macht. After that, the preface, I
think, will write itself easily; and I will send it to you. You can
send it to Mr. Jones ['who' *del.*] from whom I have just received a
note relating to it" (Yale).

The reference to Jones is to a letter that Frederick Llewellyn-
Jones of the firm of Bromley & Llewellyn-Jones, solicitors, wrote
to James from Holywell, England on August 16:

> I am acting as agent in this country for my friend Prof. *Lutoslawski*, and
> am in communication with some London Publishers with a view to the publi-
> cation of his work "The Soul's Power." Mr. Lutoslawski tells me that you
> have kindly promised to write an Introduction to the work. I shall be glad to
> know when the Introduction is likely to be written, as I do not expect any
> final arrangement can be made as to the publication of the book until the
> Introduction is sent to the Publisher (bMS Am 1092.9 [355a]).

Later, from Bad-Nauheim, James once more addressed Lutoslaw-ski, this time on August 28, 1899:

I received your letter of the 23rd. the day before yesterday, and yesterday I completed my "preface," such as it is. I didn't send it immediately, or write, because *you [*ov.* 'I'] spoke of a supplement to your letter, to be written the next day, and I wished to reply to everything together. But since the supplement does not come, I write immediately.

First, as to the preface. In finishing the reading of the book it seemed to me aesthetically absurd that so original and vital a production should be *"in-troduced"* by any third person. It is like a candle introducing an electric light, or some little schoolmaster introducing the book of revelations. Then it seemed out of place that *I* should write the introduction, because you splash round in the full deep ocean with your faith and thoughts, whilst I *wet ['we' *ov.* 'so'] my toes in the surf, and am entirely given over to all sorts of technical scruples and objections, which come up incessantly apropos of the detail of what you say. It is ridiculous. Life needs no [*'hal' del.*] introduction from half-life. Nevertheless, I fulfilled my propose [*stet*] in the only way in which I could fulfill it—disengaging my responsibility for details, and applauding the general spirit as I could sincerely and admiringly do. The result will seem, I fear, a little patronizing to you, and the compte-rendu one-sided. Therefore I simply say to you do what you like with it. Don't print it, if you have the slightest feeling that you would rather appear in *our [*error for* 'your'] own stark naked person. Max Muller published his "centennial" translation of Kant's *K. [*ov.* 'C'] d. r. V., in two volumes, of which the first *consisted [*ov.* 'considera'] of an Essay by his friend Herr Ludwig Noiré. This always seemed to me a reduplication of the famous entrance of Pontius Pilate into the creed. Now my preface has a ['simple' *del.*] similar impertinence. So I sincerely beg you to use it or throw it into your waste-paper basket, as you prefer. Or rather, if you don't use it, send it back to me, and when the book does come out, I can let most of it appear, as a review, somewhere. I suppose that from the publisher's market point of view, such a preface will be all right (Yale).

What James called in his letter of August 18 an "over scrupolos-ity [*stet*] in discussing my poor little proposed preface" seems to have continued until, on September 5, 1899, James wrote:

Just one line of reply to your letter of Aug 31. (unfinished) which I receive this A M.

I am glad that you accept the preface. I in turn accept all the suggestions of revision which you make. My omission of reference to our common *pistism* was a great mistake, and I wish amply to rectify it. I don't see what I could do better than copy some of the phrases of your letter. Our main point of agreement is one in which we do stand almost alone among philosophers:—the world is a genuinely incomplete affair, a pluralism of original agents genuinely evolving towards a difficultly attainable harmony. One reason why I did n't say this more emphatically was that I wished to leave *myself* out, as irrelevant. But it is not irrelevant, and I will put it in. [I should say that in Paulsen's "introduction" & Wundt's *"System" [*ov.* 'sy'] there is a similar Weltanschauung neutralized however in both by the enveloping Spinozism.

Renouvier is a genuine pluralist of your type]. In reading the Seelenmacht I forgot the *pistism*, you lay so much stress on the rationalism and intellectualism. I am an anti rationalist. All that shall be made good!—in proof, no need of doing anything till then (Yale).

In a letter of March 20, 1900, from Carqueiranne, James advised Lutoslawski:

I should not be too proud to accept Mr. Mercer's *offer, [*comma ov. period*] *if I were you. [*intrl.*] [for the reference, see below, ed.]. It is evidently sincere; and between America and England the book is sure to repay him. I should like to revise *my [*ov.* 'the'] preface, if the publication takes place. I fancy that what has "dished" the book is the Eleutheria part, which seemed also to me as I read it, to present many heels of Achilles to the arrows of the critic. I wish, myself, that you would revise it. It is too facile and irresponsible as it stands, and you can disarm criticism either by material alterations, or by propitiatory remarks as to its merely suggestive character. I think your mechanism of *elected [*ov.* 'electors'] electors etc. entirely nugatory. *The ['T' *ov.* 'P'] strongest force in politics is human scheming, and the schemers will capture every machinery you can set up against them. Our presidential electors were intended to deliberate freely. For 100 years now they have been merely a clumsy physical agency for recording the peoples [*stet*] vote. It will always be so (Yale).

The reference in the above letter is illuminated by a letter of April 6, 1900, sent to James by George Gluyas Mercer from his law office in Philadelphia.

I hope to have the book of our friend Lutoslawski and your preface in the hands of the printer within the next month, and shall be glad to send you proof of your introduction as requested by Prof. Lutoslawski. I return enclosed the original MS. of your introduction.

Unless advised of another wish by Prof. Lutoslawski, the book will be entitled in English "The Soul's Power". I am not sure, however, in view of the desire of our friend, that it shall have a wide circulation, whether that title is the best that could be chosen. If you are able to give such matters any attention and feel disposed to honor me with your views on this point, they will be gratefully received (bMS Am 1092.9 [356]).

The tone of Mercer's next letter of April 30, 1900, was abruptly changed. After acknowledging the receipt of a postcard from James sent on the 16th, Mercer continues:

The MS. has not yet been placed in the hands of a publisher, but I shall be prepared to bear the expense of its publication upon the return of the MS. to this country. At the request of our friend Prof. Lutoslawski, I am about to send it to him for revision. While I shall be glad to send you proofs of the American edition, I wish very much that our friend could have competent advice before the MS. is put in the hands of the printer. While I was delighted with the work upon the first reading of it, I am nevertheless convinced that the MS. *needs editing.* I have no doubt American publishers have heretofore refused it because in their judgment it would not sell. My own opinion is that it might be put in such shape as to sell by a competent editor, and that the work ought to be done *before* the MS. is put in the hands of the printer. I am not myself competent to undertake the editing. It should be done, I think, by a metaphysician.

The letter concludes with an account of how Mercer tried but failed to interest Charles M. Bakewell of Bryn Mawr College in the editing, and then with the hope that James will be able to suggest some young man for the task: "I note with pleasure your promise to reflect upon the best title for the work, and beg to assure you that I shall be glad to hear from you again" [356a].

Finally, James wrote to Lutoslawski from Bad-Nauheim on May 13, 1900, as a consequence of Mercer's second letter:

I write this morning, however, for another purpose. Mercer sent me back my preface some weeks ago, and yesterday a letter came from him speaking of your book. Since he pays for it, of course his views are entitled to great weight: he has doubtless already communicated them to you. He thinks the MS. needs *"editing"* before it goes to the printer, and I imagine he wishes I might offer to edit it. He doesn't explain whether in his ['fe' *del.*] view it is its english form, or its matter that is most in need of a finishing and revising hand. Possibly both. *I* can't touch it, being so ill; and in any case no second person can edit a living man's work. The proof-reader will care for the english, which I am sure is good *enough*. You yourself must be the editor and reviser. *I* think the book is distinctly *weedy* in form, having been composed too freely and quickly; and I think that the eleutherian part so far as it sketches a practical political constitution, is open to every sort of criticism, which will be unsparingly and immediately applied. I wish you could make it less concrete and practical, therefore, and more ideal & abstract, even at the cost of making it shorter. I should be glad to read the *proofs,* with an eye to the english style, but I can't look at the MS. Very likely after this interval you would spontaneously introduce changes—one always sees things so differently, unless indeed one has quite lost interest in the subject, then the old work stands.—I mean, if I ever live to work again, to translate and republish your Helsingfors thesis (Yale).

The letter from Llewellyn-Jones and the two from Mercer are enclosed with the manuscript in bMS Am 1092.9 (4462), at Harvard. The James Collection contains no further materials on the problems of publication, and the last word seems to be found in a letter to Schiller of October 6, 1900, from Nauheim, in which James exclaims: "Poor Lutoslawski! He is going greatly to alter the text I believe, and I wish that some one would lend a touch to the proofs. I might undertake half of them, if you would do the other half" (Stanford University Libraries). However, it was not until 1924 that the book with James's introduction was finally published by the London firm of Allen and Unwin. Whether the change at that time to the present title reflected any original suggestion by James is not known, but his reference to "The Soul's Power" in his preface remained unaltered.

The return to James on April 6, 1900, of the manuscript now preserved in the James Collection establishes that Mercer (or Llewellyn-Jones) had had a typescript made from the manuscript and that this typescript ultimately served as printer's copy for the introduction. On the other hand, no mention is made in the letter of a copy of the typescript accompanying the return of the manuscript. It seems probable, therefore, that owing to the failure to secure publication, James never saw the printer's-copy typescript before his death. The odds thus favor the working hypothesis that (except for the two pencil deletions in the MS, for which see the Textual Note to 106.14) the substantive differences between manuscript and book result from some unknown combination of typist's misreadings, Lutoslawski's own 'improvements,' and publisher's styling in 1924. No external evidence exists to connect any difference from the manuscript with James's own authority, nor are the variants of a kind that would necessarily be linked with him. Under these circumstances the manuscript is the authoritative copy-text not only for the accidentals but also for the substantives, and the book variants have been rejected in the present edition save for a few necessary corrections or normalizations.

The alterations James made in the manuscript during the course of inscription and upon review are recorded in the apparatus. The false start on fol. 3^v seems to have been the original continuation of fol. 2 but was rejected after only two lines and a word and the sheet turned over and reversed to become present fol. 3 (105.14 *nourished . . . sense:* 106.1). At a later time, the false start was deleted in pencil. The false start on fol. 7^v was also abandoned, the sheet turned over and reversed, and present fol. 7 started with *has only the unity* (106.31). Correspondingly, the deleted text on fol. 10^v is only a rejected trial for the start of the present text on fol. 10, *passion of friendship* (107.29).

EMERSON (1903).

Copy-text: (EC) "Address of William James," *The Centenary of the Birth of Ralph Waldo Emerson as Observed in Concord May 25 1903 under the Direction of the Social Circle in Concord. Printed at The Riverside Press for the Social Circle in Concord June 1903,* pp. 67-77 (McD 1903:2). This pamphlet was entered for copyright in the name of John Shepard Keyes under A66772 on

August 21, 1903; the two deposit copies were received on August 31. Reference is also made to the autograph revised typescript (TMs) in the James Collection (MS Am 1092.9 [4541]), which was the printer's copy. The address was reprinted in (M&S) *Memories and Studies,* edited by Henry James, Jr. (1911), pp. 17-34 (McD 1911:2).

On February 28, 1903, perhaps soon after his acceptance, James wrote to his brother Henry that he was to speak on Emerson, and, later, on April 7 when he was tackling the actual writing: "I have unluckily pledged myself to ['write' *del.*] give a 20 minutes address at Concord on Emerson's Centenary the 25th. Although I have been reading him lately consecutively with on the whole an enhanced opinion of his powers, my speech does n't shape itself, & I wish to Heaven that I were out of it altogether. My powers don't combine well with just that sort of thing—I only undertook it to please Alice" (bMS Am 1092.9 [2903]). Subsequently, on May 26, 1903, James described the event in a letter to Miss Frances R. Morse: "The weather, the beauty of the village, the charming old meeting house, the descendants of the grand old man in such profusion, the mixture of Concord and Boston heads, so many of them of our own circle, the allusions to great thought and things, and the old time N.E. rusticity & rurality, the silver polls & ancient voices of the *vieille garde* who did the orating (including this 'yer child) all made a matchless combination, took one back to one's childhood, and made that rarely realized marriage of reality with ideality, that usually only occurs in fiction or poetry. I let R. W. E. speak for himself. . . . Reading the whole of him over again continuously has made me feel his real greatness as I never did before" (bMS Am 1092.9 [3244]).

In the same envelope as the typescript is a copy of the program on the occasion, a four-leaf pamphlet with the title: '𝕰𝖒𝖊𝖗𝖘𝖔𝖓 𝕮𝖊𝖓𝖙𝖊𝖓𝖆𝖗𝖞 | MEMORIAL EXERCISES | IN THE MEETING HOUSE | OF THE FIRST PARISH | IN | CONCORD, MASSACHUSETTS | ON | MONDAY AFTERNOON | MAY THE TWENTY-FIFTH | NINETEEN HUNDRED AND THREE | ONE HUNDRED YEARS | AFTER THE BIRTH OF | RALPH WALDO EMERSON | ARRANGED BY THE SOCIAL CIRCLE | A SOCIETY OF WHICH HE WAS A | MEMBER FOR FORTY-TWO YEARS'. After music and a prayer the chairman Samuel Hoar delivered an introductory address, followed by addresses by Charles Eliot Norton and Thomas Wentworth Higginson. Then after the intervention of Brahms's "Song of Destiny" William James gave his address, succeeded by one by George Frisbie Hoar and finally by a reading of the Seventy-Eighth Psalm.

The typescript (TMs) headed 'EMERSON' consists of ten sheets of white wove unwatermarked paper (278 × 217 mm.) foliated [1] 2-10 but stamped by the printer first 7-16 and then numbered by hand 53-62. James made a number of ink revisions, and one in pencil, which have been listed in the apparatus under Alterations in the Typescript or added to the appropriate entries in the Emendations or Historical Collation. The text of the first page was almost entirely deleted by ink strokes but then, in the upper left corner, James wrote, circled, 'Disregard the pen lines drawn about and on this page'. Compositors' names and various printer's markings for typesetting and division into galleys are present. It is evident that James read proof and, as usual, made a number of alterations both in substantives and in accidentals. As with a number of other texts in the present edition that originate with manuscript or typescript, the care that James gave to the printed form promotes it to copy-text status above the foundation document TMs, the actual printer's copy. In preparing the text for *Memories and Studies,* Henry James, Jr., seems to have had a transcript made of TMs instead of furnishing an example of EC. The substantive readings in M&S agree with those of TMs when EC is variant, save for 111.1 and 111.4 which may represent misreadings of TMs or, more likely, editorial changes that fortuitously agree with EC.

In bMS Am 1092.9 (4514), a notebook in the James Collection contains extensive notes on Emerson, but these manifestly relate to a talk to students given at some later time and have no direct connection with the Centenary Address.

INTRODUCTION TO FECHNER'S *LIFE AFTER DEATH* (1904).

Copy-text: (F) *The Little Book of Life After Death,* by G. T. Fechner, translated by Mary C. Wadsworth (Boston: Little, Brown, 1904), pp. vii-xix (McD 1904:2), signed, and subscribed 'Chocorua, N.H., June 21, 1904.' The introduction was printed throughout in italic, which has been transliterated into roman in the present edition. The book was entered for copyright by the publishers under A 96738 on September 16, 1904, and two copies were deposited in the Library of Congress on the same day.

REMARKS AT THE PEACE BANQUET (1904).

Copy-text: (P[6]) "Remarks at the Peace Banquet," *Atlantic Monthly,* 94 (Dec. 1904), 845-847 (McD 1904:12). Reference is made to (R) "Address of Prof. William James," *Official Report of the Thirteenth Universal Peace Congress Held at Boston, Massachusetts, U.S.A., October Third to Eighth, 1904* (Boston:

Peace Congress Committee), 5 (Oct. 7, 1904), 266-269 (McD 1904:12). The report was the earlier printed and provides the original text. However, James worked this over in marking up a copy of the *Report* to send to the *Atlantic*; thus his final revised version is chosen as the copy-text.

REASON AND FAITH (1905).

Copy-text: (MS) untitled holograph manuscript (MS Am 1092.9 [4542]). Other documents collated are (MS[p]) galley-proofs filed with MS, (PU[p]) galley-proofs pasted on fols. 30-31 of Lecture VIII in the manuscript of *A Pluralistic Universe* (bMS Am 1092.6), and (P[20]) "Reason and Faith," *Journal of Philosophy*, 24 (April 14, 1927), 197-201 (McD 1927:1; wrongly listed as 1924:4).

James gave this address as part of a discussion on "Reason and Faith" at a dinner of the Pacific Coast Unitarian Club in San Francisco on February 5, 1906. On January 23, 1906, he wrote from Stanford to his old friend G. H. Howison, at Berkeley, "Do you know that I am to be joined with you as *one [*intrl.*] speech maker['s' *del.*] at the Unitarian Club dinner Feb. 5th? I have accepted, with fear and trembling, as always when speech-making is involved" (bMS Am 1092.9 [1059]). James's engagement book for the California stay notes on February 5 only, "Unitarian Club S[t.] Francis Hotel 6.30," but his general diary elaborates: "Went to San Francisco to Unitarian Club dinner. President Eells, Buckham[,] Stone, Howison, & I spoke. Poor stuff all round save for Howison's ['good' *del.*] *entrain*." The next day he wrote in exasperation to T. S. Perry, the Boston painter: "Also outside 'addresses' impossible to refuse. Damn them! 4 in the past 10 days. One last night at this Hotel, where I was one of 4 orators who spoke for 2 hours on 'Reason & Faith,' before a Unitarian Association of Pacific Coasters. Consequence: *Gout* on waking this morning! *Unitarian gout*—was such a thing ever heard of?" (#3474).

On February 7 he opened a letter to Howison with: "Here I am, laid up with *gout*, a reg'lar classical attack, orthodox, not unitarian, and which I've done nothing to merit. . . . You were in great heart that night; and the way you poured damnation and endearment over *me* in your speech, so blended that I couldnt [*stet*] tell which was stock and which was flavoring, was a unique experience. Your winding up was noble, and sure you can do *anything* with that audience—they know and love you so well." James then asserts that he thinks Howison's association of our true and eternal self with Kant's system of categories seems to him monstrous (#1060).

On February 9 Howison responds, denying that he had associated the self with the Kantian categories and explaining what it was he had intended to say, to which James replied on February 14 (#1061). (Howison's correspondence is in bMS Am 1092.9 [265-267].)

Problems then began about publication. On a postcard to Howison dated March 21 James wrote: "I have now the proof of our 'Unitarian' Symposium. It is *absolute gibberish*. I can't use a single sentence of the proof—I must ['re' *del.*] write out a speech de novo of which I have the scantiest notes. *Your* report must be worse because longer. I am proposing to Mr. Payson to let us go unprinted—what do you say?" (#1063). Another postcard to Howison, dated March 25, states only, "They wont let me off, so I also am re-writing my 'remarks'" (#1064). These postcards explain two other records. The first is the diary entry for March 24, "Writing my *remarks [*ab. del.* 'address'] at Unitarian Club dinner, of which the proof was gibberish." On the verso of the last leaf of the manuscript is the note: "Dear Mr. Payson—Here is my speech, reconstituted, with many omissions, but with what remains improved; I leave for the South and shall have no fixed address until April 8th, when I return. I can't correct the proof till then. Sincerely yours, Wm. James."

The preserved galleys are by no means gibberish, are manifestly set from the present MS, and do not appear to be revises. It seems probable that the Club had hired a reporter to record the speeches, that the transcript of his notes (which James called the proof—unless the notes had boldly been set into type) submitted to the discussants was not satisfactory, and thus that James in the manuscript 'reconstituted' from the transcript, his scanty notes, and his memory what he had said and sent this manuscript to be set into type. The preserved proofs, therefore, are not the originals but are instead the setting of James's freshly written manuscript. On April 22 (after the earthquake) James wrote Howison and in a postscript added, "I have just got proof of my 'Unitarian' speech—of course they won't print those speeches now, so I am keeping it" (#1065). In a footnote to the P[20] first publication in 1927, Henry James, Jr., remarked: "The earthquake and San Francisco fire [April 18] prevented publication. The manuscript and part of the corrected galley were brought back to Cambridge and were recently found there in a bundle of papers among which they had hitherto been overlooked."

The manuscript, signed, consists of seventeen leaves of unruled white wove unwatermarked paper, 277 × 216 mm., a vertical red rule printed 48 mm. from the left margin, foliated 1-17, centered, fol. 10 with a deleted 6 in the upper right corner, fol. 16 numbered over 15, and 17 over 16. In the upper left corner of fol. 1 are editorial directions to the printer for the typography, in pencil, and the editor's '¶ MR. JAMES.—' prefixed to James's first paragraph, an addition repeated in the proof. The manuscript is extensively revised in James's usual manner. (The alterations are listed in the apparatus to this address.) Enough evidence is present in the manuscript to indicate that not all parts of it are of a single continuous inscription. At the head of fol. 10 (deleted 6 in the right corner) are four lines of deleted text beginning with 'gious' (the last syllable of *religious*) and continuing 'conclusions, and that specific religious experiences, like mystical insights, providential leadings and conversions are not required.' These deleted lines, which occur above the present opening paragraph on the leaf (126.39 *But here I have to repeat*) are an early version of 126.34-38, written at the foot of fol. 9, immediately preceding, and thus linking with the undeleted text on fol. 10 below the excised top four lines. If the evidence of the number 6 deleted on fol. 10 were to be taken logically, we might have here a single leaf of an earlier inscription, thriftily inserted and renumbered 10 before James proceeded with fol. 11. Whether or not this is too drastic a speculation, at the least the evidence shows that present fol. 9 is a revision of a lost leaf preceding present fol. 10, and possibly fol. 8 and other preceding leaves are also revisions. In view of this evidence for a leaf numbered originally in the right corner, it may be that the original centered numbering of fols. 16 and 17 as 15 and 16 has textual significance as indicating an expansion of the text on some undetermined number of preceding leaves for which no evidence exists. But the guess may be as plausible that James, as he sometimes did, mistook the numbering of these two leaves and repaired the repeated slip.

The proofs consist of cut-up galleys pasted on sheets of typewriter paper, the first galley headed 'UNITARIAN CLUB—ONE'. The other headings have been cut off. James made a number of corrections and revisions in ink. This part of the set of galleys, identified as MS(p), contains the text of 124.1-127.22. The remaining part of the galleys (127.23-128.40) was used by James as a paste-in after seven lines of writing on fols. 30-31 in the numbered series under Lecture VII of the manuscript of *A Pluralistic Universe,* although actually starting the text of Lecture VIII as divided in the book. These pages, we know, were prepared on April 19, 1908. Before pasting these proofs on fols. 30-31, James cut them down so that the original margins were completely removed, thus removing as well whatever marginal proof-corrections had been made in the original galleys. In their turn, however, this section of the proofs, identified as PU(p), is somewhat more heavily revised than the original earlier section.

When Henry James came to provide copy in 1927 for publication in the *Journal of Philosophy*, he transcribed the text from the revised galleys up to 127.22, but then—being unaware of the continuation of the proofs in the manuscript of *A Pluralistic Universe*—he concluded with the text transcribed (not always accurately) from the manuscript. The present edition uses the manuscript as copy-text throughout, it being the only true general authority; but the alterations in the proofs (MS[p]) are incorporated to provide the authoritative final form of the text as James left it. The revisions in the sheets pasted in *A Pluralistic Universe* present a problem owing to the removal of the margins of the proofs, which destroyed the record of any marginal additions similar to those found in the earlier part. (A few simple corrections, not revisions, within the lines of the proofs are very likely original.) Fortunately, physical evidence can distinguish the three places where in the original margins James had entered revisions for the Unitarian Club proceedings from the more numerous marginal additions and alterations made for the purposes of *A Pluralistic Universe*. In both parts of these proofs when James made a marginal addition or revision he drew a guideline to the text in the margin from the desired position in the proof, usually marked by a caret. In the cutdown proofs used for *A Pluralistic Universe* the marginal additions made for the purposes of this book are readily identifiable by the continuity of line as well as by the color of the ink and the thickness of the pen when the guideline passes from the proof to the backing typewriter paper. On the contrary, whenever James made a marginal addition on the typewriter paper to fit into a guideline and caret that existed in the proofs as corrected in April 1906, some discontinuity of line as well as variation in the color of the ink and the size of the penpoint can be observed. On the basis of this physical evidence only the additions *of . . . despair* (127.29-30), *in . . . till* (127.30-31), and *in . . . coming* (128.28) can be identified with confidence as associated with the 1906 alterations, whereas the rest belong to 1908 and have no pertinence to the text of "Reason and Faith" in the form intended in 1906. One cannot be sure, of course, that the marginal additions in *A Pluralistic Universe* manuscript that tie into the 1906 carets and guidelines in the galleys are identical with the lost original text, but it is a normal assumption that they are very close when not in fact the same. A few simple corrections within the proof, such as the added comma after *experiences* (128.27), the underlining of *in spite* (128.22)—

although in error only *spite* was marked—and the alteration of the misprints *solmen* (127.35) and *evangelican* (128.15), for example, appear to have been made in 1906.

The present text restores the authoritative accidentals of the manuscript throughout, corrects the misreadings of the manuscript in the latter part of the text in the *Journal of Philosophy* initial publication, and in this latter section incorporates the hitherto unidentified proof-alterations that James made in 1906. However, the further new alterations that James made when he prepared copy for *A Pluralistic Universe,* although recorded, are not adopted in the present text, which is designed to represent the 1906 version only and not a modification of part of this for a later book.

THE ENERGIES OF MEN (1907).

Copy-text: (P^{28}) "The Energies of Men," *Philosophical Review,* 16 (Jan. 1907), 1-20 (McD 1907:1). Reference is also made to (P^{36}) "The Energies of Men," *Science,* 25 (March 1, 1907), 321-332. In the James Collection is preserved under WJ 200.145 an unopened offprint of P^{28} with James's address stamp, an unannotated copy of the issue of the *Review,* and a copy of P^{28} marked by Henry James, Jr., for reprinting in *Memories and Studies* (1911) but not used since he chose "The Powers of Men" version instead in its 1908 pamphlet form entitled (wrongly) "The Energies of Men." Despite its title, the 1908 pamphlet was a reprint of "The Powers of Men" (McD 1907:2), not of the present article, which contributed only a small part of the text.

"The Energies of Men" was James's presidential address to the American Philosophical Association meeting at Columbia University, December 28, 1906. Appendix I contains notes for a talk to the Psychology Club at Harvard on May 18, 1906; these notes form what was probably a preliminary version of the later "Energies of Men" address.

The reprint in *Science* was clearly made from a copy of P^{28} and not from a carbon, say, of the typescript presumably supplied to the *Philosophical Review.* James seems not to have revised the copy before *Science* set it, but a few alterations stem from his correction of the proof. The evidence for derivation comes at 145.24 where P^{28} had ended a sentence within the line, '*that of our means.*' In P^{36}, printed in double column, the full line reads '*our powers,* the second *that of our means.*' The next line then adds text missing from P^{28}: '*of unlocking them or getting at them.*' The easiest explanation for the preservation in P^{36} of the P^{28} period after *means* is that the line *'of . . . them.'* was added in proof and the line above not reset to remove the period. If, then, P³⁶ were read in proof but its copy P²⁸ were not revised before typesetting, the correction of the text in *Science* would have been less thoroughgoing than usual and may have covered few accidentals. Even the accidental corrections adopted in the present edition from P³⁶ may have been compositorial or editorial, though necessary ones. At any rate, a few readings from P³⁶ thought to represent James's alterations in proof (in addition to necessary corrections) have been incorporated in the present text as emendations of the copytext; but James's attention to the *Science* proofs does not seem sufficient to warrant adopting the reprint as copy-text.

The essay was so thoroughly chopped up, passages transposed, and the whole reworked as "The Powers of Men" that no collation of the two texts has been undertaken.

In a letter dated January 19, 1907, James wrote to Papini: "You have asked me to contribute to Leonardo. It seems to you barely possible that from the point of your *Uomo-Dio* theory you might like an address I *recently ['r' ov. 'g'] gave. I therefore send you a proof—the Philo[so]phic Review will probably be published in a week or ten days. [¶] Mind—I don't *ask* you translate or publish it. I send it for you to destroy if you have no room for it in Leonardo" (courtesy of Signora Paolo Casini). Papini translated "The Energies of Men," which appeared as "Le Energie delgi uomini" in *Leonardo*, 5 (Feb. 1907), 1-25.

The letter from Colonel Baird Smith, quoted at 134.15-135.17 is preserved at Harvard in the Charles Eliot Norton Papers (bMS Am 1088 [6780]). The original readings have been restored by emendation except when it seems probable that James has deliberately altered the text for public delivery.

THE POWERS OF MEN (1907).

Copy-text: (P⁴) "The Powers of Men," *American Magazine*, 65 (Nov. 1907), 57-65 (McD 1907:2, listed in error as October). Reference is also made to (EM) *The Energies of Men*, a pamphlet published in the Emmanuel Church Publications on Religion and Medicine (New York: Moffat, Yard, July 1908), pp. [1-6] 7-38 [39-40]. The essay was reprinted by Henry James, Jr., without authoritative change as "The Energies of Men" in *Memories and Studies* (1911), pp. 227-264. The discussion of the essay "The Energies of Men," immediately preceding, should be referred to as well.

The *American Magazine* added to its title, "The keys which unlock hidden energies, and stir men to achieve—such keys as love, anger, war, duty, the temperance 'pledge,' despair, crowd-contagion, Christian Science, conversion, prayer, resistance of temptation, and other excitements, ideas and efforts." It also inserted in the article a number of subheadings, manifestly not by James: 147.21+ *Getting One's Second Wind*; 148.24+ *Keeping Up a Faster Pace*; 149.21+ *Saying "Yes" and Saying "No"*; 149.34+ *Saying "Peace! Be Still"*; 150.23+ *Failing to Do All that We Can*; 151.9+ *Going Over the Dam*; 151.34+ *The Energies of Roosevelt*; 152.18+ *The Sublime Heroism of Women*; 153.10+ *Buried Coal Miner's Great Achievement*; 153.27+ *How a Soldier Survived an Awful Siege*; 154.40+ *Morbid Cases of Women*; 155.20+ *Is a "Spree" Ever Good for You?*; 156.15+ *Wonders of the Yoga System*; 157.31+ *Ideas Which Unlock Our Hidden Energies*; 158.18+ *The Power in a Temperance "Pledge"*; 159.16+ *The Value of Christian Science*; 160.12+ *Prayer as a Sleep-Producer*; 160.30+ *Trying to Work With One Finger*.

In the next year, 1908, the article was reprinted in a paperbound pamphlet with the title page: 'Religion and Medicine | PUBLICATION No. 3 | The Energies of Men | By | William James | Professor of Philosophy, Harvard University | [seal] | NEW YORK | MOFFAT, YARD AND COMPANY | 1908'. The front cover has the same text although in a different setting, within a rule-frame, with the imprint 'Moffat, Yard & Company | New York | July, 1908 | Price 25 Cents Net'.

The first printing has the contents:

p. [1]: title; p. [2]: '*And they shall call his name Emmanuel;* | *which, being interpreted, is, God with us.* | *Reprinted by kind permission of* AMERICAN MAGAZINE | [short rule] | Copyright 1907 by | AMERICAN MAGAZINE'; p. [3]: 'Religion and Medicine | Publication No. 3 | The Energies of Men'; p. [4]: blank; p. [5]: 'INTRODUCTORY. | T^{2}HOUGH it would seem that the sane and | simple message of this essay could not be | misconstrued, the fact that it has been wholly | misunderstood in newspaper comment warns us | that it is necessary to preface it by stating that | it does not counsel all persons to drive themselves | at all times beyond the limits of ordinary endur-| ance, that it is not a gospel of overstrain nor an | advocate of the use of alcohol and opium as stim-|ulants in emergencies. [¶] It states that "second wind" is a reality in the | mental as in the physical realm and that it can be | found and used when needed—nothing more. | *Publication Committee.* | [short rule] | I certify that this is Publication No. 6 of the Emmanuel | Church Publications on Religion and Medicine. | ELWOOD WORCESTER. | EMMANUEL CHURCH | Boston, Mass. | July, 1908'; p. [6]: blank; p. 7: text headed 'The Energies of Men | [short rule]' ending on p. 38; inside back cover: advertisement for *Religion and Medicine*, by Elwood Worcester, Samuel

McComb, and Isador H. Coriat, published by Moffat, Yard; outside back cover: blank. (Copy examined: Library of Surgeon General's Office, Washington, D.C.)

A later printing by Moffat, Yard is known in 1911, advertised on the title page as *A New Edition*; the verso reads 'COPYRIGHT 1907, BY | THE AMERICAN MAGAZINE | [short rule] | *Reprinted by Permission* | THE QUINN & BODEN CO. PRESS | RAHWAY, N.J.' Under the Introductory on the next page, the signature of the Publication Committee and the certification by Worcester have been replaced by a short rule, and all other evidences of the association of Emmanuel Church and its Religion and Medicine series have been removed. An entirely reset edition was published in 1926 by Dodd, Mead & Co., New York.

A small cut was made in EM at 157.3-6. The few variants do not suggest that James had anything to do with the text and thus that it is without authority. *Memories and Studies* faithfully reprints EM. Since the manuscript of Colonel Baird Smith's letter and the quotation from Pückler-Muskau have been utilized to purify the text of "The Energies of Men," the quotations in the present popularized article "The Powers of Men," have been left as in the copy-text.

THE MORAL EQUIVALENT OF WAR (1910).

Copy-text: (IC) "The Moral Equivalent of War," *International Conciliation*, no. 27 (Feb. 1910), 3-20 (McD 1910:3). Reference is also made to (MS^a) six leaves of a holograph first inscription found in the James Collection (bMS Am 1092.9 [4519]); (TMs or MS) a combination typescript and manuscript (MS Am 1092.9 [4548]); (P^{23}) "The Moral Equivalent of War," *McClure's Magazine*, 35 (Aug. 1910), 463-468; (P^{29}) "The Moral Equivalent of War," *Popular Science Monthly*, 77 (Oct. 1910), 400-410; (AR) "The Moral Equivalent of War," *Atlantic Readings*, no. 10 (Boston: Atlantic Monthly Press, 1910). The essay was reprinted by Henry James, Jr., in *Memories and Studies* (1911), pp. 265-296, from IC without reference to other authority. A few corrections, notes, and proposed revisions are marked in his private copy *AC85.J2376.911m.

In bMS Am 1092.9 (4476) of the James Collection is filed a leaf of autograph notes on stationery of the St. Francis Hotel, San Francisco, and possibly datable as written during James's stay in California in 1906. Appendix II contains these notes which were intended perhaps for some future unpublished lecture. Of interest here, however, is the series of headings on the verso of this slip:

Makers of country
Democracy
flattening out
Soldier type
Fling life away like a flower
Greek life
Find *moral [*ab. del.* 'mechanical'] equivalent for war.

The last item gives us in February 1906 the eventual title of James's 1910 essay, although in fact the phrase is met with earlier in *The Varieties of Religious Experience* (1902), p. 367.

Professor Skrupskelis has now identified the occasion for these notes on war. On February 20, 1906, the *Daily Palo Alto*, Stanford's student newspaper, announced that on the next day a student assembly would be held. "The speakers will be Dean Hodges, special Memorial Church preacher, and Dr. William James, acting head of the Department of Philosophy. The general topic on which they will address the student body is 'Arbitration in its Relations to War and Peace.' Dr. James has already announced as his particular subject 'The Psychology of the War Spirit,' . . . . [¶] Tomorrow's Assembly was called in response to resolutions passed by the famous Lake Mohonk Conference on International Arbitration, which met in the summer of 1905. These resolutions, which were sent to all the universities and colleges in the United States, request that on or about Washington's Birthday, 1906, student meetings should be held at which arbitration should be discussed by the students or lectured on by authorities on the subject. Reports of these meetings will be sent to the permanent secretary of the conference at Mohonk Lake, New York."

On Wednesday, February 21, 1906, the *Daily Palo Alto* reported James's speech:

Dr. James spoke in part as follows:
I wish simply to point out that the anti-war party has to take account of the bellicose constitution of human nature. We inherit the warlike type, and for most of the capacities of heroism, martyrdom, endurance, that the human race is now so full of, we have to thank this cruel evolutionary history. It has bred the instinct of pugnacity into our bone and marrow, and thousands of years of peace could not breed it out of us. We spend hundreds of millions as a matter of course when destructive battleships are asked for—yet universities cost no more than battleships, and last forever.

But our imagination likes all the pomp of war. The people love it. Our minds feed on the thought of war and bloodshed. The leaders are not to blame for present wars; the fault lies with public opinion. Let it reach a certain pitch of excitement and no ruler can withstand it.

What is to be done about it? Leave war for the imagination of the future to play with. Leave that possibility of romance open. But circumvent the

actual explosion. Arbitration treaties and the Hague Tribunal form an organized machinery for this purpose. To you, young men and women of the educated classes, I commend this problem. Begin at all events by speaking out as
individuals, whatever truth, however unpopular, is in you. As Emerson says,
'He who will always speak the truth will not fail to find himself in sufficiently
dramatic situations,' and I may add, warlike situations. The wars of the future
must be waged inside of every country, between the destructive and constructive ideals and forces.

The exact circumstances of the writing of "The Moral Equivalent of War" are not known, but that it was probably commissioned may be suggested by James's reference in fol. 12 of MS,
which is in a passage not printed that precedes the paragraph at
165.7 beginning *It is plain*: "Hence such *associations [*init. sg. qt.
del.*] 'for conciliation' as that which publishes this paper," a clear
reference to the fact that at an early stage he knew for whom he
was writing the piece. A few references appear in his diary. On
December 11, 1909, James noted, "Wrote [*ov.* 'Wor'] on my war
paper" and on December 13, "Finisht my article on war." On the
15th he recorded, "Mailed my article to N. M. Butler." Butler was
president of the American Association for International Conciliation.
tion. The letter of December 15 which accompanied the manuscript (preserved in bMS Am 1092.9 [822]), read as follows:

Dear President,
   Here goes all that would flow out of my pen on the subject of "Conciliation"! It contains thrice 2000 words and is a utopian speculation which goes
outside of ['you' *del.*] the immediate program of your association. Nevertheless, I think it *may* answer your purpose, so I send it. Don't hesitate to say no
if it doesn't, however, for I can easily use it elsewhere. Two magazines pester
me for articles, and I am under promise to turn over something. Would it indeed be incompatible with your propaganda to have such a thing, if you wish
it, appear *also* in the Atlantic or in the American? I doubt if the American
editors would find any objection.
   Of course I will take no 'honorarium' from your association[.]
   Please have it read and let me know as speedily as possible.

On December 17 James returned Butler's prompt reply:

   I am glad you find my utopian stuff available, and also that you are willing
"the American" should publish, if the time can be made to suit. It will save
me copying if Mr. Phillips can see the article in print, so I beg you to have
three proofs sent me, of which I will submit one to him and then the question
of date can be adjudicated.
   I am notifying him already that the thing is imminent (#823).

On December 28 the diary notes "Got proof of my war-article."
The next day James recorded that Phillips had declined the war

article. It would seem, then, that when the *American Magazine* refused, James turned to *McClure's* where in revised form the article
was published in the August 1910 issue. On January 25, 1910, the
diary records that "The Moral Equivalent of War" had appeared, a
convenient piece of evidence for its publication in IC. Unfortunately, reference ceases at this point, for one would like to know
something of the later appearances of this essay, especially the discussion that may have accompanied negotiations about its revised
form for *McClure's* (P²³).

MSª (bMS Am 1092.9 [4519]) in pencil, is without title or
foliation. It occupies the rectos of fols. 21-26 of a hardbound Partridge and Cooper notebook, with blue unwatermarked leaves
245 × 198 mm., following the complete pencil holograph of
"Bradley or Bergson?" and preceding, after an excised leaf, the
manuscript start of "A Suggestion about Mysticism." The manuscript ends after only four lines on fol. 26; the text covered is
from 162.1 *The war* to 163.14 *jingoism and imperialism.*

The first complete early text is found in TMs or MS (MS Am
1092.9 [4548]) an untitled combination of typescript and autograph on typewriter paper, foliated (typescript) [1] 2-6, 7(6),
(manuscript) 8-13, 13½, 14(13), 14½, 15a(15), 15a¹, 15b, 15c(14,
15½), 16-18, 18½, 19-21, 21½(21), 22-25, 25½, (typescript) 23,
(manuscript) 24,25(25½) (one leaf), 26-34, 36-37, 37½. The numbering is centered except for fols. 21, 25, 26 numbered in the
upper right corner. A deleted trial for fol. 15b is found on the
verso of fol. 20, but the start of 15b is then deleted and the final
text appears on fol. 15a¹. A deleted trial of the bottom of deleted
15c appears as 15cᵛ. The deleted text on the verso of fol. 36 seems
to be a trial for the upper part of fol. 25 (169.30-38) although it
does not link with fol. 24. Typewritten carbon folios 1-7 and 23
use a laid paper with vertical chainlines 25 mm. apart, watermarked
in hollow letters GLORIA LINEN and measuring 267 × 207 mm.
The holograph manuscript, starting with fol. 8, is written on a
slightly narrower wove typewriter paper (267 × 204 mm.) watermarked with a Chinese pagoda and under it CHINESE LINEN.
Alterations are made (disregarding those done in the course of writing) in dark ink, pencil, (dark ink?), light ink, and dark ink in that
order.

The first publication of the essay was in a monthly series of
pamphlets of the American Association for International Conciliation, of 20 pages, its front paper cover serving as title page:

[within single rules] INTERNATIONAL CONCILIATION | Published monthly
by the | American Association for International Conciliation | Entered as sec-

ond class matter at New York, N.Y. | Postoffice; February 23, 1909, under act of July 16, 1894 | [double rule] | THE MORAL EQUIVALENT OF WAR | [seal] | BY | WILLIAM JAMES | FEBRUARY, 1910, No. 27 | American Association for International Conciliation | Sub-station 84 (501 West 116th Street) | New York City

On the verso of the back cover is 'IRVING PRESS | 119 and 121 East Thirty-first Street | New York'. After an announcement about the Association's publications on the verso of the front cover, the text begins on page 3 and ends on 20. The inner side of the back cover contains a list of the Association's publications.

This pamphlet was reprinted without any fresh authority in October in the *Popular Science Monthly* (P²⁹) and also in *Atlantic Readings* (AR), a similar pamphlet with the cover serving as title page but in a new typesetting. On the verso of this cover is the copyright notice of the Association, and at the foot the acknowledgement of permission to reprint.

On the other hand, the readings in *McClure's Magazine* (P²³) show quite definitely that along with a considerable amount of magazine restyling of accidentals (and possibly of a few substantives) this text was printed from a copy of IC that had been authorially revised. The uncertainty that attaches to most of the accidental differences derives from the open question how much James may have troubled to alter many accidentals for another popular magazine appearance despite the care that he obviously gave to the substantives. The question is opened further by the fact that many of the accidental variants between *McClure's* and its IC copy are not especially characteristic of James and are likely to have derived from the *McClure's* editor or printer, this magazine having a strong tradition of styling authors to suit itself. These considerations encourage a conservative editorial position by which IC is retained as the copy-text on the basis of what are estimated to be its more authoritative accidentals, but the variant readings from *McClure's* that editorial judgment takes to represent James's annotations in the marked-up copy of IC he sent to the magazine (including the major excision with its bridge passage near the end) are accepted to form a selective eclectic text.

The history of this essay in England is known only sketchily. The earliest copy in the British Library (W.P.2796/2), datestamped December 14, 1943, was published by the Peace Pledge Union. An offset printing of this was republished in September 1963, again by this Union, with an introduction by Anthony Weaver. The British Library copy (8418.r.4) is datestamped October 4, 1963.

The typing errors and misspellings in the first seven leaves of the typescript part of MS are similar to those in the typescript for

Some Problems of Philosophy, known to have been typed by James's daughter Margaret (Peggy to her family). Typing initially from notebook bMS Am 1092.9 (4519), Peggy passed the end of its text in the thirteenth line of typescript fol. 3; hence some lost holograph must have intervened between the end of the notebook and the start of the preserved holograph on fol. 8 (164.18 *Our ancestors*) which continues in mid-paragraph the revised handwritten text below the typing on fol. 7 and which paraphrases the final lines of the typing that had been deleted. One may conjecture, without evidence, that when the full scope and complexity of the article impressed itself on James, he recognized that trying to write it in a notebook, even on just the rectos, made expansion by inserted leaves impracticable and otherwise inhibited free revision, and so he switched to loose sheets of paper, probably the Chinese Linen typewriter paper that we find starting with fol. 8. These have not been preserved, evidently, because they were superseded by Peggy's first typing.

The manuscript appears to have been inscribed in regular order of the folios but then materially revised and expanded by the addition and substitution of leaves. Originally a fol. 13 (now 14) had followed 12, succeeded in turn by 14 (now 14½) and 15 (now 15a), and ending with a page that seems to have been misnumbered 14, later altered to 15½ and finally to 15c. At about this point James began a major expansion after fol. 12. On the last five lines on fol. 12 only 'common sense & reason' are left undeleted and carry over to the sentence at the top of fol. 13 (now 14). The upper third of fol. 13 is a rewrite of the excision of the bottom of fol. 12 but was also then deleted. A new fol. 13 was written which was continued on a part-page 13½ (165.11 *ought . . . especially* 165.32), the new 13½ cutting in on the undeleted text left in the upper part of original 13 now renumbered 14. The inscription of substitute 13 and 13½ necessitated the renumbering of original fol. 14 as 14½. Original fol. 15 (the 5 over some undistinguishable number) was renumbered 15a. The text at the foot of this 15a had earlier been deleted in favor of an expansion heading what is now 15c. Then a revision of this text heading 15c was attempted on what is now fol. 20^v but was crossed out and another, more successful, attempt was made on 15b; however, the opening sentence of 15b not proving entirely satisfactory, James deleted it and inserted between 15a and 15b a brief substitute (166.21 *the militaristic writings* [IC *army-writings*] . . . *subject, and* 166.22) for it and the deleted foot of 15a, numbering this inserted part-page 15a^1 and changing misnumbered 14 first to 15½ and then finally to 15c, this latter leaf after further deletion now consisting of only two lines

(166.31-32 *Nations . . . ex-*) which links with fol. 16 only by reason of the insertion of *pand or shrink,* before 16's normal text starting *according to their vitality.* No explanation except a simple slip or omission seems to work for this anomaly: one can scarcely posit a missing revised page for so little text; nevertheless, such evidence as is available might suggest the possibility that there was more than one trial for what is now 15c than that preserved as 20^v, and that the misnumbering of this leaf may not have been entirely accidental. Later on, fol. 18½ (167.24 *Other . . . save* 167.29), written in dark ink but numbered in light ink, is added to substitute for deleted text at the foot of fol. 18 and the top of fol. 19.

Differences in the position of foliation may sometimes, with James, indicate leaves numbered at different times and thus perhaps substitutes. Hence the possibility exists that some disruption in the text is present in fols. 21, 25, and 26. The text of fol. 21 (168.10 *to a being . . . see the* 168.21) follows from fol. 20 without a break either in its revised form or its original opening words now deleted. However, some possible signs of substitution appear in the following leaves. Folio 21½ was originally 21, the ½ being added in light ink. Its text (168.22 *supreme theatre . . . these things* 168.34) revises the deleted foot of fol. 21 before carrying on to new matter and can have no possible relationship to fol. 20. Folio 22, numbered in the light ink (168.34 *tell but . . . rule,* 169.7), carries on with no break the undeleted text of fol. 21½, the deleted text at the foot having been broken off; and fol. 23 is linked with no break to 22 and to fol. 24 (169.19 *live in . . . transfigure it* 169.30), which in turn carries on smoothly both in its original and revised text with fol. 25, numbered to the right (169.30 *into a . . . blood-tax visible?* [IC *blood-tax?*] 170.4). The deleted foot of fol. 25 links with the deleted head of fol. 26 (numbered to the right) and fol. 27 (centered) follows on fol. 26 with no break. The evidence is very slight for a considerable rewriting in this area, but there is enough to arouse suspicion. First, we have on deleted fol. 36^v a very different form of the text now found on the upper half of fol. 25, so different as to make it possible to believe that some intermediate form might have led from one to the other. Centered 21½ is definitely an expansion and revision of the foot of fol. 21 (right corner). Its text does not link with the original deleted text at the foot of fol. 21 but starts with a paraphrase. It is odd that fol. 21½ was originally numbered 21 and only at a comparatively late stage of the revision was the ½ added; it is also odd that the 22 seems to have been added in a light ink at the head of its leaf at the same time as the addition of the ½ to 21; moreover, fols. 23-24, although numbered in dark ink, have smaller

numerals of a kind seen, for instance, in the final revised numbering of fol. 15c. Thus there is something of a possibility that the
text in fols. 21½ through 24 exists in a revised state with no evidence as to its original form.

Originally, fol. 25 lead directly into fol. 26, both numbered in
the upper right corner; but the head of 26 and the foot of fol. 25
have been deleted, and four lines written on a leaf first numbered
25½ (and then 24,25) were substituted (170.6 *Having . . . peace*
170.8). But the deletion proved to be not entirely covered by the
new text, and so James then wrote five lines on a new leaf (169.38
It . . . jelly. [IC *blubber.*] 170.1) which he numbered 25½ in light
ink and in the same ink directed its insertion in the text on fol. 25,
where in a different place it paraphrased some of the deleted text
on both leaves.

James was still not satisfied, however. Taking the carbon of a
typed part-page on the Gloria Linen paper, numbered 23, he revised it in ink, in pencil, and again in ink, added another sentence,
and inserted it between fol. 25½ (the insert) and earlier 25½ (the
revision of the bottom of 25 and the top of 26), at the time renumbering the latter leaf as combined 24,25. Curiously, although
the opening of the typescript leaf replaced the final three lines of
fol. 25½, this text is not deleted from 25½. The typed page holds
only five lines, starting with *exist to-day* and ending with *blood-tax
visible?* in which *visible?* has been deleted in ink and the question
mark inserted before *-tax.* As the sixth and seventh lines James
wrote-in the new text *Where is anything that one *feels* [*ab. del.
'is'*] *honored by belonging to?* It is significant that the typescript
was copied from the latter part of fol. 25½ and then continues
with the altered form at the foot of fol. 25 after the marked insertion. However, the revisions in the typescript both in pencil and in
ink are reproduced in the IC text, and it clearly served as the basis
for the final typescript that was the IC printer's copy. Since this
page could not have been typed until such time as 25½ had been
inserted in fol. 25, its addition to the manuscript was a comparatively late process, as was the renumbering as 24,25 (combined) of
the following leaf originally 25½ to take account of typed fol. 23.

Folio 26, numbered to the right, is succeeded by centrally numbered fol. 27 without a break. Thereafter the text proceeds nor-
mally to the end of fol. 34 *military organization* (172.37). Folio
35, which would have concluded the quotation from H. G. Wells,
barely begun on the last line of fol. 34, is missing, and was perhaps
used as a sheet with the quotation clipped and pasted on it, abstracted from the present manuscript to include in the final typescript. The text in the pamphlet is relatively close to the quotation

and could have been set from printed or specially transcribed copy. Folio 36 is written on the back of a trial that cannot be precisely placed although it is nearest to 169.31-38 *All . . . collectivity* which heads fol. 25 (the second leaf to be numbered at the right). However, fol. 24 does not link with the trial on 36^v, whereas it does with fol. 25. As remarked above, this may be part of the evidence for more extensive revision in the area than is demonstrable. Present fol. 37 (173.17 *or the . . . energy.* 173.20) is a substitute for deleted matter at the foot of fol. 36 and also at the head of original fol. 37, which has been renumbered to 37½ in two stages, first 37 in the light ink and then the ½ added in dark.

If we leave aside for the moment the problem of the typed folios 6 and 7(6), and examine typed fol. 23 in isolation, we see that it is a revision of the final forms of inserted fol. 25½ and the lower part of the manuscript of fol. 25. Its purpose, then, is one of part substitution, a verbal instruction to the typist of the final manuscript apparently replacing the marking of the manuscript by deletion for the text covered by the typing. That this leaf has not strayed into the manuscript but was designed to be a part of it is indicated by the alteration of combined fol. 24,25 from original 25½, consequent upon the insertion before it of typescript fol. 23. The typescript fol. 23 was certainly behind the final typescript made up as printer's copy for IC, and in its final revised form much worked over in pencil and in ink. The end of the typing (only five lines) corresponds to the end of fol. 25 in its revised form, taking account of the deleted text at its foot continued on fol. 26 with deleted text at its head, for both of which new part-page 24,25 serves as a substitute. The natural inference to draw from the evidence is that the typing of fol. 23 was broken off when Peggy reached the foot of fol. 25 in its revised state. Folio 23 copies the lower part of the insertion on fol. 25½ and then the rest of the text on fol. 25 but since it begins in mid-sentence it must have followed typed fol. 22 without a break, fol. 22 concluding with the start of fol. 25½ after covering the upper part of fol. 25 and the lower of fol. 24. The typescript at fol. 23 seems to be in rough balance with the text at the foot of manuscript fol. 25 and thus seems to represent a typing that had progressed regularly to this point: the manuscript leaves, although highly variable because of the revision, average out to somewhat under 145 words, whereas the typescript of the first five leaves averages about 175 words. At this rate the discrepancy between the two documents should have been in the neighborhood of somewhat over 600 words or between three and four typewritten pages, so that—given the extra space available for typewritten fols. 6-7 in their new form—the typescript is just about right at fol. 23 if it continued fol. 5 with re-typed 6-7. There can be no question, then, that this fol. 23 of typescript represents the visible conclusion of a piece of continuous typing between the end of fol. 5 and the start of 23.

The question then arises why fol. 23 was broken off. The most obvious answer is that Peggy had come to the end of the manuscript fol. 25, which had been given as her stint, and stopped because James at that moment was still making his final revision of the subsequent pages. It seems significant that though the typed fol. 23 covers the inserted fol. 25½ and the rest of the text on fol. 25, it does not take in the bridge fol. 24,25 although the original numbering of this as 25½ suggests that it preceded in composition the present inserted 25½ numbered in the light ink. For what it is worth, fol. 26 shows extremely heavy revision and fol. 27 also has a great deal of alteration, followed by the deletion of its lower two-thirds and the first line of fol. 28, although neither shows the intermediate stage of pencil alteration found on fol. 25 but not again until fol. 29.[7] The evidence does not suggest that Peggy was typing the manuscript page by page after James but instead in batches and that the end of any stint would therefore coincide with the end of a manuscript page, leaving the typescript page incomplete. This is the evidence of fols. 6-7 as well. We need not suppose that the end of every stint has been revealed by the revisions of typescript fols. 6-7 and 23 which necessitated their retyping. Presumably on some occasions she would be able to put the part-page back into the typewriter and complete it when freshly revised manuscript copy became available. The two known cases may be isolated only because in each case James decided that the part-page (and manuscript) needed such revision as to call for a fresh start. (The evidence of fols. 1-5 does not encourage the hypothesis that James broke off revising his manuscript to revise Peggy's typescript whenever she had a batch ready: the heavy revision of fols. 6-7 is not found on 1-5 although they are much altered in IC.)

The main difficulty with the reconstruction is to equate the evidence of the pencil and ink revisions on fol. 23 with those throughout the manuscript both before and after 23. Everywhere the same

---

[7]This evidence is of no significance. Actually, the pencil alteration on fol. 25 was confined to the substitution of *breasts* for *minds* (169.37) and the underlining of *such* (169.38); and that on fol. 29 does no more than substitute *last* for *the only workable* (171.3) and *subjection* for *defeat* (171.6). Thus the lack of pencil alteration on fols. 26-28 after its presence on fol. 25 has no apparent significance, for James, according to this hypothesis, would have been engaged upon the final revision which was in dark ink.

order of revision seems to be present: first (to disregard current revision during inscription) a revision in dark ink; second, minor revision in pencil, possibly but not certainly followed by another round with the dark ink; third, very minor textual alteration in a light ink which is chiefly used to put the manuscript in order by numbering a few unnumbered pages and renumbering others when necessary; and fourth, a final round of textual revision in the dark ink. That the light ink deletes an assumed error in quotation marks on typescript fol. 4 (typed double quotes are mistakenly deleted in this ink before *of* at 163.29) is of no account since James could have resurveyed this typescript at any time during the revision of the manuscript. All that this shows is that at the stage of the review of the manuscript in the light ink, typed page 4 was in existence and was considered to be an integral part of the copy, the manuscript from which it was typed not being preserved. On the other hand, the presence of pencil revisions throughout in an intermediate stage of revision, both before and after fol. 23 (the earliest on fol. 10 and then on 11, 12, 14, 14½, 16, 18, 20, 25, 29-34) appears to indicate that all these alterations were made at the same time, an hypothesis supported by light-ink alterations in the text on fols. 14, 14½ (and perhaps elsewhere when the ink is not to be identified so precisely) and in the early foliation of what became 15c, 18½, 21½, 22, 25½, and 37½. We find both pencil and later dark-ink changes on typed fol. 23, and a light-ink foliation of 25½, plus directions for the transfer on both leaves in light ink; yet the typing of fol. 23 was later than the insertion of fol. 25½ on 25.

It is true that if we owe the use of typed fol. 23 for the text here to the fact that it concluded on a part-page a full page of manuscript, and needed revision, there is no difficulty in associating its typing up of an insertion whose directions were in light ink with earlier changes in this ink on fols. 14 to 22, for these could all have been prepared before the stint of typing began that was to end with fol. 23. On the other hand, if, as seems evident, the light ink represents a third stage of the revision—one chiefly concerned with preparing the numbers of the pages for typing, one must assume that when fol. 23 was typed the further light-ink change in the number of 37 to 37½, the final leaf, had already been made. If this is so, the case is made that James completed his inscription of the entire manuscript (starting at least with fol. 8 but perhaps earlier after the end of the #4548 notebook text) before the typing began of fols. 8-37½. The more extensive evidence of the widespread pencil alterations, of a uniform kind and amount and presumably made at the same time, though earlier than the light-ink changes,[8] supports this conclusion.

If the manuscript were thus complete, the typing was not continuous, however. It is understandable that the pencil-draft notebook #4548 would have been typed early, but since the end of the notebook text comes in mid-line near the foot of typed fol. 3 and new text continues on fols. 4-5 and then 6, it is obvious that James chose to continue the notebook in some other medium, probably on loose sheets of paper. Why these sheets have not been preserved, but only the typescript made from them, is something of a mystery;[9] but the foliation of the manuscript at 8 when the autograph takes over from the typing after fol. 7, altered from 6, indicates clearly enough that Peggy had completed all of the available text with original typescript fol. 6 before changes were made that resulted in a typed fol. 7 (completed in James's hand) and the continuation of the composition of the manuscript with fol. 8 following on the end of the part-page typed fol. 7.

The casual revision of fols. 1-5 is peculiar since it consists in only a few alterations and additions made at some unknown time in a dark ink (except for the light-ink mistake on fol. 4 when James was working over the whole). But fols. 6-7 represent two different typescripts. The evidence suggests that when James started work on fol. 8 (just possibly on a lost fol. 7) he first rewrote the end of the typescript on fol. 6 (164.10 *hundred . . . Thessalonica and Lacedemon* 164.13) and added to it, including the beginning of a new paragraph, until he deleted this start and apparently discarded the leaf. Here it is difficult to be precise in reconstructing the order of events. However, it would seem that James wanted a clean copy of the typescript after fol. 5 and that Peggy tried again with a revision originally numbered 6 that omitted the mention of Brutus. The new page began with the same

---

[8] On fol. 14 two pencil alterations are deleted in the light ink, thus establishing that this ink was later than the pencil. If the evidence of fol. 23 is to be trusted, the possibility must remain that some of the pencil alterations could have been made at a later time than others. The natural inference to be drawn from fol. 23, however, is, instead, that it represents a special case and was not attached to the manuscript for very long, perhaps, before retyping.

[9] The dates in James's diary for the completion of "The Moral Equivalent" and of "A Suggestion about Mysticism" do not permit the conjecture that "A Suggestion" was started in the notebook before "The Moral Equivalent" could be continued and thus enforced the use of another medium. It is probable that the leaves of pencil inscription in the notebook represent a single day's writing. On another day he wrote elsewhere, probably for the reason that loose sheets would give him more flexibility to expand and insert.

words *hundred and fifty* and the typing ended with *this cruel history. It has bred pugnacity into our bone and marrow and thousands of years of peace won't breed it out of us.* But before James started fol. 8 he renumbered this leaf to 7, deleted the two sentences beginning *Dead men tell no tales* and combined them into one, which he transferred to come after the deletion of *It has bred pugnacity . . . us.* He then started a discussion of the fate of noncombatants (such as he had inserted after the typed text on original fol. 6) and continued with the beginning of a comment on the atrocities of the white armies in China before he broke off. It would seem that at this time the discarded fol. 6 was brought back in order to retain the reference to Brutus, and placed before revised 6 which was then renumbered 7. Finally, on fol. 8 James began the major composition with another version of *Our ancestors have bred pugnacity* (164.18-19) previously deleted on fol. 7. The revision of typed fol. 7 may not seem so strange when it is observed that James, seeing that he must revise it so extensively as to make it useless without retyping again, continued it in autograph as the first leaf of new composition. However, further deletions resulted in the material of the leaf being thoroughly rearranged, with a revision of one of its sentences heading fol. 8.

The manuscript was then completed on fol. 37½ and all of its expansions on inserted leaves were arranged. Moreover, before typing was again started, James took the opportunity to revise the manuscript throughout in pencil, to renumber its pages when needed in light ink, and, on the evidence of fol. 34 (and perhaps 14½) where dark ink deletes pencil changes, to make a further and perhaps extensive revision in dark ink. Peggy must have started her second stint at some point when this final revision had passed fol. 25. She would have first retyped fols. 6-7 and then started on the manuscript of fol. 8. The evidence suggests that her typing of part-page 23, corresponding to the foot of revised manuscript fol. 25, with its insertion of 25½, completed the batch of revised manuscript that James had given her. He himself was probably working further on in the revision; hence it is possible that he continued for some time, perhaps even completing the final revision, before he turned to her typescript and reviewed how his manuscript would continue it. At whatever point this was, he seems to have made a few changes in dark ink and then in pencil at a later time on this fol. 23. Finally, just before the start of retyping he reviewed the page again and made his last revisions in the dark ink. Peggy would have retyped this altered page as a preliminary to continuing the manuscript with fol. 24,25, and then would have gone on uninterrupted so far as one can see to fol. 37½.

The prime difficulty that must be faced is the fact that fol. 23 shares with the rest of the manuscript a mixture of pencil and ink revisions at several stages although physically it could not have undergone these stages at the same time as the earlier part of the manuscript at least. One is forced to conjecture that after whatever revision James gave typed fol. 23 when he incorporated it into the manuscript to be retyped along with the rest, he returned to it at one or more times to touch up the text before Peggy started the next stint of typing, and at one of these times he had a pencil in his hand. Since any alternatives to this hypothesis are too fantastic to contemplate, it would seem that no serious difficulty need be felt about the pencil alterations in fol. 23.

Including its preserved typed pages, the manuscript represents only a draft in comparison with the considerably revised printed text of IC. The lack of any serious or sweeping alteration in the first five pages of the carbon of the typescript gives no indication of what alterations James must have made in the ribbon copy, or whether, indeed, this original ribbon copy was so heavily revised that in turn it had to be retyped, like the preserved fols. 6-7 and 23. Speculation is useless although of some textual interest. One can say definitely that some pages of the original typescript, at least, would have needed retyping because of the heavy revision. For instance, the manuscript text (and hence the typescript) on fol. 9 beginning *At the present day* (164.29) and ending on fol. 12 with MS *-interval* (165.6) is so divergent in the IC text as to have required a new typescript. This is by no means a unique example, nor is there reason to suppose that present typed fols. 1-5, which have had no revision to speak of in their present form, were any different. But whether Peggy or a professional made a complete new typescript from the worked-over original, or only selected pages were retyped as necessary, is not to be determined. What one can say is that a comparison of Peggy's typing of the text in notebook #4548 shows that she was a relatively faithful typist despite her deficiencies in spelling and her mechanical errors. Unless the whole of her first typescript were retyped, and by another hand, the printer of IC would have been given copy that was more than usually faithful to the manuscript and to James's revisions of the manuscript both of substantives and of accidentals.

The conjectured presence of an intervening typescript that James would have corrected and even revised further reduces the possibility of utilizing the preserved early draft of this essay as copy-text, and the knowledge that James read the proofs for IC—which had been furnished what must be regarded as trustworthy copy—further enhances its authority as copy-text. The later revision of the text for *McClure's* introduces a range of altered substantives that must be accepted; nevertheless, the general accidental texture of *McClure's* is of too uncertain authority for this version to be given generally unified authority and copy-text status.

ADDENDA

LITERARY REMAINS

James wrote to Henry William Rankin on June 21, 1896 (Harvard *67 M-96, letter 20): "I wonder if you know my edition of my father's literary remains? I send you one of the only two copies procurable by me—the work is out of print. The[re] is some good english in it, whether there be good theology or no."

ROBERT GOULD SHAW

On April 28, 1897, James wrote to Benjamin Paul Blood: "I have a fearful job on hand just now: an address on the unveiling of a military statue. Three thousand people, governor and troops, etc. Why they fell upon me, God knows; but being challenged, I could not funk. The task is a mechanical one, and the result somewhat of a school-boy composition" (*Letters*, II, 59).

EMERSON

In a letter to H. W. Rankin dated February 27, 1903 (*67 M-96, letter 39) James writes: "I must likewise re-read most of Emerson, in preparation for a 1/4 part which I am to play in the Celebration of his 100th birthday at Concord—a 20 minutes address, along with 3 other Speakers. . . . I fear that poor Emerson's memory (like all things in this monstrous age) will be maltreated through quantitative excess in its celebration. Edwin D. Mead has just asked me to be one of *30* (! !) lecturers on Emerson in Boston next summer."

REMARKS AT THE PEACE BANQUET

The following is taken from the Boston *Evening Transcript* for October 8, 1904, p. 6:

THE PEACE DINNER | [rule] | Sober Warning Against Expecting Radical | Reform by Professor James | [rule]

Notable after-dinner talks by Professor William James of Harvard, Booker T. Washington, Baroness von Suttner and others marked the dinner of the peace delegates last evening in Horticultural Hall. This morning's session of the Congress being an afterthought, the dinner was intended as a farewell gathering of the peace lovers, and the speeches were, in a way, reflective of the spirit of the Congress and the hope of results to come. There was hope in the opening prayer of Dr. Edward Everett Hale; hope in the words of congratulation by the president of the Congress, Robert Treat Paine; hope in the words of Baroness von Suttner, of Rev. Charles Wagner, of Mrs. W. P. Byles, of Booker T. Washington, Miss Jane Addams, John Lund, Bliss Perry—and hope with a philosophic pessimism in the words of Professor James, the last speaker and the man who saw through the exaltation of the moment and gave some words of caution based on the reasonable limitations of human nature. For peace, he recognizes the weakness of the nations and of men. "A millenium of peace will not breed the fighting disposition out of our bone and marrow," he said, "and a function so ingrained and vital will never consent to die without resistance, and will always find impassioned apologists and idealizers. The plain truth is, that people really want war. They want it anyhow; for itself, and apart from each and every possible consequence. It is the final bouquet of life's fireworks. Born soldiers want it, hot and actual; non-combatants want it on the background, and always as a possibility to feed imagination and to keep excitement going. War is human nature at its uttermost. Society would rot without the mystical blood-payment. We do ill, therefore, to talk much of universal peace, or of a general disarmament. We must go in for preventive medicine, not for radical cure. We must cheat our foe, circumvent him, not try to change his nature. Put peace men in power. Educate editors and statesmen to responsibility. Seize every pretext, however small, for arbitration methods, and multiply precedents; foster rival excitements and diversions for the heroic energies; and from one generation to another the chances are that national irritations will grow less acute and states of strain less dangerous."

THE ENERGIES OF MEN

James addressed James McKeen Cattell on November 10, 1906 (Library of Congress): "The address I shall write for the philosophers will be of general human interest enough to do for the general S. of N—s. But it will last 50 minutes, I fear. I had hoped to do something on 'composition' in 'consciousness,' which would have been highly technical. It won't pan out in time, so I fall back on a popular talk with concrete illustrations of the reserves of energy in people that they habitually don't draw upon. I have notified you all ['that you' *del.*] i.e. Cas [*illeg. letters*] & thru him the other members of the executive committee that it need expect nothing from me as president. Angell also. As I told you, I think it likely that I may have to send my address to the philosophers to be read. Very sorry to put you out and I won't, unless compelled by *force majeure.*" [A letter to his wife of December 27, 1906 (bMS Am 1092.9 [2368]), from New York implies that contrary to his protestations, he delivered the presidential address.]

"The Energies of Men" was later reprinted with "The Gospel of Relaxation" in *On Vital Reserves* (New York: Holt, 1911).

THE MORAL EQUIVALENT OF WAR

An excerpt entitled "Professor William James's Peace Utopia" appeared in the *Advocate of Peace*, 72 (1910), 219-220. An undated pamphlet with a foreword by Albert Bigelow was perhaps distributed by the International Voluntary Service, Cabot, Vermont, 1960.

Emendations

Every editorial change from the copy-text is recorded for the substantives, and every change in the accidentals as well save for such silent typographical adjustments as are remarked in A Note on the Editorial Method. The reading to the left of the bracket, the lemma, represents the form chosen in the present edition, usually as an emendation of the copy-text. (A prefixed superior [1] or [2] indicates which of any two identical words in the same line is intended.) The sigil immediately following the bracket is the identifying symbol for the earliest source of the emendation, followed by the sigla of any later agreeing documents or by a plus sign should all succeeding documents agree with the earliest source. Readings in parentheses after sigla indicate a difference in the form of the source from that of the emended reading to the left of the bracket. To the right of this semicolon appear the rejected readings of the copy-text and of any other recorded documents, followed by their sigla; a plus sign is used after a sigil when all later documents agree with its reading. When emendations need to be made that are not drawn from any authoritative document, for convenience Henry James, Jr.'s, *Memories and Studies* (1911), in which a number of the essays in this volume were reprinted, has been utilized, and failing that, the editor's own alterations marked as H (Harvard). However, M&S is not noted in the list of Emendations except when it is an emending agent or a rejected substantive. The word *stet* after the bracket calls special attention to the retention of a copy-text reading. It may be employed to key a Textual Note, as marked by an asterisk before the page-line number. In a quotation it may indicate that James's version (differing from the source in some respect) has been retained in the edited text. It may also be used in rare instances to indicate that a possibly questionable or unusual reading has been retained in the text.

For convenience, certain shorthand symbols familiar in textual notation are employed. A wavy dash (∼) represents the same word that appears before the bracket and is used exclusively in recording punctuation or other accidental variants. An inferior caret (∧) indicates the absence of a punctuation mark (or of a footnote superscript) when a difference in the punctuation constitutes the variant being recorded, or is part of the variant. A vertical stroke (|) represents a line ending, sometimes recorded as bearing on the cause of an error or fault. A hand symbol (☞) before a page-line reference draws attention to the parenthetical listing of additional lines where the forms of emendation are identical. The mark § indicates that an MS variant is included wholly or in part in an alteration in the manuscript, the description of which has been removed to the Emendations list from the list of Alterations in the Manuscripts. The double dagger (‡) indicates that the variant in the MS is part of a larger alteration not easily transferable to the Emendations, the details of which can be found in the Alterations in the Manuscripts. Quotations within the text are identified in Professor Skrupskelis' Notes. The sigil WJ/ followed by the appropriate symbol (as WJ/MS[p]) indicates James's autograph revisions, usually found in his file sets or private copies of journal articles, and in books, proofs, or clippings.

INTRODUCTION TO *THE LITERARY REMAINS OF THE LATE HENRY JAMES*

The copy-text is LR, *The Literary Remains of the Late Henry James,* edited with an Introduction by William James (Boston: Houghton Mifflin, 1884), pp. 7-119 (McD 1884:5). Double quotation marks used for quotations in Henry James's texts are automatically reversed to single in LR and are not recorded as emendations. Accidentals in quotations from Henry James have also been emended silently.

3.11;5.3-4 *Society . . . Man,*] H;*db. qts.* (*rom.*) LR

4.18 literary] H;|iterary LR

6.20 side,] Kellogg; ~; LR

6.20 this] *stet* LR; this of itself Kellogg

6.21,22 is: ₍Given] Kellogg; ~,–given LR

6.22 Creator; to] Kellogg; creator. To LR

6.22 ²Creator] Kellogg; *l.c.* LR

6.23 doubt,] Kellogg; ~; LR

6.39 [pp. 4-5]] H;*om.* LR

7.13 insistence] H; insistance LR

8.25 hopes?] *stet* LR; ~. HJ

8.25 all] *stet* LR; all of us HJ

8.26 the shewy] HJ; a showy LR

8.29 ships] *stet* LR; worthless ships HJ

8.29 ships . . .] H; ~ ₍ LR

8.44 pp. 132-134] H; p. 133 LR

9.27 "Society"] H; ₍ ~" LR (*error*)

11.31 hindrance] *stet* LR; philosophic hindrance HJ

11.42 pp. 165-166] H; p. 185 LR

13.36 alive . . . . But] H; ~; but LR

13.41 414] H; 413 LR

14.21 In] *stet* LR; Thus in HJ

14.34 extinguish him] *stet* LR; extinguish the faintest possibility of self-consciousness in him HJ

15.4 him] *stet* LR; him at the highest HJ

15.4 vegetative] *stet* LR; vegetative and animal HJ

15.4 Creation,] *stet* LR; Creation, to be spiritual–i.e. HJ

15.5-6 creature,] *stet* LR; ~– HJ

16.28 a] *stet* LR; this HJ

16.31 truth,] *stet* LR; very truth ₍ HJ

18.2 the] *stet* LR; that HJ

18.23-24 the creature] *stet* LR; he HJ

18.28 82-84] H; 83, 84 LR

18.43 pp. 162-163] H; p. 162 LR

19.7-8 inferior . . . superior] *stet* LR; subjective or inferior . . . objective or superior HJ

19.8 appearance] *stet* LR; fact or appearance HJ

19.15-16 subjective] *stet* LR; subjective seeming, or phenomenal HJ

19.16 constitution₍] *stet* LR; ~, HJ

19.17 objective] *stet* LR; formal existence or objective HJ

19.39 185-186] H; 185, 186 LR

20.17 your] HJ; our LR

20.37 involving] *stet* LR; involving therefore HJ

20.39 vi-vii] H; 6, 7 LR

21.40 73, 72, 73] H; 72, 73 LR

22.24 Morality] *stet* LR; *ital.* HJ

22.25 that of any] *stet* LR; every HJ

22.26 gives us] *stet* LR; merely gives us on the contrary HJ

23.35 [But . . . so,]] H; ₍ ~ . . . ~,₍ LR

24.6 the] HJ; *om.* LR

24.13 dignity . . .] H; ~,– LR

24.14-15,15-16,16 He would have] *stet* LR; We should have had HJ

24.17   he would be] *stet* LR; we should have been HJ

24.18   he would lack] *stet* LR; we should have lacked HJ

24.19   his spirit] *stet* LR; our spirits HJ

24.20   his] *stet* LR; our HJ

24.38   pp. 120-121] H; p. 120 LR

25.28,32   is] HJ; was LR

25.31   feels] HJ; felt LR

26.2   depths . . .] H; ~,– LR

26.6   chatters.²¹ . . .] H; ~.¹ ∧ LR

27.20   when] *stet* LR; When HJ

28.11   conviction] *stet* LR; previous conviction HJ

28.12   [and make him]] H; ∧ ~~~ ∧ LR

28.16   revolves∧] *stet* LR; revolves about this centre, HJ

28.31   shall stand] *stet* LR; stands HJ

28.33   penitence, thus] *stet* LR; ~; these HJ

28.35   moral and religious] *stet* LR; religious HJ

28.40   pp. 10-11] H; p. 10 LR

32.10   us] *stet* LR; you HJ

35.16   an] *stet* LR; this HJ

35.26   feeling] HJ; feelings LR

38.21-23   "When . . . hell."] *stet* LR; Swedenborg makes nature the realm of *uncreation*: and by that unexpected word sends a breath of health to the deepest heart of hell. HJ

38.36   instinct] *stet* LR; the scientific instinct HJ

39.1   authenticated and unchecked,] *stet* LR; authenticated by science, and unchecked by conscience, HJ

39.5   intimate] *stet* LR; most intimate or HJ

39.6   when . . . are] *stet* LR; having had one's eyes once HJ

39.8   ere] *stet* LR; before HJ

39.39   pp. 361-362] H; p. 361 LR

41.14   alternated] HJ; alternated with LR

41.25   although] HJ; though LR

42.6   I am] *stet* LR; personally I am HJ

42.7   ambitions,] *stet* LR; ~– HJ

42.20   hell] *stet* LR; it HJ

42.21   sedulously] HJ; seduously LR (*error*)

42.22   it] *stet* LR; hell HJ

42.22   Swedenborg] *stet* LR; In short, Swedenborg HJ

42.28   their] *stet* LR; *om.* HJ

43.1-2   universe . . .] H; ~, LR

43.30   they . . .] H; ~ ∧ LR

43.31   enfeeble . . .] H; ~ ∧ LR

43.36-44.2   which . . . man] *stet* LR; *all ital.* HJ

43.37   pp. 17-18] H; p. 17 LR

43.38   pp. 106-107] H; p. 107 LR

44.35   pp. 78-79] H; p. 78 LR

44.36   pp. 251-252] H; p. 251 LR

47.6-8   birth I had . . . have . . . had] *stet* LR; birth till now I have . . . have had . . . have HJ

47.8   upon] *stet* LR; upon my mere fantastic want, HJ

47.12-14   had . . . had] *stet* LR; have . . . have HJ

47.14   that] HJ; of that LR

47.18-19   ignorance . . . . But] H; ~; but LR

47.22   women,] *stet* LR; women∧ every way my equals, in many ways HJ

47.25   infancy. . . .] H; ~. ∧ LR

48.5   towards] HJ; toward LR

48.40   devil] HJ; devils LR

49.19   170-176] H; 170-175 LR

49.22   Don't] HJ; Do not LR

49.31   pride] *stet* LR; evil HJ

49.39   200-203] H; 201, 202 LR

50.4   church . . .] H; Church∧ LR

50.6   put herself] *stet* LR; delighted to put herself again HJ

50.7   led] *stet* LR; lead HJ

50.8   sullen] *stet* LR; sombre and sullen HJ

50.9   world. . . .] H; ~. ∧ LR

50.16   toward] HJ; towards LR

50.16   *reality*] *stet* LR; *natural reality* HJ

50.44   270, 268-269] H; 268-270 LR

51.9   the] HJ; this LR

51.10-11   limitations] HJ; limitation LR

51.29   religion . . .] H; ~ ∧ LR

51.39   374, 373] H; 373, 374 LR

52.40   pp. 40-42] H; p. 42 LR

53.24   doesn't] HJ; does not LR

53.36   pp. 503-504] H; p. 503 LR

54.40   pp. 520-521] H; p. 520 LR

56.5,6   one's self] HJ; oneself LR

56.8 reader,] *stet* LR; reader then, HJ

56.37 pp. 209-210] H; p. 209 LR

57.45 pp. 294-295] H; p. 293 LR

59.23 pp. 214-217] H; p. 217 LR

59.31 this] HJ; his LR

59.41 pp. 200-201] H; p. 200 LR

60.19 naive] H; *naïve* LR

ROBERT GOULD SHAW: ORATION BY PROFESSOR WILLIAM JAMES

The copy-text is M, the Oration in *The Monument to Robert Gould Shaw* (Boston: Houghton Mifflin, 1897), pp. 71-87 (McD 1897:2). Revisions from WJ/M, James's annotated copy of the Houghton Mifflin printing of M, are incorporated. Reference is made to P[13], "II. Oration by Professor William James," *Harvard Graduates' Magazine*, 6 (September 1897), 28-37, and to TMs, the draft typescript in the James Collection (MS Am 1092.9 [4538]). James's autograph revisions of typed copy can be identified by the indication of ink or pencil. When a variant is noted from James's handwritten pages, it is identified as TMs(MS); alterations noted in these sections are to be taken as made in ink unless otherwise stated. One correction by Henry James, Jr., in James's annotated copy of M is noted as HJ/M. The posthumous reprint in M&S, "Robert Gould Shaw," *Memories and Studies*, edited by Henry James, Jr., pp. 35-61 (McD 1911:2), is noted only for substantive variants from the copy-text in connection with an entry except for the one correction drawn from it. All alterations in TMs or TMs(MS) are recorded here or in the Historical Collation. Purely typographical corrections, whether type over type or ink over type, are not noted.

[*begin* TMs]

64.9 Wagner ₐ] TMs,P[13]; ~, M

64.9 *et seq.* Fifty-fourth] TMs; 54th M,P[13]

64.20 revery] TMs; reverie M,P[13]

64.21 anyone] TMs; any one M,P[13]

64.23 May ₐ] TMs; ~, M,P[13]

65.1-2 Mayor ... Governor ₐ] TMs; mayor ... governor, M,P[13]

65.8 *et seq.* (*except* 71.20) Colonel] TMs; *l.c.* M,P[13]

65.8 battle—] H; ~,— TMs+

65.9 lost—] TMs; ~,— M,P[13]

65.11 significance] WJ/M(*penc.*), M&S; importance TMs(MS),M,P[13]

65.13 imagination ₐ] TMs(MS),P[13]; ~, M

65.14 grecian] TMs(MS); *cap.* M,P[13]

65.15 people ₐ] TMs(MS),P[13]; ~, M

65.20 history.] WJ/M ('It ... States.' *penc. del.*; 'More ... meaning.' *ink del.*); M&S; history. It set the country free from Slavery, the social plague which until then had *made [ab. del.* 'frustrated *the [ab. del.* 'all'] pos- sibility of'] real [*penc. ab. del.* 'nor-

mal'] political ['t' *ov.* 'c'] *develop- ment impossible [*ab. del.* 'f life'] in the United States. More and more, as the years pass, does that meaning *stand forth [*ab. del.* 'remain'] as the sole meaning. TMs(MS); history. It freed the country from the social plague which until then had made political development impossible in the United States. More and more, as the years pass, does that meaning stand forth as the sole meaning. M,P[13]

65.28 security,] WJ/M(*ink*); M&S; con- sciousness of legalized possession) TMs(MS); security of legalized pos- session, M,P[13]

65.32 fortune ₐ] TMs(MS); ~, M,P[13]

65.40 traveller] TMs(MS); traveler M,P[13]

66.1 swamp ₐ] TMs(MS); ~, M,P[13]

66.4 muzzled—] TMs(MS); ~,— M,P[13]

66.12 casual ₐ] TMs(MS); ~, M,P[13]

66.13 able] WJ/M(*ink*); M&S; unques- tionably able TMs,M,P[13]

66.14 situations ₐ] TMs; ~, M,P[13]

66.17 so called] TMs(*penc. intrl.*); ~ - ~ M,P¹³

66.27 soldier's ‸] TMs(Soldiers'); ~ - M,P¹³

66.30 soldier's ‸] TMs(*cap.*); ~ - M,P¹³

66.38 founders] WJ/M(*ink*);M&S; founders of the Union TMs,M,P¹³

66.39 wrought] WJ/M(*ink*);M&S; wrought and spread ['in its vitals' *penc. del.*] TMs;M,P¹³ (spread,)

67.8 the times demand,] WJ/M(*in penc. for ink del.* 'occasion serves,'*)*;M&S; occasion serves, TMs,M,P¹³

67.12 repeat:] WJ/M(*in penc. for ink del.* 'say ... poet:'*)*;M&S; say with the poet: TMs,M,P¹³

67.13 nor] Halleck; none TMs+

67.15 cheerful] WJ/M(*ink*);M&S; *cheerful [*penc.*] ready [*ab. del.* 'resolute'] TMs(MS);M,P¹³

67.29 Captain] TMs(MS) ('C' *triple underl.*); *l.c.* M,P¹³

67.29 Second‸] TMs(MS),P¹³ ; ~, M

67.31 ‸ for a moment‸] TMs(MS), P¹³; , ~~~, M

*67.35 inevitable, ... certain,] TMs (*tr. by penc. guideline*); cértain, ... inevitable, M+

68.10 picket‸] TMs(MS); ~ - M,P¹³

68.11 our Second Regiment] WJ/M (*ink*) (regiment);M&S; the Second Massachusetts Infantry TMs(MS), M;P¹³ (2d)

68.16-17 *Peninsular War ... Idylls of the King*] H; *no qts. (rom.)* TMs; *db. qts. (rom.)* M,P¹³

68.17 amongst] TMs; among M+

68.20-21 enemy— ... reverse—] TMs; ~,— ... ~,— M,P¹³

68.27 Major] TMs; *l.c.* M,P¹³

69.16 -martialled] TMs; -martialed M,P¹³

69.21 staunch] TMs; stanch M,P¹³

69.26 Tenth] TMs; 10th M,P¹³

69.28 Division] TMs;*l.c.* M,P¹³

69.37 *et seq. (except* 70.29) Adjutant] TMs; *l.c.* M,P¹³

70.1,24 General's] TMs;*l.c.* M,P¹³

*70.1 writes the Adjutant,] *stet* M,P¹³

70.2 Twenty-fourth] H; 24th TMs+

70.28 General] H; *l.c.* TMs+

70.29 Adjutant] H; *l.c.* TMs+

71.16 eighteen] TMs(MS),P¹³ ; 18 M

71.20 Colonel] H; *l.c.* TMs(MS)+

71.25 shovelled] TMs(MS); shoveled M,P¹³

71.33 ‸ indeed ‸] TMs(MS) (*intrl.*); , ~, M,P¹³

72.11 In . . . events] WJ/M(*penc. insrtd. for ink ov. penc. del.*);M&S; [¶] *Ah! my friends, [*penc. intrl.*] (Ah, my friends, M,P¹³) And (and M,P¹³) may the like of it never be required of us again! It ([¶] It M,P¹³) is hard to end a discourse like this ['one' *ink del.*] without *one [*ink ab. del.* 'a'] word of *moralizing; [*ink semicolon ov. period*] and [*ink intrl.*] TMs;M,P¹³

72.11 distinguished] WJ/M(*bef. ink ov. penc. del.*);M&S; in *all [*ink ab. del.* 'the'] events [*penc. ab. del.* 'acts'] *like those [*ink intrl.*] we are commemorating (commemorating, M) TMs;M,P¹³

72.12 from the] WJ/M(*penc.*) (from ['and' *ink del.*] the);M&S; on *the [*ink ov.* 'one'] one [*ink insrtd.*] hand, and on the other the physical TMs;M,P¹³

72.20 treasure‸] TMs; ~, M,P¹³

72.20 war-] TMs; ~ ‸ M,P¹³

72.25 our pugnacity] WJ/M(our [*ink*] pugnacity [*penc.*]);M&S; military virtue TMs,M,P¹³

72.26 virtue] WJ/M(*ink*);M&S; kind of virtue [*ink* '*most instinctive, [*penc. del.*] and' *del. intrl.*] TMs;M,P¹³

72.34 ¹courage] WJ/M(*penc.*);M&S; valor TMs,M,P¹³

72.34 peace-] TMs(*hyphen ink insrtd.*); ~ ‸ M,P¹³

73.22 Robert] WJ/M(*penc.*);M&S; *om.* TMs,M,P¹³

[*end* TMs]

73.37 had] HJ/M(*ink*);P¹³,M&S; have M

74.9 life—] H; ~,— M,P¹³

74.14 innings‸] WJ/M(*ink*); ~; M,P¹³

74.14-15 —it ... Nation.] WJ/M(—it was by [*ink ab. del. penc.* 'By'] *breaking ['away' *del.*] (breaking away M&S) from **this [*ink alt. fr.* 'the'] ['one' *ink del.*] habit the (that

271

the M&S) ***slave ['s' *uncertain l.c. or cap.*] States nearly wrecked our Nation. [*penc.*]);M&S; *om.* M,P¹³

74.15   The other is] WJ/M(*ink*);M&S; and the other, M,P¹³

74.16   who] WJ/M(*penc.*);M&S; who overstep the lawful bounds of fairness or M,P¹³

74.17   peace∧] H; ~. M,P¹³

74.17-18   —it . . . life.] WJ/M(*—it was

[*insrtd.*] By [*unreduced in error*] [*ink insrtd. aft. del. of* 'By' *outside guideline in preceding insert* (74.14-15)] *holding* ['strenuously' *del.*] (By holding M&S) to **this [*ink alt. fr.* 'the'] habit [*ink ab. del.* 'other'] the free states saved her ['from perdition.' *del.*] life. [*penc.*]); M&S; *om.* M,P¹³

74.17   States] M&S; *l.c.* WJ/M

HUMAN IMMORTALITY

The copy-text is HI, *Human Immortality: Two Supposed Objections to the Doctrine* (Boston and New York: Houghton Mifflin, 1898) (McD 1898:5). The copy-text for the "Preface to Second Edition" is the 1899 second printing.

75.4   'transmission-theory'] H; "~ - ~" HI

75.20-21;76.6   'mother-sea'] H; "~ - ~" HI

☛ 78.35-36   *Critical . . . Life,*] H; *sg. qts.* (*rom.*) HI (*similar* 89.28-29; 94.26;100.14-15)

82.38   Dühring] H; *Duhring* HI

82.39   169] H; 168 HI

83.13;89.36   pre-exists] H; preëxists HI

83.45,46   that∧] Clifford; ~, HI

83.46   does] Clifford; Does HI

84.16   connexion] Clifford; connection HI

85.16-19   place— . . . consciousness— . . . emotion—] Spencer; ~; . . . ~; . . . ~,— HI

85.17   light,] Spencer; ~ ∧ HI

85.23   must] *stet* HI; can and must Büchner

85.25   muscle-] Büchner; nerve- HI

85.26   universal∧] Büchner; ~ - HI

85.27-28   experimentally] *stet* HI; *ital.* Büchner

85.29   occupies . . . second] *stet* HI; *all ital.* Büchner

85.30   242] H; 241 HI

*85.35   red-white] H; white HI

85.42   inside] Lowell; inside of HI

86.30   Eternity] Shelley; *l.c.* HI

94.4   mother-] H; ~ ∧ HI

94.24   life."] H; ~. ∧ HI

94.37   lucidity] *stet* HI; *ital.* Schiller

94.40   inverting] *stet* HI; *ital.* Schiller

94.41,42;95.18   Consciousness] *stet* HI; *l.c.* Schiller

94.42   it∧] Schiller; ~, HI

95.20,24   favour] Schiller; favor HI

95.21   'supernatural.'] *stet* HI; "~." Schiller

95.23   tenable∧] Schiller; ~, HI

95.27   consciousness] Schiller; the consciousness HI

95.29-30   man∧ . . . time∧ . . . less∧] Schiller; ~, . . . ~, . . . ~, HI

95.33   that∧ . . . time∧] Schiller; ~, . . . ~, HI

97.14   triumphantly] H; trimphantly HI (*error*)

98.7   *saecula saeculorum*] H;*secula seculorum* HI

PREFACE TO STARBUCK'S *PSYCHOLOGY OF RELIGION*

The copy-text is S, *The Psychology of Religion,* by Edwin Diller Starbuck (London: Walter Scott, Ltd.; New York: Charles Scribner's Sons, 1899), pp. vii-x (McD 1899:5).

102.6 *et seq.*   Dr.] H; ~ ∧ S

104.24   VII∧] H; ~. S

Emendations

PREFACE TO LUTOSLAWSKI'S *WORLD OF SOULS*

The copy-text is MS, the holograph manuscript preserved in the James Collection at Houghton (bMS Am 1092.9 [4462]). Reference is also made to L, Wincenty Lutoslawski, *A World of Souls* (George Allen & Unwin, 1924), pp. 5-8 (McD 1899:12).

105.2   *The ... Plato*] L; the Logic of
    Plato MS
105.12   *The Soul's Power*] L; "The
    Soul's power" MS
*‡106.14   quality.] *stet* MS; quality.
    Witness Goethe, Emerson, Carlyle,
    Matthew Arnold, and nowadays in
    Germany Nietzsche. L
106.31   monadologist.] L; ~: MS (*error*)
107.8   non-uniformity] L; ~ ∧ | ~ MS

*107.9   science] *stet* MS,L
107.14   Professor] H; Prof. MS
107.14-16   *Ueber ... Weltanschauung*]
    L; Grundzüge einer individualisti-
    schen Weltanschauung MS
‡107.16   (Helsingfors, 1898.)] L; ∧ ~,
    ~. ∧ MS
107.20   Professor] H; Prof. MS;
    Wincenty L

EMERSON

The copy-text is EC, "Address of William James," published in *The Centenary of the Birth of Ralph Waldo Emerson as Observed in Concord May 25 1903 under the Direction of the Social Circle in Concord*, printed by the Riverside Press for the Social Circle in June 1903, pp. 67-77 (McD 1903:2). Reference is made to TMs, the autograph-revised typescript contained in the James Collection (MS Am 1092.9 [4541]) and, for substantives only, to the reprint entitled "Address at the Emerson Centenary in Concord" in M&S, *Memories and Studies*, edited by Henry James, Jr., pp. 17-34 (McD 1911:2).

109.0   Emerson] TMs; Address of Wil-
    liam James EC; Address at the
    Emerson Centenary in Concord M&S
* § 109.7   shrunk] H; shrunk *into the
    phantom of an attitude, [*del. intrl.*]
    TMs; EC, M&S
109.12;114.15   today] TMs; to-day EC
110.20   said;] TMs; ~: EC
110.30   with ... space] *stet* TMs,EC;
    But these stoopings and scrapings and
    fingerings in a few square yards of
    garden Emerson
110.31   narrowing and poisoning] *stet*
    TMs,EC; dispiriting, drivelling Emer-
    son
110.38   free] Emerson; face TMs+
110.38   negroes] Emerson; *cap.* TMs,EC
110.39   thoughts ∧] *stet* TMs,EC; spirits,
    imprisoned thoughts, Emerson
110.39   man] *stet* TMs,EC; man,—far
    retired in the heaven of invention
    Emerson
110.39   which ∧] *stet* TMs,EC; which,

    important to the republic of man,
    Emerson
110.40   me] *stet* TMs,EC; I   Emerson
111.12;115.18   man!] *stet* TMs,EC;
    ~,   Emerson
111.19-20   brain, ... heart,] Emerson;
    ~ ∧ ... ~ ∧ TMs,EC
111.20   City] Emerson; city TMs,EC
111.26   exists,] Emerson; ~ ∧ TMs,EC
111.34   Each one of us] *stet* TMs,EC;
    but we also   Emerson
111.34   rises] *stet* TMs,EC; rises for-
    ever   Emerson
111.35   eastern sea] Emerson; Eastern
    Sea TMs,EC
111.35   himself one of] *stet* TMs,EC;
    ourselves   Emerson
111.36   thyself:] Emerson; ~, TMs,EC
111.36   string. ...] H; ~. ∧ TMs,EC
§ 111.37   every] Emerson; each [*ab.*
    del. 'every'] TMs; EC,M&S
111.37   arrives] Emerson; must arrive
    TMs+

111.38 that . . .] H; ~ ∧ TMs,EC
111.38 that] Emerson; when TMs+
111.39 ∧ or worse ∧] *stet* TMs,EC;
, for worse, Emerson
§ 111.39 and know] *stet* TMs ('&' *ab.*
del. 'I');EC; *om.* Emerson
112.2 is given to] Emerson; it was
given TMs+
§ 112.9-11 ∧If . . . him, ∧] H; "~ . . .
~," [*qts. insrtd.*] TMs;EC (*para-*
phrase of Emerson)
112.9 anyone] TMs; any one EC
112.11 'My] *stet* TMs,EC; 'Cut away;
my Emerson
§ 112.11 Ygdrasil—] Emerson; Ygrasil
[*insrtd. in space left in line*], TMs; ~,
EC
112.11 life.' . . .] H; ~.' ∧ TMs,EC
112.13 ¹and ∧] Emerson; ~, TMs,EC
112.13 that] *stet* TMs,EC; *om.* Emerson
112.13 here,] Emerson; ~ ∧ TMs,EC
112.14 ever] *stet* TMs,EC; *om.* Emerson
‡ 112.15 God";] H; ~;" TMs,EC
112.29 hour,] Emerson; ~ ∧ TMs,EC
112.31 acted,] Emerson; ~ ∧ TMs,EC
112.32 good,] Emerson; ~ ∧ TMs,EC
112.36 soul] Emerson; Soul TMs,EC
112.36 had] Emerson; has TMs+
112.37 here. Shall] Emerson; here, and
shall TMs+
112.40 developes] TMs; develops EC
113.1 your] *stet* TMs,EC; his Emerson
113.1 thoughts! ∧ Hide] Emerson; ~ !—
hide TMs,EC
113.2-3 ¹They . . . . They] *stet*
TMs,EC; Thought is all light, and
publishes itself to the universe. It will
speak, though you were dumb, by its
own miraculous organ. It Emerson
113.4 manners,] Emerson; ~ ∧ TMs, EC
113.4-5 *say . . . are*] Emerson; say . . .
are TMs+
113.4 things.] Emerson; ~: TMs,EC
113.5 while,] Emerson; ~ ∧ TMs,EC
113.6 hear] Emerson; say TMs+
§ 113.6 a man *is*] *stet* TMs ('*is*'
underl.);EC; he is Emerson
113.7 upon him ∧] *stet* TMs,EC; on his
face, on his form, on his fortunes,
Emerson

113.8 nothing;] Emerson; ~, TMs,EC
113.9 eyes; . . . smiles; . . . salutations;]
stet TMs,EC; ~, . . . ~, . . . ~, Emerson
113.11 him;] Emerson; ~, TMs,EC
113.12 his . . . his] Emerson; the . . .
the TMs+
113.12 cuts] Emerson; casts TMs+
§ 113.13 on] Emerson; upon [*ab. del.*
'is'] on [*undel. in error*] TMs; upon
EC,M&S
113.14 writes ∧] Emerson; ~, TMs,EC
113.15 any] Emerson; a TMs+
113.15 it. A] Emerson; ~; a TMs,EC
113.17 see. . . .] H; ~.— TMs,EC
113.17-18 concealed! . . . concealed!]
Emerson; ~? . . . ~? TMs,EC
113.17 ²a man] Emerson; he TMs+
113.20 ground,] Emerson; ~ ∧ TMs,EC
113.22 , that,] Emerson; ∧ ~ ∧ TMs,EC
113.22 withhold] Emerson; withstood
TMs+
113.23 act,] *stet* TMs,EC; ~ ∧ Emerson
113.24 peace,] Emerson; ~ ∧ TMs,EC
113.25 aim,] *stet* TMs,EC; ~ ∧ Emerson
113.25 proclamation] *stet* TMs,EC;
proclamation of it Emerson
113.35 woods,] Emerson; ~ ∧ TMs,EC
113.37 the] Emerson; The TMs,EC
114.5 idea,] Emerson; ~ ∧ TMs,EC
114.5 execution;] Emerson; ~: TMs,EC
114.9 pain, ∧] Emerson, TMs; ~,— EC
114.10 of] Emerson,TMs,M&S; *om.* EC
114.11 past,] Emerson; ~ ∧ TMs,EC
114.12 Byron,] Emerson; ~ ∧ TMs,EC
114.13 day,] Emerson; ~ ∧ TMs,EC
114.13 day,] *stet* TMs,EC (~ ∧); day,
through wisdom and justice, Emerson
114.18-19 ∧The . . . doomsday. ∧] H;
"~ . . . ~." TMs,EC (*paraphrase of*
Emerson)
115.5 this] *stet* TMs,EC; *om.* Emerson
115.5 this, . . .] H; ~, ∧ TMs,EC
115.5 for] *stet* TMs,EC; Yet Emerson
115.6 sea ∧] Emerson; ~, TMs,EC
115.7 around] Emerson; round TMs+
115.7 universe] Emerson; *cap.* TMs,EC
115.8 where] *stet* TMs,EC; there where
Emerson

Emendations

INTRODUCTION TO FECHNER'S *LIFE AFTER DEATH*

The copy-text is F, *The Little Book of Life After Death* by G. T. Fechner, translated by Mary C. Wadsworth (Boston: Little, Brown, 1904), pp. vii-xix (McD 1904:2); James's introduction was printed throughout in italic.

116.2 *Büchlein . . . Tode,*] H; *db. qts.* F (*similar* 117.39[*both*] ; 119.36-37)

119.37 *Appearance and Reality*] stet *ital. title* (*no qts.*) F

119.38 *Elements of Metaphysics,*] H; *Elements of "Metaphysics,"* F (*no surrounding qts.*)

REMARKS AT THE PEACE BANQUET

The copy-text is P[6], "Remarks at the Peace Banquet," *Atlantic Monthly*, 94 (December 1904), 845-847 (McD 1904:12). Reference is made to R, "Address of Prof. William James," *Official Report of the Thirteenth Universal Peace Congress* (Boston: Peace Congress Committee), 5 (October 7, 1904), 266-269 (McD 1904:12).

120.10 Africa $_\wedge$] R; ~, P[6]

120.14 partiality $_\wedge$] R; ~, P[6]

120.16 cupidities $_\wedge$] R; ~, P[6]

120.17 forlorn-] R; ~ $_\wedge$ P[6]

123.15-16 anyone's] H; any one's R,P[6]

123.27 civilization.] R; ~ $_\wedge$ P[6] (*error*)

REASON AND FAITH

The copy-text is MS (MS Am 1092.9 [4542]). Reference is also made to MS(p), a set of incomplete pasted-up galley proofs in the same file; to PU(p), the latter part of these proofs pasted in the manuscript of *A Pluralistic Universe* (bMS Am 1092.6); and to P[20], "Reason and Faith," *Journal of Philosophy*, 24 (April 14, 1927), 197-201 (McD 1927:1; wrongly listed as 1924:4). Autograph alterations in the proofs are designated as WJ/MS(p) or as WJ/PU(p). The original proofs are to be taken as agreeing with MS unless otherwise indicated.

[*begin* MS(p)]

124.1 I] P[20]; ¶ MR. JAMES.– I MS (*editor*)

124.9 [2]Reason] MS(p),P[20];*l.c.* MS

§124.14 that] WJ/MS(p),P[20]; *as, that [ab. del. doubtful '–']* MS

124.14-15 , for example,] WJ/MS(p), P[20]; *om.* MS

124.17 *exist*] WJ/MS(p),P[20]; *rom.* MS (*similar* 124.17[*two words*] ; 125.24,25[*four words*],26[*first*] ; 127.9)

*125.3 this strict] *stet* MS;WJ/MS(p) (*alt. to* 'the stricter' *but alt. del.*); the strict P[20]

125.3 [1]of . . . inference] WJ/MS(p), P[20];*om.* MS

‡125.5 solid $_\wedge$] MS(p),P[20]; ~ - MS

§125.8 *Life of Reason,*] P[20]; "*Life ['L' ov. 'l'] of Reason,"* MS

125.17;127.22 Faith] MS(p),P[20]; faith MS

125.19 [1]Faith] H; faith MS+

125.24 world:] WJ/MS(p),P[20]; ~, MS

125.24 It] WJ/MS(p),P[20]; it MS

125.27 "for] MS(p),P[20]; $_\wedge$~ MS

125.30 it the] WJ/MS(p),P[20]; it the 'faith-process,' or the MS;MS(p) (*db. qts.*)

125.39 so] MS(p),P[20]; So [*cap. doubtful*] MS

275

126.16-17 fornicating . . . ['forbid,'
  del.] denounce,] WJ/MS(p),P²⁰; *om.*
  MS

§126.19 left] MS(p),P²⁰; lift [*intrl.*]
  MS

127.1 men's] WJ/MS(p),P²⁰; our MS
  [*end* MS(p); *begin* PU(p)]

127.29-30 of . . . despair] WJ/PU(p);
  om. MS,P²⁰

127.30-31 in . . . till] WJ/PU(p); before
  MS,P²⁰

127.31-32 character ᴧ] PU(p),P²⁰; ~,
  MS

127.34 life,] PU(p),P²⁰; ~ ᴧ MS

‡128.9 bankruptcy] PU(p),P²⁰; bankuptcy MS

128.16-17 'Mind-cure' . . . 'New-
  Thought.'] H; *db. qts.* MS+

§128.22 *in spite*] H; in *spite* WJ/PU(p);
  *in spite [*underl. del.*] MS;P²⁰

§128.24-25 paganism,] PU(p),P²⁰; ~ ᴧ
  ['ism' *ab. del.* 'ism'] MS

‡128.27 experiences,] WJ/PU(p),P²⁰;
  ~ ᴧ MS

128.28 in . . . coming] WJ/PU(p); *om.*
  MS,P²⁰

§128.30 experience,] PU(p);P²⁰ (~ ᴧ);
  experiences, [*comma alt. fr. semicolon*] MS;WJ/PU(p)

128.31 'natural'] H; ᴧ ~ ᴧ MS+

*128.32 experience] *stet* MS,PU(p),
  P²⁰; experiences WJ/PU(p) (*caret
  added and 's' intended*)

128.37-38 'religious experience,'] H;
  "~~," MS,P²⁰; ᴧ ~~, ᴧ WJ/PU(p)

128.38 so-called] H; ~ ᴧ ~ MS+

THE ENERGIES OF MEN

The copy-text is P²⁸, "The Energies of Men," *Philosophical Review,* 16
(January 1907), 1-20 (McD 1907:1). Reference is made to P³⁶, "The Energies
of Men," *Science,* 25 (March 1, 1907), 321-332. The quotations from Baird
Smith (BS) and Pückler-Muskau (P-M) are identified in the Notes.

*130.28;131.3,4 everyone] H; every
  one P²⁸,³⁶

130.38 important] P³⁶; imdortant P²⁸
  (*error*)

131.24 sympathies,] P³⁶; ~ ᴧ P²⁸

132.22 fatigue-] P³⁶; ~ ᴧ P²⁸

133.13 than] H; then P²⁸,³⁶

134.11;136.4 Baird Smith] H; ~ - ~
  P²⁸,³⁶

134.16 left] *stet* P²⁸,³⁶; left her BS

134.17 Camp Scurvy] BS; camp-scurvy
  P²⁸,³⁶

134.18 body ᴧ] BS; ~, P²⁸,³⁶

134.19 livid] BS; sores and livid P²⁸,³⁶

134.20 ancle ᴧ] BS; ankle- P²⁸,³⁶

134.21 itself] *stet* P²⁸,³⁶; itself however BS

134.23 me ᴧ] BS; ~, P²⁸,³⁶

134.24 ancle] BS; ankle P²⁸,³⁶

134.26 no,] BS; ~; P²⁸,³⁶

134.26 tho'] BS; though P²⁸,³⁶

134.26-27 horrible ᴧ] BS; ~, P²⁸,³⁶

134.28 ground ᴧ] BS; ~, P²⁸,³⁶

134.29 arm] *stet* P²⁸,³⁶; left arm BS

134.30 sprain ᴧ] BS; ~, P²⁸,³⁶

134.31 To] *stet* P²⁸,³⁶; And to BS

134.32 catalogue ᴧ] BS; ~, P²⁸,³⁶

134.32 diarrhœa ᴧ] BS;P³⁶ (~,);
  diarrhea, P²⁸

134.33 opium] *stet* P²⁸,³⁶; opium with
  as little effect BS

134.34;135.1 However,] *stet* P²⁸,³⁶;
  ~ ᴧ BS

134.36 heart ᴧ] BS; ~, P²⁸,³⁶

134.38 cholera] *stet* P²⁸,³⁶; Cholera—
  the Engineer Brigade lost some of its
  very best men by it BS

134.39 me] *stet* P²⁸,³⁶; me as Chief BS

134.39 twenty-seven] *stet* P²⁸,³⁶; 27
  BS

134.39 present ᴧ] BS; ~, P²⁸,³⁶

134.39-135.1 muster only] BS; only
  muster P²⁸,³⁶

135.1 fifteen] *stet* P²⁸,³⁶; 15 BS

135.1 operations] *stet* P²⁸,³⁶; conduct
  of the operations BS

135.2 ¹done ᴧ] BS; ~, P²⁸,³⁶

135.3 Siege ᴧ] BS; siege, P²⁸,³⁶

135.4 little time before,] *stet* P²⁸,³⁶;
  time before it ᴧ BS

135.4 Brandy] BS; *l.c.* P^{28,36}

135.5 none$_\wedge$] BS; ~, P^{28,36}

135.6 life$_\wedge$] BS; ~, P^{28,36}

135.7 say$_\wedge$] BS; ~, P^{28,36}

135.8-11 *The ... life.*] *stet* P^{28,36}; *all rom.* BS

135.9 *it$_\wedge$*] BS(it$_\wedge$); ~, P^{28,36}

135.11 weak$_\wedge$] BS; ~, P^{28,36}

135.13 Delhi$_\wedge$] BS; ~, P^{28,36}

135.15 , till] BS; $_\wedge$ until P^{28,36}

135.16 stimulate$_\wedge$] BS; ~, P^{28,36}

135.27 ^{3}eats,] P^{36}; ~$_\wedge$ P^{28}

138.5 problems....] P^{36}; ~ ... P^{28}

138.8 ever....] P^{36}; ~ ... P^{28}

139.26 'suggestive therapeutics.'] P^{36}; "~~." P^{28}

139.33 bodies'] P^{36}; body's P^{28}

140.21 earth....] P^{36}; ~ ... P^{28}

140.32 religious-] P^{36}; ~$_\wedge$ P^{28}

142.22 Pückler-] H; Pueckler- P^{28,36}

142.23-24 artificial resolution] *stet* P^{28,36}; *ital.* P-M

142.24 which] P-M; that P^{28,36}

142.25 device] *stet* P^{28,36}; device then P-M

142.25 this:-] P-M; ~:$_\wedge$ P^{28,36}

142.26 myself, to do, ... undone,] P-M; ~$_\wedge$ ~~$_\wedge$ ... ~$_\wedge$ P^{28,36}

142.27 cautious] *stet* P^{28,36}; cautious and discreet P-M

142.27 expedient ...] H; ~, P^{28,36}

142.28 the ... given] *stet* P^{28,36}; it is done P-M

142.28 if] P-M; though P^{28,36}

142.30 result....] H; ~.$_\wedge$ P^{28,36}

142.31 my word] *stet* P^{28,36}; it P-M

142.32 myself;-] P-M; ~- P^{28,36}

142.33-34 [When ... pronounced,]] H; $_\wedge$ ~ ... ~,$_\wedge$ P^{28,36}

142.34-35 views- ... impossibility-] P-M; ~, ... ~, P^{28,36}

142.36 I] *stet* P^{28,36}; I, on the contrary, P-M

142.36 thought,] P-M; ~$_\wedge$ P^{28,36}

142.37 weapons] *stet* P^{28,36}; such weapons P-M

142.39 thereby] *stet* P^{28,36}; hereby P-M

143.24 has termed] P^{36}; calls P^{28}

143.24-25,25 fearthought] P^{36}; fear thought P^{28}

143.30 temper;] P^{36}; ~, P^{28}

144.3 purviews] P^{36}; previsions P^{28}

145.14 *pragmatic*] P^{36}; *cap.* P^{28}

145.24 ^{2}of ... ^{2}them] P^{36}; *om.* P^{28}

145.26-27 ophthalmologist's] P^{36}; ophthamologist's P^{28}(*error*)

THE POWERS OF MEN

The copy-text is P^4, "The Powers of Men," *American Magazine*, 65 (November 1907), 57-65 (McD 1907:2). Reference is made to EM, *The Energies of Men*, a pamphlet published in the Emmanuel Church Publications on Religion and Medicine (New York: Moffat, Yard, July 1908) and to the reprint appearing under the title "The Energies of Men" in M&S, *Memories and Studies*, edited by Henry James, Jr., pp. 227-264 (McD 1911:2). EM and M&S have been collated for substantives only with the exception of the one correction drawn from M&S. The quotations from Baird Smith and Pückler-Muskau, which have been purified in respect to the originals in "The Energies of Men" in this volume, have been left here as they appeared in the copy-text.

150.27,28;160.27 Everyone] H; Every one P^4

153.32;155.21 Baird Smith] H; ~ - ~ P^4

156.21 practice] M&S; practise P^4

156.39 fourth-] EM,M&S; forth- P^4 (*error*)

158.26 Pückler-] H; Pueckler- P^4

160.13 Theophilus] H; Thomas P^{24}, EM,M&S

THE MORAL EQUIVALENT OF WAR

The copy-text is IC, "The Moral Equivalent of War," *International Concili-ation*, no. 27 (February 1910), 3-20 (McD 1910:3). Reference is made to MS[a], six leaves of a holograph first inscription found in the James Collection (bMS Am 1092.9 [4519]), to TMs (or MS), a combination typescript and manuscript (MS Am 1092.9 [4548]); to P[23], "The Moral Equivalent of War," *McClure's Magazine*, 35 (August 1910), 463-468; and to P[29], "The Moral Equivalent of War," *Popular Science Monthly*, 77 (October 1910), 400-410. The reprint in AR, *Atlantic Readings*, no. 10 (Boston: Atlantic Monthly Press, 1910) has been collated for substantives only. Reference is also made to the reprint in M&S, *Memories and Studies*, edited by Henry James, Jr., pp. 265-296 (McD 1911:2), which has also been collated for substantives only. AR and M&S are used as emending agents in accidental entries when they agree with what would otherwise be a Harvard (H) emendation.

[*begin* MS[a],TMs]

162.11 excentrics] MS[a],TMs; eccentrics IC+

162.17 woman] P[23,29],AR; women IC,M&S

162.18 tho'] H; though MS[a]+

162.22 men;] P[23]; ~, MS[a],TMs,IC,P[29]

‡163.6-7 To show war's . . . has] P[23]; Showing war's . . . is of MS[a] (hor-rors);TMs (Showing man's irration-ality and horrors); IC,P[29],AR,M&S

‡163.8 *extremis.* War-] P[23] (war ∧); extremis; war ∧ MS[a],TMs; ~; war-IC,P[29]

163.10 show] P[23]; show us IC,P[29],AR, M&S

163.13 greek] MS[a]; Greek TMs+

[*end* MS[a]]

163.17 'history'] AR('~,'); ∧~ ∧ TMs; "~" IC,P[23,29]

163.18 which] P[23]; *om.* TMs,IC,P[29], AR,M&S

163.18 was] P[23]; *om.* TMs,IC,P[29],AR, M&S

163.23 'Venus of Melos'] AR (Milo); *db. qts.* IC,P[23,29]

163.23 Melos] P[23]; Milo IC,P[29],AR, M&S

163.23 found),] P[23,29]; ~, ∧ IC (*error*)

163.23-24 acknowledge] P[23]; own TMs, IC,P[29],AR,M&S

163.26 a] P[23]; *om.* TMs,IC,P[29],AR, M&S

163.29 [*second*],34 gods] *stet* TMs+; Gods Jowett

163.29-30 believe, . . . know,] Jowett; ~ ∧ . . . ~, TMs; ~ ∧ . . . ~ ∧ IC,P[29]; ~, . . . ~ ∧ P[23]

163.30 ∧ by . . . nature ∧] Jowett, TMs; , ~ . . . ~, IC+

163.32 who] Jowett; to TMs+

163.32 it, . . .] H; ~, ∧ TMs+

163.38 age,] Jowett, P[23]; ~ ∧ TMs,IC, P[29]

163.39 colonised] Jowett; colonized TMs+

164.6 Aemilius ∧] P[23];[29] (Æmilius); Aemilus, TMs; ~, IC

164.7 'giving'] H; "~" IC+

164.10 Aetolia] P[23]; Etolia TMs,IC, P[29]

164.11 'the . . . all,'] TMs; "~ . . . ~," IC+

‡164.11 yet] P[23]; but TMs,IC,P[29],AR, M&S

‡164.12 he] P[23]; he similarly TMs,IC, P[29],AR,M&S

164.15 capacity] P[23]; capacities TMs, IC,P[29],AR,M&S

§164.16 of which . . . full] P[23]; that . . . *full of [comma del.] [aft. ink del.* 'now so'] TMs;IC,P[29],AR,M&S

[*end* TMs; *begin* MS]

164.17 tribes] P[23]; any tribes MS,IC, P[29],AR,M&S

164.18 this,] P[23]; ~ ∧ MS,IC,P[29]

164.23 bluff;] P[23]; ~, MS,IC,P[29]

164.23,30 they] P[23]; *om.* MS,IC,P[29], AR,M&S

164.23 there-] P[23]; ~, MS,IC,P[29]

164.25-26 ²in . . . months] P²³; for three months in every newspaper MS,IC,P²⁹,AR,M&S

☛164.36 'peace'] MS ('~,'); *db. qts.* IC+ (*similar* 164.37;165.1[*two words*];166.2,4,5;167.11-12;168.9, 21;169.27)

164.36 'peace';] P²³ ("~";); '~,'– MS; "~," IC,P²⁹

*164.38 *et seq.* to day] MS; ~ - ~ IC+

‡164.38 'war expected.'] AR; ∧~~.∧ MS; "~~." IC,P²³,²⁹

§164.39-40 sincerely wishing peace] P²³; wishing [*ab. del.* 'really aiming at'] peace *sincerely [*insrtd.*] MS;IC, P²⁹,AR,M&S

165.4 is the] P²³; *ital.* IC,P²⁹

165.4 permanent] P²³,²⁹; permament IC (*error*)

165.5 military] P²³; *om.* IC,P²⁹,AR, M&S

165.6 'peace'-] AR; "~"- IC;P²³ ("~"∧);P²⁹

165.8;173.12 european] MS; *cap.* IC+

165.10 (to . . . it)] P²³; ∧~ . . . ~∧ MS,IC,P²⁹

165.11 tho'] H; though MS+

§165.13 in] P²³; in *such [*ab. del.* 'this'] MS;IC,P²⁹,AR,M&S

165.14 far as] P²³; *om.* MS,IC,P²⁹,AR, M&S

165.15 together.] P²³; ~, and MS,IC, P²⁹,AR,M&S

165.21,25 shall] P²³; will MS,IC,P²⁹, AR,M&S

165.26 so] P²³; *om.* MS,IC,P²⁹,AR, M&S

165.28 anyone] MS; any one IC+

165.30 all] P²³; every MS,IC,P²⁹,AR, M&S

165.31-32 -minded] P²³; ∧~ every where MS; - ~ everywhere IC,P²⁹, AR,M&S

‡165.36-37 in their] P²³; on this MS, IC,P²⁹,AR,M&S

§165.38 All reflective . . . day] P²³; Reflective ['R' *ov.* 'r'; *aft. del.* 'The'] . . . day all MS;IC,P²⁹,AR,M&S

165.39 to them] P²³; *om.* MS,IC,P²⁹, AR,M&S

§165.39 sacrament; its] P²³; ~. ['Quite apart from' *del.*] Its MS;IC, P²⁹

166.4 consumers'] P²³,AR; consumer's MS,IC,P²⁹,M&S

166.8 healthy-] P²³; ~∧ MS,IC,P²⁹

‡166.9-10 partaking . . . degree] P²³; to some degree partaking of it MS, IC,P²⁹,AR,M&S

‡166.11 without] P²³; with no use for MS,IC,P²⁹,AR,M&S

166.13 *et seq.* everyone] MS; every one IC+

166.17 perfection-] P²⁹; ~,∧ MS; ~,– IC,P²³

‡166.20 feeling] P²³; sort of feeling MS,IC,P²⁹,AR,M&S

166.27-28;‡167.20-21 *The Valor of Ignorance,*] H; 'the Valor of Ignorance,' MS (∧~~~~ ∧∧ *at* 167.20-21); "the Valor of Ignorance," IC; "The Valor of Ignorance," P²³,²⁹

☛167.5 that] P²³; which MS,IC,P²⁹, AR,M&S (*also* 169.36;170.28; 173.21)

167.6 Islands] MS,P²³; *l.c.* IC,P²⁹

167.7 Oregon∧] MS,P²⁹; ~, IC,P²³

167.7 California∧] MS,P²³; ~, IC,P²⁹

167.9,‡22 japanese] H; *cap.* MS+

167.9 and] P²³; *om.* MS,IC,P²⁹,AR, M&S

167.14 absolutely] P²³; *om.* MS,IC,P²⁹, AR,M&S

167.17 There] MS,P²³; But there IC, P²⁹,AR,M&S

167.17 , after all,] P²³; *om.* MS,IC,P²⁹, AR,M&S

167.19 characters should appear] P²³; come MS,IC,P²⁹,AR,M&S

‡167.23 in disregarding] P²³; to ignore MS; to disregard IC,P²⁹,AR,M&S

§167.25 *Philosophie des Krieges*∧] H; ∧~ *~ ['d' *ov.* 'D'] ~ ∧∧ MS (*rom.*); "~~~," IC+ (*rom.*)

168.1-2 ordeal, . . . be] P²³; ordeal is MS,IC,P²⁹,AR,M&S

168.4 develope] MS; develop IC+

168.5 'degeneration.'] AR; "~." IC, P²³,²⁹

‡168.7 upshot, . . . can] P²³; upshot can, it seems to me, MS,IC,P²⁹,AR, M&S

‡168.10 untrained to] P²³; wielding no MS,IC,P²⁹,AR,M&S

168.11 *the*] MS; the IC+

168.12 *-régime*] MS;P²³(ˆ~);P²⁹;
-regime IC

168.12 militarist attitude] P²³;whole
situation MS,IC,P²⁹,AR,M&S

168.12 phrase:] P²³;~;MS,IC,P²⁹

‡168.15 in ... will] P²³;as I will in
my mind MS,IC,P²⁹,AR,M&S

168.16 esthetic,] P²³ (~ˆ);P²⁹;
aesthetic, IC

168.17 first,] MS,P²³;~ˆ IC,P²⁹

168.20 tragically ˆ] MS;~, IC+

§168.23 remain] P²³;keep [*ab. del.*
'remain'] MS;IC,P²⁹,AR,M&S

168.24 to] P²³;*om.* MS,IC,P²⁹,AR,
M&S

168.25 insistencies,] P²³;~ˆ MS,IC,P²⁹

§168.28-29 it is a question] P²³;the
[*ab. del.* 'it's a'] question *is [intrl.]
MS;IC,P²⁹,AR,M&S

‡168.34-35 these things] P²³;them
MS,IC,P²⁹,AR,M&S

§168.35 wars] P²³;its [*intrl.*] wars
MS;IC,P²⁹,AR,M&S

168.37 afford] MS,P²³;*ital.* IC,P²⁹

169.1 substitutes] P²³;substitute MS,
IC,P²⁹,AR,M&S

§169.2 the ... ¹war] P²³;war's *disciplinary [*ab. del.* 'ancient educa-
tive'] function MS;IC,P²⁹,AR,M&S

169.5 penalties ˆ] MS,P²⁹;~, IC,P²³

169.24 Hounds] P²³;Dogs MS,IC,P²⁹,
AR,M&S

‡169.30 'the service,'] AR; ˆ~~,ˆ
MS; "~~," IC,P²³,²⁹

‡170.3 'yes' ... 'no,'] H;*no qts.* TMs;
db. qts. IC+

‡170.5 honoured] H;honored MS+

170.6-7 and ... to,] P²³;*om.* MS,IC,
P²⁹,AR,M&S

170.8 ultimate] P²³;*om.* MS,IC,P²⁹,
AR,M&S

170.19 nations] P²³;countries MS,IC,
P²⁹,AR,M&S

170.20 among] P²³;as between MS,
IC,P²⁹,AR,M&S

170.26-27 to be] P²³;*om.* MS,IC,P²⁹,
AR,M&S

§170.36 is] P²³;*should ['get' del.]
anywhere get [*ab. del.* '['should' del.]
gets ['s' *added*]'] MS;gets IC,P²⁹,
AR,M&S

170.39 altho'] MS (~ˆ);although IC+

171.2 universal and enduring] P²³;
general MS,IC,P²⁹,AR,M&S

§171.28 get no] P²³;never *get [*ab.
del.* 'gets'] any MS;IC,P²⁹,AR,M&S

171.28 all—] P²³,²⁹; ~,— MS,IC

*§171.28 *this*] *stet* IC+;*this* *fact [*ab.
del.* 'fact'] MS

171.31 have] P²³;*om.* MS,IC,P²⁹,AR,
M&S

171.34 *nature*] MS (*rom.*); P²³,²⁹;*cap.*
IC

171.35 benefits] P²³;goods MS,IC,
P²⁹,AR,M&S

171.38 ¹blind,] P²³;~ˆ MS,IC,P²⁹

171.40 solid] P²³;sour MS,IC,P²⁹,AR,
M&S

*‡172.7 in] MS;in the IC+

§172.12 moral] P²³;many [*ab. del.*
'secondary'] moral MS;IC,P²⁹,AR,
M&S

172.18 'moral equivalent'] AR; ˆ~~ˆ
MS; "~~" IC,P²³,²⁹

172.25-26 Tho' ... it] P²³ (Though ...
Utopia); It MS,IC,P²⁹,AR,M&S

172.26 skilful] MS,P²³;skillful IC,P²⁹

§172.37 ¶ "In] P²³;H. G. Wells, as
usual, *sees [*ab. del.* 'puts his finger
upon'] the *centre [*ab. del.* 'soul']
of the *situation. [*insrtd. for del.*
'number [*ab. del.* '['s' del.] analogy']'] "In (*no* ¶) MS;IC;P²⁹
(center);AR,M&S

172.37 says H. G. Wells] P²³;he says
MS,IC,P²⁹,AR,M&S

172.37 organisation] Wells; organization MS+

172.39 street ˆ] Wells, P²³;~, IC,P²⁹

173.6-9 -seeking."² ... emphasizes.
Wells (*no* ¶)] P²³(*no fn.*);-seek-
ing.ˆˆ And ... things."* [¶] Wells
IC,P²⁹,AR,M&S (*see* Historical Collation)

§173.16 english or american] H;our
[*bef. del.* 'souls'] MS; English or
American IC+

173.24 'Meat! meat!'] MS; "Meat!
Meat ˆ" IC; "Meat! Meat!" P²³;
"meat! meat ˆ" P²⁹

173.24 'general-staff'] MS; "~ - ~"
IC; "~ ˆ~" P²³,²⁹

173.26 bridged ˆ] MS,P²³,²⁹;~. IC
(*error*)

Textual Notes

67.35   inevitable, . . . certain,]   In TMs the typed text reads 'loneliness was certain, ridicule inevitable,' which is also that of M followed by P[13] (and M&S). However, James circled 'certain,' and 'inevitable,' in pencil, and affixed a '2' above 'certain,' and a '1' above 'inevitable,' to indicate the transposition to the order he preferred. Although it is possible that he changed his mind in the final lost typescript from which, presumably, the oration was delivered and which served as printer's copy for M, it is also possible that the typist of this final script did not understand or observe the markings and that James did not notice the failure of his revised intentions. It is not perhaps too finicky to suggest that the revised order has a logical descending progression from *inevitable* through *certain* to *possible* that is superior to the original. The presumed reasoning behind the revision of the present TMs leads the textual editor to adopt the revised reading on the assumption that the typist missed or did not follow James's system for marking the interchange of the two words.

70.1   writes the Adjutant,]   This phrase was added in ink to TMs, at first positioned with a caret after 'regiment,' although James neglected to add the closing double quotation marks after 'regiment,' and the opening marks before 'the'. At some indeterminate later time he adjusted the initial guideline to bring the interlineation over to follow 'Infantry,' still without appropriate quotation marks. However, he failed to delete the initial caret and short guideline after 'regiment,'. It would have been a legitimate conjecture that the later typist, puzzled, opted for the original interlined position and James did not notice the change from his revised intention. However, the restoration in the later copy (unless its typing is to be imputed to error) of the phrase 'one of the best that had so far faced the rebel foe,' which had been pencil deleted earlier than the ink interlineation about the adjutant, quite alters the situation. If James restored this change in his revised intentions, it is probable that simultaneously he returned 'writes the Adjutant,' (in case it had after all been typed in the revised position) to its original status. The case is not truly certain, since the position of 'writes the Adjutant,' in the lost typescript may be in legitimate doubt; however, the attention that James paid to restoring deleted 'one . . . foe,' would seem to give superior authority to the placement of the interjection in M than to the altered position in revised TMs.

74.14-15   —it . . . Nation.]   The order of the separate parts of the revision in WJ/M needs explanation. The original alteration was the deletion of the semicolon after 'innings' and the change of 'and the other' to 'The other is'

281

followed by the deletion of 'overstep the lawful bounds of fairness or'. Then the contrast between North and South was elaborated. In the margin James at first extended the paragraph by writing after 'public peace.' the addition 'By breaking ['away' *del.*] from the one habit the slave States nearly wrecked our Nation. By holding ['strenuously' *del.*] to the other the free states saved her ['from perdition.' *del.*] life.' James then broke up this marginal addition into two parts by guidelines. The first ('By breaking . . . Nation.') was moved to follow 'innings' before 'The other is'. To the second he prefixed 'By' to replace original 'By' which had been excluded by the first guideline but was too close to it to be included clearly in the second. This remaining part was then moved by a guideline to follow 'peace.' Finally, in the same ink with which he had drawn the guidelines, James completed the revision, first by deleting the initial 'By' and substituting '—it was by', in the process altering 'the one' to 'this', and then by inserting '—it was' before the second section's added 'By' (left capitalized in error) and altering 'the other' to 'this habit'.

85.35 red-white] The French of J. Luys reads 'rouge blanc'. See 85.39 for another use of this phrase, which James translated correctly.

106.14 quality.] In MS the following sentence is deleted in pencil but is reproduced in L: 'Witness Goethe, Emerson, Carlyle, Matthew Arnold, and now-a-days in Germany Nietzsche.' ('nowadays' L). One could rationalize this discrepancy by speculating that the typist had ignored James's pencil deleting line; yet such a guess becomes difficult to defend when one observes that 'Christian' before 'theological' at 106.35 is also deleted in pencil but reproduced in L. These are the only pencil alterations in the manuscript text itself except for a circled 'Plato' in the margin at the foot of fol. 10 opposite 107.38-39 and its reference to utopias. It thus becomes more probable that after the return of his manuscript James made these two pencil deletions and the pencil note, perhaps in anticipation of proofs that never came. The pencil deleted trial on fol. 3^V and the words deleted in pencil in the ink deleted trial on fol. 10^V need have no relation in point of time to the two text deletions in pencil and they manifestly occur during the course of composition. In the nature of the case, of course, the two pencil deletions in the text cannot be so positively dated. Nevertheless, the evidence—such as it is—suggests that they were made after the manufacture of the typescript. Since the MS is the copy-text, James's final intentions must be respected and the two deletions observed.

107.9 science] In MS the word resembles 'Science', but James often made his lower-case 's' as if it were a capital; and indeed, such an ambiguously formed letter begins 'statistical' only a few words later. James was not in the habit of capitalizing 'science' as a concept.

109.7 shrunk] A series of pen lines drawn through portions of the first two paragraphs of the Emerson essay along with an ink note 'omit' and an ink line next to the texts in the margin indicated James's original intention to begin the address with the third paragraph. He then deleted the word 'omit' and added a circled note at the top of the page, 'Disregard the pen lines drawn about and on this page,' but the printer followed the instructions too literally and set the deleted interline 'into . . . attitude,'. James clearly hadn't intended to include this in his final text as it essentially repeats the phrase at 109.4 'The phantom of an attitude'.

125.3   this strict] MS(p), like MS, read 'this strict'. James at first altered 'this' to 'the' and 'strict' to 'stricter' but then deleted the changes, a change not observed by P[20] for 'this'.

128.32   experience] In altering the proof for PU, James changed the singular 'experience' at 128.30 to the plural to agree with the plural 'religious experiences' at 128.27-28. However, at 128.32 he inserted a caret between final 'e' and the comma of another singular, but inadvertently neglected to add 's' in the margin, as would be required by his other changes to the plural.

130.28;131.3,4   everyone] Since James's characteristic 'everyone' appears in its first use in 129.19, it is a reasonable assumption that copy was followed there but that thereafter compositorial styling substituted 'every one'. The occurrence of 'everyone' permits emendation to what was undoubtedly James's manuscript form, although he sometimes spaced the word in such a manner that it could be mistaken as two.

164.38   to day] James's usual manuscript practice varies between 'to day' and 'to-day', but in the present manuscript he consistently writes 'to day'. The hyphen, however, is found in the typescript at 169.39 (although the parallel MS text has 'to day'), probably the typist's own preferred form, and the conventional hyphen presumably enters IC either from the lost typescript that was its copy or from the IC compositor's styling.

171.28   *this*] In MS 'fact' is interlined above deleted original 'fact', but the interline is greatly obscured by a preceding interlineation 'of . . . life' and so may just possibly have been overlooked by the typist and thereupon not recognized by James as missing.

172.7   in] James originally wrote 'in the immemorial', deleted 'the' and substituted 'man's' below it, then deleted 'man's' and wrote in 'the' again above the original deleted 'the'. He finally deleted the second 'the' and made a stroke indicating the joining of 'in' and 'immemorial', but the printer either overlooked the mark or restored 'the' on his own authority. James's original intention has been restored here.

Historical Collation

This list comprises the substantive and accidental variant readings that differ from the edited text in the authoritative documents noted for each essay. Included for their intrinsic interest are the substantive variants (less bibliographical additions and cross-references) in the collection of James's essays, *Memories and Studies* (M&S), edited by Henry James, Jr. (1911), in which a number of the essays in this volume were reprinted. The reading to the left of the bracket is that of the present edition. The rejected variants in the noted documents follow in chronological order to the right of the bracket. Any collated texts not recorded are to be taken as agreeing with the edition-reading to the left of the bracket: only variation appears to the right, except for the special case when James restored the original copy-text reading in an annotated copy of private marked copies at Harvard, indicated as WJ/ followed by the sigil for the periodical, book, proofs, or clipping. The noting of variant readings is complete for the substantives and for the accidentals. To save space, however, both substantive and accidental variants are omitted in the Historical Collation whenever the copy-text has been emended and thus when the details may be found recorded in the list of Emendations. Otherwise the noting of variant readings is complete for the substantives save for the special cases of the editorial references and other strictly editorial changes in M&S, and save for the rejected readings of the sources for James's quotations, which are also confined to the Emendations list. The rejected accidental variants in collated texts are also complete except for one special circumstance: trivial differences in the accidental bibliographical details of footnotes such as in the typography, punctuation, abbreviation, and forms of references and dates are ignored. James's occasional inscription in manuscript of more than the usual three or four dots indicating ellipsis (unless the manuscript is the copy-text and is emended, in which case the emendation is accidental and confined to the Emendations list) and such purely typographical matters as the use of an asterisk instead of a number for a footnote are not recorded.

The headnote to the Emendations list may be consulted for general conventions of notation, and the Note on the Editorial Method outlines types of variants which are not recorded. One special feature appearing in the Historical Collation, as in the Emendations, is the use of *et seq*. When this phrase occurs, all subsequent readings within the essay are to be taken as agreeing with the particular feature of the reading being recorded (save for singulars and plurals and inessential typographical variation, as between roman and italic), unless specifically noted to the contrary by notation within the entry itself, or by the use of *stet* within the apparatus. Readings grouped together with multiple page-line references may also be concerned with only the particular feature being recorded and not with inessential types of variation. A plus sign signifies all collated texts later than the text identified by the sigil. Other arbitrary symbols employed in the Historical Collation when a document other than the manuscript is the copy-text include the § and the ‡. As in the Emendations, the § mark indicates that the variant is included wholly or in part in an alteration in the manuscript, the description of which has been removed to the Historical Collation from the list of Alterations in the Manuscript. The double dagger (‡) indicates that the variant in the MS is part of a larger alteration not easily transferable to the Historical Collation, the details of which can be found in the Alterations in the Manuscripts. When used together, the two symbols show that the variant occurs both in a unique alteration and as part of a larger alteration. To find the details of the larger alteration the reader should consult the Alterations in the Manuscripts. In those cases when another document agrees with a revised manuscript variant, a semicolon separates that document's sigil from the listing of MS; this emphasizes the agreement of the document(s) with the final reading of the MS.

Occasionally a variant reading between an article copy-text and MS occurs because James has made a simple error, as in putting a caret in the wrong position to indicate an interline, or in failing to omit a word or punctuation mark in an otherwise deleted passage, or in deleting a word or punctuation mark in error and not restoring it. Such mistakes, if linked to an alteration, are recorded as part of the entry for the passage in the Alterations list instead of in the Historical Collation.

Manuscript ampersands and variant spacing (as sometimes appears in words like *is n't*) are not recorded.

For conventions of description in alterations see the headnote to the list of Alterations in the Manuscripts.

ROBERT GOULD SHAW: ORATION BY PROFESSOR WILLIAM JAMES

The copy-text is M, the Oration in *The Monument to Robert Gould Shaw* (Boston: Houghton Mifflin, 1897), pp. 71-87 (McD 1897:2), with reference to TMs, the draft typescript in the James Collection (MS Am 1092.9 [4538]). James's autograph revisions of typed copy can be identified by the indication of ink or pencil. The typescript is interspersed with substitute pages and part pages of handwritten substitutes for deleted typed passages, some replacing leaves of the typescript that have been removed. Readings in these passages are identified as TMs(MS); alterations noted in these sections are to be taken as made in ink unless otherwise stated. For the system by which autograph alterations whether in TMs or in TMs(MS) are recorded, see F. Bowers, "Transcription of Manuscripts: The Record of Variants," *Studies in Bibliography*, 29 (1976), 212-264. All alterations in TMs or TMs(MS) are included here or in the Emendations list. Purely typographical corrections, whether type over type or ink over type, are not noted. Accidental as well as variant substantive readings of P[13], "II. Oration by Professor William James," *Harvard Graduates' Magazine*, 6 (September 1897), 28-37, are also recorded, but only variant substantive readings from the posthumous reprint in M&S, "Robert Gould Shaw," *Memories and Studies*, edited by Henry James, Jr., pp. 35-61 (McD 1911:2), are listed.

[*begin* TMs]

64.0 Robert . . . James] *ORATION.*
TMs; ROBERT GOULD SHAW M&S

64.1-6 Your . . . generation.] [¶] The death struggles of one generation become the material for the works of art of the next. Thirty-four years ago a certain negro regiment was *armed [*penc. ab. del.* 'raised'] and drilled in Boston, and four months later led the way in the unsuccessful storming of a Battery in *Charleston Harbor. [*penc. ab. del.* 'South Carolina.'] To the colonel of this regiment, and to its officers and men who now lie buried without ['coffin or' *penc. del.*] tombstones [*final* 's' *penc. added*] in the sands near Battery Wagner, some of our citizens have wished that a *permanent [*penc. intrl.*] memorial should be set up *on Boston Common. [*penc. intrl. bef. del. penc.* '*our midst [*ab. del.* 'in Boston.']'] The admirable monument which *Augustus [*ink insrtd. in blank space left*] Saint-Gaudens has created and which we unveil today shows how well *these [*alt. fr.* 'this'] friends ['of ours' *del.*] have been [*penc. ab. del.* 'they were'] inspired. First of all, then, thanks to them and to him for the noble work of bronze [*penc. insrtd.* 'which,' *del.*] with its basis and inscriptions, [*penc. del.* 'will' *ab. del.* 'which will'; 'which' *not restored in error*] stand here for centuries to come a priceless *ornament [*penc. ab. del.* 'decoration'] to our city. [*del. ink in left mrgn.* 'See other side.'; *in right mrgn. circled ink* 'Turn over'] TMs [*fol.* 1 *verso, insertion as marked on fol.* 1 *recto; in upper left mrgn. circled* 'Insert:'] In *these [*alt. fr.* 'this'] unveiling *exercises [*penc. ab. del.* 'ceremony'] the ['humble' *penc. del. intrl.*] duty *falls [*ab. del.* 'falls'] to [*ov. doubtful* 'on'] me of ['recalling' *del.*] expressing in ['as' *del.*] simple words *some of [*penc. ab. del.* 'as possible'] the feelings that *have [*insrtd.*] actuated the givers of the monument, and of ['reminding a' *del.*] ['recalling' *del.*] briefly recalling the ['events which it perpetuates.' *penc. del. aft. being tr. to foll.* 'recalling'] *history of Robert Shaw and of his regiment. [*added in penc. but intended to subst. for tr. del.* 'events . . . perpetuates.'] to the memory of *our [*ab. del.* 'a'] somewhat forgetful generation. TMs(MS) [*fol.* 6½ *verso del.* TMs(MS) *trial for the above*] [¶] In *this [*alt. fr.* 'the'] unveiling ceremony the duty has fallen to me of expressing in simple *words, [*ab. del.* 'language,'] but in this public *fashion, [*ab. del.* 'manner,'] the ['feelings and' *del.*] thoughts and feelings which may have actuated the donors of the monument. TMs(MS)

64.3 Gaudens'] Gaudens's P[13]

64.9 Regiment] regiment [*ink. intrl.*] TMs

64.9 afoot,] *ink comma* TMs

64.10 battle] *penc. ab. del.* 'assault' TMs

64.11 men] *penc. ab. del.* 'regiment' TMs

64.11 there] *penc. ab. del.* 'then' TMs

64.11 the] *typed* 'the' *ink alt. to* 'that' *and then penc. alt. to* 'the' TMs

64.12 twilight, . . . wet,] *ink commas* TMs

64.17 nor] or TMs

64.18 Many] *ink insrtd. for del.* 'Various' TMs

64.23 future May] *penc. ab. del.* 'distant June' TMs

65.3 ceremony,] *ink comma* TMs

65.3 meet] *penc. ab. del.* 'gather' TMs

65.3 conduct] *penc. ab. del.* 'exploit' TMs

65.4 their] *penc. alt. fr.* 'them' TMs

65.4 memory] *penc. intrl.* TMs

65.6 the war] our war TMs

65.8-9 , moreover,] ₌ ~ ₌ TMs

65.9 should] *cap.* TMs(MS) (*error*)

65.12 material] *penc. ab. del.* 'physical' TMs(MS)

65.14 Hill] 'H' *ov.* 'h' TMs(MS)

65.15 defeat;] *ab. del.* '['defeat;' *del.*] a small affair of arms, and also a defeat.' TMs(MS)

65.15 but] 'b' *ov.* 'B' TMs(MS)

65.17 The] ['['Throughout ['out' *bel.
del.* 'all']' *del.*] The ['T' *ov.* 't'] whole
[*intrl.*] dilatory length of' *del.*] The
['T' *ov.* 't'] TMs(MS)

65.18 Union] 'U' *ov.* 'u' TMs(MS)

65.18 all] *aft. del.* 'its questions of constitutional law issues, and its shifting
military' TMs(MS)

65.19-20 military ... meaning] *martial lessons which ['it took' *del.
insrtd.*] it gathered **in [*penc. insrtd.
for penc. del.* 'in its dilatory length,']
has [*ab. del.* '*lessons which it gathered [*ab. del.* 'military experiences
['and' *del.*] which it garnered in
*throughout its dilatory length
[*intrl.*]'] *together, has [*ab. del.*
'['now' *del.*] ['means but one ess'
del.] stand for']'] TMs(MS)

65.21 better] *ab. del.* 'as well' TMs(MS)

65.21 than] *ab. del.* 'as' TMs(MS)

65.22 constitution] constition TMs
(MS)

65.22 Northern] *l.c.* TMs(MS)

65.23 ¶ Look] *no* ¶ TMs(MS)

65.23 that] the TMs(MS),M&S

65.24 elements] *final apostrophe del.*
TMs(MS)

65.24 vividly] *aft. del.* 'f' TMs(MS)

65.25 go] *insrtd.* TMs(MS)

65.26 almost] 'al' *insrtd. for del.* 'al-'|
TMs(MS)

65.26 ²State] *poss. l.c.* TMs(MS)

65.27 had] *del.* TMs(MS)

65.27-28 The ... security,] The *name
[*ab. del.* 'phrase'] by which the
Southern leaders ['in Congress' *del.
ab. del.* 'mo'] ([*paren ov. dash*] insolent *with [*ab. del.* 'in'] their consciousness of *legalized [*ab. del.*
'entrenched legal'] possession) [*dash
del.*] TMs(MS)

65.29-30 by ... property."] ['in public
debate was "this peculiar sort of
property."' *del.*] was *the [*ab. del.*
'a'] contemptuous['ly' *del.*] [*intrl.*]
collective *epithet [*ab. del.* 'phrase']
of "this peculiar *kind [*ov.* 'sort [*ab.
del.* 'kind']'] of property." TMs(MS)

65.30 There] *aft. del.* '['Yet there they
*march, [*ab. del.* 'are']' *del.*] Troop-

ing ['T' *ov.* 't'] together from their
humble homes, *they [*intrl.*]
offer['ing' *del.*] their lives for a
higher civilization.' TMs(MS)

65.30-31 warm-blooded cham] *warm
blooded [*intrl. aft. del.* 'cham-'|]
cham [*insrtd.*] TMs(MS)

65.31 for man] *intrl.* TMs(MS) (Man)

65.31 horseback,] ~ ∧ TMs(MS)

65.32 in] *ov.* 'si' TMs(MS)

65.32 blue-] *ab. del.* 'gray- [*aft. del.*
'blue-']' TMs(MS)

65.33 they] *ov. doubtful* 'all [*ab. del.*
'they']' TMs(MS)

65.38-39 Since ... ¹and] *penc. intrl.*
TMs(MS) (²question ∧)

65.38 ¶ Since] *no* ¶ TMs(MS)

65.38-39 'thirties ...'fifties] ∧~ ...
∧~ P¹³

65.38 had] had had TMs(MS) (*error*)

65.39 by] By TMs(MS) (*error*)

65.39 end ... our] *ab. del.* 'date of
1860 the' TMs(MS)

65.40 it] the slavery question TMs(MS)

66.1 through] *aft. penc. del.* 'raging'
TMs(MS)

66.2 Abolition] abolitionist TMs(MS)

66.3 South] 'S' *ov.* 's' TMs(MS)

66.3 the Abolitionists] *the abolitionists [*penc. ab. del.* 'those fanatics']
TMs(MS)

66.3 could] would M&S

66.6 madness. "Every] ~: "every
TMs(MS)

66.6-7 Phillips] Philipps TMs(MS)
(*error*)

66.8 final] *ab. del.* 'last' TMs(MS)

66.8 Sumter,] Sumter["s wall,' *del.*],
[*comma insrtd.*] TMs(MS)

66.10 law and reason] Law & Reason
TMs(MS)

66.11 now] *aft. del.* 'at' TMs(MS)

66.13 destroying] furiously destroying
TMs

66.15 or] *ink ab. del.* 'and' TMs; of
M&S (*error*)

66.15 perversity] 'ty' *penc. del. but
then del. erased* TMs

66.16 ¶ Our] *no* ¶ TMs

66.16 its very origin] *penc. ab. del.*
'the outset' TMs; its origin M&S

66.17 freedom,] ~ ∧ TMs

66.17 A] A ['self' *penc. intrl. and erased*] TMs

66.17 boastfully so called,] *boastfully [*ink ov. penc.*] so called ˄ [*penc. intrl.*] TMs

66.18 at last] *ink ab. ink del.* 'finally [*penc. insrtd. for penc. del.* '*at last [*penc. insrtd. for ink del.* 'at last']']' TMs

66.19-20 what . . . but] *penc. ab. del.* 'was *in reality [*ink intrl.*]' TMs

66.20 falsehood] *bef. erased penc. intrl.* 'indeed' TMs

66.20 and] *bef. erased penc. intrl.* 'a' TMs

66.20 -contradiction?] – ~. TMs

66.21 kept] *penc. ab. del.* 'held' TMs

66.22 policy . . . concession.] patch-work, [*'policy and' ink del.*] compromise, [*ink comma ov. period*] *and concession. [*ink intrl.*] TMs

66.22 last] the last M&S

66.22 that] *that* TMs

66.24 truth!] ~!– TMs

66.24 though] tho' TMs

66.26 And . . . is] *And this [*penc. insrtd.*] *Fellow ['F' *unreduced in error*]-citizens, [*ink insrtd.*] ['This' *penc. del.*] is TMs

66.27-28 soldier's monuments] common-[*hyphen penc. insrtd.*] Soldiers' Monuments TMs

66.28 we have] *penc. ab. del.* 'our city has at last' TMs

66.29 Robert . . . his] Shaw and Shaw's regiment TMs

66.29 the subjects of] *penc. ab. del.* 'what we may call' TMs

66.30 raised] *penc. alt. fr.* 'reared' TMs

66.33 the . . . meaning] ('meaning' *ink ov. penc.*); *penc. ab. del.* 'and distinctness the deeper *significance [*ink ab. del.* 'meanings']' TMs

66.33 cause] *cap.* TMs

66.34 nation] Nation [*penc. ab. del.* 'country'] TMs

66.35 baptized] *penc. ab. del.* 'born' TMs

66.35-36 a . . . master] a [*ink intrl.*] man [*penc. alt. fr.* 'men'] requires ['s' *ink added*] no master['s' *ink del.*] TMs

66.36 him] *ink ab. del.* 'them' TMs

66.37 But the] But [*ink intrl.*] The [*unreduced in error*] TMs

66.38 not . . . great] *not dared to touch [*penc. ab. del.* 'tolerated'] the *great ['and' *penc. del.*] [*ink ab. penc. del.* 'one'] TMs

66.39 and . . . wrought] and ['Slavery,' *ink del. intrl.*; *guideline drawn first bef.* 'and' *but then del. and placed aft.* 'and'] slavery [*ink ab. del.* 'this'] had *wrought [*penc. ab. del.* 'worked'] TMs

66.39-40 only . . . die.] ['Nation's' *penc. del.*] only alternative *for [*penc. insrtd.*] *the ['of the' *penc. insrtd., ink del.*] Nation["'s' del.*] [*ink intrl.*] *was to fight or die. [*penc. ab. del.* 'was death or the amputating knife.'] TMs

67.1 Americans] *ink ov.* 'men' TMs

67.1-2 complexions and] *ink intrl.* TMs

67.2 meet death] *face death [*penc. ab. del.* 'perish'] TMs

67.3 religion] ['deeper American' *penc. del.*] ['dear' *ink del. insrtd.*] religion TMs

67.3 our] *final 's' ink del.* TMs

67.3 native land] *ink intrl.* TMs

67.4 the] *om.* M&S

67.4 earth] Earth TMs

67.5 religion;] ~, TMs

67.6 Robert] *ink intrl.* TMs

67.7 may hope to] *may hope to ['be' *del.*] [*ink ab. del.* 'in our'] TMs

67.7-8 be . . . measure] ['may' *ink del.*] be faithful *in our [*ink insrtd.*] measure [*tr. by ink guideline fr. bef. del.* 'may' *to aft.* 'faithful'] TMs

67.8 we wish his] *penc. ab. del.* 'his' TMs

67.9 ¹to] *penc. ab. del.* 'shall' TMs

67.11 ¶ Shaw . . . little] (*no* ¶) Shaw [*penc. ab. del.* 'He'] was young, ['he saw things simply and he saw them truly,' *ink del. ab. del.* 'he was pure, he was true;'] and he thought little TMs

67.11-13 himself . . . praise."] himself. *But he had a **personal charm [*ab. del.* 'grace of nature'] which, . . . him ˄ . . . name['d' *penc. del.*] . . .

praise." [*ink added*] [*del. earlier ink addition in left mrgn.* '(I shall revise this characterization, which leaves the martial quality out too much.)'] TMs

67.13-14 grace of nature] *ab. del.* '*personal charm [*ab. del.* 'grace of nature']* ' TMs(MS)

67.14 ²in] *penc. insrtd.* TMs(MS)

67.14 a filial heart] ('filial' *penc. ab. del.* 'dutiful'); *tr. by ink guideline to foll.* 'will,' [67.15] *but then line del.* TMs(MS)

67.15 that ... and] *penc. ab. del.* 'singularly' TMs(MS)

67.15 fair.] *period alt. fr. semicolon insrtd. for undel. colon* TMs(MS)

67.15 And] *ink ov. penc.; ab. penc. del.* 'So ['S' *ov.* 's'] that,' TMs(MS)

67.16 came,] ~ ∧ TMs(MS)

67.16 that] ['His own heart was loving, his will resolute and his intellect singularly fair.' *ink del. insrtd. at head of typed page*] [*ink del.* 'He honored his parents, and he instinctively *kept God's commandments. [*ab. del.* '*kept God's [*underdotted for stet*] commandments.'] He had a grace of nature that made all who *trod the path of right [*ink ab. del.* 'knew him'] love him. And when great things were doing of the *sort [*penc. del., aft. erased penc. insrtd.* 'kind']'] that TMs

67.17 help] *penc. ab. del.* 'aid' TMs

67.18 heaven] *cap.* TMs

67.20 leave] *aft. ink del.* 'shall' TMs

67.20 writ] *aft. ink del.* 'to be' TMs

67.21 water ... marble] *typed* 'marble' *and* 'water' *tr. by ink guideline and mrgn. note* 'tr' TMs

67.22 path.] path. Fortune sends an opportunity, but the man's sense for what is vital in things must be alert to take it up. (*begin indep. ink del. of an autograph revised typed passage*) Shaw recognized the vital opportunity: *He saw that the [*penc.*] time [*ink ov. penc.*] had come **when [*ink ov.* 'for'] the ***colored people [*penc. ab. del.* 'negroes'] ****must put the country in their debt. [*ink subst. for ink del.* 'to help *in [*ink

ov. penc.* 'it'] *the [*insrtd.*] salvation of the country. [*penc.*]'] [*ink intrl.*] *Colonel Lee has just told us of the obstacles which this **idea then [*insrtd. for del.* 'experiment'] had ['still' *del.*] to overcome. For a large party of us at the [*ink insrtd. for del.* '*He was only a captain in the Massachusetts Second when Governor Andrew offered him [*penc. del.*] *the headship of this first **colored [*penc. ab. del.* 'black'] regiment. [*ink ov. penc. del.*] *To many at that time [*penc. intrl.*] The [*unreduced in error*] use of colored troops seemed *a most [*penc. ab. del.* 'then a'] hazardous experiment. ['On the military side,' *penc. del.*] The [*penc.* 'T' *ov.* 't'] soldierly qualities of negroes were *unproved, [*penc. comma ov. semicolon*] and [*penc. ab. del.* 'On the civil side,'] a large party of us at the'] North (good unionists as any) [*ink del.* 'were still protesting against fanaticism, *still [*penc. intrl.*] insisting that'] this was *still [*ink intrl.*] exclusively a white man's war. If *colored troops were tried, and failed, [*ink ab. del.* 'the experiment should not succeed,'] confusion would grow worse confounded. *Shaw [*aft. large ink brkt.; in left mrgn. circled ink* '¶'] was ['only' *del.*] a captain [*comma del.*] *in the Massachusetts Second when Governor Andrew offered him the headship of this first colored regiment. [*penc. added*] [*fol. 8*] *Sure as he was of the principle, he was [*ink ab. del.* '*He was [*ink ab. del.* 'and']'] very *modest, [*ink comma*] *that he [*ink ab. del.* 'of his powers, and'] doubted for a moment his (*end del. passage for which* TMs(MS) *fol.* 7½ 'Shaw ... moment his' [67.22-33] *is a substitute*) TMs

67.23 opportunity: he] ~. He TMs(MS)

67.23 saw] saw clearly TMs(MS)

67.23 when] *aft. del.* 'fo' TMs(MS)

67.25 with] *intrl.* TMs(MS)

67.26-27 contend ... war;] *contend. There were still many of us who

thought that this was exclusively a
white man's war. [*ab. del.* 'overcome.
For a large party of us at the North
(good Unionists as *any [*ab. del.*
'ever,']) this was still exclusively a
white man's war.'] TMs(MS)

67.27 war; and should] war. *Should
['S' *ov.* 's'] TMs(MS)

67.28 not succeed,] *insrtd. for del.*
'fail,' TMs(MS)

67.30 invited . . . experiment.] offered
him the headship of this first colored
regiment. TMs(MS)

67.31 own] *ink insrtd.* TMs

67.33 doubts.] doubts. [*penc. period*]
['about [*penc. ab. del.* 'against'] the
new outpost duty so suddenly calling
him to its *lonely [*penc. intrl.*] service.' *penc. del.*] TMs

67.33 Regiment,] ~ ∧ P13

67.34 sure] *aft. penc. del.* 'certainly'
TMs

67.35 venture,] ~ ∧ TMs,P13

67.38 life.] life*'s wall [*penc. intrl.*].
TMs

67.38 But whatever] But [*ink intrl.*]
Whatever ['W' *unreduced in error*]
TMs

67.39 him,] *bef. ink del.* 'however,'
TMs

67.39 day,] *ink comma ov. period* TMs

67.39-40 for . . . resolves.] *for ['he
[*ov.* 'Shaw']' *ink del.*] ['was one of the
resolute kind' *penc. del.*] he [*ink
intrl.*] *inclined naturally towards
difficult resolves. [*penc. insrtd.*] TMs

67.40 towards] toward M&S

68.1 moment] *bef. penc. del.* 'onward'
TMs

68.1 object] *penc. ab. del.* 'purpose'
TMs

68.3 ¹his] Robert Shaw's TMs

68.3 family] *bef. ink del. comma* TMs

68.4 of April] *penc. intrl.* TMs

68.4 when,] *ink comma* TMs

68.4 a] *om.* TMs

68.4 Seventh] 7th P13

68.5-6 Some . . . ¹for] ('Some [*ink* 'S'
ov. 's']' *aft. ink del.* 'and'; 'for' *ink
added*); *penc. intrl.*; *orig. intrl. aft.*
'tone, [*penc. comma ov. period*]'
[68.6] *but then moved by ink guide-*

line to bef. 'they [*ink* 't' *ov.* 'T']' '
TMs

68.7 if . . . element,] *ink ov. penc. ab.
del.* 'a duck takes to water, for military ideals were in his *character
[*penc. ab. del.* 'nature']' TMs

68.7 were] was P13

68.8-13 make . . . discipline of] (*begin
indep. ink del. of an autograph revised typed passage*) make arms his
permanent profession. ['Those were
the days of drill and order and pride
in the *gradually forming character
[*penc. ab. del.* 'discipline and temper'] of one's regiment. Interminable
marching and countermarching and
picket duty on the upper Potomac as
lieutenant in the Massachusetts
*Second, [*ink comma ov. period*]'
penc. del.] *to which **post [*penc.
insrtd.*] he soon had been promoted.
[*penc. intrl.*] Drilling and disciplining, *pride at [*ink ov. penc.* '*satisfaction with [*ab. penc. del.* 'pride
at']'] the discipline attained *by the
Second Massachusetts Regiment, in
wh. he had soon become a lieutenant,
[*ink intrl.*] and horror at the bad
discipline of *other regiments
[*undel.*] *interminable marches and
picket **duties ['ies' *ov.* 'y'] on the
upper Potomac, as lieutenant in the
2nd Mass, [*ink intrl.*] (*end del. passage for which* TMs(MS) *fol.* 8½
'make . . . discipline of' *is a substitute*) TMs

68.9 disciplining;] ~, TMs(MS)

68.11 *et seq.* Second] 2d P13

68.12 promoted;] ~, TMs(MS)

68.13 by the Second,] *penc. intrl.*
TMs(MS)

68.13 other regiments;] *ink del.*
TMs(MS) (regiments,); *present in*
TMs (regiments,)

68.14 ²the] *om.* M&S

68.15 occasional] *aft. penc. del.* 'the
recital of' TMs

68.15 incidents,] incidents, [*penc. del.*
'baskets [*ink ov. penc.*] *from home
[*penc.*] and [*ink ov. penc.*]' *ab. penc.
del.* 'such as'] TMs

68.16 Virginian] Virginia P13

68.16 the . . . like] the [*ink intrl.*]
reading of *miltary [*penc.*] **books—
[*ink*] [*intrl.*] TMs

68.17 or the] *ink insrtd. for del.* 'and'
TMs

68.17 *Idylls*] *poems, like the [*penc.
insrtd.*] Idylls TMs

68.17 *King,*] King,– [*penc. dash
intrl. bef. del.* 'baskets from home,']
TMs

68.17 Thanksgiving] *l.c.* TMs

68.17 feasts] feats M&S (*error*)

68.19 opens,] opens for the *Second
[*penc. insrtd. for del.* 'regiment'],
TMs

68.19 thickens ∧] ~, TMs

68.21 amid] through TMs

68.21-22 death, . . . devastation ∧] ~,
. . . ~, [*ink commas*] TMs

68.22 that . . . of,] that *his pen soon
has [*penc. insrtd. for del.* 'he
*erelong [*ab. del.* 'soon'] had'] to
*write [*penc. ab. del.* 'tell'] of,
[*penc. comma ov. period*] TMs

68.22 unfailing] *penc. ab. del.* 'a steady
spirit of' TMs

68.24 After] *aft. ink insrtd. brkt. for*
¶ TMs

68.24 it,] ~ ∧ P13

68.24 Robert Shaw's] Shaw's [*penc.
ab. del.* 'his'] TMs

68.25 Second] the ['glorious' *penc.
intrl. del.*] old Second TMs

68.25 Months] *paragraph indent removed by ink guideline and mrgn.*
'tr' TMs

68.25 later,] ~ ∧ P13

68.25 in] *aft. ink del.* 'already' TMs

68.25-26 with . . . -fourth,] *ink intrl.*
TMs (54th ∧)

68.28 pleasure,] ~ ∧ TMs

68.30-31 Poor . . . slaughtered!"] *ink
insrtd.* TMs

68.32-33 do their duty] *ink ab. del.*
'face the music' TMs (*their*)

68.36-37 Robert Shaw . . . discipline.]
Shaw["'s' *ink del.*] was [*undel. in
error*] quickly [*penc. ov. erased
illeg. penc. word and* 'to' *ab. del.*
'a temperament that'] inspired ['d'
ink added] [*penc. intrl.* 'and he'
erased] ['in' *ink del.*] others *with

**his [*undel. in error*] [*penc. insrtd.*
'and to' *erased*] his own love of
***discipline. [*ov. erased illeg. word
and* 'g and'] [*penc. ab. del.* '['both'
del.] strenuous['ness and' *del.*] good-
will'] TMs

68.38 men] the men TMs

68.40 had good success,] *ink ab. del.*
'succeeded: [*ink colon*] ['in their
mission;' *del.*] ' TMs (success;)

69.1 became] *aft. penc. del.* 'quickly'
TMs

69.3 his men] *penc. ab. del.* 'the regiment' TMs

69.4 their . . . their] *penc. ab. del.* 'its
. . . its' TMs

69.4 duty, . . . war,] *ink commas* TMs

69.4 seat of war] Seat of War TMs

69.6 department] *cap.* TMs

69.6 sack and] *penc. intrl.* TMs

69.6 inoffensive] *penc. intrl.* TMs

69.7 coast] *cap.* TMs

69.7 fear,] ~ ∧ TMs

69.13 Virginia,] ~ ∧ TMs

69.15 expeditions,] ~ ∧ TMs

69.17 Fortunately] *ink* 'F' *ov.* 'f'; *aft.
ink del.* 'He wrote two semi-official
letters of similar purport; but' TMs

69.19 the Sea ∧] *the Sea- [*penc. ab.
del.* 'St. Simon's and St. Helena's']
TMs

69.27 would] should TMs

69.30 . . . .] *ink added aft. penc. del.*
'The other regiments lost three men
wounded, we lost (forty-three in all,
of whom seven were killed.)' TMs

69.34 pleasure,] *ink comma* TMs

69.37 The] *ink* 'T' *ov.* 't'; *aft. del.* 'A
passage from a narrative by' TMs

69.37-38 Fifty-fourth, . . . well] *ink
insrtd. for del.* 'Fifty-fourth *in describing this skirmish [*ink intrl.*]'
TMs (54th. *and* Gen.)

69.39 still] *penc. ab. del.* '*until then
**had [*ab. del.* 'had'] [*penc. insrtd.
for del.* 'up to that moment']' TMs

69.39 command:—] command. [*ink
del.* 'After describing this *skirmish,
[*ink comma*] he tells how *He [*ink
'H' *ov.* 'h'] *went to [*ink intrl.*]
make [*ink* 'k' *ov.* 'd'] report of
*what had happened **to [*undel.*]

[*ab. del.* 'it'] to General Terry
[*comma ink del.*] whose headquarters were under a great live oak
tree a third of a mile to the rear.']
TMs

70.1   The General's] *ink ab. del.* 'His'
TMs

70.1   writes the Adjutant,[1]] *ink intrl.*
TMs (*fn. number and fn. om.*); *in*
TMs *the intrl. w. a caret came first
after* 'regiment' (*no db. qts. bef. or
aft.*) *but then the guideline extended
to place the intrl. aft.* 'Infantry,'

70.2-3   one . . . foe,] *penc. del.* TMs

70.5   us— . . . justly—] *us,* [*ink underl.
added*] ['though perhaps not altogether justly,' *ink del.*] TMs

70.8   the advance] advance M&S

70.9   lookers-] ~ ˄ TMs

70.9   Can] ['I appeal to you then,' *ink
del.*] Can [*ink* 'C' *ov.* 'c'] TMs

70.9   then] *ink intrl.* TMs

70.10   imagine the pleasure] *ink ab.
del.* 'share with me that indescribable
sensation' TMs

70.13-14   a single] an TMs

70.15   and] and and TMs

70.17   You] ['I believe' *ink del.*] You
[*ink* 'Y' *ov.* 'y'] TMs

70.19   The] *aft. ink insrtd. del.* 'So
much for *his [*alt. fr.* 'the'] pride.'
TMs

70.19   this episode] *ink ab. del.* 'this'
TMs

70.20   at noon] *ink intrl., first a part
of the ink intrl.* 'was able' [70.21]
*but then moved by ink guideline in
error to bef.* 'and', *then guideline
del. and another line drawn placing
it aft.* 'and' TMs

70.21   was able] *ink ab. del.* 'went' TMs

70.21   their] *ink* 'its' *ov. penc.* 'their'
ab. del. 'this' TMs

70.21   General Strong,] ['the' *penc.
del.*] general *Strong, [*penc. insrtd.*]
TMs

70.22   [2]was] *ink ab. del.* 'had been' TMs

70.23   earthwork] *aft. penc. del.* 'single'
TMs

70.24   the General,] the [*ink intrl.*]
General, [*ink comma*] ['Strong
[*ink alt. fr.* 'Story'],' *ink del.*] TMs

70.25   "Colonel,] *penc. intrl. bef.*
'"Fort [*db. qts. undel. in error*]'
TMs

70.28   he] "he [*db. qts. in error*] TMs

70.30   immediately.'"] immediately.' ˄
[*db. qts. om. in error*] [*ink del.*
'General Seymour, who commanded
the attack, thus explains *in his report [*penc. intrl.*] his choice of them
as leaders. "It was believed*," he
says, "[*ink insrtd.*] that the Fifty-
fourth was in every respect as efficient as any other body of men;
and, as it was one of the strongest
and best officered, there seemed
no good reason why it should not
be selected for the advance."'] TMs

70.31   This . . . and] *ink insrtd.* TMs

70.31   just . . . made.] The *attack,
[*ink comma*] was ['not' *penc. del.*]
made *just before nightfall. [*penc.
ab. del.* 'till towards dusk.'] TMs

70.32   knew . . . and] *om.* TMs

70.33   end] death TMs

70.33   the] *penc. ab. del.* 'his' TMs

70.36   Forward!"] *exclm. mk. alt. fr.
period and db. qts. added in ink* TMs

70.36   [2]and] And TMs

70.37   the colors] colors TMs,M&S

71.1   ¶On] *no* ¶ TMs

71.2   double quick] ~ - ~ [*ink hyphen*]
TMs

71.2   chevaux de frise] ~ - ~ - ~ P[13]

71.3   it, . . . could,] it, ['then' *penc.
del.*] TMs

71.3   [2]and . . . rampart;] 'and [*penc.
intrl.*] . . . rampart,' *moved by penc.
guideline fr. aft.* 'frise,' *to bef.*
'with' TMs

71.4   Sumter,] ~ ˄ TMs

71.4   which . . . [1]them,] *penc. ab.
del.* 'and the batteries of the islands'
TMs

71.5   one mighty] *a [*ink ov. penc.*
'an'] ['immense' *ink ov. penc., penc.
del.*] mighty [*penc.*] [*ab. ink del.*
'one'] TMs

71.6   successfully] *om.* TMs

71.7   -fourth!] - ~, TMs

71.8   fell] fell (*begin indep. ink del. of
an autograph revised typed passage*)
headlong [*penc. insrtd. for del.* 'back

[*ink ab. del.* 'forward,']'] *into the fort, [*ink insrtd.*] with a bullet through his heart. Thirteen other officers, *making with him, [*penc. insrtd.*] two-thirds of their whole number, and two hundred and fifty-six ['men' *del.*] out of the six hundred *men [*ink intrl.*] who were in action fell killed or wounded beside him within the rampart or on the field. It was good behavior for a regiment *whose first recruits had been mustered in [*penc. insrtd. for del. ink intrl.* 'which had been'] only eighteen weeks *earlier [*penc. insrtd. for penc. del. ink* 'in existence'] and [*ink*] [*ab. ink del.* 'old'] which had smelt the enemy's powder for the first time only two days before. "The negroes fought gallantly," wrote a Confederate officer, "and were headed by as brave a Colonel as ever lived." Shaw was buried the next morning by the enemy, half-naked, in the same trench with his dead soldiers, without a stake or stone to mark the spot. [¶] Though it was bravely seconded, the attack had been *very [*penc. insrtd.*] badly planned. Regiment after regiment hurled themselves for two hours upon its ramparts, but Fort Wagner for that night stood safe. It succumbed only seven weeks later to a regular siege in which the Fifty-fourth Regiment did the heaviest share of work, and in which *its [*penc. ab. del.* 'the'] Confederate defenders of the fortress showed an almost incredible fortitude under the extremity of their sufferings from the blistering sun, *the suffocating bomb proofs, [*penc. intrl.*] the incessant shelling, the starvation and the putrefaction of the unearthed dead. [¶] *My friends, as we sit here, [*ink ab. del.* 'On'] this *morning, [*ink comma*] of 1897, the sands *still [*ink intrl.*] are shining, the waves sparkling and the seagulls circling *and swooping [*ink intrl.*] around Fort (*end del. pas-*

sage for which TMs(MS) *fols.* 16-18 'headlong . . . Fort' [71.8-35] *are a substitute*) TMs

71.8 headlong,] headlong into the fort ᴧ TMs(MS)

71.9 nigh] near TMs(MS)

71.9 Regiment] *aft. del.* 'The' TMs(MS)

71.10,12 Fifty-] fifty ᴧ TMs(MS)

71.10 but] *aft. del.* 'and' TMs(MS)

71.11 was . . . for] *penc. ab. del.* 'for' TMs(MS) (defended ᴧ)

71.12 five ᴧ] ~ – TMs(MS)

71.13 twelfths ᴧ] ~, TMs(MS), P[13]

71.13 or . . . half] *or nearly one half, [*intrl.*] of TMs(MS)

71.13 men ᴧ] ~, P[13]

71.13 shot . . . bayoneted] ['lost' *del.*] struck down TMs(MS)

71.14 before] upon TMs(MS)

71.15 regiment] *ab. del.* 'body of troops' TMs(MS)

71.15 whose . . . ²had] *whose soldiers had carried [*ab. del.* 'whom had carried'] TMs(MS)

71.15 in his hands] for TMs(MS)

71.16 seen the] *ab. del.* 'met an' TMs(MS)

71.16 ²the] *intrl.* TMs(MS)

71.18 ¶ "The] *no* ¶ TMs(MS)

71.18 Confederate] *l.c.* TMs(MS)

71.20 the Colonel,] *ab. del.* 'Shaw,' TMs(MS) (colonel)

71.22 him,] ~ ᴧ TMs(MS), P[13]

71.22-23 half . . . clothing,] stripped half naked, TMs(MS)

71.24 together,] ~ ᴧ TMs(MS)

71.27 Man] man M&S

71.27 lover] 'l' *ov.* 'L' TMs(MS)

71.30 and its gales] *and **its gales [*added*] [*ab. del.* '['There let its breezes' *del. insrtd.*] sigh or'] TMs(MS)

71.31 while] *alt. fr.* 'whilst' TMs(MS)

71.31 bronze] *aft. del.* 'marbl wonderful' TMs(MS)

71.31 keep] *ab. del.* 'publish' TMs(MS)

71.32 alive] *intrl.* TMs(MS)

71.32 you] you [*penc. intrl.* 'who' *erased*] TMs(MS)

71.32 and all] *intrl.* TMs(MS)

71.32 meet] [*penc. intrl. doubtful*

'spent' *erased*] meet [*ab. del.*
'stand'] TMs(MS)

71.33 are] *bef. del. intrl.* 'greater'
TMs(MS)

71.33 things] *ab. del.* 'lives' TMs(MS);
beings P[13]

71.33 meet] stand TMs(MS)

71.34 the Southern] *no doubt the
Southern [*ab. del.* 'my friends, the
['winds' *del.*] breezes are blowing
over'] TMs(MS)

71.34 their] *penc. ab. del.* 'Shaw's'
TMs(MS)

71.35 [1]and] *ab. del.* 'and' TMs(MS)

71.35 sparkling] *aft. del.* 'are' TMs(MS)

71.35 [2]and] *bef. del.* 'without doubt'
TMs(MS)

71.35 circling] *ab. del.* 'swooping'
TMs(MS)

71.37 cannon,] *ink aft. del.* 'artillery,
[*comma undel.*] [*ink ab. del.* 'cannon,']' TMs

71.38 for ... space] *penc. intrl.* TMs

71.38;72.10 far-] ~ ∧ TMs

71.39 evening] summer [*penc. intrl.*]
evening TMs

72.2 'sixties] '60's TMs; ∧sixties P[13]

72.4 history,] *ink comma* TMs

72.5 feel] *penc. ab. del.* 'recollect' TMs

72.6 erelong] ere | long TMs

72.7 books ... and] *penc. ab. del.*
'abstract names, pictures and' TMs

72.7 monuments like this] such [*penc.
insrtd.*] monuments *as this [*penc.
intrl.*] TMs

72.8 tale. The] ~—the TMs

72.8 great] *penc. intrl.* TMs

72.8 war] War TMs

72.8-9 [2]will ... it] ('siege' *ov. poss.*
'war'); *ink intrl.* TMs

72.9-10 old, unhappy,] ~ ∧~ ∧ TMs

72.11 two] Two TMs

72.12 fortitude] *penc. ab. del.* 'brav-
ery' TMs

72.12 display.] *penc. insrtd. for del.*
'embody. [*ink ab. ink ov. penc. del.*
'show['ed' *del.*]']' TMs

72.13-14 as ... virtue;] *tr. with penc.
guideline from aft.* 'War'; *penc. semicolon insrtd. aft. del. comma* TMs

72.15 ago,] *ink comma* TMs

72.17 one to] *penc. tr. fr.* 'to one' TMs

72.18 sink] *penc. ab. del.* 'forget' TMs

72.18 their] *bef. penc. del.* 'personal'
TMs

72.18 in] *penc. ab. del.* 'for' TMs

72.19 whether] *ink ab. del.* 'be' TMs

72.19-20 be ... -blood,] ('in life-
blood' *penc.*); *ink ab. del.* 'in *in
[*ink insrtd.*] blood, [*ink comma*] or
be it in treasure,' TMs

72.19 [2]in] in | in TMs

72.21 will] *penc. intrl.* TMs

72.21 otherwise,] *ink comma* TMs

72.24-25 animal; ... us;] animal;
[*penc. semicolon ov. period*] *centuries [*ink* 'c' *ov.* 'C'] of peaceful
history could not breed [*penc. intrl.*]
the [*ink ov.* 'The'] battle-instinct
*out of us; [*penc. ab. del.* 'is bred
in the bone of him;'] TMs

72.26 reinforcement by] *penc. bef.
del.* '*strengthening by [*ink ab. del.*
'reinforcement from *deliberate
[*penc. del.*]']' TMs

72.27 orator's] *aft. ink del.* 'the' TMs

72.27 or poet's help.] *or poet's help.
[*penc. insrtd.*] [*penc. del.* 'or poet's
help. Centuries of peaceful history
could not *breed [*ink insrtd. for del.*
'take [*penc. insrtd. for del.* 'get']']
it out of us. The traditions of military science might conceivably be
lost; but the innate capacity for
valor *and for ['warlike' *ink del.*]
stratagem [*ink ab. del.* 'and for *in-
venting [*ab. is erased penc.* 'the in']
new stratagems'] and methods of
destruction would be there as fresh
as ever when the need of *them [*ink
ab. del.* 'the war regimen'] returned.']
[*ink del.* 'We can count with absolute
certainty on *brave soldiers, [*penc.
intrl.*] martial valor, be our cause
*Justice or injustice, [*penc. ab. del.*
'wisdom or folly,'] be it truth or
delusion, and be our country what
it may.'] TMs

72.28 we ... need] *we really ['need
do' *del.*] need [*penc. intrl.*] TMs

72.28 help] *bef. penc. del.* 'really are
needed' TMs

72.29 , then,] *ink commas* TMs

72.29 common and] *ink intrl.* TMs

72.29 gregarious] 'and instructive' *tr.
by penc. guideline fr. aft. to bef.
'gregarious' but then ink del.* TMs

72.29-30 Robert] *om.* TMs

72.30 Seventh] 7th P[13]

72.31 that] *ink alt. fr.* 'the' TMs

72.32 warm] *penc. ab. del.* 'safe' TMs

72.32 Second] *bef. penc. del.* 'Massachusetts' TMs

72.32-33 your dubious] your [*ink ab.
del.* 'the'] dubious [*penc. intrl.*] TMs

72.33 negroes of the] *penc. ab. del.*
'[*ink intrl.* 'men' *del.*] of the dubious
and unpopular' TMs

72.33,34 kind] sort TMs

72.34 courage (civic . . . -times)]
valor, [*comma undel. in error*]
*(~ . . . -~) [*ink parens; closing
paren ov. comma*] TMs

72.34 peace-times] times of peace M&S

72.36 reared, for the] *reared,* [*penc.
comma ov. period*] for [*penc. intrl.*]
The [*unreduced in error*] TMs

72.36-37 bred . . . beings] ['yet' *penc.
del.*] bred *it [*penc. ab. del.* 'civic
valor'] into *the bone of [*penc.* 'Man
['M' ov. 'm']' *ink del.*] [*ink* 'men'
penc. del.] human beings [*penc. ab.
del.* 'our bone and fibre'] TMs

72.38 battery . . . others] Battery
*along with others [*penc. ab. del.*
'Wagner'] TMs

72.39 ready] ready *all alone [*penc.
intrl.*] TMs

72.39 fortunes] hopes and fortunes
TMs

72.39-40 all . . . resisting] *['all alone'
del.] reisting [*error*] [*penc. ab. del.*
'in fighting'] TMs

72.40 abuse.] abuse. ['Civic valor *is
what save nations from the [*ink del.*]
does [*undel.*] away with the necces-
sity of civil wars.' *ink insrtd. and
penc. del.; ink qst. mk. in mrgn.*]
TMs

72.40-73.3 The . . . saved.] [*begin
indep. ink del. of penc. false start on
fol. 21½ verso which was a subst.
for ink del. on TMs fol. 22:* 'Civilization is always in danger from some
enemy, and nations never grow beyond the need of being saved. The']

The worst enemies of nations are
*always those [*ink ab. del.* '*the
passions and delusions [*ink ab. del.*
'those, [*ink comma*]']'] that dwell
*within ['hin' *ink ov. penc.*] their
borders, and from these *enemies
[*ink ov. penc.*] civilization is always
in need of being saved. [*end del.
passage for which* TMs(MS) 21½
recto "The . . . . The" (72.40-73.3)
is a subst.] TMs(MS)

72.40 deadliest] 'de' *ov.* 'wor'
TMs(MS)

73.2 civilization is] *ab. del.* 'nations
are' TMs(MS)

73.3 blest above all] truly blest beyond other TMs

73.3-4 civic . . . does the] *civic [*ink*]
genius [*ink ov. penc.* 'unity' *or* 'unit-
ing'] **of the people does the [*penc.*]
[*intrl.*] TMs

73.4 saving] saving ['goes on' *penc.
del.*] TMs

73.4 without] *aft. ink del.* 'mostly' TMs

73.6 swiftly] *penc. ab. del.* 'promptly'
TMs

73.6-8 by good . . . nations] *['it is
*by [*del. in error*]' *del.*] good temper
between parties; [*ink ab. del.* 'by
judges giving *wise [*ink ab. del.*
'terse'] decisions;'] *by the people
[*ink insrtd. for undel. in error* '*by
trained **& disciplined [*insrtd.*] [*ink
insrtd. for del.* 'by citizens']'] knowing [*penc. ab. del.* 'instructively
recognizing'] *true men **when
they see them, [*insrtd.*] & preferring
them ***as leaders [*insrtd.*] to rabid
partisans or empty quacks. [*ink
insrtd. for del.* 'rightful leaders and
distinguishing *these ['patriots'
del.] from rabid partisans ['or [*ov.*
'and'] quacks' *del.*] & vulgar quacks
[*ink ab. del.* 'charlatans from honest
men, *or [*ink del. intrl.*]']'] *Such
nations [*ink insrtd. for del. in error*
'Such nations'] TMs

73.12 of all] *penc. intrl.* TMs

73.13 in time] *ink underl.* TMs

73.13 great.] great. [*ink del.* 'Our
fathers ought never to have suffered
things to drift and *slip, [*penc.*

comma] *from one false step to another until [*penc. ab. del.* 'to such a pass that'] after Lincoln's election *nothing [*ink intrl.*] less than four years of bloodshed could suffice to *put right. [*penc. ab. del.* 'set them straight.']'] No [*penc. intrl.; undel. in error*] *one can believe the [*erased penc. intrl.*] TMs

73.14 cannot] *ink ab. del.* 'does not' TMs

73.14 love] *penc.* 's' *added, undel. in error* TMs

73.14 -postponed] ∧postponed [*penc. insrtd.*] TMs

73.14-15 or . . . settlements.] *ink intrl. ab. del. comma or semicolon* TMs

73.15 And surely He] and *surely [*penc. intrl.*] he TMs

73.15 all] *ink intrl.* TMs

73.16 situation] *aft. penc. del.* 'economical and political' TMs

73.17 its] *aft. ink del.* 'all' TMs

73.17 rancors] *aft. erased penc. intrl.* 'new'; *bef. penc. del.* ', miseries' TMs

73.17 what . . . outcome] *what is it but the **outcome [*penc. ov. illeg. erasure which had guideline bef.* 'of the'] [*ink ab. del.* 'is the direct heirloom'] TMs

73.18 added . . . government,] *penc. insrtd. for erased penc.* '*governmental duties, of the [*ab. del.* 'taxes and financial measures,']' TMs

73.18 the corruptions] *the finances [*ink ab. del.* 'the speculations'] TMs

73.19 war?] ~. TMs

73.19 miserable legacies] miserable [*ink intrl.*] legacies [*penc. ab. penc. del.* 'heirlooms [*comma ink del.*]'] [*ink* 'of misery' *del. intrl.*] TMs

73.20 future war] *ink insrtd. for del.* 'anarchy [*ink ab. del.* 'future war']' TMs

73.20-21 save the State] *ink ov. penc.; ab. penc. del.* 'and their leaders make things right again' TMs (state)

73.22 ¶ Robert Shaw] *no* ¶ Shaw TMs

73.22 then] *ink intrl.* TMs

73.23 , so] *ink ab. penc. del.* 'he' TMs

73.23 he now] *penc. intrl.* TMs

73.23 us] *bef. penc. del. ink intrl.* 'now' TMs

73.24 lesser] *aft. ink del.* 'present' TMs

73.25 You] *ink ov.* 'We' TMs

73.25 I] *ink ov.* 'we' TMs

73.27 mourning] [*poss.* 'private' *penc. del.*] mourning [*ink* 'ing' *ov.* 'ers'] [*comma ink del.*] TMs

73.27 brides,] *ink comma* TMs

73.27 or] *foll. by penc. caret but no intrl.* TMs

73.28 ²the] *ink intrl. ov. erased penc. illeg. word and poss.* 'be' TMs

73.29 natural] *aft. penc. del.* 'rightful' TMs

73.29 country] *penc. ab. del.* 'land can' TMs

73.29 counts] 's' *ink added* TMs

73.30 but] *penc. ab. del.* 'but' TMs

73.30 poor] poor, *ghostly [*ink ab. ink ov. penc. del.* 'faint, ['shrunken' *penc. del.*]'] TMs

73.30 "the . . . dead,"] *om.* TMs

73.31 echoes] *aft. ink ov. penc. del.* 'faint' TMs

73.31 air.] air. (*begin ink del. of an autograph revised typed passage*) [¶] But [*ink insrtd.*] So, [*unreduced in error; ink comma*] and so *only, [*ink comma*] was it written that she should grow sound again. Even that fatal earlier constitutional unsoundness those deaths have bought for North and South together permanent release. No future problem can be like that problem, no task laid upon our children can possibly compare in difficulty with the task with which their fathers had to deal. Can we prize too highly, can [*cont. on fol. 3½ verso*] we guard too zealously a treasure for which so dear a price was paid? No. (*end del. passage*) [*ink note added and del.* 'One page more of peroration inspiring to avert all future civil wars will close the thing. I shall write that page later on.'] TMs

[TMs *ends*]

73.33 bought] brought M&S (*error*)

74.1 won] have won M&S

74.16 towards] toward M&S

PREFACE TO LUTOSLAWSKI'S *WORLD OF SOULS*

The copy-text is MS, the holograph manuscript preserved in the James Collection at Houghton (bMS Am 1092.9 [4462]), with reference to L, Wincenty Lutoslawski, *A World of Souls* (George Allen & Unwin, 1924), pp. 5–8 (McD 1899:12).

105.1;106.17 preface] Preface L
105.2;106.25 english] English L
105.2 *Plato,* ∧] ∼,¹|¹ *The Origin and Growth of Plato's Logic, with an Account of Plato's Style and of the Chronology of his Writings.* (London, New York and Bombay: Longmans, Green & Co., 1897) Quoted in this volume as *Plato's Logic.* L
105.4 much abused] ∼ - ∼ L
105.6 six] five L
105.6-7 languages, . . . french,] ∼−. . . French− L
105.6-7 latin . . . french] Polish, German, Russian, Spanish ∧ and French L
105.8 In (*no* ¶)] ¶ L
105.14 being ∧] ∼, L
105.16 form;] ∼, L
105.17 objections,] ∼ ∧ L
105.18 *ex cathedrâ,*] ex-cathedra ∧ L
105.19 thing ∧ . . . responsibility ∧] ∼, . . . ∼, L
105.19 naively] naïvely L
105.21 *et seq.* Professor] Wincenty L
106.4 attitudes . . . faiths] attitude . . . faith L
106.5 and must be] *om.* L
106.9-10 is, . . . sphere ∧] ∼ ∧ . . . ∼, L
106.14 have] has L
106.20 and non-ratiocinatively] more than ratiocinatively L
106.21 natural,] ∼ ∧ L
106.22 a] *om.* L
106.24 that] the L
106.26-27 us, . . . individuality,] ∼ ∧ . . . ∼ ∧ L
106.28 hierarchic] hierarchive L
106.29 words ∧] ∼, L

106.29 no] not L
106.30 monist,] ∼ ∧ L
106.33 bottom ∧] ∼, L
106.34 we] we all L
106.35 "the Creator"] the "Creator" L
106.35 theological] Christian theological L
107.8 behavior;] behaviour, L
107.8-9 Nature ∧ . . . leans ∧] nature− . . . ∼− L
107.10 number] numbers L
107.11 Nature,] nature ∧ L
107.12 Nature] *l.c.* L
107.12 *a priori*] *om.* L
107.13 a] the L
107.14 Professor Lutoslawski:] the same author, L
107.17 more] *om.* L
107.19 meagerest] meagrest L
107.22-23 men, . . . class-rooms,] ∼ ∧ . . . classrooms ∧ L
107.24 believes:] ∼; L
107.24 immortality, to souls] immortality ∧ L
107.27 polish] *cap.* L
107.28,32 *really*] *rom.* L
107.35 kingdom] *cap.* L
107.36 course ∧] ∼, L
107.36 out] up L
107.37 program] programme L
107.37 utopian] *cap.* L
107.38 utopias] *cap.* L
107.39 reproach.−] ∼. ∧ L
107.40 "livres . . . foy,"] ∧*livres de bonne foy,* ∧ L
108.1 of] of the L
108.1 critics,] ∼ ∧ L
108.2 others;] ∼, L
108.3 Surely if] If L

EMERSON

The copy-text is EC, "Address of William James," published in *The Centenary of the Birth of Ralph Waldo Emerson as Observed in Concord May 25 1903 under the Direction of the Social Circle in Concord*, printed by the

Riverside Press for the Social Circle in June 1903, pp. 67-77 (McD 1903:2). Reference is made to TMs, the autograph-revised typescript contained in the James Collection (MS Am 1092.9 [4541]). Misspelled words in TMs are recorded in this collation but not simple mechanical errors like the transposition of letters. Reference is also made to the reprint entitled "Address at the Emerson Centenary in Concord" in M&S, *Memories and Studies*, edited by Henry James, Jr., pp. 17-34 (McD 1911:2). M&S has been collated for substantives only.

‡ §109.8 phrase,] ~ ∧ [*insrtd. in ink*; *not* WJ] TMs

‡109.10 abridgment] abridgement TMs

§109.11 singularity,] personality, [*comma ov. period*] TMs;M&S

‡109.17 dust;] ~, TMs

109.22 combination] singularly harmonious combination TMs,M&S

109.23 known] accurately known TMs, M&S

110.2 students;] ~, TMs

110.3 life ∧] ~, TMs

110.3 ¹type] personal type TMs,M&S

§110.4 scholar] Scholar ['S' *ov.* 's'] TMs

§110.14-15 his genius was] genius, [*comma insrtd.*] *as he said, [*intrl.*] is TMs;M&S

110.15 his] *om.* TMs,M&S

110.15 had] has TMs,M&S

110.19 otherwise ∧] ~, TMs

110.25 it] this duty TMs,M&S

110.26 and] *om.* TMs,M&S

‡ §111.1 his] his *own [*aft. del.* 'his'; *bef. del.* 'troubled'] TMs;M&S

§111.1 conscience. To] conscience; [*semicolon ov. comma*] *–but [*ab. del.* 'and'] to TMs

111.4 unavailable; but we] unavailable. We, however, TMs

111.4 perspective ∧] ~, TMs

111.5 unqualifiedly] unqualifiably TMs,M&S

111.7 them ∧] ~, TMs

111.9 followed ∧] ~, TMs

111.10 verse] verses TMs,M&S

111.19 galaxy] galoxy TMs

111.25-26 writes Emerson.] Emerson writes; TMs,M&S

112.1 kernel] kernal TMs

112.18 desecrator] dessecrator TMs

§112.20 world] World [*bef. del.* 'that'] TMs

112.21 being ∧] ~, TMs

112.26 ²small ∧] ~, TMs

112.38 super-serviceableness] superserviceableness TMs

112.38 pretense] pretence TMs

113.16 desert] dessert TMs

113.31 genuine:–] ~: ∧ TMs

113.34 the Fifth] The Fifth TMs

114.15 Thus does "the] "The TMs, M&S

114.15 receive] receives thus TMs,M&S

§114.30 were] *were* [*underl. added*] TMs

115.23 time] times TMs (*error*)

§115.24 enmity ∧] ~ [*alt. fr.* 'emnity'], TMs

115.25 lasts,] ~ ∧ TMs

REMARKS AT THE PEACE BANQUET

The copy-text is P⁶, "Remarks at the Peace Banquet," *Atlantic Monthly*, 94 (December 1904), 845-847 (McD 1904:12). Reference is made to R, "Address of Prof. William James," *Official Report of the Thirteenth Universal Peace Congress* (Boston: Peace Congress Committee), 5 (October 7, 1904), 266-269 (McD 1904:12). Reference is also made to the reprint in M&S, *Memories and Studies*, edited by Henry James, Jr., pp. 299-306 (McD 1911:2) which is collated for substantives only.

120.1 I] *Mr. Chairman, Ladies and Gentlemen:* I R

120.2-4 do . . . always] do, and that is, to R,M&S

120.11 Nature's] *l.c.* R
120.11 any] only R,M&S
120.14 one another] each other R,M&S
120.15-16 is∧ . . . be∧] ~, . . . ~, R
120.17 ²a] *om.* M&S
120.20 the] this R,M&S
121.3 grow,–bit] ~. Bit R
121.5 the . . . and] *om.* R,M&S
121.6 task,] ~; R
121.9 noted] rooted R,M&S
121.10 in] into R,M&S
121.11 simply] *om.* R,M&S
121.12 its] his R,M&S
121.13 *status*] *rom.* R
121.25 Great-] ~∧ R
121.28 Brandenburg] Brandeburg R
121.28 soon, . . . hope,] possibly soon
        R,M&S
121.29 made] *om.* R,M&S
121.33 where] when R,M&S
121.34 view,] ~∧ R
121.40 leash,] ~∧ R
122.2 habits,] ~∧ R
122.3 Habit's] *l.c.* R

122.8 fascination. With] fascination of
        R,M&S
122.9 progress] process R,M&S
122.9-10 world, there] ~. There R
122.15 *saecula saeculorum*] *saecula
        saeculorum* R
122.20 itself;] ~, R
122.27 , they feel,] *om.* R,M&S
122.28-29 , they think,] *om.* R,M&S
122.30 fancy] think, therefore R,M&S
122.32 politically . . . action] circum-
        vent him in detail R,M&S
123.3 But (*no* ¶)] ¶ R
123.5 peace-] ~∧ R
123.6 responsibility;–how] ~. How R
123.10 excitements∧] ~, R
123.11 another,] ~∧ R
123.11 irritations] irritation R,M&S
123.13 will fire] fire R,M&S
123.23-25 It knows . . . civilization.]
        om. R,M&S
123.25 , to be sure] *om.* R,M&S
123.26 of the word] *om.* R,M&S

REASON AND FAITH

The copy-text is MS (MS Am 1092.9 [4542]), with reference to MS(p), a set of incomplete pasted-up galley proofs in the same file, to PU(p), the latter part of these proofs pasted in the manuscript of *A Pluralistic Universe* (bMS Am 1092.6), and to P[20], "Reason and Faith," *Journal of Philosophy,* 24 (April 14, 1927), 197-201 (McD 1927:1; wrongly listed as 1924:4). Autograph alterations in the proofs are designated as WJ/MS(p) or WJ/PU(p).

[*begin* MS(p)]
124.10 faculty∧ . . . facts∧] ~, . . . ~,
        P[20]
124.11 cannot] can not P[20]
124.14 other,] ~; P[20]
124.15 follow∧] ~, MS(p),P[20]
125.8,9 colleague∧] ~, P[20]
125.30 *sorites*] *Sorites* MS(p),P[20]
125.34 lies,] ~; MS(p),P[20]
126.20 ¹∧Reason∧] "~" P[20]
126.21 ∧indeed∧] , ~, P[20]
126.21 be] is P[20]
126.23+ [*space*]] *circled* 'blank line' *in*
        MS *mrgn.*; *no space* MS(p) (*uncer-
        tain*);P[20]
126.24 altogether] atogether MS(p)
        (*doubtful*)
126.25 ¹Reason] *l.c.* MS(p)

126.25 (*twice*) versus] *ital.* MS(p),P[20]
126.25 rather] WJ/MS(p); faher MS(p)
126.26 think] WJ/MS(p); thnk MS(p)
126.29 From] From ['all' *del.*]
        WJ/MS(p)
126.29 thinks,] ~. P[20]
[*end* MS(p); *begin* PU(p)]
127.25-26 death and termination]
        death and determination PU(p);
        deathlike termination WJ/PU(p)
127.27 run] ran P[20]
127.34 The] Mr. Chesterton says some-
        where, I think, that the WJ/PU(p)
127.35 solemn] WJ/PU(p); solmen
        PU(p)
127.36 gods] Gods P[20]
127.38 extremest] WJ/PU(p); extremist
        PU(p)

127.39 say∧] ~, PU(p); ~— P20
☛128.1 Church-Christianity] l.c.
   WJ/PU(p) (*similar* 128.14,17,33)
128.6-7 -sufficiency. He thought] - ~,
   thinking WJ/PU(p)
128.9 standards] WJ/PU(p); standard
   PU(p)
128.10 cannot] can not P20
128.10-11 -sufficingness] -sufficiency
   P20
128.12 currently] correctly P20
128.13 To] Sincerely to WJ/PU(p)
128.15 evangelical] WJ/PU(p); evangelican PU(p)
128.16 now-a-days] nowadays PU(p)
128.16 Mind-cure] mind-cure WJ/PU(p)
128.19 literal] literal and legal
   WJ/PU(p)

128.25 naturalism∧] ~, PU(p),P20
128.25 pin ... on] put ... in P20
128.26 other] WJ/PU(p) *underl. but*
   del. and marked for rom.
128.29 existence,] ~∧ P20
128.29 with] with our WJ/PU(p)
128.29 'natural'] WJ/PU(p); "~"
   PU(p); ∧~∧ P20
128.30 its] their WJ/PU(p)
128.30 come] actually come WJ/PU(p)
128.30 given] given to us WJ/PU(p)
128.31 Creation] l.c. WJ/PU(p),P20
128.32 so-called] ~ ∧~ P20
128.35 Reason] Science WJ/PU(p)
   (*poss.* science)
128.39 everyone] every one PU(p)
128.40 religious] *om.* WJ/PU(p)

THE ENERGIES OF MEN

The copy-text is P[28], "The Energies of Men," *Philosophical Review*, 16 (January 1907), 1-20 (McD 1907:1), with reference to P[36], "The Energies of Men," *Science*, 25 (March 1, 1907), 321-332. The use of asterisks in P[36] to indicate ellipses instead of the dots used in P[28] is not noted in this collation.

129.6-7 "Sketch ... Psychology,"] *sg.*
   qts. P36
☛129.7 "the ... attitude"] *sg. qts.*
   P36 (*similar* 135.32;143.24-25,25-26)
129.22 Presidential Address] l.c. P36
130.35 *et seq.* cannot] can not P36
131.2+ *et seq.* space] *no space* P36
131.10 half-] ~∧ P36
132.28 ¶ Either] *no* ¶ P36
133.9 city-] ~∧ P36
133.10 country-] ~∧ P36
133.37 fine] late P36
133.37 "The ... Builder,"] *sg. qts.* P36
134.14 follows:-] ~:∧ P36
134.15-135.17 "My ... me."] ∧~ ...
   ~.∧ P36 (*smaller type*)
134.40 Quincey.∧] ~.–W. J. P36
136.38 corroboration,] ~∧ P36
136.40 *et seq.* practice] practise P36

137.17 ago.] ~: P36
137.18-139.11 "Thus ... complete
   ——."] ∧~ ... ~ ——.∧ P36 (*smaller*
   type)
137.18-19 'Practice ... matter.'] "Practise ... ~." P36
138.22 been not] not been P36
138.40 March.∧] ~.–W. J. P36
140.1 fastings,] ~∧ P36
140.6-36 "You (*no* ¶) ... training."]
   ¶ ∧~ ... ~.∧ P36 (*smaller type*)
141.2 travelled] traveled P36
141.2 third class] ~ - ~ P36
141.3 fourth class] ~ - ~ P36
141.30 negations,] ~∧ P36
143.21-22 Buddhism,] ~∧ P36
144.9-10 coördination] coordination
   P36
145.16 physic,] ~∧ P36

THE POWERS OF MEN

The copy-text is P[4], "The Powers of Men," *American Magazine*, 65 (November 1907), 57-65 (McD 1907:2), with reference to EM, *The Energies of Men*, a pamphlet published in the Emmanuel Church Publications on Religion and Medicine (New York: Moffat, Yard, July 1908), and to the reprint entitled "The Energies of Men" in M&S, *Memories and Studies*, edited by Henry James, Jr., pp. 227-264 (McD 1911:2). EM and M&S have been collated for substantives only.

152.5   than] as EM,M&S
152.36 virtue's] virtues EM,M&S
154.33 past] passed EM,M&S
157.3-6 Compared . . . imperious.] *om.*
   EM,M&S

158.38 views] view EM,M&S
161.4 impression] an impression EM,
   M&S

THE MORAL EQUIVALENT OF WAR

The copy-text is IC, "The Moral Equivalent of War," *International Conciliation*, no. 27 (February 1910), 3-20 (McD 1910:3), with reference to MS[a], six leaves of a holograph first inscription found in the James Collection (bMS Am 1092.9 [4519]), and to TMs (or MS), a combination typescript and manuscript (MS Am 1092.9 [4548]). Reference is also made to P[23], "The Moral Equivalent of War," *McClure's Magazine*, 35 (August 1910), 463-468, to P[29], "The Moral Equivalent of War," *Popular Science Monthly*, 77 (October 1910), 400-410, and to AR, "The Moral Equivalent of War," *Atlantic Readings*, no. 10 (Boston: Atlantic Monthly Press, 1910). The *Atlantic Readings* reprint has been collated for substantives only as has the reprint in M&S, *Memories and Studies*, edited by Henry James, Jr., pp. 265-296 (McD 1911:2). One correction in Henry James's private copy of M&S is marked as HJ/M&S. Other annotations have been omitted. All alterations in MS[a] are confined to the Alterations list.

[*begin* MS[a]; *begin* TMs]
162.0 War] WAR[1] | [*fn.*] [1]This article, published last February by the American Association for International Conciliation, is here reproduced as a tribute to the memory of William James. It was written at the suggestion of the editor of THE POPULAR SCIENCE MONTHLY. P[29]
‡162.1 The] This MS[a],TMs
162.1 against] agst. MS[a]
162.4-5 nations ∧ . . . individuals ∧]
   ~, . . . ~, P[23]
‡162.5-6 ups . . . trade] vicissitudes of trade and the ups and downs of politics MS[a],TMs
162.6 modern] Madeson TMs (*error*)
162.7 north . . . south] *each cap.* P[23]
162.8 war] War P[23]
162.13 spiritual] *cap.* TMs
162.14 out] out to win it MS[a],TMs
162.14 Yet ∧] ~, P[23]

162.15 ∧ in cold blood ∧], ~~~, P[23]
162.16 now ∧] ~, P[23]
162.16 another] a P[23]
‡162.16 possession,] ~ ∧ MS[a]
162.17 or woman] *om.* MS[a],TMs; or women IC,M&S (or woman HJ/M&S)
§162.17 modern] the modern man's MS[a]; ['the' *ink del.*] modern *men's [ink alt. fr.* 'man's'] TMs
§162.18 wars] the wars MS[a]; ['the' *ink del.*] wars TMs
‡§162.19 the ideal harvest] exerting military energies and virtues MS[a]; showing [*ink ab. del.* 'exerting'] military *energy [ink alt. fr.* 'energies'] and *virtue['s' *ink del.*] TMs
162.19-20 one, . . . alternative,] one by an enemy's injustice MS[a],TMs
162.20 a] *om.* P[29]
162.22-23 village] villages P[29]
162.22-23 village ∧ . . . females,] ~, . . . ~ ∧ P[23]
‡162.24 exciting,] exciting ∧ MS[a]

162.24 of] to TMs

§ 163.1 selected,] ~; [*ink semicolon alt. fr. comma*] TMs

‡163.2 came to mingle] mixed MS[a], TMs

163.4-5 avenue to plunder;] means of plunder, MS[a],TMs

163.8 *strong*] strong TMs

163.8 *in*] in MS[a],TMs

‡163.9 pay,∧] ~;∧ P[29]; ~,– MS[a]

163.9-10 as . . . show.] grumble they may, but they don't hesitate. Look at our naval budget, look at our Panama canal bills, met because of military necessity. MS[a],TMs

163.12 *killed*] rom. TMs

‡163.14 jingoism] pure jingoism MS[a] [*end* MS[a]]

§ 163.14-15 imperialism—war] ~ , [*ink comma ov. period*] war ['w' *in ink ov.* 'W'] TMs

163.15-16 reading,] ~ ∧ TMs

163.16-17 all— . . . 'history'—] ~ ∧ . . . ∧~ ∧, TMs; ~— . . . "~"; P[23]

163.17 the history] history TMs

163.19 ever] *om.* TMs

163.20 gold,] gold, loot, TMs

163.21 excitement,] ~ ∧ P[23]

163.21-22 , for example,] *om.* TMs

163.22-23 ask . . . found] asked the Mileans TMs

163.24 meet, and hold] met, and held TMs

163.24 debate∧] ~, P[23]

163.25 gives in full,] *om.* TMs (*error*)

163.25-26 , for . . . form,] ∧ ~ . . . ~ ∧ TMs

163.26 Matthew] Mathew TMs

§ 163.28-29 Meleans . . . "Of] Mileans declined to ['be enslaved' *typed-del.*] own Athenian lordship, saying they would appeal to the gods, the Athenians replied that [*opening db. qt. del. in light ink*] of TMs

163.31 will.∧] ~." TMs (*error*)

163.32 but] not P[23]

163.36 Meleans] Mileans TMs

163.36 refused,] ~ ∧ TMs

163.36 taken] invested so that they surrendered at discretion TMs

164.1 simple, nothing] ~. Ntohing TMs

164.3 There . . . the] The TMs

164.3 died] died his conquests broke assunder, and TMs

164.4 another.] another. There was no rational principle in it. TMs

164.5 is] is to our minds TMs

164.6 Paulus] the Roman general Palus TMs

§ 164.6-7 told . . . kingdom] ordered by the senate to reward his army for their toil by ['abandoning pirates to their mercy' *typed-del.*] making a gift to them of the province TMs

164.10 they] the soldiers TMs

§ 164.12-13 [2]the . . . fight.] Thessalonica and *Lacedamon [*ink alt. fr.* 'Lacedeemon'] [*period del. in ink*] *to ravage, if they gain the battle. [*added in ink*] TMs

164.13 ravage,] ~ ∧ P[23]

§ 164.14 societies] society [*alt. in ink to* 'societies' *and then restored in ink*] TMs

164.15 warlike] war-like TMs

164.15 type;] ~, P[23]

[*end* TMs; *begin* MS]

164.20-21 fattens] feeds MS

164.26 politician] vote-catcher MS

164.29 day,] ~ ∧ P[23]

164.32-33 Innumerable . . . service.] *om.* MS

164.33 seem] are MS,

164.35-36 we, . . . ceasing,] ~— . . . ~— P[23]

§ 164.37 glory.] ~— [*dash ov. period*] MS

‡164.40 it] its name MS

☛ ‡164.40-165.1 up-to-date] ~ ∧~ ∧~ MS (*similar* ‡169.6-7,18; ‡170.24,25[*first*];172.1-2,‡2[*first two*])

165.1 Dictionary] *l.c.* P[23,29]

§ 165.2-6 It . . . -interval.] The humanitarian sentiment so-called, ['is' *del.*] which has grown so steadily for more than a century, is another of war's obstacles. It has already made *mercy [*intrl. aft. del.* '*an obligation of [*ab. del.* 'our armies']' *and bef. del.* 'merciful [*ab. del.* '—save in']'] to non-combatants [*comma wiped out*] and neutral *provinces ['p' *ov.* 'c'] *a military obligation [*intrl.*] —save ['of course' *del.*] in countries 'beyond the pale' like China, where ['the' *del.*] white armies ['vied' *del.*] ['revert['ed' *del.*] to primeval savagery,' *del.*] ['revert' *del.*] as a matter of course *revert [*intrl.*] to primeval savagery. [¶] But the worst criticism ['modern' *del.*] war ['r' *ov.* 'y'] has to suffer from is *that **of [*undel. in error*] [*ab. del.* 'that the'] ['of economic' *del.*] of the modern economic man's *reflections. [*period added and tr. by guideline from bef.* 'of the modern'] Industrialism has become so religious, as one might say, in these days, and *national excellence [*ab. del.* 'progress'] so much identified with *constructive [*penc.* 've' *ov.* 'on'] invention [*penc. intrl.*] and accumulation, that [*del.* '*a magnificent [*ab. del.* 'an immense'] machinery ['employing' *del.*] intended solely for the destr'] to keep a *magnificent and [*ab. del.* 'magnificently costly'] machine['ry' *del.*] ['going in a state of magnificent perfection' *del.*] going *at stupendous cost [*ab. del. comma*] solely for the purpose of destroying wealth and life, appears *to economically minded ['something' *del.*] persons something **quite [*penc.*] [*ab. del.* 'anomalous [*comma del.*] not *anomalous and [*penc. del.*]'] irrational. *Might not the **interests of nations be [*insrtd. for del.* 'ulterior ends be compassed'] [*undel. in error*] [*del.* 'attained by processes less wasteful and *less painful? [*ab. del.* 'more friendly.'] Hence the Hague tribunal, and the growing *dreams [*penc. intrl. bef. penc. del. ink* 'thought [*ab. del.* 'favor']'] of arbitration as a method.'] Hence such [*opening sg. qt. del.*] associations 'for conciliation' as that which publishes this paper. MS

165.12   conflict of honest] honest conflict of MS

165.12   myself] *om.* MS

165.13   bounden] *om.* MS

165.14   , as things stand,] ∧ ~~~∧ MS

165.19 *et seq.*   utopia] *cap.* P23

§ 165.20   abstract] ['abstra' *del.*] highly abstract MS

165.22   abstract] broad MS

165.23-24   the . . . hypothesis,] *om.* MS

165.23 *et seq.*   utopian] *cap.* P23

165.25   remarks,] ~∧ MS

‡ § 165.25   tho'] *as ['tho' ' *del.*] [*ab. del.* 'as'] MS; though P23,29

‡ 165.26   war-] ~∧ MS,P23

§ 165.27   writers] writer's [*apostrophe undel. in error*] MS

§ 165.34-35   revolts, . . . higher] revolts [*final 's' del. and restored*] *it is said, the higher ['times' *del.*] [*ab. del.* 'the *ordinary ['o' *ov.* 'm'] man's'] MS

165.35   ∧ then ∧] , ~, P23

‡ 165.37   to] so as to MS

‡ 165.37   flat degeneration] utter flatness MS

☛ 165.40   victor;] ~, MS (*similar* 167.19;168.28,33;169.11)

165.40;172.20   and ∧] ~, P23

‡ 166.1   profit] profits MS

166.1   we are told,] *om.* MS

166.4   co-education] coeducation P23

166.4   zoophily] zoöphily P23

‡ § 166.6   valor ∧] ~, [*ov. del. exclm. mk.*] MS

‡ 166.6   any] *any* MS

‡ 166.7   a . . . planet] cattle MS

166.7   cattleyard] ~ - ~ P23

‡ 166.15   is . . . mankind,] *om.* MS

166.15-16   mankind, . . . stock—] ~∧ . . . ~,— P23

§ 166.16   ∧ in stock ∧—of] 'in stock' [*dash ov. comma del.*] is thus *incumbent on mankind, [*ab. del.* 'is absolute of'; *moved fr. aft.* 'duty' (166.15) *first to bef.* 'is', *then to aft.* 'is', *then to aft.* 'thus'] MS

§ 166.16   them,] ~∧ [*intrl. bef. del.* 'it [*ab. del.* 'them,']'] MS

166.17   themselves ∧] ~, P23

‡ § 166.17   as] *del.* MS

§ 166.18-19   end . . . nature.] *end by driving everything else off the planet. [*ab. del.* 'inheriting ['ing' *added*] the *entire earth. [*ab. del.* '['whole earth.' *del.*] terrestrial globe.']'] MS

‡ § 166.20-21   army-writings] ['all' *del.*] the militaristic *writings [*ab. del.* 'books'] which appear ['in such

abund' *del.*] almost as abundantly as those ['of' *del.*] that ['give voice to the oppos' *del.*] breathe the antimilitaristic spirit. MS; ~ ∧~ P23

‡166.21 authors] writings MS

‡166.22 mystical] metaphysical MS

‡166.23 necessity,] need ∧ MS

§166.25-26 for . . . fictitious.] the *justification [*ab. del.* 'reasons'] [*del.* 'pretended [*ab. del.* 'pleaded']'] ['being always absurd' *del.*] pleaded being *always [*ab. del.* 'only'] a pretense. MS

166.26 is, in short,] in short is MS

166.27 book ∧] ~, P23

166.31;167.4 General] Gen. MS

166.33 and ∧ . . . question ∧] ~, . . . ~, P23

‡166.35 conquest–] ~, MS

166.38 Hawaiian] Hawaian MS

166.38 Alaska,] ~ ∧ P29

166.39 Coast] coast P23,29

166.39 west] West MS

166.39 Passes] passes MS,P23,29

166.40 as a state] *om.* MS

166.40;172.32 state] State P23

§167.2 have,] ~ ∧ (*error*) ['nothing at present,' *del.*] MS

§167.4 corruption . . . feminism.] feminism, ['and our' *del.*] our corruption, and our *incurable [*added*] optimism. [*ab. del.* 'decay'] MS

167.7 Alaska,] ~ ∧ | MS (*error*)

167.7 Southern] *l.c.* P23,29

167.10 republic] *cap.* P23

167.12 Caesar] Caesar P29

§167.12-13 to . . . nation.] again [*intrl.*] to make *a [*ab. del.* 'a decent'] nation of it. [*del.* '*once more. [*ab. del.* 'again.']'] MS

167.14 forecast ∧] ~, P23

167.14 Yet] yet MS (*doubtful*)

167.15 Caesarian] Caesarian P29

167.15 type ∧] ~, P23

167.19 Japan ∧] ~, P23

§167.20 and . . . opportunity] *and* *find [*insrtd. for del.* 'gain'] *their opportunity* MS

‡167.22 recesses] foldings MS

167.24 moral] moral than Gen. Lea, MS

167.25 R.] ~ ∧ MS

167.25 Steinmetz ∧] ~, P23

167.26 an . . . instituted] a duty fatally intended MS

167.28 State] state P29

167.29;168.19 and] *om.* MS

167.32 conscience] dutifulness MS

167.32 economy,] ~ ∧ | MS (*error*)

§167.33 vigor–] ~,–[*dash insrtd.*] MS

☛167.35-36 *Die . . . Weltgericht*] all *rom.* MS (*similar* ‡168.34;‡171.7; ‡171.27)

168.5 The . . . 'degeneration.'] *om.* MS

168.7 account] consideration MS

168.8 Simon] Simon's MS (*error*)

§168.12 *-régime*,] *-* ~ ∧ [*bef. del. closing sg. qt.*] MS

§168.13 ¹fear] a [*ab. del.* 'and the'] fear MS

§168.16-17 imagination, . . . unwillingness] ~. ['An' *del.*] Unwillingness ['U' *ov.* 'u'] MS

168.17 moral:] ~– P23

168.17-18 army-] ~ ∧ P23

168.20 thrillingly,] ~ ∧ P29

168.21 insipidly ∧] ~, P23

§168.21 , secondly,] ∧~ ∧ [*bef. del.* 'an'] MS

168.22 theatre] theater P23,29

168.22 strenuousness] strenousness MS

168.26 *et seq.* cannot] can not P29

‡168.27 counter-insistency] ~ ∧ insistancy MS

§168.30 so much] all [*intrl.*] this ['mer attitude of' *del.*] MS

§168.31 evident] too [*ab. del.* 'only too'] evident MS

168.32-33 the bestiality nor] *om.* MS

168.33 bestiality ∧] ~, P23

168.33 horror,] ~ ∧ MS

168.35-36 protection] protections AR

168.36 and more cowardly] *om.* MS

168.37 adopt . . . -economy] go without them MS

168.38 the esthetical] militarism's aesthetical MS

168.39 of their opponents] *om.* MS

168.39-169.1 ∧Do . . . controversy, ∧ . . . ∧then . . . follow. ∧] db. qts. P23

§168.40 *then . . . point,*] all *rom.*; *intrl.* MS

169.1 follow] follow you MS

§169.2 ²of war,] *of* [*insrtd. for del.* 'for [*insrtd. for del.* 'of']'] war ∧ [*bef. del.* ', as one'] MS

Historical Collation

169.4-5 ∧ as a rule ∧], ~~~, P²³

‡169.9 spur provided] 'brace' furnished MS

§169.10 But our] Our ['O' ov. 'B'] MS

169.11 and ∧] ~, P²³

169.14 acquainted] aequainted MS

169.15 dialogue,¹] ~,∧ MS (fn. om. but empty space present between lines for including fn.)

169.17 Meanwhile ∧ ... live ∧] ~, ... ~, P²³

169.18-19 economy— ... ocean—] ~,— ... ~,— P²³

169.18 economy—for those] ~. Those MS

169.19 live] lived P²⁹

§169.19-22 the ... flavors.] *the stormy ocean, [ab. del. 'a mighty sea of struggle,'] and ['we owe our ease entirely to' del.] we owe our ease for the most part *either [intrl.] to our own *predacious & [intrl.] military *talent, [ab. del. 'and pre-|*dacious [insrtd. for del. |'datory'] character,'] or to that of *some ancestor. [ab. del. our ['ancestors.' del.] grandfather['s' del.].'] ['The whole atmosphere of' del.] U[db. underl.] topia ['s' del.]-making [intrl.] *is indeed a [ab. del. 'are the man['s' del.]'] noble['st' del.] occupation; but the whole ['moral' del.] atmosphere of *present-day [ab. del. 'our'] utopian literature is lukewarm and ['saturated with reliefless' del.] mawkish to those *who keep a taste for [insrtd. for del. '*to whom life presents [insrtd. for del. '*with taste for [insrtd. for del. 'who *['see' del.] want ['life to have a 'sense'' del.] life with a [ab. del. 'crave the']']']'] [illeg. del.] stronger ['flavor.' del.] moral flavors. MS

§169.22 , in truth,] , [comma insrtd.] *in one word, [intrl.] MS

169.23-24 keynote] ~ - ~ P²³

169.24 "Hounds ... forever?"] ∧Dogs ... ~?∧ MS

169.25 Great] Second MS

169.25 Yes,] ~! MS

169.25 utopians,] Utopians; P²³

§169.25-26 let ... ¹our] live forever, and *try to [ab. del. 'we will try to'] raise your MS

169.29 their] the MS

169.30 characteristic,] ~∧ MS

169.31 and ... that] redeeming it thus MS

169.35 confessed] confest MS

169.36 sentiment] emotion MS

§169.38 belonging to] *being owned by [ab. del. 'participating in'] MS

‡169.39 General] Homer TMs

170.2 own] one P²³

‡170.4 ¹Where] where TMs

170.6 thus] this P²³

‡170.10 is] seems MS

170.17 claims, ... them] adjustments MS

170.19 acts of] om. MS

170.24 permanently] om. MS

170.26 towards] toward P²³,AR

170.27 drifting ∧] ~, P²³

170.27 collectively] om. MS

170.30 manliness] ideals of manliness MS

§170.31 enduring ... intrepidity] cement of *the new ['kind of community' del.] [ab. del. 'communities in the new order'] as much as *of [ov. 'is'] the old. ['one.' del.] Intrepidity MS

170.32 interest] interests MS

§170.33 must] will [ab. del. 'must'] MS

§170.33 remain] *have to [intrl.] be MS

‡170.34 , indeed,] ∧~∧ MS

‡170.34-35 commonwealths] a society MS

170.35 only] om. MS

170.35 whenever] if MS

170.36 centre] center P²³,²⁹

170.37 anywhere ... neighborhood] om. MS

171.1 form ∧ are, after all,] ~, ~∧ ~~∧ MS

171.6 fend off] postpone MS

171.9 effective] strong MS

171.16 honour,] honor∧ P²³; honor,p²⁹

171.16 (second);172.29;173.16 honour] honor P²³,²⁹

171.18 war-] ~ ∧ MS,P²³

171.18 graspt] grasped P²³

171.18 us ∧] ~, P²³

171.20 burden] tax MS

§171.25 opportunity,] ~∧ [aft. del. 'lack of'] MS

§171.26 toil ‸] *comma del.* MS

‡171.27 *no* vacation,] no ~,– MS

§171.27 no more deserving] just *as good ['get' *del. insrtd.*] [*ab. del.* 'like them, *live [*alt. fr.* 'life'] in pure softness, and one [*intrl.*] taste not of this *common [*ab. del.* 'animal'] heritage at all,'] MS

§171.28 *this*] *this* *fact [*ab. del.* 'fact'] MS

§171.30 campaigning,] ~ ‸ [*comma del.*] MS

171.32 ¹conscription ‸] ~, P²³

171.33 years ‸ a] years, MS

171.37 fibre] fiber P²³,²⁹

§171.38 remain blind] remain [*intrl.*] *['be' *del.*] as ['ignorant as' *del.*] entirely [*ab. del.* 'remain uneducated entirely'] blind [*ab. del.* 'ignorant [*insrtd. for del.* 'unaware [*ab. del.* 'uneducated,']']'] MS

171.39 real] *om.* M&S

171.39 on,] ~ ‸ MS

‡172.2 clothes-washing,] ~ ‸~, MS; ~ – ~ ‸ P²⁹

172.3 -holes,] – ~ ‸ MS

§172.4 skyscrapers,] *sky scrapers, [*bef. del.* 'would accord-'|] MS

172.7 own] *om.* P²³

172.8-9 nature, . . . proudly, . . . highly,] ~; . . . ~; . . . ~; P²³

‡172.16 cheerily ‸] ~, MS

‡172.17 threatens] need MS

172.17 to] *om.* MS

‡§172.19 far,] ~ ‸ [*comma del.*] MS

§172.28-29 Strenuous] We have ['the' *del.*] ['*already the [*insrtd.*] same' *del.*] strenuous MS

172.29 abound] *om.* MS

172.31 conscious] made conscious MS

172.32-34 We . . . are.] *om.* MS

172.34 , then,] ‸ ~ ‸ P²³

§172.35 henceforward is] is *henceforward [*ov.* 'now'; *intrl.*] MS

172.37 "military] ‸~ MS (*error*)

172.37-173.6 is the . . . . -seeking."²] *fol. 35 missing in MS (including fn.; see entry 173.6-8 for remainder of probable MS text*)

172.40 underselling ‸] ~, P²³

173.2 co-operation] coöperation P²³; cooperation P²⁹

173.2 honourable] honorable P²³,²⁹

173.2-3,5 ‸ at least ‸] ,~~, P²³

173.5 services] service P²³

173.6 -forgetfulness ‸] – ~, P²⁹

173.6-8 -seeking."² . . . emphasizes.] And beside the feeble and irregular endowment of research by commercialism, its little short-sighted snatches at profit by innovation and scientific economy, see how remarkable is the steady and rapid development of method and appliances in naval and military affairs! Nothing is more striking than to compare the progress of civil conveniences which has been left almost entirely to the trader, to the progress in military apparatus during the last few decades. The house-appliances of to-day for example, are little better than they were fifty years ago. A house of to-day is still almost as ill-ventilated, badly heated by wasteful fires, clumsily arranged and furnished as the house of 1858. Houses a couple of hundred years old are still satisfactory places of residence, so little have our standards risen. But the rifle or battleship of fifty years ago was beyond all comparison inferior to those we possess; in power, in speed, in convenience alike. No one has a use now for such superannuated things."* IC,P²⁹;AR (to-|day, for . . . today); M&S (ito the progress [*error*])

173.9 adds³] ~ ‸ (*om. fn.*) MS,P²³

173.11 exertion,] ~ ‸ P²⁹

173.11 responsibility,] ~ ‸ P²³

173.13 acquisition,] ~ ‸ P²³

‡173.18 Fear] fear MS,P²⁹

173.18-19 believe ‸] ~, P²³

173.18-19 believe and] *om.* MS

173.19 stimulus] incentive MS

‡173.20 men's spiritual] human MS

173.24 cannibal] *om.* MS

§173.25-26 bridged over: the] ~. [*period undel. in error*] over, [*insrtd.*] the ['t' *ov.* 'T'] MS

§173.26 can] will *surely [*intrl.*] MS

Alterations in the Manuscripts

All alterations made during the course of writing and of revision are recorded here except for strengthened letters to clarify a reading, a very few mendings over illegible letters, and false starts for the same word. The medium is the black ink of the original inscription unless otherwise specified. It is certain that many of the alterations were made *currente calamo* and others as part of one or more reviews. The two are ordinarily so indistinguishable in the intensity of ink or in the kind of pen, however, as not to yield to systematic recording by categories on the physical evidence. In the description of the alterations, when no record of position is given the inference should be that the change was made in the line of the text and during the course of the original writing. *Deleted* or *deletion* is given the abbreviation *del.*; *over* (*ov.*) means inscribed over the letters of the original without interlining; *above* (*ab.*) always describes an independent interlineation. When an addition is a simple interlineation, either with or without a caret, the description *intrl.* is used; when an interlineation is a substitute for one or more deleted words, the formula reads, instead, *ab. del.* 'xyz'. The word *inserted* (*insrtd.*) ordinarily refers to marginal additions or to squeezed-in letters, syllables, and words that also cannot properly be called interlines but are of the same nature. When reference is made to one or the other of two identical words in the same line of the present edition, some preceding or following word or punctuation mark is added for identification, or else the designated word is identified with a superscript [1] or [2] according as it is the first or second occurrence in the line. A superscript is also used to indicate which of more than one identical letter in the same word is referred to. A vertical stroke | signifies a line ending.

In order to ease the difficulty of reading quoted revised material of some length and complexity, the following convention is adopted. The quoted text will ordinarily be the final version in the manuscript, whereas the processes of revision are described within square brackets. To specify what words in the text are being affected by the description within square brackets, an asterisk is placed before the first word to which the description in brackets applies; thus it is to be taken that all following words before the square brackets are a part of the described material. For example, at 68.2 in *Some Problems of Philosophy* James altered 'one' to 'One' when he deleted four succeeding sentences. In the first sentence, which he subsequently may have independently deleted, he wrote 'We may mean' and then interlined 'for instance', following it with 'that' and a false start 'it is our' which he deleted. For the false start he substituted 'we treat the whole of it', deleted that, and wrote above it 'the whole of it can be taken', ending the sentence with 'as one topic of discourse.'

He began the second sentence with 'We do this by the' which he deleted. He started again with 'Whenever we use the word 'universe' we' in which he wrote 'W' over 'w' in 'Whenever', interlined 'take it thus,' above deleted 'do this,', interlined 'for', continued with 'we mean that no item of reality shall', wrote 'escape' above deleted 'be left out', wrote 'from what' and inserted 'our word covers;' in the margin for deleted 'we point to,' which he inscribed above deleted 'is signified,'. He carried on beyond the semicolon with 'but this unity of abstract reference, altho it has been made much of by', crossed out 'some rationalists,' above which he wrote 'idealistic writers,' and ended with 'is insignificant in the extreme.' In the third sentence James wrote 'It carries no', altered 'other' to 'further', continued with 'sort of connection with it, and would apply as well to', interlined 'any' above deleted 'an utter', and ended with 'chaos as to our actual world.' The final sentence reads 'Both would be *knowable-together* in the same barren way.' with 'the' written over 'this'. In formulaic terms the alteration entry is transcribed as 68.2 One] ('O' *ov.* 'o'); *bef. del.* '[*del.* 'We may mean *for instance [*intrl.*] that *the whole of it can be taken [*ab. del.* '['it is our' *del.*] we treat the whole of it'] as one topic of discourse. We do this by the'] Whenever ['W' *ov.* 'w'] we use the word 'universe' we *take it thus, [*ab. del.* 'do this,'] for [*intrl.*] we mean that no item of reality shall *escape [*ab. del.* 'be left out'] from what *our word covers; [*insrtd. for del.* '*we point to, [*ab. del.* 'is signified,']'] but this unity of abstract reference, altho it has been made much of by *idealistic writers, [*ab. del.* 'some rationalists,'] is insignificant in the extreme. It carries no *further [*alt. fr.* 'other'] sort of connection with it, and would apply as well to *any [*ab. del.* 'an utter'] chaos as to our actual world. Both would be *knowable-together* in *the [*alt. fr.* 'this'] same barren way.'

In formulaic transcriptions double asterisks can also be used to set off subsidiary alterations occurring between the single asterisk and the bracketed description that applies to this single asterisk, as, for example, 'In all these modes of union *some parts **of the world [*intrl.*] prove [*ab. del.* 'several aspects seem'] to be conjoined'. Inferior brackets clarify subsidiary bracketed descriptions within or before the main bracketed entry with or without the use of asterisks according to circumstances. The full details of this system may be found in F. Bowers, "Transcription of Manuscripts: The Record of Variants," *Studies in Bibliography*, 29 (1976), 212-264.

The lemmata (the readings to the left of the bracket) are ordinarily drawn from the present edition and represent the agreement of book and manuscript. To permit condensed entries, in some cases a single dagger prefixed to the page-line reference warns the user to refer to the Historical Collation for the exact manuscript reading in simple situations when the precise form of the alteration in words or accidentals is (a) not printed in the lemma, or (b) not specified in the descriptive part of the entry. For instance, in "The Moral Equivalent of War" at 164.40 the edition-text reads 'it ever' where the manuscript reads 'its name ever'. The daggered entry †164.40 it ever] *intrl. aft. del.* '*the printing of the word ['it ever' *del.*] [*ab. del.* 'either the word war or ['of' *del.*] the word peace']' saves space by referring the reader to the Historical Collation which reads ‡164.40 it] its name MS (the double dagger in turn cross-referencing to the Alterations entry).

On the contrary, twin daggers warn the user that the lemma is not (as in every other circumstance) the reading of the edition-text but is instead that of the manuscript. This convention is employed only when the two readings are so similar that a user following the edition-text in the Alterations list will be able to identify with certainty the reading that is intended, without recourse to the Historical Collation. A simple example of an accidental difference occurs at 165.26 where the edition reading's hyphen in 'war-régime' does not appear in the manuscript. The condensed entry reads ††165.26 the war ∧ régime] 'the' *intrl.*; 'régime[')' *del.*]' *insrtd.* A simple substantive example comes at 170.24-25 where the manuscript reads 'A successful' and the edition-text has 'A permanently successful'. The alteration is noted as ††170.24-25 A successful] *ab. del.* 'The'.

In some cases either single or twin daggers may refer the reader to the Emendations list. This will occur when a source other than the MS has been used as the emending agent in an emendation or when the manuscript copy-text has been emended. In such cases, the MS reading and the emended text reading will diverge, and because emendations are not repeated in the Historical Collation, the reader must check the Emendations list for the details of variation. It is worth emphasizing that whereas the device of twin daggers saves the reader from consulting any other part of the apparatus, the details of all such variants will nevertheless appear in the Historical Collation and Emendations list should he wish to check them there. There are two instances, however, in which a twin-daggered variant cannot be found in the Historical Collation. If James has made an obvious error in the manuscript which is somehow connected with an alteration, the error is cited in the Alterations entry and is not repeated in the Historical Collation. Second, when the manuscript reading used in the lemma corresponds to a variant in the edition-text which has been silently emended or is not recorded in the Historical Collation (as indicated in A Note on the Editorial Method and in the headnote to the Historical Collation), twin daggers refer to no other section of the apparatus but merely draw attention to the easily construed variant between text and MS.

Whenever practicable, alterations in the manuscript that also comprise textual variants complete in themselves appear in the Historical Collation or in the Emendations list instead of in the list of Alterations. For the details of these entries, see the headnotes to those two sections.

The use of three dots to the right of the bracket almost invariably indicates ellipsis rather than the existence of dots in the manuscript. This is the only violation of the bibliographical rule that material within single quotes is cited exactly as it appears in the original document. In order to avoid confusion with the asterisks used in formulaic description, James's footnote markers, which are frequently asterisks, are invariably indicated by a superior '×'.

Deleted versos which do not apparently relate to revisions in the main body of the Alterations list or which are revisions of continuous deleted material already set out therein are transcribed in a separate section following the list of Alterations for the entire manuscript.

PREFACE TO LUTOSLAWSKI'S *WORLD OF SOULS*

105.0 Preface] *aft. del.* 'Pef'
105.2 that weighty] *ab. del.* 'his other'
105.2 work,] *bef. del.* 'that he'
105.3 and] *aft. del.* 'sense of that'

105.4 term.] *ab. del.* 'word. His other writings, all of them less voluminous,'
105.5 previous] *ab. del.* 'other writings'
105.6 if not] *ab. del.* 'though less'

105.6   embrace] *aft. del.* 'are'

105.6   six other] *ab. del.* 'seven different'

105.6   latin] *aft. del.* 'beside en'

105.7   spanish, and] *aft. del.* 'fren'; 'and' *intrl.*

105.8   politics.] *bef. del.* 'In the present work'

105.8   –if] *aft. del.* '–though'

105.8   term] *ab. del.* 'word'

105.9   be applied] *ab. del.* '['be' *del.*] apply [*alt. fr.* 'applied']'

105.9   so] *aft. del.* 'evidently'

105.9   the] 't' *ov.* 'a'

105.10   cosmopolitan] *aft. del.* 'idealist'

105.10   speaker] *ab. del.* 'lover of human nature, and knower'

105.11   lover of] *ab. del.* 'believer in'

105.11   takes . . . entirely] ('s' *added to* 'take'; 'the . . . and' *insrtd.*); *ab. del.* 'gets entirely the upper hand, and'

105.12   "gets away" from] '['almost' *del.*] "gets away" ['entirely' *del.*] from' *ab. del.* 'only in the most general way remains one with'

105.13   simple] *intrl.*

105.13   peculiarly] *aft. del.* 'man [*ab. del.* 'human being,'] who, with a minimum of formal reasoning, and in disregard of the critical and skeptical'

105.14   being] *bef. del.* ', who,'

105.14-15   nourished . . . now] *insrtd.*

105.15   expressing] 'ing' *ov.* 'es'

105.15   idealities] 'ies' *ov.* 'y'

105.15   are] *ab. del.* 'is'

105.15   direct] *bef. del.* 'and'

105.16   and refusing] *ab. del.* 'not allowing himself'

105.16   (for] *paren ov. comma*

105.16   time ⌄] *comma del.*

105.16-17   any . . . technical] '*any of ['all' *del.*] [*intrl.*] those [*alt. fr.* 'the'] technical [*intrl.*]'

105.17   cobwebs] 's' *added*

105.17   and] *aft. del.* 'of ['scruples and' *del.*] technical scruples'

105.17   which so] *aft. del.* 'but'; 'so' *ab. del.* '['the minds of professors of philosophy are so' *del.*] are ['to' *del.*] apt to'

105.18   philosophy ⌄] *comma del.*

105.18   that] *aft. del.* 'to such a degree'; *bef. del.* 'they hardly ever dare to say anything'

105.19   a thing['s' *del.*]] *ab. del.* 'anything'

105.19   on] *aft. del.* 'directly'

105.19-20   is . . . take.] *ab. del.* 'at all.'

105.21   Professor Lutoslawski] ('l' *ov.* 't'); *aft. insrtd.* '¶'

105.22   ¹its] *ab. del.* 'the'

105.22   traditions; but] *semicolon ov. period*; 'b' *ov.* 'B'

105.22   finds ['no' *del.*] little] *ab. del.* 'has no use for its vital'

105.22-23   for its sceptical] ('s' *added to* 'its'); *ab. del.* '['for in' *del.*] ['its' *del.*] inhibitions and sceptical ['the' *del. insrtd.*]'

105.23   is] *bef. del.* '*in short [*intrl.*]'

106.1   sense.] (*period insrtd. for *colon [*undel. in error*] insrtd. for del. colon*); *bef. del.* | 'a prophet, to those ['who' *del.*] to whom his voice may come with *the note [*ab. del.* 'accents'] of authority, and surely amongst his readers there will be many many such.'

106.1   assuredly be as] *ab. del.* doubtful 'be'

106.2   not . . . but] *intrl.*

106.4   our] *aft. del.* 'be d'

106.5   thus] *alt. fr.* 'this'; *ab. del.* 'so'

106.5   usually] *intrl.*

106.5   deeper] *aft. del.* 'far [*intrl.*]'

106.6   these latter] *ab. del.* 'our reasonings'

106.6   masquerades] *aft. del.* 'a'; *final 's' added*

106.7-8   them, and they] *comma insrtd. bef. del. semicolon bef. del. period*; 'and they' *ab. del.* 'What creates them and personal'

106.8   never bear] 'never' *bef. del.* 'enforce them'; 'bear' *ab. del.* 'force'

106.8   in upon the] 'in [*intrl.*] upon [*ov.* 'on'] the [*intrl.*]'

106.8-9   of others.] *ab. del. period*

106.9   an] *intrl. aft. del.* 'the [*ab. del.* 'another's']'

106.9   in] *intrl. aft. del.* 'for [*ab. del.* 'in']'

106.9-10 every . . . ¹of] 'every [*alt. fr.* 'everything'] sphere [*intrl.*] save [*ab. del.* 'but'] *that of [*intrl.*]'

106.12 authority.] *period insrtd. bef. del.* ', what Goethe called the demonic quality.'

106.13 charm,] *comma ov. period*

106.14 the demonic quality.] *ab. penc. del.* 'Witness Goethe, Emerson, Carlyle, Matthew Arnold, and now-a-days in Germany Nietzsche.'

106.16 his] *insrtd. for del.* 'this'

106.21 This . . . his] *ab. del.* 'Professor Lutoslawski's'

106.21-22 after all] *intrl.*

106.22 great] *aft. del.* 'the [*intrl.*]'

106.22 traditions] *aft. del.* 'beliefs and'

106.23 individual] *aft. del.* 'soul's [*apostrophe indep. del.*] as substances'

106.23 souls] *apostrophe bef. final* 's' *del.*

106.24 ; but] *semicolon insrtd. bef. del. dash*

106.24 prejudice against] *intrl.*

106.25 term] *insrtd. for del.* 'word'

106.25 english] *aft. del.* 'reader'

106.26 author's] *intrl.*

106.26 meaning,] *ab. del.* 'sense of the *author's thesis, [*ab. del.* '['affir' *del.*] affirmation,']'

106.26 each . . . inner] *ab. del.* 'in the'

106.27 is] *aft. del.* 'of each of us'

106.27 ¹permanent['ly' *del.*]ly] *bef. del.* 'active part of the universe'

106.28 great] *bef. del.* 'higher'

106.29 individual souls.] *alt. fr.* 'individualities [*alt. fr.* 'individuals'] .'

106.29 Professor] *aft. del.* 'Lu'

106.30 either] *ov. doubtful* 'a'; *aft. del.* 'but rather'

106.30-31 pluralist] *aft. del.* 'mon'

106.31 has] *insrtd.*

106.32 immense] *intrl.*

106.32 souls ∧] *comma wiped out*

106.32 from] *aft. del.* 'of which it comes'

106.32 those] *alt. fr.* 'the'

106.33 at the bottom] *intrl.*

106.34 to] *aft. del.* 'at the bottom,'

106.34 the single] *ab. del.* 'the highest god at the top'

106.34 But] *aft. del.* 'But God here'

106.35 God ∧] *comma penc. del.*

106.35 is not "the Creator"] ('the' *ov.* 'their'; 'C' *ov.* 'c'); *ab. del.* 'is not the crea as the'

106.35 theological sense;] ('theological' *alt. fr.* 'theology'; 'sense;' *ab. del.* '; and'); *aft. del.* 'sense of the ['Christian' *penc. del.*]'

106.37-39 author . . . theist.] *marked by mrgn.* '?'

106.38 under] *bef. del.* 'recogni'

106.40 instinctive] *ab. del.* 'popular'

107.1 repressed ∧] ¹'r' *ov.* 's'; *comma del.*

107.8 behavior] *aft. del.* 'cond'

107.10 statistical] *aft. del.* 'conse-quences,'

107.10 results ∧] *comma del.*

107.11 than] *bef. del.* 'con'

107.16 1898] *aft. del.* '18'

107.21 the] *bef. del.* 'outco'

107.22 their] *ab. caret ov.* 'a'

107.22 world.] *bef. del.* '—"*Ceçy ['C' *bel. del. poss. db. qt.*] est un livre de bonne foy."'

107.24 believes:] *alt. fr.* 'beliefs.'

107.24 they] 't' *ov.* 'T'; *bef. del.* 'give their'

107.24 assent] ¹'s' *ov.* 'e'

107.25 such] *bef. del.* 'as'

107.26 a faculty of] *intrl.*

107.26 that which animates] ('which animates' *ab. del.* 'of'); *aft. del.* 'Professor'

107.27 friend! He] *ab. del.* 'author! He really'

107.27-28 For him this] 'For him' *intrl.*; 't' *ov.* 'T'

107.28 relations. A] *period insrtd. for del. colon*; 'A' *ov.* 'a'

107.30 throughout] 'out' *insrtd.*; *bef. del.* 'all'

107.30 absolute] *ab. del.* 'ultimate'

107.32 ²the] *ab. del.* 'its'

107.32 of] *ov.* 'are'

107.32-33 its . . . are] *intrl.*

107.33 We] *aft. del.* '['The world may' *del.*] Potentially at least, this world is a spirtual ['universe' *del.*] republic

worthy of the name of kingdom of
heaven.'

107.34 slowly but] *ab. del.* 'evolving'

107.36 in] *aft. del.* 'the'

107.37 and romantic,] *ab. caret ov.*
doubtful comma

107.37-38 deliberately so.] *ab. del.*
'confessedly utopian *and romantic.
[*ab. caret formed fr. orig. period*]'

107.38 utopias and] 's' *ov.* 'n'; 'and'
intrl.

107.38 forces ∧] *comma del.*

107.38-39 as ... reproach.] *opp. mrgn.*
penc. note 'Plato'

107.39 that] *aft. del.* 'there'

107.40 books,] *comma insrtd.*

107.40 such ... foy,"] *intrl.*

107.40 sure] *aft. del.* 'such'

108.1 in the end] *ab. del.* ', with or'

108.1 aid] *aft. del.* 'publisher's'

108.1 , critics,] 'critics' *aft. del.* 'and';
commas insrtd.

108.1 or preface-writers.] ('or' *ov.*
period); *insrtd.*

108.2 finally] *aft. del.* 'gain their constituency wherever humanity, natural
consistency'

108.3 passionate] *aft. del.* 'a sort of';
bef. del. 'and'

108.5 sure ... advance.] *ab. del.* 'already'

DELETED VERSOS FOR "PREFACE TO LUTOSLAWSKI" MANUSCRIPT

[*del. fol.* 3ᵛ: *penc. del.*; *orig. continuation of fol.* 2] '['is not *as [*poss.* 'esp']'
del.] regardless of ['the' *del.*] all the ['possible' *del.*] technical criticisms with
which ['mere [doubtful]' *del.*] pedantic [*poss.* 'pedants']'

[*del. fol.* 7ᵛ: *earlier draft of top of fol.* 7, *corresponding to text* 106.31-32]
'*in fact [*intrl.*] has [*undel. in error*] only a collective unity. There follows
from this a sort of polytheism, in the sense that'

[*del. fol.* 10ᵛ: *earlier draft of top of fol.* 10, *corresponding to text* 107.28-30]
'passion of brotherhood, ['and human love' *penc. del.*] and friendship sings
through *his [*ab. penc. del.* 'the pages.']'

EMERSON

All alterations in the typescript are in ink unless otherwise indicated. When
the words *'bef.'* (*before*) or *'aft.'* (*after*) are used in an alteration, it is to be
understood that the lemma is a positioning word and hence is part of the original typescript.

†109.1-20 The ... generations.]
marked w. mrgn. line and 'omit' *for*
del. but restored by circled note 'Disregard the pen lines drawn about and
on this page'

109.1 one's] *ab. del.* 'a man's'

109.2-3 those ... passing,] *orig. del.*
but restored by underdotting for stet

109.3 one] *ab. del.* 'him'

109.4-7 The ... us.] *marked for del.*
but restored

109.8 suggestive] 've' *ab. del.* 'on'

109.9-10 happy ... abridgement.]
marked for del. but restored

109.12-14 taking ... but] *marked for*
del. but restored

109.15 notion] *ab. del.* 'sense'

109.15-20 The ... generations.]
marked for del. but restored

109.19 the] *alt. fr.* 'these'

110.3 own] *bef. del.* 'one'

110.4 ¹the] *intrl.*

110.11 consult] *insrtd. for del.* 'look
at'

110.11 sky,] *bef. del.* 'frequent'
110.14 ¶ This] *¶ sign insrtd.*
110.14-23 This . . . material.] *marked w. mrgn. line and* 'omit' *but then restored*
110.16 with] *ab. del.* 'for'
110.18 combination,–] *dash added*
110.27-28 associations∧ . . . functions∧] *commas del.*
110.30-31 "with . . . poisoning,"] *all db. qts. insrtd.*
110.34 The] 'T' *ov.* 't'; *aft. del.* 'Even'
110.35 itself,] *intrl. w. caret ov. comma*
110.36 this] *alt. fr.* 'the'
110.40-111.1 the . . . his] ('the . . . qu' *in penc.*); *intrl.*
111.2 such a] *ab. del.* 'this'
111.3 him] *ab. del.* 'Emerson'
111.5 must] *ab. del.* 'have'
111.5 approve] *aft. del.* 'to'
111.5 faultless] 'fault' *insrtd. for del.* 'match'
††111.9 insight & creed] *ab. del.* 'theoretic insight,'
111.9 life] *aft. del.* 'government of his own'
111.13 there] *aft. del.* 'that'
111.13 him] *ab. del.* 'this man'
111.27 in a life] *ab. del.* 'living'
111.27 there] *intrl.*
111.28 something] *aft. del. intrl.* 'always'
111.32 freshly,] *comma del. and restored*
111.35-36 light." "Trust] *db. qts. added; four intervening periods del.*
111.36 every] *aft. del.* 'then,'
112.6 future] *aft. del.* 'all'
112.7 soul] *ov.* 'core'; *ab. del.* 'kernel'
112.11 wrote,] *comma ov. colon*
†112.14-15 "Cleave . . . God";] *all db. qts. insrtd.*
112.15 so,] *comma insrtd.*
113.13 sets] *intrl.*
113.28 itself,] *comma alt. fr. period*
114.4 comparisons] *alt. fr.* 'companions'
114.10 so] *insrtd. for del.* 'do'
114.21 an optimist] *ab. del.* 'a sentimentalist ['ist' undel. in error]'
114.21 sentimental] *ab. del.* 'timid'

114.24 alike] *bef. del.* 'and common'
114.25 soon] *ab. del.* 'with a flavor'
114.25 and *as [insrtd.]* dreary.] *ab. del. period*
114.28 that indiscriminate] *ab. del.* 'vague'
114.28 ²with] *intrl.*
114.29 made] *ab. del.* 'taught'
114.29 familiar.] *ab. del. period*
114.30 indeed] *circled for poss. del. but restored*
114.32 worthy specimens,–] *ab. del.* 'genuine,'
114.33 Sentiment,] *alt. fr.* 'Sense,'
114.34 the] *ab. del.* 'what is'
114.34-35 Universe's meaning.] *alt. fr.* 'universal.'
114.35 does] *intrl.*
114.35 act] *final* 's' *del.*
114.36 connection,] *comma added*
114.36-37 (somewhat . . . confessed)] *parens ov. commas*
114.38 consistency.] *period insrtd. bef. del.* 'of method.'
114.39 perceive] *ab. del.* 'see'
115.1 easily] *del. but restored aft. intrl.* 'possibly' *del.*
115.1 found . . . saying] *insrtd. for del.* 'said'
115.3 private] *ab. del.* 'merely phenomenal'
115.3 a tedious] *alt. fr.* 'an odious'
115.11 This] *aft. del.* 'Thus do his words rekindle vital zest, thus does he fan the waning flame of men's belief in themselves and in their situation.'
115.13-14 penetratingly persuasive] 'ly persuasive' *del. but restored*
115.14 and,] *comma added*
115.15 that] *ab. del.* 'which'
115.16-17 divine,] *comma added*
115.17 individuals and] 's and' *del. but restored*
115.20 me] *ab. del.* 'us'
115.21 but] *intrl. bef. del. intrl.* 'but'
††115.21 argument,] *period alt. to comma and not restored in error when intrl.* 'rekindling vital zest, reviving our belief in ourselves and in our situation.' *del.*
115.21-22 words . . . effect] *ab. del.* 'pages [insrtd. bef. del. 'best pages'] '

115.23 Scriptures] 's' *added*

115.25 Master. As] *period aft. del.*
colon or exclm. mk.; 'A' *ov.* 'a'

115.25 English] *intrl.*

115.26 cheered ⌄] *comma del.*

115.27 noble and musical] *intrl.*

115.27 pages] *ab. del.* '*noble and musical pages sentences Sentences Sentences thoughts [*ab. del.* 'words']'

REASON AND FAITH

124.2 announced in print] *ab. del.*
'suggested'

124.3-4 sincerely] *ab. del.* 'may be
permitted to'

124.4 may] *insrtd. for del.* 'will'

124.5 question] *ab. del.* 'sufficiency'

††124.5 |sons all-... reach] ('sons'
penc. insrtd.); *ab. del.* | 'son to draw'

124.7 point.] *aft. del.* 'matter.'

124.8 all-] *intrl.*

124.11 cannot] *alt. fr.* 'can't'

124.11 exist; but] *alt. fr.* 'exist. But'

124.11 be] *aft. del.* 'exist she can ded'

124.12-13 be able,] *insrtd.*

124.13 by] *ab. del.* 'possess'

124.13 that] *aft. del.* 'that establish'

124.13 in advance['s' *del.*]] *aft. del.*
'the [*undel. in error*] relations'

124.15 and the like.] *aft. del.* 'etc.'

124.18 feel...be] *ab. del.* 'recognize
certain forms as'

124.18 and lower,] *intrl.*

124.18-19 the higher things] 'the' *alt.
fr.* 'them'; 'higher things' *intrl.*

124.19 conclusion.] *period aft. del.
comma*

124.21 parts] *aft. del.* 'only'

124.21 that] *ab. del.* 'whether'

124.22 is] *alt. fr.* 'be'.

124.22 can only] *ab. del.* 'must'

124.22 experience] *ab. del.* 'his
creation'

125.1 ¹from] *insrtd. for del.* 'by'

125.1 character] *aft. del.* 'adequate to
their'

125.1 as [*intrl.*]... cause,] ('needing
['ing' *added*]' *bef. del.* 'of'); *brought
by guideline fr. aft.* 'their'

125.1 ²from] *ab. del.* 'by'

125.2 display.] *aft. del.* 'express.'

125.3 Reason] 'R' *ov.* 'r'

125.3 sense] *insrtd. for del.* 'way'

125.4 put] *ab. del.* 'reac reach'

†125.5 on...base.] *intrl.*

125.5 pantheism] *aft. del.* 'the con-
troversies'

125.6 itself] *intrl.*

125.6 appealed] *aft. del.* 'flourished
the name of *Reason ['R' *ov.* 'r'] a'

125.7 The] 'T' *ov.* 't'; *aft. del.* 'To say
nothing of Tom *Paine's [*alt. fr.*
'Paine,'] 'Age of Reason,''

125.8 that] *ab. del.* 'my colleague
Santayana's'

125.8 by] *aft. del.* 'which I recommend you all to read,'

125.9 For my] *ab. del.* 'My'

125.9 colleague] 'ue' *ov.* 'gu'

125.10 as you all know,] *ab. del.*
'thinks that'

125.11 secure.] *period bef. del. doubtful comma*

125.11 thinkers] *intrl. bef. del.* 'men
[*ab. del.* 'colleagues']'

125.11 actuate?] *ab. del.* 'inhabit*?
[*undel. in error*]'

125.12 Speaking] 'S' *triple underl.*;
aft. del. 'If Evidently it works differently in each.'

125.13 Reason] *aft. del.* 'the'

125.14 Neither] *insrtd. for del.* 'Yet
here they are at absolute loggerheads
on *the [*ov.* 'a'] most vital religious
point. Neither'

125.14 neither] *aft. del.* 'and say that
whereas his conclusion is *one
[*intrl.*] of *Reason ['R' *ov.* 'r'], his
opponents is *only one [*intrl.*] of
*Faith ['F' *ov.* 'f']. or'

125.15 that] *intrl.*

125.15 but] *intrl. bef. del.* '*that his
rival [*ab. del.* 'or']'

125.15 blind] *ab. del.* 'mere'

125.18 Their] *insrtd.*

125.18 indicates] *bef. del.* 'a['n' *del.*]
possibility, and'

125.22 wise.] *bef. del. false start of*
'F'

125.30 ¹the] *aft. del.* 'l'

125.31 but,] *ab. del.* 'and'

125.32 live.] *aft. del.* 'lif'

125.32 no] *ab. del.* 'all'

125.32 matter] *final* 's' *del.*

125.32 can] *intrl.*

125.32-33 be more than] *ab. del.* 'can
at best be'

125.33 We use] *intrl. bef.* 'Our [*unreduced in error*]'

125.34 probability] 'y' *ov.* 'ies'

125.34 our] *aft. del.* 'we have formed'

125.34 is made,] *intrl.*

125.36 Probability,] *comma added
bef. del.* 'is math'

125.36 mathematically] *ab. del.*
'practically'

125.38-39 (...)] *parens ov. commas*

125.38 half-] *ab. del.* '½'

125.39 all);] *semicolon ov. colon*

126.1 certainty)] *paren ov. comma*

126.2 naught.] *aft. del.* 'zeroes or'

126.5 approve] *aft. del.* 'ca'

126.10 forbid us] *ab. del.* 'condemn'

126.12 must] *aft. del.* 'alone'

126.15-16 ['in' *del.*] their ... practice,]
intrl. aft. del. 'so *very* [*intrl.*] little'

126.18 Virtually] *ab. del.* 'Practically'

126.20 ¹Reason] 'R' *ov.* 'r'

126.22 a man's] *insrtd.*

126.23 obvious] *aft. del.* 'flagrant to
admit of discussion.'

126.23 further] *intrl.*

126.25 ¹Reason] 'R' *ov.* 'r'

126.25 rather] *aft. del.* 'in view'

126.25 Faith ͜] *comma del.*

126.26 ²that] *insrtd.*

126.28 about] *ab. del.* 'as to'

126.29 the facts of] *ab. del.* 'finite our'

126.29 thinks] *ab. del.* 'pretends'

126.33 physical] *aft. del.* 'the'

126.34 ¹and] *ab. del.* 'as well as'

126.37 natural] *aft. del.* 'f'

126.39 But] *aft. del.* '[*fol.* 10] | gious
conclusions, and that specific religious experiences, like mystical insights, providential leadings and
conversions are not required.'

126.39 outset.] *ab. del.* 'beginning.';
bef. del. 'Does reason, as it concretely exist force'

126.39 facts] *aft. del.* 'general'

127.1 natural] *intrl.*

127.1 Reason] 'R' *ov.* 'r'

127.3 possessing *Reason ['R' *ov.*
'r']] *ab. del.* 'being equally rational,
are led by'

127.4 facts] *ab. del.* 'aspect'

127.5 (*twice*) diversely] *insrtd.*

127.5 in this matter] *ab. del.* 'differently'

127.5-6 up ... hour.] *ab. del.* 'differently.'

127.7 ¹and] *intrl.*

127.12 the] *intrl.*

127.12 Reason] 'R' *ov.* 'r'

127.13,15 she] *ab. del.* 'it'

127.14 class of] *insrtd.*

127.15 we give her] *ab. del.* 'it have'

127.16 more] *intrl.*

127.20 religious] 're' *ab. del.* 'Re'

127.21 Reason] 'R' *ov.* 'r'

127.21 show] *aft. del.* 'open'

127.21-22 another ['a' *del.*] possibility]
ab. del. 'an opening'

127.23 Briefly,] *comma insrtd. bef.
del.* 'stated,'

127.23 I] *ov.* 'ar'

127.24 By this] *intrl.*

127.24-25 immortality] *aft. del.* 'here'

127.25 ¹death] *aft. del.* 'total'

127.25 body] *aft. del.* 'person'

127.26 mental] *intrl.*

127.26 within] 'in' *added*

127.27 and] *bef. del.* 'eventuate in
despair.'

127.28 Just] *aft. del.* 'As'

127.28 seems] *bef. del.* 'to'

127.28-29 recent literary] *insrtd. for
del.* 'modern'

127.30 seem to have] *intrl.*

127.32 will] *ab. del.* 'would'

127.32-33 inner ... ourselves] *ab. del.*
'ancient'

127.33 of ... Romans.] *ab. del.* 'the
modern inner life times'

127.33 ancient] *final* 's' *del.*

127.35 set] *aft. del.* 'folk'

127.35 The] *aft. del.* 'Good was good
and bad was bad, and moral values

brooked no irony, with them. Their pride had never crumbled. As'

127.36-37 Aristides;] *bef. del.* 'and'

127.37 were] *aft. del.* 'very'

127.38 Cato's . . . that] *intrl.*

127.38 the] 't' *ov.* 'T'

127.39 of anything] *insrtd.*

127.39 "I] *aft. del.* '"I would'

127.40 believe] *aft.* 'be- | [*undel. in error*]'

127.40 Good] *aft. del.* 'They held by naturalistic values exclusively, hypocrisy, which Church-Christianity brought with it, hardly existed,'

128.1 Hypocrisy] *aft. del.* 'Their pride and never crumbled, and the *individual, [*comma del. and replaced*] ['was deemed' *del.*] they conceived, could, if he were virtuous, fulfill all the duties that the law exacted.'

128.2-3 held . . . values] *ab. del.* 'of values held firm, and'

128.7 (. . .)] *parens ov. commas*

128.9 brings] *ab. del.* 'bankrupts'

128.9 our] *bef. del.* 'first'

††128.9 to bankuptcy.] *ab. del. period*

128.10-11 or self-sufficingness.] *ab. del. period*

128.11 the] *ab. del.* 'our'

128.12 accepted] *ab. del.* 'conventional'

128.12 our] *intrl.*

128.13 as absolute] *ab. del.* 'mere silliness and'

128.13 To give ['giving' *del.*] up one's] *ab. del.* 'Self-surrender, ceasing the foolish'

128.14 door] *aft. del.* 'way'

128.15 familiar] *aft. del.* 'things'

128.17 The] *aft. del.* 'The [*alt fr.* 'They']'

128.17 phenomenon] *alt. fr.* 'phonemenon'

128.18 succeeding] *aft. del.* 'and power and well-being'

128.18 resources] *aft. del.* 'more'

128.19 that] *ab. del.* 'than [*alt fr.* 'that']'

128.19 naturalism,] *comma added*

128.19 with] *aft. del.* 'never dreamed of'

128.19 literal] *ab. del.* 'stiff'

128.19 recks] *alt. fr.* 'recked'; *ab. del.* 'dreamed'

128.21 philistine] *ab. del.* 'ordinary'

128.21 can] *ab. del.* 'had'

128.21 imagine] *final* 'd' *del.*

††128.23 strength ʌ] *ab. del.* '['respon' *del.*] pride, [*comma del. in error*]'

128.24 responsibility] *aft. del.* 'anxiety and'

128.24 ²of] *intrl.*

128.25 naturalism and] *insrtd. bef. del.* 'and'

128.25 pin] *final* 's' *del.*

128.25 their] *intrl. bef. del.* 'its [*ab. del.* 'their']'

128.26 operating] *aft. del.* 'without'

††128.26-27 even . . . experiences ʌ] *intrl.*

128.27 inferred] *ab. del.* 'divined'

128.28 could] 'c' *ov.* 'w'

128.28 not] *insrtd. for del.* 'never have'

128.29 suspect] *alt. fr.* 'suspected [*ab. del.* 'prophecied']'

128.29 their] *alt. fr.* 'them'

128.29 existence, for] *intrl.*

128.29 they] 't' *ov.* 'T'

128.29 'natural'] *aft. del.* 'the'

128.30 ¹and] *insrtd. for del.* 'they'

128.30 its] *intrl. aft. del.* 'our [*ab. del.* 'the natural']'

128.31 Creation . . . view.] *ab. del.* 'they *make [*ab. del.* 'enlarge'] the world for us.'

128.31 ²our] *intrl.*

128.32 , so-called,] *intrl.*

128.32 be a] *insrtd. for del.* 'yield [*ab. del.* 'be a']'

128.32 of reality.] *ab. del.* '. They soften of it.'

128.33 the] *intrl. aft. del.* 'new perspectives of'

128.33 strangest] 'st' *added*

128.35 in] *aft. del.* 'on'

128.36 omit] *ab. del.* 'leave'

128.36 something,] *comma insrtd. bef. del.* 'out'

128.37 completely] *alt. fr.* 'completeness'

128.37 adequate] *ab. del.* 'in her true religious'

128.38 needs,] *ab. del.* 'must'
128.39 interpreted ₍ₐ₎] *comma del.*
128.39-40 to . . . a *true [*intrl.*]]

insrtd. for del. 'to a religious philosophy that he can call rational *to
build up a [*added*]'

THE MORAL EQUIVALENT OF WAR

a. Alterations in MSᵃ

††162.1 This] *alt. fr.* 'the'
162.2 The . . . are] ('The' *bef. del.*
'['Our' *del.*] The'); *ab. del.* 'The war-
function is'
162.2 grounded to] ('grounded' *bef.
del.* 'in man's nature'); *ab. del.*
'['rooted in human society to yield
until some worthier substitute is
found than' *del.*] give way'
162.3 place] *bef. del.* 'until some
sterner substitute is found than'
162.3 our] *ab. del.* 'human men's'
162.3 better] *insrtd. for del.* 'other
[*ab. del.* 'sterner']'
162.4 the glory] *aft. del.* '['ste' *del.*]
the market ups and downs which
in ['a state of' *del.*] peace measure
the ['height' *del.*] distance between
glory's heights and shame's abysses.'
†162.5 politics] MSᵃ 'politics.' *ab.
del.* 'the market.'
162.8 our] *ab. del.* 'the'
162.8 war] *bef. del.* 'of the rebellion'
162.9 Union] *bef. del.* ', with all its
memories,'
162.9 the record of] ('record' *ab. del.*
'memory'); *intrl.*
162.10 that of its] *aft. del.* 'its memories'; *bef. del.* 'battles and'
††162.11 & battles,] *intrl.*
162.12 ancestors,] *ab. del.* 'heroes,'
††162.12 & legends,] *intrl.*
162.12 are] *bef. del.* 'our [*ab. del.*
'the most'] sacredest ['est' *ab. del.*
'part of our'] inheritance, [*comma
ov. period*] ['They' *del.*]'
162.13 spiritual] *intrl.*
162.14 possession] *ab. del.* 'inheri-
tances'
162.15 same] *aft. del.* 'very'
162.15 start] *ab. del.* 'institute'
††162.16 to . . . possession ₍ₐ₎] ('sion'
of 'possession' *ov.* hyphen *and bef.*
'sion' *undel. in error on following*

line); *moved fr. aft.* 'whether
[162.15]' *to aft.* 'now [*caret of
guideline ov. orig. comma*]' *and bef.
del.* 'between the East and the West,
perhaps'
162.18 wars] *aft. del.* 'spiritual results
of'
162.18 they] *ab. del.* 'war'
162.18 waged . . . of] *ab. del.* 'made
*for [*undel. in error*] the mere
purpose of'
††162.18 sake of exerting] 'exerting'
bef. del. 'the'
162.19 Only] *aft. del.* 'They *no
[*doubtful*]'
162.19 upon] 'u' *ov. doubtful* 'a'
162.20 now thought] *intrl.*
162.21 men] *ab. del.* 'tribes'
162.22 the males] ('the' *alt. fr.* 'them';
'males' *intrl.*); *aft. del.* 'the men or
enslave'
162.23 females,] *ab. del.* 'women,'
††162.23-24 profitable . . . exciting ₍ₐ₎]
ab. del. 'remunerative'
162.24 living] *aft. del.* 'making a'
163.1 selected,] *comma insrtd. bef.
del.* 'for *supremacy, [*comma
insrtd. for del. colon or semicolon*]'
163.1 chiefs] *aft. del.* 'both'
163.1 peoples] 's' *added*
163.1 a] *ab. del.* '['ambition & love of
glory' *del.*] the love of plunder
*mixed with [*ab. del.* 'developed
into']'
163.1 love of] *ab. del.* 'love of'
††163.2 glory.] *period undel. in error*
†163.2-3 came . . . plunder.] *ab. del.*
'The pugnacity and glory we to day inherit, *tho ['o' *ov.* 'e']'
163.4 Modern] *opp. mrgn.* '¶'; 'M' *ov.* 'm'
163.4 we . . . be] *ab. del.* 'trade has
proved'
163.5 modern . . . all the] *ab.* 'the
[*undel. in error*]'

163.6 all the] *insrtd.*
163.6 war's ['economic' *del.*]] *ab. del.*
 'up the'
††163.7 is of no . . . him.] ('no' *insrtd.*
 for del. 'little'); *ab. del.* 'won't do.'
163.8 ¹life] *ab. del.* 'thing'
163.8 ²life] *ab. del.* 'human nature'
††163.8 extremis;] *semicolon ov.*
 colon
163.9 ones] *ab. del.* 'taxes'
††163.9 to pay,–] 'to' *ab. del.* 'about';
 'ing' *del. fr.* 'paying'; *comma ov.*
 colon; dash ov. 'a'

163.9-10 as . . . show.] 'grumble they
 may, but they *don't [*ab. del.*
 'never'] hesitate. Look at our *naval
 [²'a' *ov.* 'e'] budget, look at our
 Panama canal ['paid for as' *del.*]
 bills, ['needful as a military necessity.' *del.*] met because of military
 necessity.'
163.11 a] *ab. del.* 'one'
163.11 recital] 'c' *ov. possible* 'l'
163.11 how] *intrl.*
††163.14 pure jingoism] 'pure' *ab. del.*
 'what'

b. Alterations in TMs(MS)

[*begin* TMs]
162.12 legends,] *comma added in ink*
163.2 glory ∧] *comma ink del.*
163.20 Those] 'o' *in ink ov.* 'e'
†164.10-13 hundred . . . fight.] *fol.* 6
 insrtd. for ink del. '[*fol.* 7] hundred
 and fifty *in number. [*undel. in*
 error]'
164.11 was . . . all,'] *in ink ab. ink*
 del. 'again, the noble stoic Brutus,'
††164.11 but to reanimate] ('to' *aft.*
 del. 'to'); *in ink ab. ink del.*
 'promises'
164.12 on . . . ¹of] *in ink ab. ink del.*
 'before'
††164.12 he similarly . . . them] ('similarly' *insrtd.*); *in ink ab. ink del.* 'he
 will give them ['the' *typed-del.*] two
 cities to spoil and plunder,'
†164.13 fight.] *bef. ink del. insrtd.*
 '[¶] Such treatment of non-comba-
 tant countries has ceased since the
 ['french' *del.*] french revolution'
164.14 Such was] *in ink ab. ink del.*
 'This is'
164.14 that] *bef. ink del.* 'has [*ink*
 intrl.]'
164.14 cohesiveness.] *period insrtd.*
 in ink bef. ink del. 'in its infancy.
 Dead men tell no tales. Tribes of
 any other type than this, if there
 were any, have left no survivors, no
 defenders of their type of character.'
164.15-16 heroism] *bef. ink del.*
 ', martyrdom, endurance,'

164.16-17 history.] *bef. ink del.* 'It
 has bred pugnacity into our bone
 and *marrow, [*comma ink insrtd.*]
 and thousands of years of peace
 won't breed it out of us.'
[*end* TMs; *begin* MS]
164.17 were] *bef. del.* 'any tribes'
164.17 type] *insrtd. for del.* '*['temper' *del.*] sort [*ab. del.* 'type']'
164.18 survivors.] *period insrtd. for*
 del. ', no ['ex' *del.*] defenders of
 their type of *character– [*dash ov.*
 period] Modern *war['s' *del.*] ['is
 merciful low' *del. intrl.*] spares
 non-combatants and neutral countries: [*dash del.*] so much is gained–
 save where as in ['China' *del.*] far
 away China the people seemed so
 alien that'
164.18 Our] *ab. del.* 'Our predacious'
164.18 bred] *ov.* 'bread'
164.19 our] *ab. del.* 'the'
164.19 marrow,] *comma insrtd. bef.*
 del. 'of us'
164.20 fairly] *intrl.*
164.21 thought] *aft. del.* 'Nevertheless'
164.21 wars.] *ab. del.* 'fighting. Public
 opinion, reading the word *WAR
 [*ov.* 'war'] in capitals three inches
 high in every newspaper for three
 months overpowered the pliant vote-
 catcher McKinley'
164.21 public opinion once] *ab. del.* 'it'
164.22 fighting] *intrl.*
164.22 pitch,] *comma insrtd. bef.*

del. 'of war*-tension [*ab. del.* '['excitement' *del.*] expectancy,']'

164.23 governments] *ab. del.* 'sides'

164.24 military . . . them.] ('tension was' *ab. del.* 'excitement was'; 'them' *ov.* 'it'); *ab. del.* 'fighting instincts got away with'

164.27 eagerness,] *ab. del.* 'pressure,'

164.29 At the] 'At' *ov.* 'The'; 'the' *intrl.*

164.29 day,] *ab. del.* 'state of opinion'

164.29 is] *ab. del.* 'about war *shows [*ab. del.* 'is']'

164.29 mental] *aft. del.* 'mixture of'

164.30 The] *aft. del.* 'For more than a century humanitarianism, ['has' *del.*] so-called,'; *bef. del.* 'old'

164.30 are . . . but] *intrl.*

164.31 by] *ab. del.* 'with *a [*intrl.*]'

164.31 criticisms] *final* 's' *added*

164.31 which] *bef. del.* '['make['s' *del.*] it impossible for them to express themselves with' *del.*] *much ['impede' *del.*] [*intrl.*] their [*ov.* 'the'] ancient freedom. *To ['make' *del.*] wage a [*intrl.*] War['s' *del.*; 'W' *unreduced in error*] ['of' *del.*] purely ['ly' *added*] *for loot and glory is [*ab. del.* 'glory and conquest are'] no longer ['con-' | *del.*] justified *by conscience [*intrl.*] and the ['sentimental' *del.*] humanitarianism, so called, which for more than a century has increasingly asserted itself, has awakened'

164.31 sorely curb] *ab. del.* '['whi' *del.*] greatly bear'

164.33 morally] *insrtd. for del.* 'publicly'

††164.34 a motives,] ('a' *undel. in error; probably false start of* 'as'); *intrl. bef. del.* '*as our own motives [*ab. del.* 'motives,']'

164.34 pretexts] *aft. del.* 'it'

164.34 attributing] *ab. del.* 'charging'

164.35 solely to] *insrtd. for del.* 'upon'

164.35 we,] *comma insrtd. bef. del.* 'must arm for 'peace,' Germany and Japan it is'

164.36 authorities] *intrl. bef. del.* 'officers [*ab. del.* ', professionals']'

164.36 without ceasing,] *ab. del.* 'must'

164.36 solely] *intrl.*

164.36 Germany] *aft. del.* 'exquisite verbal discovery—'

164.37 'Peace'] *aft. penc. del.* 'In Germany and Japan one *hears ['s' *ov.* 'd'] the opposite story.'; *bef. del.* ', in our modern dictionaries'

164.38 a] *intrl.*

164.38 synonym for] *alt. fr.* 'synonymous with'

††164.38-39 expected. ∧ . . . provocative,] *ab. del.* 'in *posse*, and the dictionaries should so define it. *No [*ov.* 'A']'

164.39 and no] *insrtd.*

164.40 allow] *ab. del.* 'forbid'

†164.40 it ever] *intrl. aft. del.* '*the printing of the word ['it ever' *del.*] [*ab. del.* 'either the word war or ['of' *del.*] the word peace']'

164.40 to be printed] ('printed' *bef. del.* 'in'); *intrl.*

†164.40-165.1 Every . . . say] '['It has become a pure provocative. The' *del. intrl.*] ['The dic'| *del.*] Dictionary ['Dic ['D' *ov.* 'd']' *insrtd.*; 'y' *ov.* 'ies'] should *Every [*alt. fr.* 'Each'] up to date [*intrl.*; *placement of caret in error*] say [*ab. del.* 'take notice']'

165.1 and] *insrtd. aft. del.* 'means ['all' *del.*] the thrill of war will ['and' *del.*]'

165.2 ¹now] *intrl.*

165.2 ²now] *ov.* 'or [*ab. del.* 'and']'

165.7 civilized man] '['the' *del.*] civilized ['mind' *del.*] man' *ab. del.* 'of war *human ['h' *ov.* 'n'] nature'

165.7 developed a] ('a' *ab. del.* 'into a'); *aft. del.* 'wa'

165.8 double personality.] (*period insrtd. bef. del.* 'for itself.'); *ab. del.* 'divided self. ['No' *del.*] No [*insrtd.*] one would have past wars expunged; yet'

165.8 If we take] *penc. insrtd.*

165.8 european] *ab. del.* '['As ['A' *ov.* 'a'] among [*ab. del.* 'between']' *penc. del.*] civilized'

165.8 legitimate] *intrl. aft. del. intrl.* 'country's'

165.9 any one of them] *ab. del.* 'which

any one of them could legitimately linger,'

165.9 tremendous] *intrl. bef. del.* 'wholesale [*ab. del.* '['immense' *del.*] immensity of']'

165.10 destructions] *final* 's' *added; bef. del.* 'of value which'

††165.10 necessarily] ('t' *in error*); *intrl. bef. del. intrl.* 'needs'

165.11 common . . . reason] *aft. del.* 'some reasonable *agreement [*ab. del.* 'equilibrium'] ['might be rea' *del.*] ought always to be reacht by'; *bef. del.* '[*on fol.* 12] ['. Neverhteless [*error*] ['the' *del.*] unassuageable ambition ['of' *del.*] is the soul of patriotism' *del.*] | [*fol.* 14] ought to find a way to reach agreement in every *honest conflict of interests. [*penc. ab. del.* 'genuinely'] ['case of right.' *del.*] ['righteous case.' *penc. del.*] Yet at the same time *['extravagant' *del.*] ['inordinate' *del.*] ['unrighteous' *del. ab. del. insrtd.* 'inordinate'] [*ab. del.* 'unassuageable'] ambitions ['s' *added*] are [*ab. del.* 'is'] the soul of every patriotism; war is the *['great' *del.*] popular [*intrl.*] romance ['of history; and' *del.*] The ['T' *ov.* 't'] military-minded everywhere, ['and' *del.*] especially ['cially' *undel. in error*]'

165.16 certain deficiencies] *alt. fr.* 'a certain deficiency'

165.18 In] *ov.* 'in'; *aft. del.* 'on both sides'

165.18 the] *ov.* 'this'

††165.18-19 Both . . . ground.] ('Both [*unreduced in error*] sides are on' *ab. del.* 'We are on strictly'; *period insrtd.*); *ab. caret formed fr. orig. period aft.* 'discussion'; *moved fr. aft.* 'it.' [165.18]

165.21 characterize] *ab. del.* '['ex' *del.*] tell'

165.22 strokes] *bef. del.* 'what seem to me'

165.24 conciliation.] *alt. fr.* 'conciliatory action.'

††165.25 pacifist as I am] *intrl.*

165.25 refuse . . . of] *ab. del.* 'avert my attention from'

††165.26 the war ⌃ régime] 'the' *intrl.*; 'régime['] *del.*]' *insrtd.*

165.27 aspects] *ab. del.* 'side'

165.28 Patriotism] *aft. del.* 'Inordinate ambitions are the'

165.28 discreditable;] *semicolon bef. del.* '. Yet inordinate'

165.30 ²the . . . violent] *alt. fr.* 'death and violence'; *bef. del.* 'the and'

165.31 The] *aft. del. circled note* 'no break'

165.32 to] *aft. del.* 'for a moment to admit the supposition that'

165.33 for] *aft. del.* 'even'

165.33 war] *intrl. aft. del.* '*['it' *del.*] war [*ab. del.* 'way [*error*]']'

165.33 phenomenon in] *ab. del.* 'phase in'

165.34 social] *penc. ab. ink del.* '['social [*ab. del.* 'human']'*del.*] history. ['Such a sheep's paradise is intolerable to the' *del.*] the [*penc. del.*]'

165.34 evolution.] *period in penc. bef. penc. del.* 'of society.'

165.34 The notion of] *ab. del.* 'Such'

165.34 a] *ov.* 'be'

165.34 like that ['would' *del.*]] *intrl.*

165.35 imagination.] *period ov. comma bef. del.* '*we hear. [*penc. insrtd.*]'

165.35 Where] *alt. fr.* 'When'

165.35 then] *intrl. aft. del. intrl.* 'then'

165.35-36 the . . . life?] *ab. del.* 'the heights and depths?'

165.36 war] *final* 's' *del.*

165.36 had ever stopped,] ('ever' *ab. del.* 'never been,'); *ab. del.* 'did not exist,'

165.36 re-invent] 're-' *intrl.*

165.36 it,] *intrl. bef. del.* '*['save' *del.*] it, [*ab. del.* 'them']'

†165.36-37 in . . . to] *intrl. aft. del.* '*to [*insrtd.*] ['regain' *del.*] regain [*ab. del.* 'to save human nature']'

†165.37 redeem . . . degeneration.] *insrtd. for del.* '*get some lost [*ab. del.* 'regain the'] manliness *back into the [*ab. del.* 'of'] human *soul. [*ab. del.* 'nature, [*comma ov. period*]']'

165.39 profits are] *ab. del.* 'gains are'

†165.40-166.1 any . . . profit,] *ab. del.* 'the question of gains,'

166.1 an] *aft. del.* '*however dreadful [*ab. del.* ', at any rate']'

166.3 the] *ov.* 'a'

166.3 only . . . a] ('only' *insrtd.*; 'supposed' *aft. del.* 'of a'); *intrl.*

166.3 world] *bef. del.* '['entirely' *del.*] wherein the highest virtues would be commercial, ['of philan' *del.*] of cosmopolitanism *& [*ab. del. comma*] philanthropism, feminism, *and [*ab. del.* 'zoophily,'] co-education, ['college' *del.*] settlements, and socialism. *consumer's leagues [*insrtd.*]'

166.4 co-education] *aft. del.* 'zoophily and'

166.4 and zoophily,] *ab. caret formed fr. orig. comma*

166.5 'associated charities,'] *ab. del.* 'college settlements,'

166.5 industrialism] *aft. del.* 'industrialism and feminism'

166.5-6 unabashed] *aft. del.* 'unrebuked.'

†166.6-7 No . . . planet!] ('hardness,' *ab. penc. del.* 'callousness,'; '*any more!*' *insrtd.*; 'F' *of* 'Fie' *ov.* 'f'); *insrtd.*

166.8 So] *aft.* '¶' *insrtd. in mrgn.*

166.8 central] *intrl.*

†166.9-10 partaking . . . degree.] '*to some degree partaking of [*ab. del.* 'sharing'] it. [*period insrtd. for del.* 'strongly. War is the great']'

166.10 Militarism] *aft. del.* 'The'; *alt. fr.* 'military'; *bef. del.* 'regime is the'

166.10 is the] ('the' *ab. del. insrtd.* 'one'); *insrtd.*

166.10 of ['the' *del.*] our] *insrtd. for del.* 'and hardihoods'

166.10 of hardihood,] *moved fr. aft.* 'preserver'

166.11 human] *bef. del.* '*['life' *del.*] life with no further [*insrtd. for del.* 'nature without']'

†166.11 life without] ('life' *ab. del.* 'need for'); *ab. del. insrtd.* 'sans [*ab. del. doubtful caret or* 'A']'

166.11 contemptible] *ab. del.* '['a' *del.*] fearfully [*ab. del.* 'mawkish and'] insipid. ['thing.' *del.*]'

166.11-12 Without] *alt. fr.* 'with no

desperate'; *aft.* '—History [*undel. in error*]'

166.12 history] *intrl.*

166.12 insipid] *ab. del.* 'mawkish'

166.13 type] *aft. del.* 'certain'

166.13 military] *intrl.*

166.13 which] *aft. del.* '*fostered ['produced' *del.*] by [*ab. del.* ', bred in'] militarism alone, ['of' *del.*]'

††166.13-14 that the race,] ('the' *bef. del.* 'our'; *comma undel. in error*); *ab. del.* 'the ['s' *del.*] immediate superiority and which *mankind one feels, [*ab. del.* '['the world can never afford to lose.' *del.*] humanity']'

166.14 breed,] *comma ov. period*

166.14-15 for . . . superiority.] ('sensitive' *alt. fr.* 'sensible'); *intrl.*

166.15 of] *insrtd.*

166.15-16 military characters] ('characters ['s' *added*]' *ab. del.* 'virtues'); *aft. del.* 'the'

166.16 ends] 's' *ab. del.* 's'; *aft. del.* 'an [*intrl.*]'

166.17 themselves] *ab. del.* 'itself [*insrtd. for del.* 'themselves']'

166.17 pure . . . perfection] '['as a' *del. intrl.*] pure *pieces of [*intrl.*] perfection['s [*ab. del.* 's']' *del.*]'

††166.20 natural sort of] *ab. del.* '*simple and [*ab. del.* 'direct and'] praiseworthy'

166.20 of] *bef. del.* 'a couple of defences ['c' *ov.* 's'] of war which I have just been reading, one by an american army officer,[x] the other by a German (or dutch) anthropologist and statistician.[†] | [*fn.*] [x]Homer Lea: The Valor of Ignorance, N.Y., Harpers, 1909 | [*fn.*] [†] S.R. Steinmetz: *Die [*intrl.*] Philosophie des Krieges, Leipzig, Barth, 1907.'

†166.20-22 army- . . . and] *insrtd.*

166.21 Without] *aft. del.* 'Almost'; 'W' *ov.* 'w'

166.22 regard] *aft. del.* 'Both writers take a highly metaphysical view of their subject. Both'

†166.23 or . . . necessity,] *ab. del.* 'function'

166.23-24 psychological] *ab. del.* 'practical'

166.24 checks and motives.] *alt. fr.*
'motives and *cheeks [*error*].'
166.25 ¹the] *ab. del.* 'the'
166.26 a] *ov.* 'an'
166.26-27 permanent human *obligation.*] *ab. del.* 'obligatory and permanent function *based on [*ab. del.*
'of'] man [*alt. fr.* 'man's'; *undel. in
error*] nature *as a [*insrtd.*; *undel. in
error*] social beings, *and never to be
out-grown. [*ab. caret formed fr. orig.
period*] The American writer considers readiness for it to be the essence of nationality, and ability in it
the supreme'
166.30 nations.] *bef. del.* 'German
writers^x treat it as a duty fatally imposed by God, who weighs the na-
tions in its balance. | [*fn.*] e.g. S.R.
Steinmetz: Die Philosophie des
Krieges'
166.31 Nations] 'N' *ov.* 'n'; *aft. del.*
'[*fol.* 15c: *draft of deletion at top of
fol.* 15b; *see alts. entry* 166.22]
'Both writers take *a metaphysical
[*ab. del.* 'the religious'] view of *war.
[*period ov. comma; doubtful* 'X'
del.] ['regarding it as a fatal necessity imposed on many by God who
weighs' *del.*] The american *considers [*ab. del.* 'treats it as *the [*ab.
del.* 'a'] necessary'] *military
**agressiveness [*alt. fr.* 'aggression']
['the' *del.*] [*ab. del.* 'symptom of
health and vitality'] *to be [*intrl.*]
the essence of *nationality [¹'n' *ov.*
'a'], ['and *appetite for war [*ab. del.*
'war']' *del.*] ['as' *del.*] the ['one
symptom' *del. ab. del.* 'one mark']
['*supreme measure of [*ab. del.* 'of']
a nation's health and vitality in a'
del.] nations, ['s,' *ov.* 's'] [*del.* 'resolute deliberate pacifism spelling nothing but disease and death, the german
treats it as a fatal duty ['(and by God'
del.] imposed by man on God who
weighs the peoples in its balance and
readiness for war the supreme
mea-'|] ['measure ['mea' *insrtd.*]'
del.] of *the [*intrl.*] health *of [*ov.*
'a'] nations. [*period insrtd. bef. del.
semicolon*] The ['T' *ov.* 't'] German

treats *it [*ab. del.* 'war'] as a duty
fatally imposed ['on man' *del.*] by
God, who weighs the peoples in its
balance. As the american's *thesis
[*ab. del.* 'state of mind'] is much the
*cruder [*ab. del.* 'simpler'] I will
speak of it ['first and by itself.' *del.*]
['by itself.' *del.*] first. ['¶' *in mrgn.*]
['The boundaries of' *del.*]'
166.31-32 necessarily ... shrink,]
('necessarily ex-'| *bel. del.* 'ex-'|);
insrtd.
166.34 her] *insrtd. aft. del.* 'she should
not aspire to the mastery of the
whole pacific ocean, and impossible
being what she is that her'
166.34 long] *aft. del.* 'have'
†166.34-36 have ... which] ('foresight,' *ab. del.* 'entered'; 'vast' *aft. del.*
'adopted *a [*del. in error*]'; 'the' *ov.*
'a' *bef. del.* 'policy of which'); *ab.
del.* '['have formed a plan' *del.*] decided on a plan for possessing ['the
whole *Pacific ['P' *ov.* 'p'] Ocean'
del.] the whole Pacific Ocean, a plan
of which'
166.36 moves] *ab. del.* 'steps'
166.36 her] *ab. del.* 'the Chinese and
the Russian'
166.36 China and Russia] *penc. alt. fr.*
'Russia & China'
166.37 her] *ab. del.* 'the'
166.38 capture] *ab. del.* '['conquest of
the Ph' *del.*] capture'
166.40 ¹her] *ab. del.* 'destiny'
166.40 vocation] *ab. del.* 'destiny
requires.'
166.40 forces] *ab. del.* 'requires'
167.1 oppose] *ab. del.* 'meet'
167.2 we Americans] *intrl. for del.*
'*the United States [*ab. del.* 'we']'
167.3 nothing but] *insrtd. for del.* 'save'
167.3 conceit] *aft. del.* 'conceited
optimistic'
167.5 military strength] *ab. del.* 'force'
167.6 oppose] *alt. fr.* 'opposite'
167.6 strength] *aft. del.* 'present'
167.7 fall] *ab. del.* 'be occupied by
Japan'
167.8 that] *ov.* 'a'
167.8 must surrender] *ab. del.* 'would
yield'

167.12   until perhaps] ('perhaps'
   insrtd.); *aft. del.* 'into'
167.12   should] *ab. del.* 'should'
167.14   not] *aft. del.* 'one'; *bef. del.* 'so
   very'
167.15   mentality] *ab. del.* 'psychology'
167.15   statesmen be of] ('be of' *ab.
   del.* 'is'); *aft. del.* 'leading'
167.15   Caesarian] *aft. del.* 'only'
167.15-16   type . . . and] *ab. del.*
   'mentality [*ab. del.* 'psychology']'
167.16   all that] *insrtd. for del.* '*the
   only type [*ab. del.* 'all that']'
167.18   women . . . Napoleonic] *ab. del.*
   'the mill of human generation
   [*would have ceased to [*ab. del.* 'has
   ceased to'] produce' *del.*] will *bring
   forth [*ab. del.* 'produce'] no more
   Caesarian'
167.19   these] *ab. del.* 'they'
167.19   in Japan] *intrl.*
167.20   just] *aft. del.* 'such'
†167.20-21   *The Valor of Ignorance*]
   intrl. for del. '*this book [*ab. del.*
   'Gen. Lea our author']'
167.21   lurk] *aft. del.* 'be in reserve'
167.21   still] *intrl.*
†167.22   the . . . mentality,] *ab. del.*
   'the japanese psychology,'
167.22   may] *ab. del.* 'should'
†167.23   disregarding such possibilities.] *ab. del.* 'deny [*insrtd. for del.*
   'ignore'] ['the' *del. ab. del.* 'that']
   *all possibility of [*intrl.*] danger.
   *from that quarter. [*added*]'
167.24-29   Other . . . save] *fol.* 18½
   insrtd. for del. '[*on fol.* 18] The
   German writer's book is ['less concrete but' *del.*] more complex *&
   more moral [*intrl.*] He ['min' *del.*]
   ['weighs' *del.*] treats of war in general, & weighs its advantages *con-
   scientiously [*intrl.*] against its
   drawbacks. Its supreme *value [*ab.
   del.* 'advantage'] is that ['of' *del.*
   insrtd.] *by forcing [*alt. fr.* 'it
   forces'; *insrtd. for del.* 'of a training
   school of collective effort [', as
   distinguished from' *del.*] in which
   ['in' *del.*] the selfishness of *forces
   [*ov.* 'forcing'; *moved fr. aft.*
   'which']'] individuals into collective

service, *it [*insrtd.*] *['gets' *del.*]
lifts them out of their **inferiority
[*alt. fr.* 'inferior'] and [*ab. del.* 'and
makes them sacrifice their'] selfishness. ['Militarism is the' *del.*] The
military form is the | [*fol.* 19] [*del.*
'essential form of *nations, [*ab. del.*
'the states;'] and war is the only function in which *states [*ab. del.* 'the
states [*final* 's' *added*]'] employ['s'
del.; *undel. in error*] all *their forces
[*ab. del.* 'its *faculties ['ies' *ov.* 'y']']
['together and' *del. intrl.*] *at once
and [*intrl.*] convergently. No victory
save']'
167.24   Other] *ab. del.* 'The *Continen-
   tal ['C' *ov.* 'c']'
167.30   for which some] *ab. del.* '['save
   under' *del.*] to'
167.31   not responsible.] ('responsible.'
   aft. del. 'to blame.'); *ab. del.* '['cohesive no' *del.*] cohesivenes [*or*
   'cohesive no']'
167.31   tenacity] *aft. del.* 'in [*doubtful*] patience,'
167.32   heroism,] *bef. del.* 'honesty
   dutifulness, intelligence, economy,
   forethought, strength and health,
   there isn't a gift'
167.33   physical] *aft. del.* 'health,'
167.33   point] *aft. del.* 'environ [*ab.
   del.* 'virtue'] that doesn't *tell*, in'
167.34   when] *aft. del.* 'in the ['secur-
   ing of victories' *del.*] beating of an
   enemy.'
167.34   God] *final* 's' *del.*
167.35   peoples upon one another.]
   alt. fr. 'nations at each other's
   throats.'
167.36   believe] *aft. del.* 'belief'
167.36   in . . . run] *moved fr. bef.* 'Dr.'
   [167.36]
167.37   chance and luck] *ab. del.*
   '['accidents' *del.*] luck and accident'
††167.37   the issues ⌄] (*no period in
   error*); *ab. del.* 'victory or defeat.'
167.38   anyhow,] *comma ov. period
   bef. del.* 'They ['are all virtues in a
   state' *del.*] are virtues and'
167.39   count] *ab. del.* 'prevail'
167.40   being] *ab. del.* 'is'
167.40   intenser] *aft. del.* 'harder'

168.1 makes war] ('war' *ov.* 'a'; *bef. del.* 'an'); *ab. del.* '['so the' *del.*] is'

168.1 as a trial.] ('as' *insrtd.*); *ab. del. period*

168.2 its] *ab. del.* 'wars'

168.2 winnowings.] 's.' *ov. period bef. del.* 'Nothing hammers *['states' *del.*] men [*ab. del.* 'people'] ['into cohesion' *del.*] *into states [*ab. del.* '['natio' *del.*] ['not' *del.*] form'] like its dread necessities, and the form of the state ['makes states cohesive' *del.*]'

168.3 welder] *intrl. bef. del.* 'creator [*ab. del.* 'welder']'

168.3 men into] *ab. del.* 'the states''

168.3 cohesive states,] 'cohesive' *alt. fr.* 'cohesiveness'; '['of' *del.*] states,' *intrl.*

168.3-4 nowhere but in such] *ab. del.* 'it is only in the form of cohesive'

168.4 can] *insrtd. for del.* ', according to our author *does [*ab. del.* 'that']'

168.4 adequately] *ab. del.* 'shows its full'

168.4 develope['s' *del.*]] *alt. fr.* 'development'; *bef. del.* 'to'

168.5 capacity] *aft. del.* 'full'

††168.6 Dr. Steinmetz.,] *aft. del.* 'So *much [*ov.* 'So'] for'; *comma insrtd. aft. period, and both undel. in error*

168.6 is a] *aft. del.* '*who [*ov.* 'He'] [*ab. del.* 'is a human']'

168.6 thinker, and his] *comma ov. period ov. comma*; 'and' *ab. del.* 'and'; 'his' *ov.* 'His'

168.6 as] *insrtd. for del.* 'the [*ab. del.* 'as']'

168.7 much] *ab. del.* '['an immense n' *del.*] a multitude of elements'

†168.7 Its . . . can] ('Its' *bef. del.* 'The'); *ab. del.* '['The way of thinking which he represents' *del.*] It can all'

168.8 word] *final* 's' *del.*

168.8 mankind] *ab. del.* 'mankind'

168.8-9 was . . . *the [*penc.*]] *intrl. aft. del.* '*owes what strength it possesses [*ab. del.* '['was nurtured in' *del.*] was [*insrtd.*] nursed in a pain economy and that']'

168.10 fatal] *bef. del.* '*as he [*insrtd.*

for del. '*to a being [*insrtd. for del.* ', as he']']'

†168.10-11 [1]to . . . influences.] 'to ['such' *del.*] a being [*comma del.*] wielding [*ab. del.* 'owning, as he does,'] no powers of defense against its disintegrative influences.' *ab. del.* 'who [*insrtd.*] owns [*ab. del.* 'has *evolved [*intrl.*]'] no faculties evolved for meeting its relaxing influences.'

168.11 If . . . of] *ab. del.* '*If we say of *'fear ['f' *ov.* 'F'] ['to lose' *del.*] [*ab. del.* 'We should']'

168.12 we] *intrl.*

168.12 put] *final* 's' *del.*

168.13 regarding] *intrl. aft. del.* 'of'

168.13 [2]fear] *aft. del.* 'salutary [*intrl.*]'

168.15 Turn] 'T' *ov.* 'F'

††168.15 fear over as] *ab. del.* '['matter' *del.*] how'

168.15 lead back] ('back' *aft. del.* 'us'); *ab. del.* 'revert'

168.16 two] *ov.* 'an'; *bef. del.* 'innate ['ne' *del.*] unwillingnesses. ['es.' *added bef. del.* 'to *forfeit forever [*ab. del.* 'abolish'] the *wild [*insrtd.*] charm, on the one hand, of so many elements of the military life, and']'

168.16 unwillingnesses] 'es' *added*

168.17 in] *bef. del.* 'from [*ab. del.* 'in']'

168.17 army-] *ab. del.* '*a soldier's [*insrtd. for del.* 'the military']'

168.18 shall] *aft. del.* 'is'

168.19 the . . . peoples] *ab. del.* '['issues' *del. ab. del.* 'momentous things'] immense issues'

168.19 nevermore] *intrl.*

168.20 thrillingly, and tragically] *ab. del.* 'and excitingly,'

168.20 but] *aft. del.* 'and not by'

168.20-21 gradually and insipidly] *ab. del.* 'slowly'

168.21 by] *bef. del.* 'education and'

168.21 see the] *ab. del.* '['see the' *del.*] think *that [*ab. del.* 'of'] the splendid military aptitudes of human beings *as ['shall' *del.*] remaining ['ing' *added*] always [*intrl.*] buried in their breasts and never ['able to' *del.*]

displaying ['ing' *added*] themselves in action, an unwillingness to ['give up strenuous' *del.*] see the'

168.23-24 in . . . latency] *insrtd. for del.* '*latent and potential only, [*ab. del.* 'buried in their breasts']'

168.25 no less than] *ab. del.* 'have, it seems to me, like'

168.25 esthetic] *init.* 'a' *del.*

168.26 have . . . and] ('to be' *insrtd.*); *ab. del.* 'to be'

†168.27 mere . . . -insistency] *ab. del.* 'simply dwelling'

168.27-28 expensiveness and horror.] ('and horror.' *ab. caret formed fr. orig. period*); *aft. del.* 'horror['s' *del.*] and'

168.28 when] *aft. del.* 'expense is *nothing*'

168.29 the extremest] ('extremest' *ab. del.* 'utmost'); *aft. del.* 'human'

168.29 supremest] *ab. del.* 'most admirable'

168.30 talk['s' *del.*]] *aft. del.* 'whoever'

168.30 sounds] *ab. del.* 'is'

168.31 is] *aft. del.* 'on the part of so many ['of' *del.*] pacifists ['p' *ov.* 'to']'

168.31 pacificism] *ab. del.* 'they'

168.31 makes] 's' *added*

168.32 The . . . denies] *ab. del.* '['Horror and' *del.*] ['The horror and expenses are ['neither' *del.*] not' *del.*] Militarism ignores'

168.33-34 that these things] *aft. del.* 'that war is necessary and'; *bef. del.* 'don't incline the balance. So long as the peace-party ['makes' *del.*] offers no vision, in the pacific regime, of a ['strenuous' *del.*] kind of strenuous life'

168.34 tell but half the] ('but' *ab. del.* 'only'); *ab. del.* 'fail to tell the *whole* [*intrl.*]'

168.34 only] *intrl.*

†168.34-35 war . . . taking] *ab. del.* 'taking'

168.35 best] *ab. del.* 'its'

168.36 against] *ab. del.* 'from'

168.36 weaker] *ab. del.* 'lower'

168.36 mankind] *ab. del.* 'society'

168.38 to . . . into] *ab. del.* 'first of all to put themselves at'

168.39-40 Do . . . controversy,] *insrtd. for del.* '*First do that, then more [*ab. del.* 'Move the point,']'

168.40 says] *bef. del.* 'Dr. Cabot'

169.1 as] *bef. del.* 'the ['pacific par' *del.*] peace-party'

169.4 And] *bef. del.* 'the'

169.5 pictured in] *ab. del.* 'of all'

169.6 utopias they paint] ('they paint' *insrtd.*); *aft. del.* 'peace'

169.6 all] *intrl.*

169.6 to touch] *aft. del.* 'to s'; 'touch' *ab. del.* 'make *any [*insrtd. for del.* 'the right'] appeal to'

†169.7 -minded.] *aft. del.* '*types of [*ab. del.* 'imagination.']'

169.7 Tolstoy's] *aft. del.* 'Socialism'

169.7 is] *aft. del.* 'alone approaches'

169.9 Lord] *alt. fr.* 'lord's'

†169.9-10 furnish . . . elsewhere] '*furnish the [*ab. del.* 'wrath do'] the [*undel. in error*] *moral 'brace' furnished [*ab. del.* 'work done else-'|] else [*insrtd.*]'

169.11 instead of] *ab. del.* '['the' *del.*] the only substitute they offer for'

169.12 Lord and] *bef. del.* 'of the enemy is the fear of poverty if one be lazy.'

169.13 reckon with] ('reckon' *ov.* 'risk'); *ab. del.* 'talk of'

169.13 poverty] *ab. del.* 'small wages'

169.13 lazy] *aft. del.* 'too'

169.15 high] *final* 'er' *del.*

169.15 and] *aft. del.* 'is'

169.15 short] *final* 'er' *del.*

169.16 the only] *ab. del.* 'the only'

169.16 invoked for] *ab. del.* 'deemed sufficient to'

169.16 overcoming] 'ing' *ov.* 'e'; *bef. del.* 'the average'

169.17 repulsive kinds] ('kinds' *ab. del.* 'and dangerous forces'); *aft. del.* 'toilsome and'

169.17 men] *ab. del.* '['man' *del.*] at large mankind'

169.17 live] *final* 's' *del. insrtd. for del. final* 's'

169.17 they] *intrl. aft. del.* '['mankin *del.*] it' *ab. del.* 'he'

169.18 have] *ab. del.* 'has'

169.23 Inferiority] *aft. insrtd. vertical stroke and mrgn.* '¶'

169.23 ¹is] *ab. del.* 'must'

169.23 with] *aft. del.* 'be'; *alt. fr.* 'within'

169.23 us, ... scorn] *comma ov. period;* 'and merciless' *intrl.;* 's' *in* 'scorn' *ov.* 'S'

169.23 it] *ab. del.* 'inferiority, contemptuous and merciless treatment of it,'

169.24 the military temper.] 'the' *intrl.;* 'military temper.' *alt. fr.* 'militarism.'

169.25 shouted] *insrtd. for del.* 'said'

169.26 best] *aft. del. false start of letter*

169.27 tough] *ab. del.* 'hard'

169.28 morally ... insensitive.] '*morally **almost [*insrtd.*] as insensitive. [*ab. del.* 'callous.']'

169.28 see] *ab. del.* 'make'

169.30 it] *insrtd. for del.* 'the inferiority'

169.30 meritorious] *alt. fr.* 'meritoriously serviceable' *ab. del.* 'note of professional character and merit.'

††169.30 needed by ⌃the service,⌃] ('by' *ov.* 'in'); *ab. del.* ', no longer leave it a mark'

169.31 the suspicion] ('suspicion' *ab. del.* 'consciousness'); *aft. del.* 'inferiority'

169.31 All] *aft. del.* 'A man's'

169.32 acquire] *ab. del.* 'rise in'

169.32 that] *ov.* 'them'; *bef. del.* 'to be needed by'

169.33 that ... them.] 'that owns him' *ab. del.* 'he belongs to'; 'needs them.' *ab. caret formed fr. orig. comma*

169.34 own] *ab. del.* 'self'

169.34 is] *intrl.*

169.34 an] *aft. del.* 'th'

169.35 such] *ab. del.* 'this'

169.35 the only] *aft. del.* '['the only emotions' *del.*] ['only collectivity can' *del.*] collectivity sl'

169.36 pacific] *aft. del.* 'cosmopolitan pacifi'

169.37 breasts] *in penc. ab. del.* 'minds'

169.38 *such] penc. underl. added*

†169.38-170.5 It ... to?] '[*fol.* 25½]

It is obvious that ['to the mind of a Homer Lea,' *del.*] the United States of America ['are but a vast & i' *del.*] as they *exist to day, seem to ['th' *del.*] a mind like Homer Lea's, but a sort of vast and ignominious moral jelly. [*undel. in error along w.* 'Where ... -tax visible' (170.1-4); *see end of entry*]' *marked by light ink mrgn. note* 'insert in p. 25' *which corresponds to note in light ink on fol.* 25 'insert 25½' *insrtd. aft.* 'collectivity.' [169.38] *Fol.* 25 *followed by typed fol.* 23 *(revised in penc. and ink) fr. a later draft which reads* 'exist to-day [*comma ink del.*] impress [*ink ab. ink. del.* 'affect' *ab. ink del.* 'seem, [*comma insrtd.*] to'] a mind like Homer Lea's *as [*bef. ink del.* 'a sort of' *ab. ink del.* ', but a *like [*penc. insrtd.*]'] *so much human [*ink bef. ink del.* '[*penc.* 'so much' *del.*] sort of' *ab. ink del.* '*sort of [*ink del.*] *vast and ignominious [*penc. del.*]'] blubber. [*penc.*] [*ab. penc. del.* 'moral jelly.'] Where is the sharpness and precipitousness, the contempt for life, *whether one's own, or another's [*comma del.*]? Where is [*ink insrtd.*] the savage yes and no, the unconditional duty? Where is the conscription? where is the *blood-tax? ['?' *insrtd. for del.* 'visible?'; *ab. period undel. in error*] *Where [*cap. doubtful*] is anything that one **feels [*ab. del.* 'is'] honored by belonging to? [*ink insrtd.*]' *which is revision of* '[*on fol.* 25] *Where is the sharpness and precipitousness, the contempt for life, ['&' *del.*] the ['stern & imperious' *del.*] ['stern imperativeness,' *del.*] savage yes and no, the unconditional duty? Where is the conscription? where ['in short' *del.*] is the blood-tax *visible? [*insrtd. for del.* '?'] [*undel. in error because of probable verbal instruction to typist; see textual discussion p.* 57]'

170.6-8 Having ... peace] *fol.* 24, 25 ['½' *del.*] *orig. insertion for del.* '[*bottom fol.* 25] Instead of these, one thinks of preference['s' *del.*], and postponement['s' *del.*], *& in-

dulgences [*ab. del.* 'of inducements,']
*which [*ov.* 'not'] are not [*ab. del.*
'instead of'] commands, of flabbi-
ness, gelatinousness, | [*fol.* 26] ['and
tepid' *del.*] and tolerance of every
*weakness. [*ab. del.* 'inferiority.']
[¶] Now I devoutly believe, myself,
in the triumph of the party of peace,'
170.7 will] *ab. del.* 'may'
170.7 confess] *ab. del.* '['write down
m' *del.*] ['conf' *del.*] write down'
170.8 ¹in] *bef. del.* '['peac' *del.*]
peace'
170.9 advent] *aft. del.* 'gro'
170.9 The] 'T' *ov.* 't'; *aft. del.* 'I disbelieve in'; *bef. del.* 'religious or'
†170.10 is . . . know] *ab. del.* 'and
think'
170.11 is . . . subject] ('is' *insrtd.*;
comma aft. 'motives' *undel. in error*;
'&' *insrtd.*); *ab. del.* ', [*comma undel.*
in error] · | is just as *much ['of an'
del.] [*ab. del.* '['amenable to an' *del.*]
['the' *del.*] ordinary'] ['a' *del. insrtd.*
for del. 'a'] psychological process
*like [*ab. del.* 'as'] any other sort of
enterprise, and ['sub' *del.*] amenable'
170.11 prudential] *aft. del.* 'the same
checks and'
170.12 criticisms,] *comma ov. period*
170.12 just . . . enterprise.] ('form of'
insrtd.); *ab. del.* 'War between'
††170.12-13 And When] 'And' *insrtd.*;
'When' *unreduced in error*
170.13 the armies,] *ab. del.* 'in arms,'
170.13 the science] *aft. del.* '['is' *del.*]
intellectually [*alt. fr.* 'intellectualist']
*the science of destruction [*moved*
fr. bef. 'is'] as powerfully as the'
170.13 destruction] 'ion' *insrtd. bef.*
del. '['ion is pursued as intellectually
as the' *del.*] ion ['enlists the highest
intellectual powers' *del.*] becomes in'
170.14 intellectual['ity' *del.*] refinement
[*intrl.*]] *aft. del.* 'refinement [*ab. del.*
'elaborateness'] and'
170.14 production] *ab. del.* 'construction'
170.14-15 I see that war] *insrtd. for*
del. 'the thing'
170.15 impossible from] *insrtd. for*
del. '*grows unmanageable from [*ab.*
del. 'breaks *down [*intrl.*] with'] '

170.15-16 monstrosity.] *insrtd. for*
del. '*unwieldiness. [*period insrtd.*
for del. '& overgrowth.'] [*ab. del.*
'magnitude. ['I believe that all this
is as' *del.*] Reasonable adjustments
must displace inord'] '
170.16 will have to] *ab. del.* '['. I
must' *del.*] give place to'
170.18-19 ∧yellow∧ . . . ∧white∧]
sg. qts. del.
170.19 future] *ab. del.* 'day'
170.20 formally] *ab. del.* 'officially'
170.21 of mine put] ('put' *insrtd. for*
del. 'class [*ab. del.* 'put'] '); *intrl.*
170.21 into] *ab. del.* 'on the side
*with [*ab. del.* 'of'] '
170.22 peace] *aft. del.* 'the'
170.22 either . . . or] *ab. del.* 'party'
170.22-23 ²be . . . unless ['the' *del.*]]
insrtd. for del. '(*begin indep. del.*)
triumph, or that it ought to *be
permanent, [*ab. del.* 'triumph,']
['unless the socialistic organizations'
del.] unless [*ab. del.* 'so long as']
*the states [*insrtd. for del.* 'the
pacifically organized states'] *shall
preserve [*ab. del.* 'of the future
*respect [*insrtd. for del.* 'include'
ab. del. 'exclude']'] in [*ab. del.*
'from'] their *constitution certain
elements [*ab. del.* 'program the
ideals'] ['to whom' *del.*] *of military
discipline. [*insrtd. for del.* 'of the
more reflective militarism of our
*time. [*ab. del.* 'day.'] ['is loyal.'
del.]'] The new economy must
*not simply be a [*insrtd. for del.* 'not
*be a simple [*ab. del.* 'be purely a']']
pleasure economy. (*end indep. del.*)
*In the [*ab. del.* 'The socialistic']
more or less socialistic ['regimen to'
del.] future *towards [*ab. del.* 'to']
which *man [*ab. del.* 'history']
seems *drifting ['working' *del.*] [*ab.*
del. 'pointing'] we [*intrl.*] must
*still hold fast to [*ab. del.* 'preserve
in the administration of peace some
of'] those *severities ['features'
del.] [*ab. del.* '['ster' *del.*] elements']
which answer *to our [*insrtd. for*
del. 'to *his [*ab. del.* 'man's']'] real
['animal' *del. ab. del.* 'biological']
position on this only partly hospit-

able globe, and which *may appear [*ab. del.* 'will be'] a *worthy [*ab. del.* 'fit'] succedaneum to the ideals of life to which the military party still is so loyal.'

170.23   the states] *aft. del.* 'in'

†170.23-24   preserve . . . -discipline.] ('pre' *insrtd.*; 'old' *intrl.*); *aft. del.* 'we [*insrtd. for del.* 'the states pacifically organized shall pre-' |]'; *moved fr. bef.* '['in' *del.*] the states' [170.23] *to aft.* 'organized [*period del. by caret*]'

††170.24-25   A successful] *ab. del.* 'The'

170.25   cannot] 'can' *ab. del.* 'must'

170.25-26   In the] *insrtd. for del.* '['In' *del.*] The [*ov.* 'the']'

170.26   towards] 'wards' *insrtd.*

170.27   we] *ab. del.* ', we'

†170.27   still . . . to] ('ourselves' *insrtd. for del.* 'itself'); *insrtd. for del.* '*resign ourselves to [*ab. del.* 'keep hold of']'

170.28   our] *intrl. bef. del.* 'the [*ab. del.* 'our']'

170.28   upon] *alt. fr.* 'on'; *aft. del.* '*of even [*intrl.*]'

170.29   make] ('k' *ov. illeg. letter*); *intrl. bef. del.* 'invent [*ab. del.* 'find']'

170.29   new energies and] *insrtd. for del.* '['one' *del.*] ['other [*insrtd.*] equivalents.' *del.*] ['other hardihoods' *del.*] constructive'

170.30   continue] *insrtd. for del.* '['and *energies [*ab. del.* 'manliness']' *del.*] and *heroisms [*alt. fr.* 'heroic'] ['duties,' *del.*] *to be ['a' *del.*] [*ab. del.* 'which may serve as *a [*ab. del.* 'an equivalent and']'] *as [*undel. in error*] ['successors' *del.*] legitimate successors of [*ab. del.* 'succedaneum to']'

170.30   manliness to] ('to' *ab. del.* 'to'); *aft. del.* 'energies'

170.30-31   so faithfully clings.] *ab. del.* 'is still so loyal to.'

170.31   Martial] 'M' *ov.* 'm'; *ab. del.* 'The *old [*intrl.*] heroic'

170.32   private] *aft. del.* 'one's perso'

170.33   upon] *ab. del.* 'on'

170.33   states are] *alt. fr.* 'the state is'

170.33-34   —unless] *dash intrl.*

††170.34   ∧ indeed ∧ . . . for] *ab. del.* 'we *are ready for [*ab. del.* 'wish for']'

†170.34-35   commonwealths . . . for] 'society fit for' *ab. del.* 'population [*ab. del.* 'housekeeping'] worthy only of'

170.35   liable to] *insrtd.*

170.35   invite] 'e' *ov.* 'ing'

170.36   a centre] *aft. del.* 'ever'

170.36   for] *ab. del.* '['of' *del.*] more'

170.36   enterprise] *aft. del.* 'men should get formed'

170.38   The] *aft. del.* 'The'; *bef. del.* 'milial'; '¶' *insrtd. in mrgn.*

170.40   goods.] *ab. del.* 'values.'

171.1   specifications] *alt. fr.* 'species'

171.2   competitive] *aft. del.* 'sort of'

171.2   are its] *ab. del.* 'were the'

171.3   form,] *comma bef. del.* 'evolved,'

171.3   its last] ('last' *in penc.*); *ab. del.* 'the *only workable [*penc. del.*]'

171.4   Men] *ov.* 'We'; *aft. del.* '['Other' *del.*] Who can say that with time and ed'

171.4   now are] *alt. fr.* 'are now'

171.4   conquering] *ab. del.* 'victorious'

171.5   and . . . ¹their] *ab. del.* 'and ashamed ['of belonging' *del.*] if a defeat be not wiped out. We give our'

171.5   ²their] *ab. del.* 'our wel'·

171.6   if . . . may] ('they' *ov.* 'we'); *ab. del.* 'without a murmur, to'

171.6   subjection.] *penc. ab. penc. del.* 'defeat.'

171.6   be sure] *ab. del.* 'say'

††171.7   other] *aft. del.* '['shame at belo' *del.*] similar pride and shame over'; *bef. del.* 'merits in our ideal country'

††171.7   one's] *ab. del.* 'our'

171.9-10   some day feel] *ab. del.* 'agree'

171.10   worth] *bef. del.* 'playing'

171.10   ²a] *intrl.*

171.11   respect?] *penc. insrtd. for penc. del.* 'line whatever?'

171.11   blush] *aft. del.* 'feel'

171.12   the] *alt. fr.* 'their'

171.12-13 in ... whatsoever?] ('whatsoever?' *in penc. ov.* '?'); *ab. caret
formed fr. orig. period*

171.13 daily] *aft. del.* 'growing'

171.13 now feel] *ab. del.* 'are growing
subject to'

171.14 blowing ... spark] *ab. del.*
'spreading the contagion,'

171.15 gets] *ab. del.* 'grows'

171.15 and] *aft. del.* 'with the aspiration,'

171.15 morals] *insrtd. for del.* 'Ethics
['E' *ov.* 'e']'

171.16 a] *insrtd. for del.* '['an' *del.*] a
new and'

171.16 system of morals] *ab. del.*
'system of *Ethic ['E' *ov.* 'e'; *final*
's' *del.*]'

171.16 civic] *aft. del.* 'mil'

171.16 builds] *alt. fr.* 'built'; *aft. del.*
'in a state of peace is ['rea' *del.*]
['reared' *del.*]'

171.17 comes] *ov.* 'no'

171.17 grasps] *ab. del.* 'holds'

171.18 The] *aft. del.* 'Militarism'

171.18 graspt us] *ab. del.* 'done this'

171.19 but] *ab. del.* 'peaceful'

171.19 no less] *aft. del.* 'as imperative.'

171.21 Let me] *penc. ab. del.* 'To'

171.21 There] *penc.* 'T' *ov.* 't'; *aft.
period ov. comma*

171.24 we] *ab. del.* 'men [*ab. del.*
'we']'

171.24 mere] *aft. del.* 'the'

171.24-25 accidents] 's' *added*

171.25 have] *intrl. bef. del.* 'lead [*ab.
del.* 'have']'

††171.26-27 imposed ... no vacation,—] ('should have' *insrtd.*); *intrl.*

171.28 of ... life] ('this' *bef. del.*
'heritage'); *intrl.*

171.29 may end by] *ab. del.* 'comes
to'

171.29 seeming] 'ing' *penc. added*

171.30 to ... ¹us] *penc. ab. penc. del.*
'that conditions should be so ['un-
evenly' *ink del.*] distributed [*comma
ink del.*] that'

171.30 that] *penc. insrtd. for ink del.*
'['the [*ab. del.* 'the'] common class
should' *del.*] ['one set of people
should *lead [*ab. del.* 'have'] a life

too soft for any of the campaigning
virtues, and another set' *del.*] we
should not all be called to bear some
part in the campaigning'

171.30 ²of us] *ab. del.* 'of us should'

171.31-32 now ... were,] *intrl.*

171.32 a conscription] *aft. del.* 'there
were'; *bef. del.* 'imposed'

171.32 ²of] *ov.* 'on'

171.32-33 the ... population] *ab. del.*
'all without exception'

171.33 for] *aft. penc. del.* 'part of the
industrial army *enlisted against
[*penc. ab. ink del.* 'from']'

††171.34 part ... nature,] *penc. intrl.*

171.35 out] *aft. del.* 'arid'

171.35 other] *ab. del.* 'incidental'

171.35-36 commonwealth] *ov.* 'community [*ab. del.* 'collectivity']'

171.36 follow.] *penc. ab. penc. del.*
'accrue.'

171.36 hardihood] *aft. del.* 'hardness,'

171.37 growing fibre] *ab. del.* 'entire
youth'

171.37 people;] *penc. ab. penc. del.*
'nation;'

171.38 luxurious] *ab. del.* 'richer [*ab.
del.* 'upper']'

171.38-39 blind, to] *ab. del.* ', of'

171.39 lives] *aft. del.* 'lif'

171.39-40 to the permanently] ('to
the' *insrtd.*; 'permanently' *alt. fr.*
'permanent'); *ab. del.* 'of the'

171.40 hard] *bef. del.* '['f' *del. intrl.*]
subsoil of life.'

171.40 his] *ab. del.* 'the'

171.40 To] *ab. del.* 'In'

††171.40-172.1 & iron] *intrl.*

172.1 ¹to] *ab. del.* 'on'

172.1 ²to] *ov.* 'on'; *ab. del.* 'in
December'

172.1 in December,] *ab. caret formed
fr. orig. comma*

172.1 ³to] *ov.* 'in'

†172.2 ['and' *del.*] clothes- ... -wash-
ing ['in' *del.*]] ('and' *ov.* 'in'); *ab.
del.* '['& road m' *del.*] ['and wit'
del.] and road-mak'

172.2 to] *insrtd.*

172.3 ¹to] *insrtd. for del.* 'in'

172.3 foundries ∧] *comma del.*

172.3 ²to] *ov.* 'on'

172.4   gilded] *intrl.*

172.4   youths] 's' *added*

172.4-5   drafted . . . childishness] ('ac-
-cording ['accord' *insrtd.*] . . . choice,'
moved fr. bef. 'would' [172.4];
'childishness' *aft. del.* 'nonsense
and' *and bef. del.* '&'); *ab. del.* 'sent
[*ab. del.* 'drafted'] off to serve their
terms and ['come back' *del.*] have
the nonsense'

172.6   healthier] *ab. del.* '['various'
del. insrtd.] manlier'

172.7   They] *aft. del.* 'The temporary
nature of the service would ['deprive
it of all tendency to degrade' *del.*]
keep [*insrtd.*]'

172.7   would] *ab. del.* 'will'

172.7   done] *insrtd. for del.* 'and
played'

172.7   own] *intrl.*

172.7   in] *bef. del.* 'the [*ab. del.*
'man's' *bel. del.* 'the']'

172.8   human warfare] *ab. del.* 'human
game, and bought themselves free
struggle'

172.10   teachers] *aft. del.* 'educators'

172.10   of] *intrl. for del.* 'to [*ab. del.*
'of']'

172.10   following] *penc. ab. del.*
'coming'

172.10   generation.] *period insrtd. bef.
penc. del.* 'to come.'

172.11   a conscription,] *penc.* 'a' *ov.*
'an'; 'conscription,' *penc. ab. penc.
del.* 'institution,'

172.11   would] *ab. del.* 'should'

172.12   required] *aft. del.* 'come to'

172.12   fruits] *ab. del.* 'consequences'

172.12   bear] *aft. del.* 'bring'

172.13   the manly virtues] ('manly
virtues' *ab. del.* 'martial virtues');
aft. del. 'the most of'

172.14   is . . . seeing] *ab. del.* '['fears
that peace would ['extinguish' *del.*]
cease to foster. It would give' *del.*]
would'

172.15-16   as . . . possible,] ('criminal'
insrtd.); *insrtd. for del.* 'little [*ab.
del.* '-|out [*hyphen undel. in error*]
much'] cruelty,'

††172.16   and . . . cheerily,] *ab. del.*
'*repulsive duties [*ab. del.* 'base

work'] done cheerfully without
refusing'

†172.16-17   duty . . . threatens]
('need' *aft. del.* 'does'); *ab. del.*
'certainty of the vacation ['ahead,'
del.]'

172.17   degrade] *intrl. aft. del.* '*drag
down. [*ab. del.* '['entailing degradation because no possible release is in
sight.' *del.*] degrade']'

172.17-18   remainder] *intrl.*

172.18   So] *ov.* 'so'; *aft. del.* 'War,'

172.19   war has been] *ab. del.* ', is'

172.19-20   community, . . . an] *comma
insrtd.*; 'and . . . an' *ab. del.* 'in such
a way. Till the'

172.21   war] *aft. del.* 'the'; *bef. del.*
'party'

172.21   way.] *ab. del.* 'day.'

172.24   some other] *alt. fr.* 'another';
bef. del. 'equally'

172.24   preserving] *bel. penc. del. penc.
intrl.* 'national'

172.26   but] *ab. del.* 'merely'

172.26   skilful] '['the' *penc. del.*]
skilful ['so' *penc. del.*]' *penc. insrtd.*

172.26   opinion-] *aft. penc. del.* 'embraced by'

172.27   seizing] *ov. penc. illeg. bef.*
'historic *opportunities. ['ies.' *ov.*
'y']' *moved in penc. from aft.* 'and
of' [172.26]

172.28   The] '¶' *in mrgn.*

172.28   can . . . war.] *ab. del.* 'doesn't
require war to breed. H. G. Wells, as
usual, puts his finger on the ['truth.'
del.] centre of the situation.'

172.29   ¹and] *aft. del.* 'in many other
professions'

172.29   elsewhere] *ab. del.* 'in other
professions'

172.30   are in a fashion] ('in a fashion'
intrl.); *aft. del.* 'have it'

172.30   we should all] *ab. del.* 'every
*one [*insrtd. for del.* 'walk in life']
might grow to'

172.31   we] *ab. del.* 'he'

172.31-32   our . . . obligatory] *ab. del.*
'his walk as a consecrated public'

172.32   to the state.] *ov. del. period*

172.35   temper] *penc. intrl.*

172.36   past] *intrl.*

172.36 temper] *penc. insrtd. for penc. del.* 'imagination'

173.9 ‸the conceptions] *db. qts. del.*; 'conceptions' *ab. del.* 'ideals'

173.9 order] 'o' *ov. poss.* 'w'

173.11 which] *aft. del.* 'will remain a univ'

173.12 duty] *ab. del.* 'service'

173.12 european] *aft. del.* 'the'

173.12 nations,] *intrl. aft. del.* 'countries, [*ab. del.* 'nations,']'

173.13 when] *ab. del.* 'the'

173.14 as he does.] *ab. del.* 'with him.'

173.15 preposterous] *intrl.*

173.15 the only force] ('force' *ab. del.* 'power'); *aft. del.* 'our'

173.16 standards of] *intrl.*

173.17 by] *aft. del.* 'and'

†173.17-20 or . . . energy.] *fol.* 37 *insrtd. for del.* '[*fol.* 37½] or the Japanese. *Great indeed is fear, but it [*ab. del.* 'Fear'] is not, as the military enthusiasts *try to make us believe, [*insrtd. for del.* 'would ['insist,' *del.*] ['believe' *del.*] have us think,' *ab. del.* 'imagine'] the only incentive ['available [*ab. del.* 'possible']' *del.*] for awakening *our manlier energies [*ab. del.* 'man's

higher activities'].' *subst. for del.* '[*on fol.* 36] or [*undel. in error*] | the Japanese. *Fear is not, as the military party **dreams, [*bel. del.* 'thinks'] the only incentive to man's higher activities. [*insrtd.*] The *alteration [*ab. del.* 'change'] in public opinion which *my utopia [*insrtd.*; *poss. underl. del.*] postulates is infinitely *less [*ab. del.* 'smaller'] than the difference between the mentality of any 'general [*hyphen and closing sg. qt. del.*] Staff' *of a contemporary nation [*ab. del.* 'at the present day,'] and that of the black warriors on the Congo who used to pursue Stanley's party with the war cry of 'Meat!' Meat!' Evolution has bridged the one interval, it will bridge the *other *still [*intrl.*] more easily. ['still.' *del.*]'

173.20 amount of] *intrl.*

173.22 those] *alt. fr.* 'the'

173.23 who] *aft. del.* 'on the Cong'

173.24 'Meat] 'M' *ov.* 'm'

173.24 and] 'n' *ov. poss.* 't'

173.25 History] *insrtd. for del.* 'Evolution has'

173.26 2over] *ab. del.* 'still'

DELETED VERSOS FOR "THE MORAL EQUIVALENT OF WAR" MANUSCRIPT

[*del. fol.* 15cᵛ: *new trial for end of deletion on fol.* 15c ('As the american's . . . first.'); *see alterations entry* 166.31] 'The american's state of mind is the simplest so I will speak of it'

[*del. fol.* 20ᵛ: *draft for deletion on fol.* 15c; *see alterations entry* 166.31; *corresponds to text* 166.21-26] 'Both writers take a highly metaphysical view of war, *and [*intrl.*] regard['ing' *del.*] it [*ab. del.* 'it as a sort of'] ['not as ['a thing' *del.*] subject to the usual *reasonable ['rea' *undel. in error*] ['motives' *del.*] causes' *del.*] as *a [*intrl.*] biological ['rather than psychological. It is a' *del.*] function, *uncontrolled by the ['psychological' *del.*] [*insrtd. for del.* 'fatally to be exerted when the time is ripe, *['unintell' *del.*] independently ['ly' *ab. del.* 'ly'] of the ordinary psycho- [*intrl.*] ['and the alleged' *del.*] to which the psychological'] practical [*intrl.*] motives and checks *that govern peaceful enterprises. [*ab. del.* 'which govern peaceful enterprises are inapplicable.'] When the *time is ripe, [*ab. del.* 'fateful [*alt. fr.* 'fatal' *ov.* 'future'] hour has struck'] the war must come, *reason or no reason, the reasons [*ab. del.* 'and the occasions'] pleaded *being [*ab. del.* 'are a'] ['*only a [*intrl.*] mere pretence' *del.*] always *fictions. [*ab. del.* 'mere inventions.'] It is an ['absolute necessity,' *del.*] an eternally' [*del. fol.* 36^v: *probable earlier form of upper half of fol.* 25, *related to text* 169.31-38] 'the only workable form simply because it was the form developed earliest. Most men ['are' *del.*] are proud of belonging to an admirable collectivity of any kind, and ashamed when *the [*alt. fr.* 'their'] ['class is' *del.*] body that owns them is inferior.'

Word-Division

The following is a list of actual or possible hyphenated compounds divided at the end of the line in the copy-text but which were not confirmed in their forms as printed in the present edition either because the copy-text did not derive from a learned journal or manuscript at that point or because the journal or manuscript gave the form as two separate words which was not adopted as an emendation. In a sense, then, the hyphenation or the non-hyphenation of possible compounds in the present list is in the nature of editorial emendation. When the compounds were divided in the copy-text at the ends of lines but their probable form was evidenced in the source, this edition prints the reading of the source (unless emended by record), and no list is provided here.

5.11 deathbed	97.7 prehistoric
65.30 warm-blooded	98.18 to-night
66.25 hell-fire	110.8 snow-flake
86.17 psycho-physiologist	118.6 self-same
87.34 one-sided	121.25 Great-mindedness
94.17 non-appetitive	139.27 self-suggestion

The following is a list of words divided at the ends of lines in the present edition but which represents authentic hyphenated compounds as found within the lines of the copy-text. Except for this list, all other hyphenations at the ends of lines in the present edition are the modern printer's and are not hyphenated forms in the copy-text.

3.15 foot- |notes	81.8 crack- |brained
5.39 counter- |theories	82.30 -an- |sich
7.32 brain- |spinning	86.11 air- |chest
8.3 Sisyphus- |labor	89.40 transmission- |theory
11.26 self- |seeking	90.11 wave- |scheme
31.12 self- |control	91.19 psycho- |physical
33.36 ill- |qualified	91.34 *over-* |*waves*
50.30;59.24 self- |love	92.27 discretely- |feeling
62.22 prison- |inmates	93.10 brain- |action
62.29 well- |doing	99.29 saturation- |point
70.19 Fifty- |fourth	106.10 opinion- |confirming
72.5 leaden- |footed	107.25 dead- |and-

131.1   mind- |curers
132.18 fatigue- |obstacle
132.22 fatigue- |distress
137.11 over- |animation
152.8   crowd- |pressure
156.30 posture- |gymnastics

159.26 self- |suggestion
165.31 romantic- |minded
166.8   healthy- |minded
166.20 army- |writings
172.26 opinion- |making

The following are actual or possible hyphenated compounds broken at the end of the line in both the copy-text and the present edition.

10.39   *self-* |*hood* (i.e., *selfhood*)
20.22   week- |day (i.e., week-day)
92.31   psycho- |physically (i.e., psycho-physically)
125.37 half- |action (i.e., half-action)
126.21 faith- |process (i.e., faith-process)
128.10 self- |sufficingness (i.e., self-sufficingness)
164.40 up- |to- (i.e., up-to-)
168.17 army- |life (i.e., army-life)
172.1   dish- |washing (i.e., dish-washing)

Index

This index is a name and subject index for the text of *Essays in Religion and Morality* and Appendixes I and II.

It is an index of names only for the "Notes," "A Note on the Editorial Method," and "The Text of *Essays in Religion and Morality.*" Names of persons, localities, and institutions and titles of books are indexed. However, such items are not indexed if no information about them is provided—if they are only a part of the identification of a discussed item or are only used to indicate its location. This excludes, most of the time, names of editors, translators, and libraries and titles of reference books consulted by the editors of the present text. Also not indexed are titles of articles in periodicals, except those by James, and references to William James.

Not indexed is the Introduction added to the present edition.

Index

Abolitionism, 66
Absolute, the, 111
Académie Française, 152
Across the Plains (R. L. Stevenson), 99n, 187
Action, 125-126, 145, 199
Activity, 132, 147, 149
Adam, 24n, 180
Addams, Jane, 265
Aesthetics, 116
Aetolia, 164
Agassiz, Louis, 220
Ajax, 163
Alaska, 166, 167
Alexander the Great, 164
Alger, William Rounseville, 78, 184
Allen, Gay Wilson, 192, 195, 201
Alnwick Castle (F. Halleck), 182
American Association for International Conciliation, 252, 253
Americanism, 66-67
American Magazine, 252-253
American Philosophical Association, 129n, 199, 247
Andrew, John Albion, 67, 182
Angell, James Rowland, 192, 266
Angels, 42-43, 59n
Animals, 97-98
Antietam, 67
Anti-Imperialist League, 195
Antinomianism, 7, 42
Appearance and Reality (F. H. Bradley), 119, 190
Aristides, 127
Arnold, Matthew, 163, 192
Artist, the, 110
Asceticism, 136-137, 156-157
Ashburner (unidentified person), 200
Asia, 60
Association, 80n, 129
Atheism, 7, 11, 125
Athens, 163, 202

Automatisme psychologique, L' (P. Janet), 192

Baird-Smith, Richard. *See* Smith, Richard Baird
Bakewell, Charles Montague, 239
Bancroft Library, 184
Barber, Francis, 218
Barber, John, 218
Barber, William, 218
Beinecke Library, 187
Berkeley, Calif., 201n
Berkeley Club, 183, 234
Berton (unidentified person), 153
Bible, H. James on the, 53, 57n
Bigelow, Albert, 266
Blacks, 65, 67, 68-70, 71
Blindness, human, 98-99
Blood, Benjamin Paul, 264
Body, 82n-83n, 94
Boer War, 164
Boston, Mass., 39, 52, 65, 70, 181
Bourget, Paul, 152, 194
Bowers, Fredson, 178, 195, 207n, 210n
Bradley, Francis Herbert, 119, 190
"Bradley or Bergson?" (W. James), 253
Brahms, Johannes, 241
Brain: and consciousness, 75, 83n, 88-89; and thought, 79-82, 84-86; and transmission, 87; and abnormal mental states, 93
Brandenburg, 121, 191
Brave Black Regiment, A (L. F. Emilio), 181, 222
British Guiana, 191
Brutus, Marcus Junius, 164, 261
Büchlein vom Leben nach dem Tode, Das (G. T. Fechner), 116, 190
Büchner, Ludwig, 85n, 185
Buckham, John Wright, 191, 243
Buffon, Georges Louis Leclerc de, 188
Bunker Hill, 65

Burchard, Peter, 181
Butler, Nicholas Murray, 252
Byles, Mrs. W. P., 265
Byron, Lord (George Gordon), 21

Cabanis, Pierre Jean Georges, 84n–85n, 185
Cabot, James Elliot, 189–190
California, 167
Carlyle, Thomas, 4, 178, 214, 218
Carpenter, Edward, 131, 160–161, 193
Carpenter, Frederic I., 188
Catholicism, 200
Cato, 127
Cattell, James McKeen, 265
Cedar Mountain, 67
Certainty, 125
Cerveau, Le (J. Luys), 85n, 185
Chaix, Jeanne, 152–153, 194
Chapman, John Jay, 168–169, 196
Character, 80–81, 112–113
Charlton, D. G., 179
Chesterton, Gilbert Keith, 131, 160, 192
China, 166, 195
Christ, 48, 56–59, 181
Christianity: and H. James, 6, 20, 46–52, 56–59; and creation, 9; and pluralism, 60; and religious experience, 128
Christianity the Logic of Creation (H. James), 8n, 24, 42–43, 44–46, 56–59, 179, 180, 181
Christian Science, 143, 159
Church of Christ Not an Ecclesiasticism, The (H. James), 46n, 181
Civilization, 73, 121, 123, 165, 170, 202
Civil War, 65–66
Clairvoyance, 93
Clemens, Samuel, 202
Cleveland, Grover, 191
Clifford, William Kingdon, 83n–84n, 185
Columbia University, 247
Common Sense, 82n, 86, 106–107
Concord, Mass., 109, 241
Conduct of Life, The (R. W. Emerson), 188
Confessions of an English Opium-Eater (T. De Quincey), 193
Conscience: H. James on, 10–12, 24, 26–28; and vitality, 131
Consciousness: and brain, 75, 83n, 84, 88–89; and transmission, 86–87; nature of, 88; and threshold, 89–92; Fechner on, 117; and the unconscious, 118
Constable, Archibald, and Co., 232
Conversion, 93, 126, 143, 159, 199, 200
Coriat, Isador H., 250
Cornell University, 187
Courage, 72–73

Courrières, France, 153, 194–195
Creation, H. James on, 4, 6, 8–12, 14–16, 17–18, 19, 20, 40, 43
Creator, the, H. James on, 7, 35
Crepuscolo dei filosofi, Il (G. Papini), 194
Critical History of the Doctrine of a Future Life, A (W. R. Alger), 78, 184
Critique of Pure Reason (I. Kant), 186
Cromwell, Oliver, 134, 153

Darien, Georgia, 69, 182
David (Biblical king), 38
Davidson, Thomas, 184, 215
Death, 109, 115, 118–119, 127, 128
Degeneration, 168
Deism, 50
Democracy, 74, 202
Dependence, 82
De Quincey, Thomas, 134n, 154, 193
Dewey, Edward Hooker, 157–158, 195
Dewey, John, 192
Dewhurst, Stephen (pseudonym), 3
Diary (W. James), 195
Dickens, Charles, 193
Dickinson, Goldsworthy Lowes, 169, 196
Diogenes, 38
Diomedes, 163
Disarmament, 122
Discours sur le style (G. L. L. de Buffon), 188
Discrimination, 129
Divine-Natural Humanity, 12–13, 14n, 45
Dualism, 82n–83n
Du Bois-Reymond, Emil, 88, 186
Dühring, Eugen Karl, 82n, 185
Duty, 152–153

Eby, Samuel Clarence, 178
Ecclesiasticism, 46–52, 53–56, 77
Economy, 169
Eddyism, 200
Education, 149, 202
Eells, Alexander G., 243
Effort, 132, 151, 200
Einige Ideen zur Schöpfungs- und Entwickelungsgeschichte der Organismen (G. T. Fechner), 190
Elder Henry James, The (A. Warren), 178
Elemente der Psychophysik (G. T. Fechner), 89, 90n–92n, 186
Elements of Metaphysics (A. E. Taylor), 119, 190
Eliot, Charles William, 221
Ellis, Havelock, 234–235
Emanuel Swedenborg (W. White), 178
Emerson, Edward Waldo, 188
Emerson, Ralph Waldo: his personality, 109–111; his creed, 111; on individual-

ity, 111–112; on character, 112–114; his optimism, 114; his vision, 115; H. James on, 220; quoted, 89n, 101; notes on, 186, 187–189; mentioned, 106, 178, 241, 242, 252, 264

"Emerson" (W. James), 240–242, 264

Emerson in Concord (E. W. Emerson), 188

Emerson's Complete Works, 188

Emilio, Luis F., 181, 183, 222

Emotion, 80

"Energies of Men, The" (W. James): notes for, 199–200; textual documents, 247–258; James on, 265–266; mentioned, 192

Energy, human: spiritual, 100; levels, 130–132, 147–149, 150–151, 200; reserves, 133–135; and asceticism, 136–137, 156–157; and Yoga, 137–141, 156–157; and suggestion, 139; and ideas, 141–142, 157–159; and mind-cure, 143–144, 159–160; mental, 144–145; study of, 145–146, 150, 161; and training, 149; and effort, 151; and duty, 152–153; and excitement, 153–155; and will, 155–156

England, 32, 121, 123, 164, 166, 202

Epaminondas, 112

Epictetus, 38

Epirus, kingdom of, 164, 195

Equality, 44

Equilibrium, 133, 148

Essays (R. W. Emerson), 186, 188, 189

Essays in Philosophy (W. James), 186, 190, 194

Essays in Radical Empiricism (W. James), 228n

Europe, 60

Eve, 23, 24n, 180

Evil, 40, 44–46, 73

Evolution, 10, 96–97, 116

Evolutionism, 7

Excitement, 122, 132, 133–136, 151, 153–155

Exercises at the Dedication of the Monument to Colonel Robert Gould Shaw, 182, 219

Experience, 117–118, 126–128

Faith, 106, 124–126, 141

Faith-ladder, 125–126

Fatigue, 129, 130, 132, 133, 147, 151, 199

Fear, 31, 168, 169

Fearthought, 143, 159

Fechner, Gustav Theodor: on threshold, 90n–92n; his philosophy, 116–118; on immortality, 118–119; on God, 119; his personality, 132; notes on, 186, 190; mentioned, 89, 242

Feeling, and immortality, 78

Field, Horace, 178

Finiteness, 95

First and Last Things (H. G. Wells), 172–173, 196

First Principles (H. Spencer), 85n, 185

Flechsig, Paul Emil, 80, 184–185

Fletcher, Horace, 143, 157, 159; note on, 194

Force and Matter (L. Büchner), 85n, 185

Formation, 9

Fort Sumter, 66, 71

Fort Wagner, S.C., 64, 68, 70, 71, 73, 181, 182, 219, 222

Fourier, François Marie Charles, 13, 179

Frederick the Great, 169

"Frederic Myers' Services to Psychology" (W. James), 186

Freedom, 45, 107, 199

Function: kinds of, 83n, 84, 85–86, 87; in science, 88

Garibaldi, Giuseppe, 142, 158, 193

Gehirn und Seele (P. E. Flechsig), 80n, 184–185

Genesis, book of, 30

Germany, 164

Gilbert, J. Allen, 194

God: H. James on, 6, 10, 19–22, 33, 40–42, 51, 60–61; and pluralism, 60; and love, 100; Lutoslawski on, 106; Fechner on, 119; existence of, 124. *See also* Creation

Godwin, Parke, 215

Goodness, 44

"Gospel of Relaxation, The" (W. James), 194, 266

"G. Papini and the Pragmatist Movement in Italy" (W. James), 194

Grant, Ulysses Simpson, 134, 153

Grattan, Clinton Hartley, 178

Great Britain, 191

Greece, 163, 164, 202

Greg, Walter Wilson, 207n

Grenzen geistiger Gesundheit und Krankheit, Die (P. E. Flechsig), 80n, 184–185

Grimm, Herman, 187

Grundriss der Psychiatrie (C. Wernicke), 80n, 184

Gunn, Giles, 178

Gustav Theodor Fechner (K. Lasswitz), 190

Gustav Theodor Fechner (W. Wundt), 190

Habit, 122, 144, 151, 202

Habit-neurosis, 132–133, 151, 199

Hague Tribunal, 252

Hale, Edward Everett, 265
Halleck, Fitz-Greene, 182
Hallowell, Edward Needles, 70, 183, 222
Happiness As Found in Forethought Minus Fearthought (H. Fletcher), 194
Harvard University, 77, 184, 199, 233
Hawaiian Islands, 166, 167
Healthy-mindedness, 62
Heaven, 96
Hector, 163
Hegel, Georg Wilhelm Friedrich, 8, 179
Hegelianism, 7, 8
Hemispheres, cerebral, 80n
Henry James, Sr. and the Religion of Community (D. W. Hoover), 178
Henry James, Sr.: A Selection (G. Gunn), 178
Heredity and Social Progress (S. N. Patten), 196
Heretics (G. K. Chesterton), 192
Higginson, Thomas Wentworth, 241
History: meaning in, 65; and war, 72, 73, 121-122, 163-164, 166; scale of, 97
History of the Fifty-fourth Regiment (L. F. Emilio), 222
History of the War in the Peninsula (W. F. P. Napier), 68, 182
Hoar, George Frisbie, 241
Hoar, Samuel, 241
Hodge, C. W., 184
Hodges, George, 195, 251
Hodgson, Shadworth Hollway, 214, 216
Holmes, Oliver Wendell (senior), 201
Honor, 142, 158
Hoover, Dwight W., 178
Houghton, H. O., 227, 231
Houghton Library, 177, 178, 184, 212, 227
Houghton Mifflin Co., 214, 215, 217, 227, 228, 230
Howison, George Holmes, 124, 222, 234, 243, 244; notes on, 183-184, 191
Human Immortality (W. James): critics of, 75-76, 184; textual documents, 229-234; mentioned, 183, 187
Hypnosis, 139
Hypothesis, 88
Hyslop, Theophilus Bulkeley, 160, 195

Idealism, 7, 86, 89, 117-118
Ideas, 132, 141-142, 151, 157-160
Identity, personal, 76
Idylls of the King (A. Tennyson), 68
Ignatius Loyola, Saint, 136, 156
Iliad (Homer), 163
Immortality: and the transmission theory, 75-76; and organized religion, 77-78; James's view, 78, 202; studies, 78-79;

physiological objection, 79-82; and brain functions, 83n, 87-88; and mind-stuff, 83n-84n; and materialism, 84n-85n; and soul, 94; and the self, 95-96; and size of population, 96-101; and common sense, 107; Fechner on, 118-119; and experience, 127
Immortal Life (H. James), 178, 215, 217
Individualism, and immortality, 76
Influx, 93
Ingersoll, Caroline Haskell, 184
Ingersoll, George Goldthwait, 77, 78, 79, 184
Inhibition, 129, 131, 133, 151
Insanity, 80n
Institutions, Emerson on, 112
International Voluntary Service, 266
Introduction to Philosophy (F. Paulsen), 190

James, Alice Gibbens (wife), 188, 220-221, 233, 241, 266
James, Garth Wilkinson (brother), 69-70, 220, 222, 229; notes on, 182, 183
James, Henry (brother), 215, 216-217, 220-221, 221-222, 226, 241
James, Henry (father): his literary remains, 3-4, 214-219; his thought, 4-5, 6-8, 12-13, 37-38, 39-40, 46, 60-63; and theology, 5-6; on creation, 8-10, 14-16, 19; on selfhood, 10-11, 16-18, 22-24, 29-30, 38-39; on religion, 11-12, 24-28; on God, 19-22, 40-42; on morality, 22-23, 28; his religious development, 28-29; his conversion, 30-37; his antinomianism, 42-46; on ecclesiasticism, 46-56; and Christianity, 56-59; and Swedenborg, 59-60; notes on, 178-181
James, Henry (son), 228, 242, 244, 246, 247, 248, 250
James, Margaret (daughter), 255, 258, 259, 261, 262, 263
James Collection, 177, 212
Janet, Pierre: on psychasthenia, 129-130, 135, 155; notes on, 192, 193; mentioned, 199
Japan, 121, 164, 166-167, 191
Job (Biblical person), 101
John (book of the Bible), 112
Jones, Iredell, 183
Judaism, 9, 60
Justice, 47
Justice and Liberty (G. L. Dickinson), 169n, 196

Kant, Immanuel, 94, 186, 237, 243, 244
Kellogg, Julia A., 6, 178, 181

Index

Keyes, John Shepard, 240
Kleine Schriften von Dr. Mises (G. T. Fechner), 190
Kraft und Stoff (L. Büchner), 185
Kritik der reinen Vernunft (I. Kant), 94n, 237

Lake Mohonk Conference on International Arbitration, 251
Lasswitz, Kurd, 117, 190
Law, 27, 37, 66, 77
Lea, Homer, 166–167, 170, 195
Lectures and Biographical Sketches (R. W. Emerson), 188, 189
Lectures and Essays (W. K. Clifford), 83n–84n, 185
Lectures and Miscellanies (H. James), 46n, 181
Lee, Henry, 67, 182, 221
Leonardo, 248
Leonidas, 65
Letters (R. G. Shaw), 182
Letters and Social Aims (R. W. Emerson), 188, 189
Letters of Henry James, The, 180
Letters of William James, The, 184, 192, 193
Leuba, James Henry, 104, 187
Life of Reason, The (G. Santayana), 125, 191
Limits of Evolution, The (G. H. Howison), 183
Literary Remains of the Late Henry James, The, James's Introduction to, 178, 179, 214–219, 264
Literature and Dogma (M. Arnold), 192
Little Book of Life After Death, The (G. T. Fechner), James's Introduction to, 190, 242
Llewellyn-Jones, Frederick, 236, 239, 240
Locke, John, 76
Logika ogolna (W. Lutoslawski), 138, 193
Love: H. James on, 11, 12, 18n, 25n, 43, 50n; divine, 100
Lowell, Percival, 85n, 185
Lund, John, 265
Luther, Martin, 6, 127, 128
Luther et le serf-arbitre (J. Milsand), 6n, 178
Lutoslawski, Wincenty: his thought, 105–108; regeneration of, 137–141, 156–157; and James, 235–240; notes on, 187, 193; mentioned, 141, 200
Luys, Jules, 85n, 185

McClure's Magazine, 253, 254, 264
McComb, Samuel, 249–250
McDermott, John J., 211

McKinley, William, 164
Man: H. James on, 7, 27, 40–42, 44–45; evolutionism on, 10; and war, 72, 121–122, 162–163, 166; and merit, 97; blindness, 98–99; and reason, 120–121; and levels of energy, 130–132, 144, 147–148; powers of, 150, 152–154
Mann, Charles Holbrook, 178
Martin Chuzzlewit (C. Dickens), 193
Materialism, 84n–85n, 87–88, 89, 117
Mead, Edwin D., 264
Meaning of Truth, The (W. James), 228n
Mediumship, 93
Melos, Island of, 163
Memoir of Ralph Waldo Emerson, A (J. E. Cabot), 189
Memories and Studies (W. James), 184, 186, 228, 229, 241, 242, 247, 248, 250
Menticulture (H. Fletcher), 194
Mercer, George Gluyas, 238–239, 240
Merit, and immortality, 97
Metaphysics, 116
Militarism, 165–168, 169–170
Mill, John Stuart, 152, 194
Milsand, Joseph Antoine, 6n, 178–179, 214
Mind: and body, 82n–83n; and abnormal states, 93–94, 135–136; and the unconscious, 118; and psychasthenia, 129–130, 135, 155; and energy, 132, 147; and work, 144–145; and activity, 149
Mind-cure, 128, 131, 143–144, 159–160
Mind-stuff, 83n–84n
Miscellanies (R. W. Emerson), 188, 189
Monadism, 106–107
Monism: and Christianity, 60; in H. James, 60–61; and pluralism, 61–62; and religion, 62; and immortality, 75–76
Montgomery, James, 182
Montyon, Jean Baptiste Antoine Robert Auget, baron de, 152, 194
Monument to Robert Gould Shaw, The, 219
"Moral Equivalent of War, The" (W. James): origin of, 195, 196, 201–202; textual documents, 250–264, 266
Moralism, 62, 63
Moralists, 131
Morality, H. James on, 10–11, 22–23, 28, 29–30
Morris Island, S.C., 64, 70
Morse, Frances R., 241
Müller, Friedrich Max, 237
Munk, Hermann, 80n, 185
Münsterberg, Hugo, 199, 200
Myers, Frederic William Henry, 92, 186
Mysticism, 37–38

Napier, William Francis Patrick, 68, 182
Nations, 72–73
Natural History of Intellect (R. W. Emerson), 188, 189
Naturalism, 7
Nature: H. James on, 9–10, 14n–15n; uniformity of, 107; and reason, 120; war against, 171
Nature, Addresses, and Lectures (R. W. Emerson), 188
Némy (unidentified person), 153, 195
New Jerusalem, the, 55–56
New Thought, 128, 143, 159, 200
Noiré, Ludwig, 237
Norton, Charles Eliot, 134, 153, 193, 241, 248

Obsessions et la psychasthénie, Les (P. Janet), 192
Occult Japan (P. Lowell), 85n, 185
Official Report of the Thirteenth Universal Peace Congress, 191
Olivier, Sydney Haldane, 133–134, 193, 200
O Logice Platona (W. Lutoslawski), 187
One Gallant Rush (P. Burchard), 181
"On Some Hegelisms" (W. James), 179
"On Some Mental Effects of the Earthquake" (W. James), 193
On Vital Reserves (W. James), 266
Optimism, 7, 25n, 114
"Oration by Professor William James," 219–229, 264
Oregon, 167
Origin and Growth of Plato's Logic, The (W. Lutoslawski), 105, 187
Osgood, James R., and Co., 214, 216, 217

Pacific Coast Unitarian Club, 201, 243
Pacificism, 165, 168–169
Pain, 132
Paine, Robert Treat, 265
Pantheism, 7, 9n, 60, 75–76, 125
Papini, Giovanni, 145, 146, 248; note on, 194
Paris, 121
Patrick, George Thomas White, 148, 194
Patriotism, 165, 170–171
Patten, Simon Nelson, 168, 196
Paul, Saint, 112, 128
Paulsen, Friedrich, 117, 190, 237
Paulus, Aemilius, 164, 195
Payson, W. H., 244
Peace: and human nature, 121; how attained, 122–123; and war, 164–165; prospects for, 170; and martial virtues, 172–173
Peace Pledge Union, 254

Peloponnesian War, 163
Perry, Bliss, 265
Perry, Ralph Barton, 177, 178. See also *Thought and Character of William James*
Perry, Thomas Sergeant, 243
Pessimism, 7, 25n
Phenomenism, 82n–83n
Philippi, battle of, 164
Philippines, 115, 166, 195
Phillips, John Sanborn, 252
Phillips, Wendell, 66, 182
Philosophical System of Antonio Rosmini-Serbati, The (T. Davidson), 184
Philosophie des Krieges, Die (S. R. Steinmetz), 167, 196
Philosophy: and pluralism, 60, 61; and science, 89; and skepticism, 105; types of, 117; function of, 120; religious, 128; and pragmatism, 145
Philosophy of Henry James (J. A. Kellogg), 6n
Philosophy of Henry James, Sr., The (F. H. Young), 178
Phocion, 127
Physiology, 79–82
Piedmont, 121, 191
Pilate, Pontius, 237
Pledge, the, 142, 158
Pluralism, 60, 61–62, 106–107
Pluralistic Universe, A (W. James), 179, 181, 186, 190, 192, 193, 243, 245, 246, 247
Poems (R. W. Emerson), 187, 188
Polytheism, 60, 106–107
Positivism, 7, 81n–82n
"Powers of Men, The" (W. James), 247, 248–250
Pragmatism, 145, 200
Pragmatism (W. James), 181
Pratt, James Bissett, 184
Prayer, 93, 132, 160
Premonitions, 93
Preyer, Wilhelm Thierry, 117, 190
Prince, Katharine James, 216
Prince, Morton, 135, 154, 199
Principles of Psychology, The (W. James), 83n, 184, 185, 186, 192
Probability, 125
Proprium, 22, 29
Protestantism, 102–103
Psychasthenia, 130, 135–136, 155
Psychical research, 81, 92
Psychology: and immortality, 79–82; methods, 102–103; described, 104, 199, 200; and Fechner, 116; types of, 129–130; and mental energy, 145–146, 161
Psychology Club of Harvard, 192, 199, 247

Psychology of Religion, The (E. D. Starbuck), James's Preface to, 187, 234–235
Psychophysics, 89–90
Pückler-Muskau, Hermann Ludwig Heinrich von: quoted, 142, 158–159; note on, 193–194; mentioned, 250

Questionnaires, 102

Radicalism, 52
Rankin, Henry William, 264
Rapports du physique et du moral (P. J. G. Cabanis), 84n–85n, 185
Rationalism, 126
Reality, 86–87, 128
Reason: and war, 66; and faith, 106, 124–126; and human nature, 120–121; and experience, 126–128
"Reason and Faith" (W. James), 192, 201, 243–247
Redemption, 9, 16
Reincarnation, 76
Relaxation, 150
Religion: H. James on, 10–12, 24–25, 28, 46–52, 54; and pluralism, 60; and healthy-mindedness, 62; and moralism, 63; and immortality, 77–78; study of, 102–103; and science, 103–104; and war, 122; and fact, 124–125; and experience, 126–128
Religion, a Criticism and a Forecast (G. L. Dickinson), 196
"Remarks at the Peace Banquet" (W. James), 242–243, 264–265
Remarks on the Apostolic Gospel (H. James), 179
Renouvier, Charles, 238
Rest, 148–149
Revelation, 53
Revivalism, 52
Riddles of the Sphinx (F. C. S. Schiller), 94n–95n, 186
Ritual, 52, 54
Riverside Press, 231
Rome, 121, 164
Roosevelt, Theodore, 166, 194, 201, 202, 249
Royce, Josiah, 119, 125, 190
Ruskin, John, 25n, 214
Russia, 166

Saint Francis Hotel, 201, 250
Saint-Gaudens, Augustus, 64, 181, 220, 221
Salter, William Mackintire, 233
Sanford, Edmund Clark, 129, 192
San Francisco, Calif., 134, 167, 193, 244

Santayana, George, 125, 191
Sarpedon, 163
Schiller, Ferdinand Canning Scott, 94n–95n, 233, 239; note on, 186–187
Schiller, Friedrich, 196
Scholar, the, 110
Science: and immortality, 79, 81; and dualism, 82n; described, 88; and philosophy, 89; and religion, 103–104
Science and a Future Life (F. W. H. Myers), 186
Scientists, 132, 160
Scudder, Horace, 217
Second wind, 132, 147, 199
Secret of Swedenborg, The (H. James), 14–16, 19, 20, 25n, 26–28, 43–44, 46–49, 55–56, 179–180, 181, 214
Seelenmacht (W. Lutoslawski), 187, 236, 238
Self-consciousness, H. James on, 10–11
Selfhood, H. James on, 8n, 11, 15–16, 16–18, 22–24, 26, 28, 29, 36, 38–39, 49n, 52
Selfishness, 22–23, 28, 42–43, 49n–50n
Sensation, 93
Sexuality, 199
Shaw, Anna Haggerty, 182
Shaw, Francis George, 183
Shaw, George Bernard, 131, 160, 192
Shaw, Robert Gould: his military career, 67–71; his burial, 71; notes on, 181–183; mentioned, 64, 66, 72, 73, 220, 221, 222, 223, 229
Shaw, Sarah Blake Sturgis, 181
Shelley, Percy Bysshe, 86, 186
Sieben Welträthsel, Die (E. Du Bois-Reymond), 186
Skrupskelis, Ignas K., 201, 251
Slavery, 65–66, 110–111
Sleep, 160
Smith, Richard Baird: quoted, 134–135, 153–154; note on, 193; mentioned, 136, 155, 248, 250
Socialism, 169
Society, H. James on, 9–10
Society and Solitude (R. W. Emerson), 189
Society the Redeemed Form of Man (H. James), 3, 5, 11n, 18n, 21–22, 30–37, 38–39, 40–42, 44, 49n–50n, 51–52, 57n, 178, 179, 181
Some Problems of Philosophy (W. James), 186, 187, 191, 192, 255
Soul, 82, 87, 94, 106
South Carolina, 66
Space, 96
Spain, 164
Sparta, 164

Spencer, Herbert, 85n, 117, 185
Spiritual Creation (H. James), 178
Spiritualism, 106
Stanford University, 191, 192, 195, 201, 243
Stanley, Henry Morton, 173, 196
Starbuck, Edwin Diller, 102–104, 187, 234
Statistics, 120
Steinmetz, Sebald Rudolf, 167–168, 195–196
Sterling Memorial Library, 184
Stevenson, Robert Louis, 99, 187
Stewart, Balfour, 83n, 185
Stone, George W., 191, 243
Strong, George Crockett, 70, 182, 183, 222
Stumpf, Karl, 216
Subjection of Women, The (J. S. Mill), 194
Substance, 18n, 106
Substance and Shadow (H. James), 16–18, 20–21, 22–23, 25–26, 28, 29–30, 53–54, 180
Suggestion, 139, 141–142, 157
"Suggestion about Mysticism, A" (W. James), 253, 261n
Suttner, Baroness von, 265
Swedenborg, Emanuel: his philosophy, 33–34; on selfhood, 38; on indifference, 42–43; and Swedenborgianism, 56; and H. James, 59–60, 179, 181; quoted, 186; mentioned, 12, 13, 14n, 15n, 16, 24n, 27, 29, 30, 45, 178
Swedenborgianism, 55–56, 179
Swedenborgians, 93
Swedenborg School of Religion, 178
Sydney Olivier (M. Olivier), 193
Sympathy, 98–101
System der Philosophie (W. Wundt), 100n, 187

Tagesansicht, Die (G. T. Fechner), 117, 190
Tait, Peter Guthrie, 83n, 185
Talks to Teachers on Psychology (W. James), 194, 201n
Tapley, Mark (literary character), 193
Taylor, Alfred Edward, 119, 190
Temperance, 142, 158
Tennyson, Alfred, Lord, 68, 183
Terry, Alfred Howe, 69, 70, 182, 229
Thayer, William Roscoe, 220
Theism, 6, 60, 125
Theology, 5, 9, 36
Thermopylæ, 65
Thessalonica, 164

Thilly, Frank, 190
"Thomas Davidson" (W. James), 184
Thought, 79–82, 84–86
Thought and Character of William James, The (R. B. Perry), 178, 181, 184, 185, 187, 191, 192, 194, 196
Three Jameses, The (C. H. Grattan), 178
Threshold, psychophysical, 89–92, 200
Through the Dark Continent (H. M. Stanley), 196
Thucydides, 163
Thucydides (B. Jowett), 195
Time, 96–97
Titchener, Edward Bradford, 192
Tolstoi, Lev Nikolayevich, 169, 196
Tour in England, Ireland, and France (H. L. H. von Pückler-Muskau), 142n, 159n, 194
Tracts for the New Times (H. James), 179
Transcendentalism, 89n, 105–106
Transmission theory: critics of, 75–76; described, 83n; and consciousness, 86–87; and threshold, 89; and psychical research, 92; and abnormal states, 93–94; and immortality, 94–95
True Christian Religion, The (E. Swedenborg), 186
Truth, H. James on, 33

Über die Grenzen des Naturerkennens (E. Du Bois-Reymond), 186
Über die Grundvoraussetzungen (W. Lutoslawski), 107, 187
Unconscious, the, 118
Uniformity, 107
Unitarian Club of California, 191
Unitarianism, 25n
United States, 66–67, 73–74, 164, 167, 169–170, 202
Unity, kinds of, 106
Universal Peace Congress, 120n
Universe, the, 86, 99, 101, 117
Universities, 77
Unseen Universe, The (Tait and Stewart), 83, 185
Utopia, 107
Utopianism, 169

Valor of Ignorance, The (H. Lea), 166, 167, 195
Varieties of Religious Experience, The (W. James), 186, 187, 191, 192, 194, 196, 251
Vastation, 33
Venezuela, 123, 191
Virtue, 167–168
Vivekananda, Swami, 137, 193

Index

Wadsworth, Mary C., 190, 242
Wagner, Charles, 265
Walsh, Catharine, 216
War: and justice, 66; and history, 72, 73;
 and human nature, 121-122; and peace,
 122-123, 164-165; and energy, 134,
 153; attitudes towards, 162-163;
 modern view of, 165-168; and
 discipline, 167-168; moral equivalent
 for, 169-173, 202
Warren, Austin, 178, 179
Washington, Booker T., 220, 221, 265
Washington, George, 43
Watt, A. P., and Son, 232
Weaver, Anthony, 254
Webb, Miss (unidentified person), 200
Wells, Herbert George: quoted, 172-173;
 notes on, 193, 196; mentioned, 131,
 161, 192, 201, 202, 257
Wernicke, Carl, 80n, 184
Werth des Lebens, Der (E. K. Dühring),
 82n, 185
West Riding Asylum, 160
What Constitutes the State? (H. James),
 179
White, William, 178
Whitman, Walt, 114
Widener Library, 177

Wilkinson, James John Garth, 178, 179,
 181
Will, 136-141, 155-156, 200
William James (G. W. Allen), 192, 201
Will to Believe, The (W. James), 179, 186,
 196
*Wissenschaftliche Briefe von Gustav
 Theodor Fechner und W. Preyer,* 190
Wolcott, Roger, 219
Women, 152
Worcester, Elwood, 249
Wordsworth, William, 183
Work, 133, 144-145, 148, 149
World, the, 106, 117-118
World and the Individual, The (J. Royce),
 119, 190
World of Souls, The (W. Lutoslawski),
 James's Preface to, 235-240
World-soul, 83n
Worship, H. James on, 20, 21
Wundt, Wilhelm, 100, 117, 186, 237;
 notes on, 187, 190

Yoga, 136-141, 156-157, 200
Young, Frederic Harold, 178, 181

Zend-Avesta (G. T. Fechner), 117, 190